2002
COACH OF THE YEAR CLINICS
FOOTBALL MANUAL

Edited by Earl Browning

www.coacheschoice.com

ISBN: 1-58518-644-9
Library of Congress Control Number: 2002104653

Transcription: Tom Cheaney and Larry Kindbom
Diagrams: Steve Haag
Developmental Editor: Kristi Huelsing
Book layout and cover design: Jennifer Bokelmann

Cover photo: courtesy of University of Miami SID
Back cover photo of Larry Coker: courtesy of University of Miami SID
Back cover photo of Bo Schembechler: courtesy of Allsport

Special thanks to the Nike clinic managers for having the lectures taped.

Coaches Choice
P.O. Box 1828
Monterey, CA 93942
www.coaceschoice.com

Contents

Contents

ACCOUNTABILITY AND MOTIVATIONAL TECHNIQUES

University of Colorado

How many of you won a state championship last year? How many of you made the playoffs? Okay, the rest of you are trying to get to the championships. Originally, I was asked to talk about training the quarterbacks. I asked Don Lessner, the Clinic Director, if I could change my topic, and he agreed to allow me to change my topic to a certain degree. When you get a topic such as training the quarterbacks, it has an adverse effect on some of the coaches attending the clinic. First, all of the defensive coaches do not come to the session. They go to gambling tables. Then all of the offensive-line coaches go join the defensive coaches at the gambling tables. That leaves me with the quarterback coaches and receiver coaches for the lecture.

I would like to address some of the things we did to turn our program around from 3-8 the year before to a national championship contender this year. I will talk about some of our offense later if I have time. I would like to walk you through some things that are really critical in developing your team to the point where they become playoff contenders and possible championship teams. The things we did were the same things we have done at four schools now. The same philosophy was used at each stop. I coached high school football for 13 years, was a small-college coach for two years, an assistant coach at Colorado for eight years, the head coach at Northwestern University for seven years, and now I'm in my second year as head coach at Colorado.

The things we had to do this year fell right in line with the things I have had to do at all of the other places where I have coached. All of the programs were down when I went there to coach. In the first year at the University of Colorado, we were 1-10. Most people know that Northwestern was down when I went there. The small college that I coached at had never won a league championship. Over the years, I have developed some things that I think are critical to building a championship football team. First, I would like to share some of those thoughts with you.

I always like to tell a story about a couple of my players before I get to the meat of the things we have done over the years. In 1989, we played Notre Dame in the Orange Bowl for the National Championship. Colorado was the favorite to win the game and the Championship. We were 11-0 and ranked number one in the country. We lost that game to Notre Dame. It was the last game on New Year's night, and everyone in the country was watching the game. We were supposed to win the game, and we lost. We were really dejected and disappointed after the game.

We got back to the hotel late and went straight to bed so we could get some sleep before we returned to Colorado the next morning. About four in the morning, I heard a large commotion in the hall outside my room. I walked out in the hall and found two of my players, a quarterback and a running back, in the hall. They were giving high fives and low fives. They were really excited and very loud. It was only three hours after we had just lost the national championship, and they were having a blast in the hotel.

I approached them and asked them, "What has gotten into you two?" They replied, "Coach, we have just finished putting together a jigsaw puzzle." I said "WHAT!?" They replied they had just finished a jigsaw puzzle. I asked them when they had started this jigsaw puzzle. They replied, "August." I said, "You started in August and now it is January 2, and you just finished the puzzle? You guys are excited about that?" They said, "Yes, coach. The outside of the puzzle reads 'two to four years.'"

I tell this story because of what it conveys: If you take the box top off the jigsaw puzzle, you find a whole lot of individual pieces of cardboard. The pieces are supposed to fit together. The only way you are going to know how those pieces fit together is to go back and look at the front cover of that box. On the front cover of the box is a beautiful picture of what the puzzle is supposed to end up looking like. There is a thing called jigsaw-puzzle management. There are strategies that apply to solving jigsaw puzzles that also apply to management. The strategies apply to teams or to business.

Have any of you ever worked a jigsaw puzzle? Do you know the first thing you look for? First you look for straight edges. The straight edges create the border of the jigsaw puzzle. Then you put all those pieces together by color. The colors are a puzzle within themselves.

What I have done at each of the schools I have coached at is to approach things with that same concept and same philosophy. When I went to Northwestern, I had no idea what I was getting into. I did not know anything about the Big Ten, and I knew nothing about Northwestern. I did not know they had lost a lot of games in the past years. I did not have a clue when I went there.

I first sat down with my assistants and told them what we were going to do was what everyone had told us was impossible to do. "If you can't see the invisible, you can't do the impossible." They introduced me at a basketball game at halftime. I walked out to the center of the floor and told the crowd, "We are going to take the Purple to Pasadena for the Rose Bowl." Of course everyone went nuts. I heard a lot of the people talking after the game. "That dumb football coach does not know what the hell he is talking about. He must be drinking or smoking dope." They had a losing season for 22 straight years.

When I made the statement at the basketball game, I created a lid for our football team. I created an image of what that program was going to look like. The next day I ordered a banner from a 1949 Rose Bowl that Northwestern had played in. I hung it in the athletic building. I got a ticket from the 1959 Rose Bowl and put it on my desk. A high school coach sent me a silver rose and I put it in a crystal bowl in the middle of my desk. I got a poster from the 1949 Rose Bowl and put it up on my wall in the office. I had some-

one take a picture of a road sign with an arrow on it pointing to Pasadena. I put that picture on my west wall in my office. You could not walk into our athletic facility or our office without knowing where our program wanted to go.

I did the same thing when I went to Colorado three years ago. In the early 1990s, from 1991 to 1994, Colorado was a dominant football program. There is a bus line that runs throughout the whole state of Colorado that is called RTD. It stands for Rapid Transit Department or something to that effect. At my first press conference, when I came back as head coach at Colorado, I said we are going to take this program and we are going to RTD it. What I was meaning by that acronym was this. "We are going to RTD or Return to dominance." We were going to take our program back to what it was in the early 1990s when Bill McCartney was coaching at Colorado. That was between 1989 and 1994.

Once again, I had come into a jigsaw puzzle. The RTD created a box top for our jigsaw puzzle. Once you create that vision, it drives you in how you make your decisions. At Northwestern our decisions related to how we were going to get to the Rose Bowl. At Colorado every decision we made about our program was based on the question of how to get our program back to that type of dominant position. It is like having a mission statement. It is about who you are. It is easy when you have a vision like that. You have it written out and then everyone starts buying into it.

When you come into a new program you inherit what was left in that program. The people left do not have the new coach's personality. Most coaches will have some adjustments to make in a new program. I had to make adjustments in Chicago with Northwestern, and at Colorado as well.

To go to our locker room at Colorado you have to go down a set of stairs. To go to the classrooms you have to go up a set of stairs. There is a landing between those stairs. There is a wall. I put three signs on that wall on the landing. I made the signs as big as I could make them. First I put the years that Colorado had won league championships. Then I put Big Twelve on the sign with a big question mark. The players saw the signs every day.

In the middle of the wall, I put the national rankings of the University of Colorado for the last 50 years. For the first year I was there, which was 1999, I put a question mark. After that year was over, I put up the year 2000 and put up a question mark. This past year I had the year 2001 on the wall with a question mark. I wanted the team to be thinking about where we were going to be ranked at the end of the year.

I had a third sign that had National Championship on it. It had the year 1990, when we won the National Championship, and then I had a big question mark. The players saw those three signs every day when they came to our facility or when they went to class. That was my way of letting the players know what my vision was for the Colorado football program.

In our team room, I have our schedule of games printed out from the bottom to the top. The first game on our schedule is printed on the bottom. The second game is the second from the bottom and on up the schedule. Our schedule goes all the way up to the Championship Saturday date. That is for the players to think about and to see each time they are in the team room. I want them to talk about the schedule constantly.

I put a big gold square around the November games. To me, in college football, championships are crowned in November. This is when the games really count. If you lose a game in November, you are out of it. We want to draw special attention to the November games. I put those games in gold to get the players to notice them.

How do you determine how you are going to get those things set up and get them to work? You must have a certain philosophy on the coaching staff. You must decide how you are going to coach the players. The first thing we said was this: "Coaching is taking players where they cannot take themselves." It is the same for teaching and leadership. We can all take ourselves just so far. We hit a spot where we need a mentor, or a coach, or a leader, or someone to get us beyond that point. That is what our jobs were at Colorado. We had to take them where they could not take themselves.

The second thing we stressed was this: Every player deserves a coach that believes in them. If they were going to come to our meetings, practice with us, and wear the Gold and Black, then we were going to believe in them. They needed to know we believed in them, and we were going to treat them that way. It did not matter if they were a walk-on or the 115th player out for the team, we were going to try to show them that we believed in them, no matter what.

The third point that we stressed was this: I firmly believe attitude and chemistry are the keys to winning, regardless of the talent level. You saw a great example of this in the Super Bowl this past year. Nothing better has happened in football than to have the New England Patriots win the Super Bowl. To have the entire team introduced as a team to start the game rather than have individuals introduced was a big statement about their attitude. Being introduced on national TV for the Super Bowl was not as important to them as it was to be one unit for that game. Not many people gave them a chance to win that game. It confirmed what I believe in: Attitude and chemistry is where it really counts. You must have some talent, but that just gives you a chance. You do not win championships without having a great attitude and great chemistry on the team.

The fourth point we stressed was the fact that football is a hard game. In college it is really hard. One day the reporters asked Bear Bryant how he could continually turn out winning football teams. He replied, "I am a plow hand from Arkansas, and I do not know a whole lot about football. But I do know a little about people and teams. Some people you have to build up, some you have to settle down. But at the end you must get the entire team playing with one heartbeat." From the time I heard that story it has been a constant for us. In each program I have been in, we have stressed that we are going to operate the team as one heartbeat. I take this one step further. I have a sign up that indicates this fact.

"A man will do so much for a dollar, more for another man, but he will die for a cause."

As a head coach, I spend my time creating causes for my teams. It may be a weekly, monthly, or yearly cause. I spend my time creating causes to get that right attitude and chemistry that is really needed.

Once you decide on what you want to do, you must decide on how you are going to go about solving that jigsaw puzzle. How are you going to find those straight edges and those corners of that puzzle? In any company, there are five basic ingredients that you must have. One, you must create an atmosphere where there is great trust and respect. If you do not have number one, there is no reason to go to the other four items. Trust is faithful, caring, and predictable. You must have this in your football team or in your business if you are going to succeed. This is not easy to do. Trust is not an easy thing to explain, especially to a young person. You must work at doing it to be successful. I found this out when I went to Northwestern. I thought I could get everyone to follow me when I went there. I had a championship ring from Colorado and I thought they would jump on my bandwagon. They just did not do that. I had to earn their trust and respect.

I said if I ever got into that situation again, I would go meet every parent of all of the players. When I went to Colorado, I went to visit almost every player on the team. I missed two players. I went to their homes to see what the family liked or disliked about our program at Colorado. I wanted to see how that kid was motivated. I wanted to see how they were educated and what was important in their homes.

If I am going to believe in that player, I must have enough information about him to know how he thinks. It was a tough job to make all of those trips. It did not pay off the first year. However, it did pay off this year. I had to be patient with it, but it paid off.

The second basic ingredient you need to be successful is to create an atmosphere where the things you are doing are important to the players. If it is not important for them to play football in your school, they are not going to give you everything. In Chicago we had to find ways to make football important because it was not important to most people there. It may be the special teams. For example, we take three buses to the games. The special-team players go on the first bus. They get the first and best of everything. We want to draw attention to the special-team players. We did it in many different ways this year. You must find ways to do this. The players are not going to find this. You must find it. It becomes part of your responsibility to solve that part of the puzzle.

To be successful, you must create work habits and standards. We have standards in our program; we do not have rules. When someone operates below a standard, I go to them and discuss what they did that was below our standards. I do not talk about rules. That is how I hand out the discipline.

We coach character every day. The players cannot get enough of hearing what is right. I have been coaching 32 years now. People ask me how the kids have changed over the years. Kids have not changed. No! The adults have changed. The adults today will not hold the kids to the same standards we did 15 to 20 years ago. If you want the same standards, then the adults must hold the kids to those standards. Kids are going to do what you let them do. Your kids trust you. Whatever you ask them to do, they will try to do it. But because people are so concerned about the self-image, we have forgotten that we need to hold kids to certain standards. Kids will climb to whatever standards we set for them.

The fourth basic need to be successful is a system. You must have a system. You must be patient with your system. All systems work. I am in my fourth offense. All four of the offenses have produced league championships. We went to Northwestern and put in our defense. In the first year, we were last in the NCAA ranking on scoring defense. We were 117th out of 117 teams. The second year we were 86th in defense. The third year we were 48th on defense. The fourth year we were 1st in the NCAA in scoring defense. This was in a school that was not supposed to do this. Nothing changed including the coaches and most players. The system stayed the same. We believed in the system, and we were patient with the system.

The fifth ingredient is very important. It is having the right people around you. In our business, it is recruiting. In your business, it is your choice of coaches and the kids you choose to have on your team. We look for competitors. I look for kids that love to play the game. At the Division I level, there is a difference between givers and takers. Some kids go to certain schools to get out of the school what the school can give them. I believe you bring in kids to your program that want to give to your program. They want to make a difference at the school. It is not what the school can do for the player, but it is what the player can give to the school. We feel it is hard to make a championship team out of a group of takers. It is much easier to do it with a group of givers.

There are three values your program must have. First is trust. I use every story I can to try to give the players a picture of trust. Patience is the next value you must have in a program. This is often lost in the shuffle. Try to explain what patience is to a 17-year-old kid.

The third thing you must have is faith. The definition of faith for me is this: "belief without evidence." There are so many different ways this comes into being important.

Before we went to the Rose Bowl at Northwestern, we had to call the reporters to get them to come out to visit with us. When we practiced, we would come together and form a huddle. We would put our hands together and everyone would yell out "Rose Bowl." We had two reporters from the Chicago Sun Times and one from the Chicago Tribune lying on the ground laughing when our team came together and gave the yell "Rose Bowl." They were laughing at us. They asked me what kind of evidence they had that they could go to the Rose Bowl. I told them they would have to wait and see because our players honestly believe it. I told them they had put in three hard years now and the payoff would come this year. We did indeed go to the Rose Bowl that year.

We had a 3-8 season a year ago. In my first team meeting this past year, I talked about accountability. Our big problem was this. We had a handful of really good players. But they were more concerned with who was going to win the national awards at the end of the season. Actually, we had played as a selfish team and the fact we were 3-8 proved that. When I met with the team last year, I started hammering this home.

In our off-season workouts, we go at 6:30 a.m. We have six stations, and we go for five minutes at each station. We have two teams at each station. There are three competitions within the five minutes. It is all change of direction and footwork kind of drills. All of our coaches are at the drills, and we are yelling and screaming. There is a winner and a loser three times at every station. The loser had to do up-downs and the winner had his name posted on the winner's list on our board. That forced the players to be ac-countable to their teams.

At the end of those drills, we did what we called Big-Twelve Sprints. We would do 12 sprints at a distance of 10, 20, or 30 yards, depending on the mood I was in. We never did 10-yard sprints. We had them line up, and on the whistle they had to sprint the distance we were running that day. If the players had a hand across the line, were slow getting off the ball, or did not run all the way through the line, all of them ran again. Each assistant coach had a yellow flag. They would throw the yellow flag and comment: "Jim Jones did not run all the way through the line. Billy Bob was slow coming off the ball." We had a person charting all of those flags and each run. If they got a flag on the play they had to run it over. They had to run 12 perfect plays. The first day, it took us 36 sprints to get the 12 perfect sprints in. At the end of the day we posted the names in the locker room of the players that made the team run more. Things started taking care of themselves when that list started appearing on the bulletin board. We could see our leaders starting to emerge on the team. We spent the entire pre-spring running the "Dirty Dozen." We had tremendous things happen related to this drill. We had accountability and competitiveness going on during this period.

Before last year in spring football, we were always concerned about getting players hurt. We went to spring football last year, and I said I was not going to sacrifice the team to keep from getting someone hurt. We had the most physical spring practice I have ever had. We had the best practice tempo I ever had. The seniors told me it was because of the drills we did in the indoor program and in particular the "Dirty Dozen." You had to come up to the standard of the team, or they were going to throw you out. However, I will say the players were fair about this, and they did encourage the young players and worked with them.

In the summer, we had everyone come back to school after a two-week break. We had three t-shirts made up. One read, "Power of the Buffalo - Big-12 Northern Champion." I hung this t-shirt in the weight room. A second t-shirt read, "Colorado - Big-12 Champions 2001." A third shirt had "Colorado Buffalos - National Champions - 2001." I put those three shirts in a prominent place of the weight room so they would see them every day when they worked out during the summer.

During the summer, our receivers ran hills by themselves every Wednesday. We have some great hills in Boulder. They did this on their own. Our linemen bear-crawled up and down the stadium steps four days a week. They wanted to do something different. The linemen lifted weights at 5:30 a.m. They did this, not because anyone told them to, they decided to do this on their own. They took the responsibility for their own success.

We have three plush fields for practice. During the summer, our strength coach made the team earn the right to go work out on those green, grassy fields. He took them to the baseball diamond and made them work in the sand pits until they earned the nicer fields. It took them two-thirds of the time in the summer to get to the grassy fields. He has a fence around the sand pits. He would lock the gates when the workout started. If you came late, you had to crawl over the fence. Everyone knew if you were late. Some of this we planned, but some of it we just fell into.

In July we have a media day in Dallas for the Big 12 Conference. Each coach brings two players from his team and you have meetings with all of the press people. The reporters ask the same questions to each coach and their two players. All the writers do is to look at your stats from the year before and try to assess how they will do for the upcoming season.

We landed in Dallas and drove to the Media Day hotel. From the airport, we passed Texas Stadium where the Big 12 Conference Championship was to be played in December. I asked the person that was driving us to the meeting if he could get us into the stadium after the meeting. He assured me he could. I told him I wanted our two players to see where they would be playing in December, where they would dress, the sideline we would be on, and the seats our supporters would sit in.

We went to the meeting and it was the same old stuff. However, I told the reporters they had no idea how good our football team was going to be in the fall. "I can tell you right now, we are going to be back here December 1st in the Big 12 Championship game."

I took our two players and went back to Texas Stadium. The players were not prepared for this. When we got back to Boulder, the first thing the two

players did was to tell our seniors what I had done. They told the players that I had told the reporters that I said we would be at Dallas for the Big 12 Championship in December. We had set the standard for the team. I could feel this running through the team.

One of our coaches recruits the Dallas area. They have a miniature of the Dallas stadium. I had the assistant coach pick up one of those miniatures of the stadium. At our first meeting in the fall, I sat the plastic model in front of me.

The first meeting in the fall is the most important meeting that we hold. I am sure most of you do the same thing. I work all summer on this meeting. I read all summer things that might help me say the right thing or create the right *cause* I need to develop.

I am going to give you a couple of books to read. Hopefully you are readers. First is a book by Billy Packer entitled *Why We Win.* He has introduced 20 coaches that have won world championships or other NCAA Championships. It includes coaches in soccer and others that have won two championships. He includes Bill Walsh, Bobby Knight, and Joe Paterno. He asked all of them the same exact questions. One thing Billy asked these coaches was how important were halftime adjustments compared to pre-game preparation? Not one coach listed halftime adjustments as being more important than pre-game preparation. The second question asked of the coaches was, "What is your biggest concern as a coach?" Every one of the coaches said the fear of failure was what motivated them.

A second book I read last summer helped me a lot. It is by Brian Billick of the Baltimore Ravens. It is titled *Competitive Leadership.* I got one of the best ideas I have ever gotten from Brian and his book. I will cover that point later.

I started our first meeting with this statement on the overhead.

"First, you think of yourself as a team of destiny. Second, you develop a sense of family." From day one, in that first meeting, I convinced our players they were a team of destiny. After we lost the first game of the year we sat in the locker room and I told the players they were a "team of destiny." I reiterated this every week. On Thursday after practice is when

I create my *cause*. That is when I go over several things with them. I remind them of who we are, where we are going, and how we are going to get there. Then I talk about the upcoming game. I tell them our game plan and how we are going to get there. I tell them who has to do what in that game.

The next thing I tell the players is this: Opportunities do not occur in life just because you want them to. You do not deserve anything special. "Just because you are at Colorado does not mean you deserve anything special." You do not get the opportunity just because you want it, you have to go out and make it. "*Only those who risk going too far can possibly find out how far one can go.*" This is a quote by T. S. Eliot. When I told the players we were going back to Texas Stadium I know I hung my butt out. But, I knew we would never get there unless we said it. We were not going to get to Texas Stadium unless we took the risk of saying that we were going to do it. You are the handicap you must face. You are the one that must overcome this situation. Faith without work is not true faith. Individual honors are mostly political. But in winning and losing there are no politics, only numbers.

I said this specifically to those team members that had individual national goals before team goals the year before. I followed this up with a positive statement. "If you will identify the team goals first, the individual goals will follow." They did just that. I told them we could not trip on something that was behind us. We were 3-8 the year before. I did not care what happened the last year.

I gave them two formulas for a championship. The first formula was 90 - 10. Any successful business spends 90 percent of its time chasing its goals, and 10 percent of its time on internal issues. An average team spends 50 percent of its time chasing its dreams, and 50 percent of its time on internal issues. The real bad team spends 10 percent of its time on chasing its dreams, and 90 percent on internal issues. They are more concerned over what color pants or jerseys they are going to wear. This past year we were 95 percent working on our dream, and 5 percent on issues. The only internal issue all year was what color pants we were going to wear for the Nebraska game.

The second formula is one that I have used everywhere I have coached. "There are seven todays in a row." We use it as today, plus today, plus today, plus today. Take them one day at a time and one play at a time.

The next thing I did at the meeting was to tell them a story. "How many of you saw the movie *The Fugitive*?" Tommy Lee Jones and Harrison Ford are the stars in the movie. Harrison Ford was a doctor whom they claimed killed his wife. Tommy Lee Jones chased him for five years all over the country. Tommy Lee finally cornered Harrison Ford in a big sewer in the movie. There was no escape for Ford. Tommy Lee Jones pulled his gun and pointed it at Ford and told him he was under arrest. Tommy Lee slipped and dropped his gun. Harrison Ford picked up the gun and pointed it at Tommy Lee Jones and told him he did not kill his wife. Jones replied, "I DO NOT CARE!"

So now, we evoke the Fugitive Rule at Colorado. We do not care about that. That means we do not care if you have problems. We do not want any excuse for losing. If the players came to me with a problem, I told them I was going to ask them if they saw *The Fugitive*. "I DON'T CARE." That became our mantra for the year. If something went wrong on the field, we simply said, "Did you see *The Fugitive*?"

On Monday I do a scouting report. If the opponent has a great player I talk about him. I would tell them a certain back was the best running back we would face all year. I would give that player's stats and point out how good he was. The players would look at me and reply. "Coach, did you see the movie *The Fugitive*?"

This mantra really came into play because we lost our first game to Fresno State. We got beat up after that game by the media. In our meeting after the game I told them they still were a team of destiny. "We have no one but us. Everyone is after us." We had five days to get ready for Colorado State, a team that had beaten us two years in a row. We put a big sign in the locker room that said we did not care about all of the other things. We took the attitude if you were not with us you were against us. We did manage to defeat Colorado State this year.

At Colorado we have a tunnel that goes out to the field. It is made of concrete bricks that are painted over. Several years ago, they started a tradition of painting one of the bricks gold when we beat a team that was in the top 25 in the nation, or if we beat a big team that really meant something special. It became a brick wall of fame in a way. I painted a black brick on the wall that read "NEXT." I wanted the team to start thinking who would be the next team on that wall. We put five new bricks on the wall this past year. I think the fact they knew where the next brick was going to go made a difference.

When we played our first conference game against Kansas, after the game the players got the trophy case with the miniature Texas Stadium and told the team they were going to put a team sticker of Kansas on the trophy case. They announced they were going to put a school sticker up for each school as they beat them.

The next week we played Kansas State. It had been a tough place for us to play over the years. It was a tough game and we were very worried about it. In the meeting on Thursday night, I had a 10-foot, 2-by-6 plank. I put it on the floor. I put a dollar bill at the end of the 2-by-6. I called one of the players up and told him if he would walk the plank and pick up the dollar bill without falling off he could have it. He had no problem doing that. Then I raised the plank three feet off the floor and put two dollars at the end of the plank. Again, he tip toed down the plank and picked up the two one-dollar bills and put them in his pocket.

Then I raised the plank to 12 feet. I put two ladders up and put the plank on the ladders. I put a $20 bill at the end of the plank. I told the player the same story. He was a little shaky but he did manage to make it over to get the $20. The team just knew they had ripped me off for $23, which they had. I asked the player to tell me what he thought about as he walked the plank.

He said on the first plank for the one dollar it was no problem. The second plank at three feet was a little different. He said he had to really concentrate on the $20 bill when the plank was at 12 feet.

I asked the team if I put the plank at 100 feet and put $100 at the end, how many of them would try for the money. Not many of them were interested in making that effort. I told the team the Kansas State game was going to be played at 100 feet high. I told them the plank was the same length at 100 feet as it was when it was lying flat on the floor. I told them the secret to success is to concentrate on what you want and not to look down. We went to Kansas State and played the best defensive game of the year. We won the game and put the Kansas State sticker on the Texas Stadium trophy case. By this time we were taking the trophy case on the plane with us so we put it on the case just after the game.

We had to play Kansas State, Texas A&M, and Texas in a row. One of the things for me in coaching has been that I have gotten my teams too high for games. I know this has happened. I wanted to make sure it did not happen this year. We could not afford to be high for one game and low for another game, so we talked about finding a level we could play at consistently over the year. We went to Texas A&M and beat them. We played Texas and turned the ball over five times and got beat by a good football team.

Nebraska is a very, very big game for us. We had lost to Nebraska on the last play of the game the last two years in a row. Nebraska is a game that we put in RED on our schedule and really look to that game. We do not allow anyone to wear red in our building. None of our coaches have red cars. It is a big deal for us. For us to play in the Big Eight Championship game in Texas Stadium we had to win all of our other games after we lost to Texas, and we had to beat Nebraska.

We beat Missouri and Oklahoma State. We got down to the Iowa State game before the Nebraska game. At our meeting on Thursday night before the Iowa State game, I took that board and put it on the ladders at 12 feet. I put the Texas Stadium trophy case with all of the decals on it at the end of the plank. This time I called up a player that was deathly afraid of heights. I had no idea that he was afraid of heights when I called him up. I told him to take the decal and walk the plank and put it on the trophy case. He got up on the plank, and then he really started shaking. The players went up to the ladder and held it for him as he walked that plank. He sweated all the way across the plank. There was no way he was not going to put that decal on the trophy case. It took him a minute and a half to walk the plank. As he put the decal on the trophy case, I knew there was no way we were going to lose that Iowa State game. That set us up for the Nebraska game and that is what we had been shooting for.

It was the first time in 10 years that Colorado had been in position to earn a ring for a championship. On Thursday night, I had all the assistant coaches bring in all of the rings they had earned. We had one coach that had a Super Bowl ring, and other coaches had league-championship rings. I had the players come up and try on the rings. We had a sample of the Big 12 Championship ring. It was a vision I wanted them to see. I wanted them to know they were the Team of Destiny.

The Nebraska game was quite a game. In the middle of the second quarter the score was 35-3. One of the coaches came up to me and asked me what I thought about the game. I told him it was like the first time Adam saw Eve. "Stand back, I do not know how big this thing is going to get."

We had a great week of practice before the game. It was 17 degrees that week in Boulder and we do not have an indoor facility. But we had a great week of preparation because the game meant a lot to us. After that 62-36 win over the number one team in the country the media was all over us. I was so impressed at the way our kids handled the Nebraska game. A lot of the success we had related to the leadership on our team.

We traveled with 70 players this year. In each game, we averaged playing 65 players per game. The average is about 45 players a game for most teams. Everyone on our team this year knew their role, and they accepted it and handled it with great dedication. They had a very positive attitude about their role. We lost three of our best players in the fourth game. But we had other players step up and make plays. There was no excuse for us not winning the games. It was the Fugitive Rule coming into effect.

We played Texas for the Championship in December. Tennessee had just beaten Florida that afternoon. If Texas beat us, they would play Miami for the National Championship in the Rose Bowl. I did not know that Tennessee had beaten Florida. Someone told me this just as we were going on the field against Texas. We had a great game plan and defeated Texas. I almost screwed it up when I called the fake punt. The field goal kicker saved my butt when he kicked the winning field goal. It was a great atmosphere after the game. Then we went to the New Year's bowl and messed in our pants.

We finished .05 points away from playing Miami for the National Championship. That is only one play. We were only one play away from playing for the National Championship. In the 1992 Olympics there were only 16 inches between the first and fifth place in the women's 100 meters. There is a fine line between winning and losing. You cannot tell me we could not have made one more play last year. This year we will have a lot of signs up at our place that has .05 on them. Everyone will know what that means. We had a great year and a lot of it was because we had so much accountability.

Those of you that want to get to the championship game at your level just remember this: It is not about schemes or systems. It is about all of the other things. It is about creating the right attitude, developing that chemistry, getting the kids to be accountable to each other, and creating that attitude of trust. Finally, you must have a belief that it can all happen.

MAINTAINING THE WINNING TRADITION

University of Oregon

Men, I am not going to show any film. I am not going to draw any X's and O's or diagram a play. I want to talk about the most important things I do as a head coach. If you are not a head coach, I am sure you will find these things important.

Each year the people want to know if we have the talent to win. They want to know if the quarterback is going to be good, if the linebackers will be good enough to win with. When I took over at the University of Oregon in 1995, we had just come off a trip to the Rose Bowl for the first time in 37 years. A lot of my friends told me that was not a good time to take a program over. Most people would prefer to take over a team when it is near the bottom and then move the program up a bit. But I could not take a chance and turn down the opportunity to coach in the PAC-10. The chance to coach in the PAC-10 does not come around very often. For me, the challenge was not to change anything. I had been a part of that winning staff. For me the challenge was this: How could I keep that same chemistry the team had, the confidence and trust they had in the program?

I truly believe we were not the most talented team in the PAC-10 Conference when we won the Championship in 1995. If you make a list of the players we have on our team and rate them on their talent we may not be rated at the top of the PAC-10 very many years. But, in the last eight years we have won more games in the PAC-10 than anyone else.

I do not have all the answers but I do know something about players and coaches. We have won 25 of the last 26 games at home including 23 games in a row. Why have we been able to accomplish this? Our field is a different field than our opponents were used to playing on. Some of it was due to our great fan support. If you have been to our stadium you know what I am talking about. It is a very difficult place to play. We love this and it is something we promote.

This past year we had six ranked teams from the PAC-10 Conference. It is a very good league. We have been on TV in a bowl game 10 of the last 13 years. I speak at other Nike clinics and I have to tell the coaches of other parts of the country that we actually do get on TV. If their kids come to our place, they can still be on TV.

We finished number two in the national ranking this year. That was not a miracle as far as we were concerned. It represents a lot of hard work, a lot of perseverance, and a great effort by our staff. I want to recognize our staff today. (Introduction of Oregon Staff followed.)

I am going to talk more than lecture. I think these points are applicable for all levels. When I took over at Oregon, I put up a sign in the coaches' locker room and one in the players' locker room. Basically, the sign read, "Be positive, enjoy yourself, and make it fun for everyone." Those signs are still up. At times we tend to forget that it is supposed to be fun. It is supposed to be a game. At my level, it is not a game. At this level you have to win, or you lose your job. I say this, but I know it is my responsibility and my concern. It should not be my assistant coaches' problem or my players' problem. I want my players to have fun and to enjoy themselves. We must have that facet when we go out on the football field. Most of the high school coaches do a great job of keeping the fun in the game and the love element in the game. I say "love," and I can go into more detail on this subject later.

One of the factors a new coach must consider when he comes into a new program, or is elevated to the head coach from the present program, is this. What consistency factors can we live with in the new era? I can say that because I can recall when I was the offensive coordinator, if practice did not go well, I would get mad. The madder I became, the less communicative I became. As such, I was not much good to anyone. I was not any help to my quarterback, and I was not any good to myself.

I realized this when I became the head coach. I said this was something I would have to change. I decided if I was going to ask for a maximum effort and maximum commitment from my players, I would have to do the same thing in practice.

When I was the offensive coordinator, I got the chance to go visit other programs. I went to Florida and Miami. I talked with the coaches, and I watched the kids practice. It was amazing to watch those teams practice. I realized we were not going to be a good football team until our players took ownership for our practice and for the work ethic in the weight room. The same thing was true in the summer programs. They had to take ownership of the program when the coaches were not there. The players must be involved and they must be willing to say, "This is the level we are going to practice and play." I felt we could not be successful until our players bought into this idea. I knew no amount of yelling by me was going to make a difference. We needed a group of kids to set the standards and the level of expectations that would enable us to win and to continue to win. If we could do that, we would have a chance to be successful.

Let me talk about the things we demanded as a coach. At times there are things that go wrong in practice. Sometimes a drill will not work the way you want it to work. Sometimes the assistant coaches do not get across to the athletes what you wanted to convey to them. How do you handle that situation? First of all you try to get that solved and worked out in the war room before you go on the field. That is why there is no detail too small to go over to make sure everyone is on the same page. The amount of time you spend on those small details will pay off in the long run for you and the staff. You have a limited amount of time on the practice field with your athletes. When you are on the practice field you must make sure you are prepared, organized, and detail-oriented. If you do that, you can demand the same respect from the players.

For example let's say we are going to make practice hard. I do not think making practice hard is necessarily a lot more physical work. It can be mentally hard. You can be tough on kids. You can have positive reinforcement or negative reinforcement. Some of our coaches are awesome in that respect. Some of our coaches send the players up the stadium stairs. That is negative reinforcement. Some of the coaches talk to the players in a great manner. I may want them to yell more at the players but they don't. They know what motivates their individual kids. Coaching styles and methods are different. You must be comfortable at the end of the practice that you have gotten a requisite amount of work and teaching accomplished in that practice. You must be comfortable you have gotten a reasonable amount of repetitions on the ideas you wanted to accomplish that day. If you demand those things in practice, it is what you will get in the game.

I think this same principle is true in working with the community. I say this for the following reason. This is my 30th year of coaching football. More and more I realize my job is not just X's and O's, it is not just setting up a practice, and it is not just coaching the coaches. My job is to try to make a difference in the lives of those young men. This may sound altruistic and idealistic, and it is. Every year this gets a little harder and harder. That is because kids change. When I started coaching 30 years ago, when I walked into a room, the players would jump up and say, "Yes, sir." Now you must earn that respect. It does not come just because we wear the title "Coach." I think this is very important for coaches to know.

Kids are looking at the coaches for an example. They are looking for an example of a work ethic, for an example of honesty, and an example of what they hope to be someday. The consistency factor is very important. What can you live with first. What will you demand of yourself, what will you demand of your assistant coaches second, and what will you demand of your players? You must get all of these things rolled together.

I am going to jump to a lot of different subjects, so bear with me. The first subject relates to team rules. I am talking about accountability and responsibility. You can have as many rules as you want or as few rules as you want. Unfortunately, over the years, our list of rules has grown. I have tried to create some flexibility in the rules. But every time we do that, there is another gray area that occurs. I think it is important to make the kids accountable and responsible. That is a tough thing to accomplish. We get players that have never had to be at school on time. They did not have to show up for practice all of the time. Now, this may sound foreign to you, but it is really true. Some of the players we get are ready. They want to be on time and they want to practice when they are scheduled to practice.

We have had kids that want to skip practice. We talk about those situations and hope the kids will learn their lessons on this matter. The problem with this is that there comes a time when they are no longer freshmen. You must create a structure of responsibility. The more I coach the more I realize that kids want a structure and they want discipline. They want everyone to be treated equally. They do not want a star system. They want to know if they work hard, they will have a chance. They need to know if they do not work hard, they will not have a chance. They want to know that a player that slips by will not have the same chance the players that work hard have.

We talk about treating each other like family. I talk to our players about treating everyone like brothers. The players look at me and tell me they are not going to love some of the players. They tell me this is not going to work. I assure them they do not understand what I mean. "I am talking about the fact that you do not always like your real brother or sister because sometimes they make you mad. But underneath we always love them because there is a respect for a mutual goal and a common ground that we all work toward." This is something we work very hard to create so the kids will never let their fellow teammates down. This is very, very important.

We have 30 out of 37 games that have been decided by one touchdown or less since I have been the head coach. I really believe this is because our kids believe in each other and trust each other and trust the coaches. I think the trust and respect must go both ways. I do not think we practice any different than other teams. But when it is crunch time and it is time to make a play, our kids find a way to pull together.

A few years ago, I stole something from another coach in the PAC-10. It was called the *Team Pledge*. I decided we were going to have something like that for Oregon. We tweaked it a couple of times and this is what we came up with. I would encourage you to do something like this for your own team. It does not have to be what we selected for our pledge. It can be what-ever you want. Whatever you want done, you had better be willing to live up to it and to demand that of your kids. When we started the pledge, we only had four or five things on it. But now we have several items covered.

> **I promise to play the game with great courage and never make excuses. I will play with great intensity and give everything I have. I will finish plays and never give up. I will take responsibility for my actions and inactions. I will continue to push my teammates and myself to be the best in athletics, academics, and in life. I will support my teammates and treat them like family. I will enjoy myself and make football fun for everyone.**

I got tired of hearing kids make excuses. They had excuses for everything they did not want to do. These things are easy to ask of the kids but making them happen is another thing.

We talked a long time about finishing plays. We said we were going to finish plays on offense, defense, and special teams. We point out in a positive and negative mode when someone is standing around on the field. We do the same thing when someone runs halfway across the field and blocks two men. We are going to jump up and down and pat those kids on the back. We are not going to let the kids get away with less than their best effort. It is easy to take responsibility for your action. That is an easy thing to understand. But, they must also take responsibility for their inactivity and the things they do not do. It comes back to the first statement: no excuses. They are responsible for what they do and what they do not do, or what they do not get done.

It is not a pledge for the individual and what he will do. They must agree to push their teammates as well. They want to do what they can to be better in life. I have covered what they must do in the community. "We are all higher than the buildings in town." It does not matter what level we are on, if one of the athletes gets in trouble it makes front-page news. The athletes must understand with their stardom comes that ironclad agreement of responsibility that they have agreed to live with. It is important for them to know if they can get the job done on the football field, it does not stop there. When they walk off the field, they do not stop being a person that wants to be the best they can be. We push them in the classroom, and we expect them to be a model for the community.

When we first had the pledge set up, we decided to have everyone on the team sign it. So we had a signing party after fall camp. Now we have two of these signing parties. We have one after spring practice and one after fall camp. The players that are newcomers get to sign on with us. It is like signing the Magna Carta.

The first time we did it the players asked if the coaches were going to sign the pledge. I assured the players the coaches would sign the pledge with them. We all sign the pledge and hang it in our locker room. It is a big sign. It is four feet by six feet. We all have our signatures on it. We have all pledged what we are going to do to make our team better and make each person a better person. That is our credo. That is what we must do to be successful.

What you have on the pledge is really not that important. It must be what you believe in and what you consider important to your program. You must hit a nerve with your players. You must get them to respond and want to live by the pledge.

Let me talk about captains for a second. In 1993 we had year-long captains at the University of Oregon. Up to that time, it was a hit and miss proposition. Some years the captains did a good job and some years they did a poor job. In 1993 we had a player quit the team after being a captain. I think it was a combination of things that caused this to happen. He told me he got tired of being put between the players and coaches. He was tired of trying to get the players to see the side of the coaches, and tired of trying to get the ideas of the players to the coaches. I saw his point. It was not my decision at the time, but now we do not have year-long captains. We have game captains. Each week we have four captains. Typically we try to select seniors but it does not always happen that way. We try to reward the players that have played well. We try to have a player from offense and one from defense and someone from the special teams.

The most important thing about the captain situation is that we have changed the leadership dynamic for the team. Leadership is a shared commodity on our team. Every single person can be a leader. On different days, individuals feel they can be leaders. We feel picking the players that have played well in the previous game is a good way to reward the players. It does not have to be a starter each week. It does not necessarily have to be a senior. It is someone that has done something in practice, in a game, in the weight room, or in the off-season program. Selecting captains in this manner also is a way to motivate some of the individuals on the team. We have weekly captains, and we believe leadership is a shared commodity. I think this has made a difference in our program. We will repeat captains as we do not have a rule that a person cannot be a captain more than once.

The one area where the senior leadership comes into play is in the off-season. I know that some teams select season captains for that reason, and I understand that situation. But we simply tell our seniors they must be the leaders in the off-season.

Let me talk about the practice player versus the game player. You get some players that will tell you not to worry; they will have it all down by the time the game comes around. They make a statement like this: "I will show them on game day." I tell them, "Bullshit!" I do not believe that. I want to see the effort and success every day in practice. I want to know the kid knows how to do something right. I do not care if he gets bored learning how to do something. I want to make sure he knows how to do it full speed. I want to know how long it takes for him to get tired and how he reacts in adverse conditions. I do not believe that guys can just show up on game day. I do not believe in players that do not think they need to practice. I do not want players that do not believe they should be accountable for the same rules and regulations as their teammates. If a player has not practiced by Wednesday, he does not start for us. If he does not practice by Thursday, he does not play. He does not even make the trip if he is not at practice by Thursday.

A few years ago we had some people getting upset on our team because we would not protect our stars in practice for a couple of days, and then put them in the game to play. They wanted us to let the stars take it easy in practice a couple of days and just play in the games. Sometimes the stars play well, but the players that worked hard for practice were not getting to play in the games. Sometimes those stars would play poorly. We figured out that we were not helping ourselves by pampering the stars. But playing the stars that had been rested for three days did not get it done for us. The player was better physically, but he was not ready to play as much as the player that had practiced for three days. The kid that had practiced may not have the same ability, but he had practiced and he had great desire. So now we have those rules about practice.

Here is my favorite maxim in life. *Don't get by — get better.* We all know we can walk into a meeting like this, walk into a classroom, walk onto the practice field, and do the least amount and still get by. We can work just enough to make the others think we are working. We can do the same type of thing in practice. We can tell the other players that we are going to "take it easy this play, and I will take it easy on you the next play." That is bull crap. If you just get by, you will not get any better. It does not take that much more effort, concentration, and focus to get better.

When I visited Florida and Miami, the thing I saw that really made an impression on me was the tremendous amount of competition in practice. They were really going at it. They were players that had tremendous pride and would not take a down off.

Now I think our program is getting closer to that attitude. We have kids on our team that do not take downs off. We have players that get into the game and bust their tail on every play. It is fun to watch those kids play. The kids across from those players know they had better get going, or they will kick their tails. This is the attitude we want with our players. We do not want the buddy system where they take it easy on each other. We used to have that system. We do not have it now, but I am not stupid. I know it can happen at times.

We want our practice to be intense. We do not practice that long. We are only on the field two-and-one-half hours, and this includes stretching and conditioning. We do not practice that hard for a long duration of practice. We tell them, "Don't get by — get better."

One other point I want to make before I close. Players want ownership in the team. Players want a voice

in the team. They want to know that the coaches care about what they think. They want to feel they are important. Basically we have two groups. We have the seniors that always get involved in any major policy decision. I say this to the degree that I will always listen to them and I will ask their advice. I may not always agree with them but I give them a voice.

We have created a Team Council. That council is made up of representatives from different positions on the team. I will get together with them and ask them what type of meal they want after the game. I may ask them what color socks they want to wear for the home game coming up. We have our options on the socks.

I have had the council come to me to talk about problems. I may ask them about discipline situations. I will get them together and tell them what a player did to break a rule that does not fit into the present rules that we have. I will ask them what we should do for punishment for that situation since it is not covered in our rules. It is amazing because most of the time they will be a lot tougher on a player than I would have been. They will come to me and tell me something like this. "Coach, get him out of here. If he does not want to do it our way, he should be gone."

While I am shocked at the players' strict punishment, I know they welcome the opportunity to have input on their team. It is their team. Coaches get carried away at times dealing with their own ego value to a football program. We would not be there without the players. We call plays, but the players make the plays. It took me 10 years in coaching to realize that *it is the players and not the plays that win games.* I used to think if I could get the chalk last, I could beat you. I could always draw up a better play on the napkin than the previous coach did. It is not about the plays that you draw up on napkins. There have been some great plays that started out on those napkins. There have been some great coaches that were great teachers. The coaches draw up the plays, but the players execute the plays. If it were not for the players, we would not have a job.

Phil Bennett

STOP THE RUN WITH THE EAGLE DEFENSE

Southern Methodist University

My topic tonight is stopping the run. The first thing you have to do is to develop a philosophy that will accomplish that goal. I view all coaches as teachers. To be a good teacher, you need to have a lesson plan. I'm going to start off tonight with a progression of teaching that I have used over the years.

I break down every defensive play we run using five steps. The first thing is *alignment.* As a coach, the hardest thing for me to accept is getting beat before the ball is snapped. That happens each time your defense lines up wrong. The one thing you need to do on defense is align perfectly. There is a saying in this business, "You work alignment to assignment." Before you can do your job as a defensive player, you have to line up correctly.

To be a good coach, you must coach the *stance.* The stance of a player is critical to his ability to play the game. I'll give you an example. As I grade my players, they are either in control or out of control. Stance is crucial to that point. I have had good tackling teams and bad tackling teams. The thing that all the good teams had in common was they had players who played under control. Their stances were good, and the pad levels they played with were excellent. Their change-of-direction skills were outstanding. All those qualities in a defensive player start with his stance.

I'm going to talk about our linebacker stance. When I teach our linebackers, I start with a shoulder-width stance. I want their knees bent and their back flat. I don't want the arms hanging down. I want them to play with a slight bend in the elbow and their fingers pointing forward. I want them to look like they are playing the piano with their hands and arms. There is a good reason for that. I think it eliminates wasted movement. Football is a game of inches. We lost and won football games this year by inches. A wasted step can cause players to make a play late. Instead of stopping the third-down play, we give up the first down.

The next step to playing good defense is *a defensive key.* Everyone on the defensive team has to have an initial key. Someone on the offensive team has to give the defense a run-pass key. Someone on the offense will give a defensive player the proper angle to take and the proper fit into his pursuit scheme.

Defensive players must have *reaction.* Reaction goes back to getting in the proper stance. I am fortunate to have coached a lot of good linebackers. I had a kid at Texas A&M who ran about 4.7 seconds in the 40-yard dash. But in reaction time, he played like a 4.3 player. He never wasted a step. A player's stance can create problems for that player. A good coach puts his players into a position to be fundamentally sound. If you can get your players to play fast and eliminate wasted steps, you are a pretty good coach.

The final thing I consider in defensive evaluation is *tackling.* If you tackle well as a team, you have a chance. Good tackling occurs when players are under control. Having a good base and playing under control are essential to tackling. When we teach tackling, we overemphasize the wrap-up. Make your tackling drills relative to what you are asking your players to do.

I was working at LSU six years ago. We had a strength coach who made the players work with hand grippers all the time. He felt like our players didn't work on strength in the hands and wrist. He thought football was a game that demanded strength in the hands and wrist, and we didn't focus on it enough. From that point on, everywhere I've been in my coaching career, I've made my players squeeze those grippers. The wrap-up in tackling comes from strength in the hands and wrist.

I start my defensive philosophy with those five points. That is how I start teaching run "fits." Our defense at Kansas State was very good. We had good players. I'll be the first to admit that. But, we've always had a philosophy. Our philosophy was to teach *fit*. We taught run-fit every day. Before practice each day, I took 15 minutes to walk through our defensive run-fits. I took the top five running plays from our upcoming opponents and had a defensive walk-through of our defensive run-fits for each play. It is not contact, it is a mental approach to the running game.

You cannot be a good run-stopping defense, unless you know what your footwork is going to be. That is something a walk-through can give your players. It gives your players a mental vision of what is going to happen when the drill goes full speed. We did it every day, and it was very good for us.

Kansas State was the best third-down percentage defense in the nation. We gave up 18 percent first downs on third-down plays. That was good, but third down was not the down that concerned me. The down that I talked to my players about was first down. I want us to be a great run/pass defense on first down. If you can put a team into second and third down and long yardage, your chance for success on third down goes up considerably.

Our goal on first down is simple. We want to give up no more than 2 yards on first down. Any offensive coach will tell you, it is harder to call a play in that situation. If you can get the offense into a third down and 4 yards or greater, your chance for success rises.

I'm going to give you one of our defensive packages today. That package is our *eagle defense*. To be a good run-stopping defense, you have to involve your safeties in run support. This is the way we taught the defense the last four years at Kansas State, and the way we are going to teach it at SMU.

The first thing I'm going to talk about is the fit and alignment of the defense. We number our defensive techniques and letter defensive gaps. The gap between the center and guard is called the A gap. The guard-tackle gap is called the B gap. The gap between the tackle and tight end is called the C gap. Anything outside the tight end is called the O gap. The gaps are the same to the right or left of the center.

Our defensive techniques are numbered as to the alignment of the offensive linemen. On our eagle defense, I'll start from the open side to show you our

alignments. The end to the open side aligns in what we call a 7-technique. Although it appears he is on the outside shoulder of the tackle, he is wider. We want to make sure the defensive end knows his alignment is not a 5-technique, but wider.

The defensive tackle to the open side is in a 3-technique, which is the outside shoulder of the guard. The Will linebacker is off the line of scrimmage in a 1-technique, which is the inside shoulder of the guard. Since he is off the line of scrimmage, we add a zero to the alignment. His alignment is called a 10-technique.

Our nose guard is in a shade technique. I don't give that alignment a number. His alignment is a shade alignment to the tight end. That means he is aligned on the shoulder of the center toward the tight-end side.

The Mike linebacker is in a 40-technique. He is head up the offensive tackle and off the line of scrimmage. The end to the tight side is in a 5-technique, and the Sam linebacker is in a 9-technique.

EAGLE DEFENSE

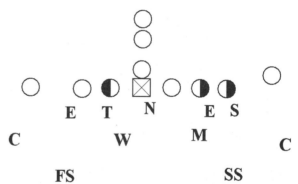

That group is called our front seven. To the front seven we add the two safeties. When the defense breaks the huddle, the only thing they know about the offense is the personnel grouping in the game. They don't know how the offense is going to line up and what distribution they will see. When the offense aligns, it always gives the defense an attack point.

If the offense comes out in a pro-I formation, we will be in our eagle defense. The alignment of the eagle defense means there are bubble areas where the two linebackers are aligned. That becomes the attack point for the offense. They will attack the areas where there is no lineman on the line of scrimmage.

The B gap to the strongside and the A gap to the open side are the attack points.

In run defense, everyone knows the strengths of the defense. What you need to know is the weaknesses. I'm going to give you some of my thought process on the eagle defense. If we are playing a two-back offense, we are going to be in a nine-front defense. That means our safeties are going to play a major role in the run defense.

Our strong safety alignment is going to be 7 to 8 yards deep. We have a couple of Nebraska coaches in the room. Dan Young, the offensive line coach at Nebraska, wouldn't believe that. I moved them up to about 3 yards when we played them, because they didn't throw the ball much. I want our safeties to be effective in stopping the run for short gains.

The free safety's alignment will be somewhat tighter than the strong safety. The strong safety has a vertical threat with the tight end. For that reason, he has a deeper alignment than the free safety. The strong safety has to be hesitant with his reaction up to the line of scrimmage.

Our strong safety keys the tight end to the strong tackle. If the tight end is releasing and the tackle has a pass set, he plays the pass. If he sees the tight end base blocking or blocking down, and the tackle with a low helmet run block, he plays run.

The free safety always keys the end man on the line of scrimmage to his side. In the case of the pro set, he is keying the offensive tackle to the open side of the set. He is looking for a high or low hat by the offensive tackle. The high hat means the tackle is getting into a pass set. The low hat means the tackle is run blocking. The high hat is easy to see because the offensive tackle gets depth immediately backing off the line.

When I play my safeties down, I teach them as if they were linebackers. The keys for the linebackers and safeties are the same. There are four kinds of flow by the offense. There is inside flow toward and away, and there is outside flow toward and away.

The safeties and linebackers are getting the same kind of cutback reads. If the Mike linebacker reads inside flow toward him, he wants to take away the quickest north-south running route. He forces the ball to go in an east-west direction. He spills the ball outside. He fits the fullback in what we call an *underneath fit*. We don't want to give up a linebacker in a 1-for-1 block. If the Mike linebacker takes his outside arm across the fullback's block, he is out of the play. I don't want that. The linebacker uses his fit technique, forces the ball to spill, and gets back to the ball.

When the linebacker crosses his shoulder to spill the ball, he becomes a perpendicular player. That means he is not parallel to the line of scrimmage and becomes a one-way player. We want him to use his hands, stay square to the line, and force the ball out.

The strong safety becomes the *hit man*. When he sees inside flow toward him, he has to fit off what he sees in front of him.

The Will linebacker and free safety are reading inside flow away. The free safety has what we call a *buzz technique*. He is shuffling toward the strongside and becomes the inside-out player to the ball from the backside.

We teach our defensive lineman blocks and name them. A base block to the defensive lineman is a run block that attacks the inside shoulder of the defensive tackle trying to drive him off the ball. The reach block tries to get to the outside pad of the defensive lineman. The offense is gaining ground on the block and trying to get outside. The offensive lineman is trying to get his body between the defensive lineman and the ballcarrier. On the cutoff block, the offensive blocker is trying to get to the inside pectoral muscle of the defensive player. He is trying to stop the pursuit of the defensive player.

On a down block the vision zone of the offensive blocker focuses on another defender. The new blocking scheme now comes from the bucket step of the offensive lineman. A lineman using the bucket step gives the impression that a reach block is coming. The offensive blocker, however, is not trying to gain ground. He wants to force the defenders wide, so the offensive back can cut north-south.

The Will linebacker is a slow player. He knows the Mike linebacker has a safety playing down to his side. He is playing slow through the backside A gap. If the ball cuts back, he is the *hit man*.

INSIDE FLOW STRONG

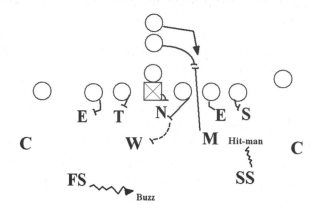

I'm going to show you the outside flow toward with a pulling guard. The Mike linebacker and strong safety read the outside flow toward them. The strong safety reads the reach blocks by the tight end and tackle. He is in what we call *fit support.* That means he is fitting off the 9-technique. As long as the 9-technique is keeping outside leverage, the strong safety is fitting up to what he sees. If he sees the Sam linebacker has been reached, he fits outside of him. As long as the Sam linebacker continues to keep outside leverage, he fits inside of him.

Our free safety has what we call *primary support.* That is the difference between the two-man blocking side and three-man side. We don't want the free safety working off the defensive end. It may happen, but we don't teach it that way.

As the free safety reads the outside flow away he has to be aware that the ball could cut back at anytime. He is the inside-out player on the ball at all times until the ball is committed to the outside. The worst thing that could happen is the ball gets underneath the free safety.

OUTSIDE FLOW STRONG

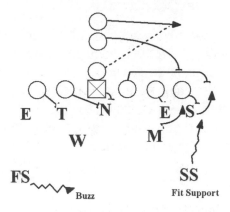

On inside flow to the weakside, the attack point of the offense probably will be in the A gap. If the ballcarrier bends his run back to the strongside, he will probably bend into the B gap. The double team goes on the noseguard with one blocker coming off on the Mike linebacker. The offensive guard and tackle blocks the 3-technique and the 7-technique to the outside. The Will linebacker has to make sure he has a down safety. The Will linebacker takes the inside fit. He doesn't cross shoulders. He fits inside and stays square. If the ball breaks inside, the linebacker makes the play because he has taken an inside position. If the ball goes outside, the linebacker is still alive to pursue the ball.

I don't want to ever tell a linebacker that giving himself up is the way to play the block. I want him to take the block on as deep as he can, but stay alive in the block so he can pursue.

The free safety is the hit man and fits outside the Will linebacker. The strong safety is the buzz player, but has a slightly different responsibility than the free safety in the buzz technique. He has to know that the cutback by the running back could be a direct seam to him. The Mike linebacker is going to play over the top of the double team and fits outside. We have two guys looking for the spill to the outside. The strong safety is the cutback player.

When you put nine players in the box, there are two players the offense can't block. But the defenders can't take themselves out of the play because of an alignment error, or by not having the progression read that the linebackers have. The safeties have to read like a linebacker.

INSIDE FLOW WEAK

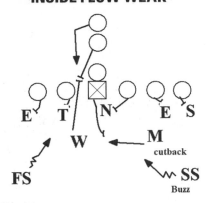

On the outside flow to the weakside, the free safety is *primary support*. Primary support means that the free safety has to turn everything back inside. Nothing can get outside of him. All his help is inside. The Will linebacker becomes the inside-out player. He always fits underneath the free safety. When the strong safety knows he has full flow away, he can be more aggressive. Since he doesn't have the threat of the cutback, he can come faster.

Teams will zone the noseguard and let him go. They tell their tailback if the noseguard tackles him, he is going to the bench. The offense is going to do everything they can to block the Mike linebacker. The Mike linebacker has to do everything he can to get over the top and fit into the outside.

OUTSIDE FLOW WEAK

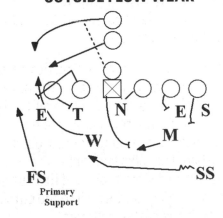

It is important that you stunt out of your base front. We want to make the blocker have to adjust to our movement on the run. If a fullback or pulling guard has to read a different defensive look while he is running, you have made him a softer player. He has to go on a search for his blocking assignment. When he is looking for his assignment, he is not going to be as downhill in his attack.

If we were having problems with the Mike isolation play, we would call an *exchange*. The 5-technique tackle stems to a 4-eye technique and becomes a B-gap player. The strong safety has to change one part of his fit. On inside flow away, he covers the C gap instead of the B gap. The strong tackle is taking the cutback run in the B gap on inside flow away. This stunt is called *eagle rip*.

We build our system with hot words. As soon as the strong safety hears *eagle rip*, he knows on inside flow toward him the ball is going wider. The fullback on the isolation play has to adjust his path to get to the Mike linebacker. The Mike linebacker fits into the C gap and plays his spill technique. One of the hardest things the offensive tackle has to do is take his initial step to a block, then make an adjustment because his block is slanting inside.

EAGLE RIP

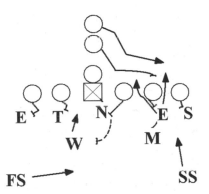

This becomes a major adjustment for the offensive blocking scheme, but only a minor adjustment to your defensive fit. The ball automatically has to move wider, which is where we want it to go in the first place. This line stunt protects your Mike linebacker from getting hammered all the time.

In our game plan, we use these stunts early in the game. If a team has four bread-and-butter plays, I will have four base fits that we are going to use to stop them. In the first series of downs, I'll use all of our defensive stop calls. I want them to know from the first series how we are going to play them.

I want them to know from the first series that we are not going to allow them to run their base offense. They are going to have to adjust and find another attack point. Some people call it making a right-handed team become left-handed. If you are going to be a good defensive team, you have to cancel their best running play. The offense has to go to something they are not as good at doing. That gives your defense a chance to be successful.

The stunt to the other side is called *eagle tam*. The 3-technique tackle is slanting into the A gap, and the Will linebacker is fitting outside in the B gap. Nothing has changed on our fit scheme. The free safety is primary support. If the offensive tackle blocks out on the defensive end, the free safety fit is inside, off the Will linebacker. The Mike linebacker is playing over the top, and the strong safety is buzzing to the B gap for the cutback.

EAGLE TAM

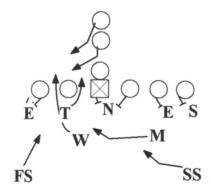

I like to get the noseguard involved in our stunting game. We call this stunt *eagle nose*. If a center has a shade noseguard aligned on him, the first thing he looks for is the attack angle of the noseguard. I want to make a point that I left out earlier. This is a big point on run defense. The defense can dictate the depth of the offensive lineman. I expect the umpire to tell me two to three times a game that our players are in the neutral zone. I want our defensive front to crowd the ball as much as they possibly can. To get the angles they want in blocking, the offensive line has to move back off the ball in their alignment. That means before the ball is snapped, the defensive line has taken half a yard from the line of scrimmage.

The eagle nose stunt is a cross-gap stunt. This protects your Will linebacker. The noseguard attacks across the face of the center into the open side A gap. The Will linebacker's gap responsibility is the strongside A gap on inside flow away. Nothing else changes in the defensive fit scheme. The safeties are fitting exactly where they did in the base defense.

EAGLE NOSE

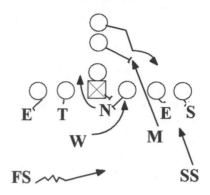

Our defensive linemen are what we call anchor points. They can't let the offensive linemen get off to the second level of our defense. These stunts change up the zone-blocking scheme for the offensive linemen. It gives us a different look. I like to do things that are minor moves for us, but are moves that don't affect your secondary coverage or run-fit schemes.

We have another line stunt we call *eagle tuff*. The noseguard is still in a shade position on the center, but he is playing heavier in the A gap. The strong tackle moves into a 4-eye technique. Our Mike linebacker shifts to a 50-technique stack on the tackle. This alignment gets the defense into a version of the double-eagle defense.

The offensive line has some decisions to make. If the offense uses a zone-blocking scheme, they have to develop a scheme to get to the second level to block the Mike linebacker. People think it is a good adjustment for a strongside run. However, I believe it is better against a weakside run. When we make these technique moves, we stem to them. The 5-technique tackle stems to the 4-eye alignment before the ball is snapped. The cutoff block is almost impossible to make. If the ball is run to the weakside, the backside defensive tackle is turned loose in the backfield. The offensive guard and center is scoop blocking the noseguard. That leaves a big gap for the 4-eye tackle to slant into. He becomes a big disrupter for the offense.

EAGLE TUFF

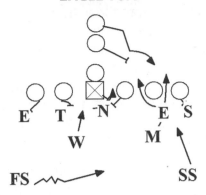

EAGLE MIKE

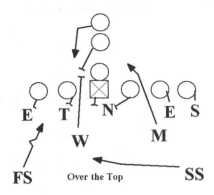

Another simple adjustment is to use the word *stem* as part of our stunt. If we call *stem eagle tuff*, the 5-technique tackle aligns in a 4-eye technique and stems back to our base defense. The stem call tells our secondary there is no adjustment being made.

The next thing I'm going to talk about is what we call our *plug defense*. This is a force-fit technique for us. I don't like to call this stunt a blitz. We are taking a linebacker and telling him to ignore the flow of the offense. He is going to fill his gap on the snap of the ball. I only use this against a two-back set and with our eagle package. On this stunt, we are trying to make something happen. We are looking for penetration.

In this stunt we will be in man-to-man coverage in the secondary. The call to the strongside would be *eagle Mike*. That means we are playing eagle defense and the Mike linebacker is going to plug the B gap. The strong safety plays normal on any flow toward him. On flow away, he has no cutback responsibility. He is playing over the top to the weakside. He has to be a factor to the weakside run game.

The Mike linebacker plays everything the same as far as his fit on the fullback on flow toward him. However, if inside flow comes toward him, he is hitting the fullback deeper and forcing the back to redirect immediately. He becomes the aggressor on the fullback because he is coming full speed unblocked into the backfield. On flow away, he has a chance to run plays down from the backside. The offense is going to continue to block the play the same way. That means the Mike linebacker can come clean on his force fit and disrupt plays run away from him.

The stunt to the other side is called *eagle Will*. I like to run this stunt against teams that are running the inside isolation to the strongside. It gives us a chance to run the Will linebacker through from the backside of the combination block on the noseguard. There is a possibility that the center will miss the plug because he is doubling with the guard on the noseguard. This stunt will make the center's block on the noseguard softer because he is looking for the run-through of the Will linebacker.

EAGLE WILL

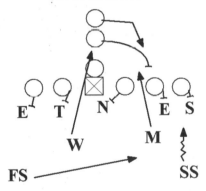

Our Will linebacker at Kansas State this year was a little kid. He was about 6'0" and 195. He was absolutely the biggest playmaker I've ever coached. He had great timing for this stunt.

The plug stunts fit well against inside runs and power plays. But if you end up getting perimeter plays, you need to get out of them. You have to teach your Mike and Will linebackers how to come out of the stunts when they see perimeter plays.

The play I want to show you is the power play. On this play the offensive line to the strongside is blocking down. The center is blocking back with the backside guard pulling. The fullback is leading toward the defensive end for a kick out or log block on the Sam linebacker. We have to make this play bounce to the outside. One of our defenders in the blocking progression has to occupy two people. In this case it will be our Sam linebacker. When the Sam linebacker sees the departure angle of the tight end, he has to get deep enough upfield to occupy two blockers.

The strong safety is in fit support. When he sees the down block by the tight end, he starts up. When the Sam linebacker disappears, he knows he is primary support and the hit man. The Sam linebacker has to make the ball bubble out to the hit man. The free safety is reading inside flow away. He is the shuffle player and an over-the-top player.

The Will linebacker sees the pull by the guard and becomes the free player to the ball. If the Sam linebacker can't occupy two blockers, we have a problem. We have lost our angles and our extra hitter. Our backside safety is nothing more than a linebacker. He has to come downhill and fit inside-out on the ball. He is the defender they can't get a hat on.

EAGLE POWER

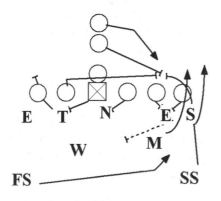

In closing, if I could stress anything to you, it would be going back to those five opening thoughts. Alignment, stance, key, reaction, and tackling are of paramount importance in any defensive scheme. Always do drills that are relative to what you are teaching. That gives you credibility with your players. When they can see on game film the skills that you are teaching in practice they understand the importance of the drills.

When I started back in the late 1970s, whatever you told the kids to do, they tried to do it. In these times, it is not that simple. Your players now want to know why they are doing things. When they can see the skills you are teaching working on the game field, it gives you credibility as a coach.

When you do your defensive drill work, make sure the last part of that drill is to finish with a tackle. That becomes a realistic game situation. We have a drill circuit that we go through. I take a lot of pride with that. The last three years, we have been the only defense to finish in the top five nationally in every defensive category. We lost eight starters from last year's defense. Seven of the eight went to the NFL. People didn't think we were going to be any good this year. We were every bit as good as we were the previous year. We finished third in the nation in team defense. If our offense hadn't given up some scores, we would have finished first in the nation in scoring defense. We ended up second in scoring defense. Our kids bought into what we were selling. We taught fundamentals and put our kids into positions where they could be successful.

I appreciate your time tonight. High school coaches are special to me. Our world right now is on the verge of being chaotic. Coaches work with the kids that are going to be our saviors. If it weren't for what you are doing, we would all be in a big bag. I appreciate your efforts and thank you for coming tonight.

REVIVING AN ESTABLISHED PROGRAM

University of North Carolina

Thank you. This is my second Nike clinic. I spoke about a month ago in Cincinnati. I'm going to talk to you about taking over a program that has been a good program but has fallen on hard times. I think this might help you if you have been in a similar situation. I've got some of my ex-players here this evening. They will tell you I probably haven't changed much.

Coming back to this area is like coming home. I spent 20 years here during my playing and coaching career. I stayed in this very hotel the night before our ball games. This was our team hotel. I am very familiar with being here. There were a lot of great games and great memories attached to this area. They asked me about handling the press when I interviewed for the job at UNC. I told them I spent 20 years in Philly, so I won't have a problem with handling the press.

I spent some time as head coach of a little university called Glassboro State. I was very happy there. I really thought I would never leave. Friends of mine told me I should move on to a bigger program. I really didn't want to coach Division I football because of the problems at that level.

I have really learned to love coaching. I found out I could do this job for a living. At one point, I didn't want to coach for a living. I got into a situation where I was part of a staff that was not together. They had nothing that resembled teamwork. But I found out eventually I could make those things work. I got back into pro ball for 13 years, 11 years in the NFL and two years in the USFL. I went back and coached with Jim Mora at the Saints for one year, and I enjoyed that.

After that, I went to the Browns. I came to realize two things that I wanted to do in my life. I wanted to get back to the Super Bowl, and go back and coach at my alma mater. I accomplished the first goal with the Rams, and then was hired last year at UNC. I feel real good about that so far.

Taking the job with North Carolina this past year is probably going to be the biggest job of my life. There are a lot of things to do down there to get the program back to where it used to be.

Since I returned to North Carolina last year, there has been a whole lot of things happen. Some good things have happened and some bad. The good thing is we won the Peach Bowl. I should have retired after we won that game. Since then I've had two coaches quit and we had two starters quit the team. I lost my starting left tackle, who had two years of eligibility left, the day he came back to start the second semester. His explanation for quitting was that he wanted to graduate in three years and get on with his life. He was not interested in playing pro ball and was tired of playing. One of my coaches left and went to Vanderbilt as an assistant head coach. My defensive coordinator moved to Georgia Tech as defensive coordinator. On Monday I had a press conference to announce the transfer of my starting quarterback. I'm not sure many people have done that before. But we had to get that done.

I used this saying frequently last year with my staff and my players. I really believe in this. *You can never let yesterday take up too much of today.* You better understand this if you are going to be an effective coach. I think that is essential for me to believe in right now with this program.

When you deal with kids on a daily basis, don't let yesterday take up too much of your time. You can't hold grudges with a kid, unless he keeps on giving you problems. If that happens he is out of here.

I tried to use my background to introduce the fundamentals and techniques I have learned. I have learned a lot over the years from some great coaches. I want enthusiasm in the program and to be known as the *football coach* at North Carolina. North Carolina is a basketball school and the ACC is a basketball conference.

I believe with the advantage of the technology that has come into the football program, you can really be creative. The players have more and more ways to be distracted. Before I sign a kid to a scholarship, I look him right in the eye and ask him, "Do you really love football?" I don't want them if they don't love the game.

I want guys that want to play the game. Does that mean they want to practice every day and go to school? No, because it is hard work. I want them to love to get involved in the community and young kids. That's when it becomes a lot of fun.

My game day checklist is something you might want to take a look at. I got totally involved this year with our team on pre-game because our players didn't take the field with any enthusiasm. They weren't excited about playing the game. I watched it happen on game day. We have an old landmark on the campus at Chapel Hill. The bus would unload the team on game day at the landmark and our players would walk from that landmark down through the campus to the stadium.

It started out with 2,000 people gathering along the way to cheer our players as they walked to the stadium. From 2,000 people the numbers grew bigger and bigger. Finally we had 10,000 people aligning the course that our players took to the stadium. That was exciting to walk through all those people. It made your blood run and the hair stand up on the back of your neck. That is what I wanted to create in our players.

I'm going to list these things for you. Some of them might be important to you and some may not, but you can pick and choose what you like.

- Notify inactive players and arrange sideline passes
- Identify opponent's inactive players
- Notify officials; quarterbacks 1-2-3 plus inactives
- Pre-game introductions, special events, National Anthem
- Check primary phone systems (press box and sideline)

- Identify location and specific phones for each coach
- League designee (uniform violation)
- Check backup phone system
- Check number of footballs plus air pressure and rub down
- Check for field equipment and bench location (kicking net, tee)
- Game-day ball boys
- Check video systems and Polaroid
- Arrange for runners as needed
- Training room procedures – taping schedule
- Coordination of medical staff and procedures
- Check players' numbers for substitutions
- Check game uniforms (league regulations)
- Arrange for a backup signaling system
- Locker room assignments (offense, defense, coaches)
- Identify sideline support personnel and responsibilities
- Check for sideline-authorized personnel
- Players' locations on sideline
- Captain's pictures
- Security check for authorized personnel in locker room
- Detail halftime procedures
- Review substitutions
- Coordination in the press box and communications with the sideline
- Post the pre-game warm-up schedule
- Coordinate warm-ups and coach locations
- Coordinate with trainers/doctors in respect to questions on injured players

- Schedule pre-game prayer and talk in coordination with taking the field (2-minute warning)

- Sideline coordination as it relates to play calling, substitutions, injuries, officials, and game situations is vital

- Situation checklist

- Identify responsibilities for coaches

- Communicate with officials: captains, special players, and substitutions

- Meet with captains to coordinate strategy

- Meet with coordinators for last-minute adjustments

- Anticipate post-game atmosphere — take control and give direction

- Coordinate specific coaches' game-day responsibilities

- Direct coaches/players as it relates to their sideline posture and communications

- Game management

Anything that is important to you should be written out. Print it up, and put it on paper. Decide what you want to do on defense, and make a chart for everyone to see.

On defense you have to stop the run. You have to tackle on defense. If you put things down on paper it makes you look accountable and makes the players more accountable. You have to have a walk-through to accomplish understanding. Show lots of video. Kids love to see film of the team and themselves. That is a great teaching device. The films don't lie.

I've been around coaches who know the game. They can talk to other coaches about things and know exactly what to do. But they cannot communicate it to their players, and their players can't play.

When I start out talking to our players about defense, I give them the playbook on the 4-3 defense. I give them the stunts that are run and the blitzes we call. You want to give your stunts and blitzes names that are catchy, but are names they will understand.

If you are an offensive coach or a defensive coach, the most important thing you can communicate to your team is the importance of turnovers. You win and lose games by the turnover margin. If you give it up on offense, you are going to lose the game. If you can't take it away on defense, you have less chance of winning.

I'm going to show you some tape of a great player. This first shot you are seeing is me playing in a 50-defense when I was a freshman at North Carolina. The freshmen players were not eligible to play varsity football back when I started. The next year, I moved up to varsity ball. The coaching staff had gone out to Missouri and picked up what was called a split-8 defense. We had eight people on or close to the line of scrimmage. We had two inside linebackers, two 3-techniques, two 7-techniques, and two outside linebackers outside of them. We played zero coverage on every play. The corners had the wideouts. The safety had the tight end, and the outside linebacker on each side had the first back out of the backfield. It was very simple and great for option football.

Players learn from video. They love to watch themselves play. That goes for years ago, to right now in our present times. Today's teams have so many more advantages because of the specialization that has taken place in the film market. If you have good video guys, they can create special film for your players to watch on a weekly basis.

I have played for some great coaches, starting with my older brother who coached me in little-league baseball. He turned me on to competition. He was one of the biggest inspirations in my life. If you are an athlete and have the opportunity to coach, don't pass it up because you can help an awful lot of kids. My other brother was a wrestler and went to school on a wrestling scholarship and is now a teacher. My daughter is a teacher.

Your family, coaches, and teachers have a big effect on young people growing up. That is so important to have those people in their lives. I can remember my first coach at Philadelphia; he was quite an inspiration with his enthusiasm. I remember Mike McCormick, John Sandusky, and one of the greatest coaches of all time in my opinion, Dick LeBeau. He was my first special-teams coach. I have been around some great coaches to learn from. Of course Dick

Vermeil and Jim Mora made a tremendous impression on me.

I believe in trying to do different things. I try to keep guys involved and their interest high.

Monday I had a press conference. Tuesday I flew to Philadelphia for the Maxwell Club Dinner. Wednesday I flew back and spent the day on campus. Thursday I spent the day in Virginia. Friday I came home and had some dinner with my kids. I'm up here today and I am going back tonight. On Thursday, in morning conditioning drills, we had a linebacker lost for the season with a knee injury. He was my starting middle linebacker who is gone for next season. Never let too much of yesterday take up today. This has been a tough week for me.

When I took the football program over in December of last year, I told my football players my goals were high. The key to reaching those goals is performance. We are in a high-performance business. Nothing happens by accident. To be successful, you must have talent. I asked them if they were strong, tough, athletic, smart, and if they were conditioned enough to play a 60-minute game. This football team has never played a 60-minute game in the last three or four years.

Having good talent only provides a team with the chance to win. Utilizing that talent to play at the highest and most consistent level is what is important. People that perform at that high and consistent level are motivated. Those that are self-motivated are the ones who will thrive in our new program. The ones that are not as motivated will have to learn to be motivated. The ones that won't be motivated or only occasionally motivated will be eliminated from our program.

Motivation is driven by attitude. Good decisions and positive actions are a direct result of attitude. Once decisions are made or commitments defined, a person with attitude will succeed. Attitudes can change for better or worse. The choices you make control attitude.

The power of *choice* is the greatest power you have. The final link to the whole thought process is recognizing what controls attitudes. It has always been my belief that attitudes are controlled by *choice*. The power to determine what we allow to enter our minds leads to the formation of our attitudes. The power to align priorities, pull together, and care about a teammate is a *choice*. The power to be unselfish, be held accountable, and make a commitment is a *choice*. This comes right out of Dick Vermeil's playbook. That man was so special to me.

When we went to the Peach Bowl, we were taking our team to Atlanta for four days. I hadn't done anything like that in a long time. My staff was advising me on things to do. I listened to what everyone had to say, and then I made a decision based on those recommendations. I don't always make everyone happy, but I do make decisions.

I got everyone together when we first got to Atlanta. I wanted everyone to know why we were there and what we were going to do. I had the manager, trainer, medical staff, and security there, in addition to our team and coaches. There were 150 people in that room. I brought our own security to take care of the rooms just like I had done in the pros. They were going to walk the halls and take care of the rooms. When they found one of my players with a girl in his room, I fired him the next day. I sent him back to Chapel Hill the next day. We had a curfew of two o'clock the first night. The second night the curfew was one o'clock. The third night they had to be in by twelve o'clock.

I have had several views written down together for years in my playbooks, but I fine-tuned them for the Peach Bowl. These are simple non-compromising ideals. *Punctuality* is the first thing. Be ahead of time for all meetings. It is better to be an hour early, than be one second late. Don't waste my time or the time of your teammates. Don't put yourself before the team. Be a team player.

Concentration is the second point. In all meetings, practices, and film sessions, pay attention to what is going on. Don't ask questions of a teammate while something is being explained or demonstrated. If you have a question, ask the coach. Don't daydream when something is going on. Be a participant not a spectator. If I don't have an answer for you when you ask a question, I'll get it for you.

There is no substitute for *effort*. Lay it on the line every day. Do things our way not yours. Your effort must be 100 percent physically and mentally. Don't let anyone give more effort than you do and be relentless.

We started out 0-3. We lost to Oklahoma at Oklahoma. We lost to Maryland. We lost to Texas at Texas. No one gave us a chance to be successful after that start. We had a chance against SMU, but that was the weekend after 9/11, and we postponed that game. That brought Florida State up on the schedule. Everyone thought Florida State was going to kick ass. I've got the whole building in a meeting. I got the secretaries, equipment managers, trainers, and everyone I could find in that meeting. I told them to stay the course. We were not going to give an inch. We beat Florida State and that started us on an upturn for about six weeks.

Communication is tremendously important. Ask questions when you don't understand or you are confused — then listen. We will discuss questions in meetings, and we work on the field. If you have a problem, don't let it build up. My time is yours anytime you want to talk about a problem.

You have to be *dependable*. Your teammates are counting on you. On every play on defense, 10 other guys are expecting you to do your job, so they can do theirs. Don't put yourself before the team, and always be a team player.

Respect your coaches, teammates, and yourself. Don't do things to hurt any of them. You don't have to like a person, but in order to be a team, we must respect each other's feelings and goals. Make winning your number one priority, and everyone will gain.

Mental toughness is a big part of every team's makeup. No one ever said it would be easy or fair. You have to play with pain, suffer in silence, never show pain to the enemy, and never ever give up. Make the other guy quit because he knows you never will.

Special teams are extremely important to any program. In our practices, we want to practice all kinds of kicking game situations. I spend 20 to 25 minutes a day on our kicking games. I go through three phases of it every single day. We go from one to the other and keep the players involved.

We have checklists for every phase of our offense, defense, and kicking games. We go through each situation that may occur in a game and cover any

unusual play that could occur. Don't wait until it happens in a game to think about a reaction to it. Practice situational football to be ready for what happens in the game. Have everything you do in practice written down, so when you get on the field you don't have to do too much thinking. If you have someone hurt or want limited time for a particular player, put it on the schedule.

Just remember, football players come in all shapes and sizes. If they want to play ball, there is probably a place for them. Our leading special-team player this past year was 5'6" and 155 pounds. He was a walk-on cornerback. He ran back punts and kickoffs for us. He was a flier. If you have guys who want to play, it doesn't matter what size they are.

Let's watch some more film. Taping your drill work can become an invaluable tool. Showing a guy a picture is worth a thousand words. They can see the visual technique.

When I teach linebacker drills, I want the linebacker's cleats close to the ground. I don't want him on his toes. I want all his cleats in the ground when he makes cuts. I work a lot of drills with the hands behind the back, so they get the feel of training the legs. When we do the shuffle drill, keep the feet apart. Don't click the heels together. Don't do drills that don't relate to something that occurs in the game. I don't do drills that have no carryover value for something that happens in the game. If you are crossing bags or cones, get the feet back on the ground. If the feet are in the air, you can't cut. I don't do any high stepping drills. We want to play in a football position all the time. That means the knees are bent, the back is straight, and the eyes are up.

A linebacker can't make a tackle with his foot off the ground. He has no power. We want to keep the feet moving, but not in the air. Never let the feet go dead. We tamp the feet. We do a drill where we tamp the feet and accelerate for 5 yards, tamp the feet again, and accelerate for 5 more yards. We do that drill for 40 yards.

When we get into a change of direction drill, we want to finish the drill. At the last change of direction, sprint hard out of the drill. You can do these drills with pads or without pads. We teach the linebacker to pivot, cross over, and get downhill to attack a blocker. If a linebacker is playing a back, I let him take the back on with his shoulder. But if he is facing a lineman, he uses his hands. If the linebacker tries to use a shoulder on a lineman, the lineman will hold the linebacker.

I believe in tackling every single day. We practice ball drills every day. Linebackers are notorious for dropping interceptions. Work on their hands in ball and catching drills. Get the linebacker 10 yards away from you and throw the ball as hard as you possibly can. That is the way it will come in a game. Make the linebackers catch a one-handed pass. That works on his eye contact with the ball.

Anytime I can have fun with my players, I do. We had a situation that occurred in the East Carolina game that showed up on ESPN. They were returning a kickoff, and they had broken it, and were going in for a touchdown. One of our corners didn't give up on the play and knocked the ball out of the ballcarrier's hands right before he scored. The ball rolled through the end zone for a touchback. We won the ball game because of the play this player made.

The special-teams coach for the New Orleans Saints is a good friend of mine. He saw the story on ESPN. He showed that clip to the Saints that night and showed them how that had won the game for us at North Carolina. Al made a big deal about this play to the Saints the night before they played the Vikings. As luck would have it, a similar play happened in the Saints-Viking game. He sent me a voice message the next day and I played it for my team. That is having fun with your players because they, at times, relate to the pro game.

It is fun for me to have relationships with other coaches who call and talk about the game.

Like I said we started our season 0-3. From that point, we won five games in a row before losing a tough one to Georgia Tech. People were wondering how we would come back after that bitter loss. We played Wake Forest the next week. We jumped in front 24-0 but lost the game 32-31.

We started 0-3 then won five in a row, and thought we were going to the Orange Bowl. When we lost those two games to Georgia Tech and Wake Forest, I got a bad letter. I don't know if it was from a Carolina fan or not. The letter read as follows.

"It would make us fans sick if you accepted any bowl invitation. Mr. Bunting, you showed us last Saturday that we do not deserve to go to any bowl. You were a joke, an enigma, an aberration, and a total fake, and so was Carolina's football team. Wake Forest fans will be celebrating for years. There is no heart, soul, or character in our team, and they are a bunch of losers. Last Saturday, we saw the end of Carolina football. If you don't believe me, just wait and see. You and Carolina football are finished. You are history, Mr. Bunting."

Well, he called me mister. At least that was nice. You are going to get stuff like that. You have to take the good with the bad. Obviously he didn't sign his last name.

The first time I met with my football team, I talked to them about having great performances. When I started the spring with our staff, I talked to them about how important they were. I really believe in my staff. I think I did a great job of hiring a great staff. I think we will develop loyalty, trust, and chemistry. The three most important things to me are loyalty, dedication, and honesty. I think my staff knows I am tired of lazy, selfish, and undisciplined decisions or choices. I will attack those problems, not the individuals. If an individual refuses help, he will be gone, regardless of whether he is a player or a coach.

I want my coaches to stress team discipline. I want every coach to be consistent with his demands. Respect the personality of the players because all of them are different. I have a list of *do's and don'ts* for my coaches. There are 10 items on both lists.

The do's include the following:

- Get excited and get the players excited.

- Keep your players proud and positive.

- Demand a lot, have high expectations.

- Be on time. Have a plan for today and tomorrow.

- Make sure individual work is organized and *football* related. Don't waste time on the field explaining a drill.

- Be organized with the managers. Make them feel appreciated. Same with the trainers and staff.

- Make sure your players are in Carolina issue.

- Cooldown period is important. Talk to your players *after* cooldown.

- Build up (to players) other coaches. Impart respect.

- Always encourage: Play hard, fast, smart for 60 minutes.

The don'ts on the coaches' list are as follows:

- Don't curse the players.

- Don't get in a pissing contest with a player (or coach on the field). Let JB handle those problems.

- Don't coach other coaches' players.

- Don't humiliate a player.

- Don't grab a player.

- Don't complain about anything around players.

- Don't react (the wrong way) to adversity.

- Don't panic.

- Don't bluff. Remember, you might not know every answer to every question.

- Don't be closed-minded or thin-skinned.

A coach has to develop unconscious confidence. Being negative all the time is not being disciplined. That is not discipline. That is just being negative. Be positive whenever possible, especially with the second- and third-team players. It is easy to coach the first-team guys. Anybody can do that. Our strength team coach has prepared the players, but still, hard work is relative. I told our players and coaches that they have not worked hard in years at North Carolina. They have forgotten how to work. You have to emphasize fundamentals. Small wins on a daily basis add up. Utilize meetings and walk-throughs to the highest level in all phases of the game. Remember that the offense, defense, and special teams are all new to your players. Encourage understanding and demand focus from all your players. Be prepared every time you walk on the football field.

I am in this game for the fun of it. I have coached eight years in the pros, and I had fun there. I coached five years at Division III and had an absolute blast. I haven't coached high school, but maybe I will someday. But I do believe coaching is working with people. When you get an opportunity to work with young people, it is extremely important. I really believe this statement:

"A hundred years from now, it will not matter what my bank account was, what sort of house I lived in or what kind of car I drove. But the world may be different because I was important in the life of a child."

I think that is the most important thing we could all do on the face of this earth at this time in our great country. I have enjoyed being here. Hope you enjoyed it and learned something.

THE UNDER DEFENSE AND BLITZES

University of Southern California

Thank you. I am really excited to be here. I want to thank Nike for putting these clinics on. It gives us a chance to exchange ideas, have some fun, and talk about the game we love. It is a great pleasure to come to Hawaii and have a chance to share with you some of our ideas.

I'm thrilled to be here. I love coming to the islands. I've been doing it for years. It's great fun for me. My wife is out running around and spending money while I'm here speaking. It's a great opportunity for her too.

I'm here today to talk about defense. But before I get to that, I want to reflect on my years of coaching. I spent 10 or 11 years in college football coaching before I went to the NFL. I spent 16 or 17 years coaching in the NFL. I had a wonderful time coaching at both levels.

When I coached in college the first time, my children were young, and I didn't know much about being a father. What was exciting about the NFL was the opportunity to coach mature players who were more deeply involved with their football and making money. It was a nice step up at the time.

I had a couple of opportunities to come back to college football, but the timing of the close of the pro-football season never fit those opportunities. By the time I was free to interview for a job, the jobs always seemed to be filled. I finally had the opportunity to take a college job and landed at USC. I thought I knew what I was getting into. I was really excited about it and jumped in with both feet.

I put a good staff together, but it took me until the middle of the season to realize how foreign college football was and how different it was than what I had remembered. It was different because my perspective had changed so much. It was a much different experience than I ever anticipated. It has been so much fun because you compete on so many different levels. It is not just football. You have to compete in recruiting. You compete in academics, so your players can make it through college. Now I am representing the University, and it has been a blast and so much fun.

I have no desire to go back to the NFL. I don't want any part of it. I'm having such a good time in college football. That is not to say I didn't have a good time in the NFL, because I did. But coming back to college coaching has been a real pleasure for me. I'm pumped up about it, and as long as you guys want to talk about it, I'll be here.

The topic I want to share with you today is defense. I've been coaching defense for a long time. I have been on the defensive side of the ball for my entire career, with the exception of a couple of years. I was primarily a secondary coach. I had the good fortune of coaching with the top-ranked teams in the NFL. I was on the Minnesota staff and coordinated the defensive staff at San Francisco when those teams were really good. I get excited talking about that because it took a long time to develop the stuff we do on defense.

I'll try to give you some general thoughts that might help you. I'm not trying to convince you to change defenses, but I'll show you what we are doing.

To be successful on defense, you need to develop a philosophy. You have to know what you want to do, how you want it to look, and how you want it to feel. A philosophy is like a railroad track. You have a clear-cut direction in which you are going. If you start to get off the track, it gets real obvious to you. If you don't know what you want and what you are about, you won't know when you are off course. If you do realize you are off course, you won't know how to fix the problems you are having without a philosophy.

If you can't write down your philosophy, you still have some work to do. If you don't have a clear view of your philosophy, you will be floundering all over the place. If you win, it will be pure luck. One year you will run a 3-4 defense, and the next year you will run a 4-3 defense. You will never get zeroed in on what is important.

I am an example of a person who really got zeroed into a philosophy early. I went to Arkansas several years ago to work for Lou Holtz. Monte Kiffin was his defensive coordinator. He had just come from Nebraska to take that job. He is now the defensive coordinator with the Tampa Bay Buccaneers and is one of the best coaches that has ever lived. He is extraordinary. I was a part-time coach working with the secondary.

Monte ran an under defense. That was his base defense. That was the first time I started to get hold of something that had a philosophy to it. I started to grow with this defense. After all the years I've been in football, I've never coached anything but the under defense. I know this defense inside and out. I know the good side of the defense. I know the problems and weaknesses of it. I have done all the complements to the defense. I have played the defense from a one-gap principle to two-gap principles. When I was at San Francisco, we played a combination of both principles.

What I bring to you is a real base understanding of this front and what you can do with it. I am not trying to sell you on this being the best defense. What I am saying is I know this defense the best. The reason I run this defense is I know how to fix any problem that may be created.

I want to start you out with the basic front and coverage. I want to cover one more sidelight before I go on with my topic. When I went to the NFL with the Minnesota Vikings, Monte Kiffin was there and we got together with a guy named Floyd Peters. He was from the Northern California area. He played for the Browns and had coached all over the NFL. He had 27 years in the league and was always an under-defensive guy. He was one of the greatest pass-rush specialists that has ever been around. He believed the under front was the best front to use to rush the passer.

When we were all together with the Vikings, Floyd had some really interesting concepts. This defense has been in the pros and college for a long time. It has staying power. This is the defense I'm going to show you today.

This defense has evolved and adjusted over the years. There are some different ways to do things from it. The presentation I'm going to give you today is the one-gap approach. This is the scheme everyone seems to be talking about today.

We want to give our football players a chance to know exactly what they have to defend. We want to give them an attitude in which to do that. We want to always be an attacking, aggressive football team. We don't sit and read. We get off the ball and attack the quarterback.

The big problem with one-gap control is it allows a ballcarrier to get into the secondary if one guy makes a mistake. No matter how aggressive the defense is, there is a great amount of discipline that goes with the defense. You have to be very strict about your positioning and placement of your players. You have to have the ability to maintain relative spacing between your players.

When we talk about the front, all the gaps are lettered to give us a reference point. We letter the gaps on each side of the center as A, B, C, and D. The Sam linebacker controls the D gap to his side. He is in an inside-foot to outside-foot alignment on the tight end. He can never get reach blocked by the tight end. He is the force player and turns everything back to the pursuit.

The end to the tight-end side is a C gap control player. He is in an inside-foot to outside-foot alignment on the offensive tackle. If the tackle blocks inside, the defensive end has to close down with him to keep relative control on the C gap.

The nose tackle plays in the A gap to the tight-end side. We have done a number of things with this position. We have put him in the gap, cocked him on the center, and played a shade on the center. The way we play him in our base defense is an inside-foot to outside-foot alignment on the center toward the tight-end side.

The prime spot on this defense is the B-gap player to the open side. He is an inside-foot to outside-foot alignment on the offensive guard. He has B-gap control, but he can't get hooked. The whole scheme of this defense is based on not getting hooked.

The best pass rusher on the team has to be the defensive end to the open side. He is C-gap control, but his alignment is a little wider. He is an end that can play in space. We align him about a yard outside the offensive tackle. He is playing C-gap control, but at the same time, he is rushing the passer like it is third and ten on every single snap. He has to close down if his tackle blocks down.

The front five players are playing aggressive defense with their outside arms free. The only thing that can't happen to them is to get reach blocked.

The strong B gap and open A gap is played by the Mike and Will linebackers. The Mike linebacker is in an inside-foot to outside-foot alignment on the offensive guard off the line of scrimmage. The Will linebacker is heading up the offensive guard off the line of scrimmage. He is basically a protected player and should make a lot of plays. He has to control his A gap and work relative to his Mike linebacker and free safety.

The free safety is the force player to the open side of the ball. He works off the defensive end's play. The defensive end works for leverage and force. The free safety works off the defensive end and fills wherever he is needed. The strong safety has the middle third on coverage, but fills off the Sam linebacker's play. If the Sam linebacker gets hooked, the strong safety will make the tackle. The offense will make some yardage off the play, but that is how we control the line of scrimmage if there is a breakdown.

The two safeties are fill-where-needed players. They have to keep everything on the inside shoulder. All the players in this defense keep the blocks on their inside shoulders and force the ball back inside to the next player.

UNDER DEFENSE VS. PRO SET

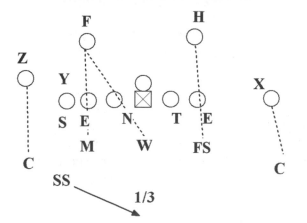

If you look at this under front, it is an eight-man front. This is a stop-the-run-first type of defense. We want to outnumber the offense to each side of the ball. We call the alignment of the front *under* and the coverage *flex*. The open side of the alignment is the flex side and the tight-end side is the solid side. Those are our terms for the tight-end and split-end sides of the defense.

The defense is a man-to-man coverage scheme for the corners. If we call a cover-one flex, we are man-to-man on the corners with the strong safety into the middle of the field. The free safety or flex safety is down in run support. The Sam linebacker has the tight end man-to-man in coverage. He has him anywhere he goes. He never switches up with anyone. If the tight end goes in motion, he goes with him.

The Mike linebacker plays the first back out of the backfield to the strongside. The free safety plays the first back out of the backfield to the weakside. The Will linebacker plays the short middle. That gives us a man in the hole in the short-middle area of the field. If we get a full flow by the backs to the strongside, the Mike linebacker takes the first back and the Will linebacker takes the second back out of the backfield. The free safety becomes the short-middle player.

If it is full-flow weak, the free safety has the first back, and the Will linebacker has the second man to the weakside. The Mike linebacker becomes the short-hole player. In theory the middle-hole player helps with the tight end, but in reality he is the second line of defense against any breakdown in the pass rush. They can help on the draw play, scramble by the quarterback, or screen passes that they can see developing.

If the offense comes out in a different look, the basic core of the defense stays the same. There are no adjustments to be made. The defenders take their men in coverage regardless of where they line up. The Mike linebacker has help in the middle from the short-hole player. However, he can't get beat in the flat. The play-action pass is a problem for this defense. That is an area on which you really have to focus. That is probably the most critical aspect that you have to get accomplished.

UNDER DEFENSE VS. TWINS

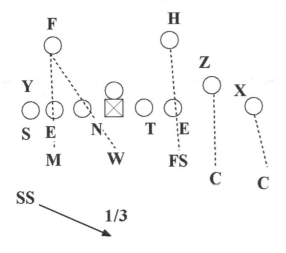

Before we go any further, let's talk about personnel. You want to try to get your best football players on the field. The open-side end has to be one of your best football players. The size doesn't matter. We want an athletic player who can move around.

At the nose tackle, you have to find a player who likes to mix it up. We want a big guy here who likes to get down and dirty. He is going to get doubled on run and pass and is going to get down blocked a lot. He has to be a tough player. This guy can be a short and stubby type of player.

The premier pass rusher on the down line is your 3-technique tackle. He gets a lot of 1-on-1 blocks. At SC this year, we played with a converted end at our 3-technique. He found a home there.

The defensive end to the tight-end side is a defensive lineman that can play the run. He doesn't have to be a big-time pass rusher. He has to be able to play in the C gap and stop the run.

The Mike linebacker is a traditional linebacker. He is instinctive and makes a lot of calls for the defense. He may be the guy with the most experience or the best feel for the game.

The Will linebacker can be small. At our level we can play with a player who is 200. The Will is protected and doesn't have to take on line blocks. All you want him to do is flow and chase the football. We want our fastest linebacker at this position.

The Sam linebacker has to be a good contain player. He has to be strong enough to play on the edge of the tight end. He has to be able to run in pass coverage also.

The defensive backs that are the best run defenders play our safeties. The free safety is the player who makes a lot of tackles for us. He has to have good instincts. He is what we call a natural player. You don't have to coach this player too much. He has a feel for everything and understands the whole picture.

The corners have to run fast if you plan on playing bump and run. If they don't run fast, you can still play with them. But if your corners are not faster than the receivers they are covering, don't play bump and run. It is a race when you play bump and run technique. If you can't win the race, don't play bump and run.

If you have a million reads for your secondary people, you are crazy. They don't need that. All they need to know is their primary responsibility. At the highest level in the NFL, the pass game is about as complex as you can imagine. If a defender can play the post route and seam route, they can play at that level. The thing that breaks the defense down the quickest is a ball being thrown over the defender's head for a touchdown.

Teach your player to play deep middle and forget about all the rest of the rules. The guy who is playing in the middle of the field has to figure out who can get into the middle. We want our safety to play in the middle of the two receivers that can run the post route. He wants to split a relationship with anyone who can get down the middle.

When we play pass defense with our corners, we play as tight as we can. We are going to beat the hell out of the receivers as they go down the field.

If we get a one-back or ace set, the safeties are going to take care of it. Everything else in the defense stays the same. The Mike and Will linebackers take the back out of the backfield. If he goes to the strongside, the Mike linebacker takes him. If he goes to the weakside, the Will linebacker takes him. The linebacker that is not involved in coverage drops into the middle-hole on pass coverage. The free safety adjusts down to take the second tight end.

UNDER VS. ACE

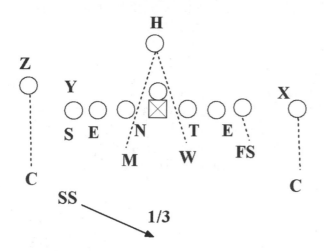

UNDER VS. TRIPS

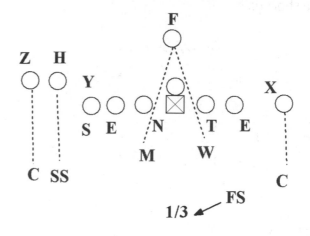

If the offense spreads out, we don't make any adjustments except to match up man-to-man with the safeties. Everything else on the defense remains the same. Everyone is playing their gap control and support schemes. If the back goes in motion to leave the empty set, the linebacker to the side of the motion takes him. The remaining linebacker bumps over to balance the defense and plays football.

UNDER VS. DOUBLE

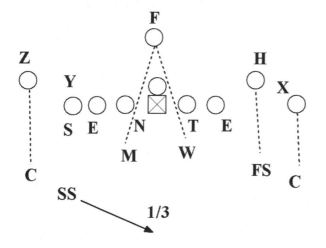

If the offense comes out in a trips set, the adjustment is made by the safeties. In this case, the strong safety goes out to cover the third receiver to the strongside. The free safety moves to the middle of the field and plays the middle third. Everyone else stays the same with the linebackers playing the remaining back the same way.

For a base defense to hold up, you have to have some things that you use to complement it. When you play Southern Cal, every single player on the field is going to have a blitz pattern. The offense has to account for every player on the defense in his pass protection.

The next thing I'm going to show you is different combinations of pass rushes that fit with the under defense. I want to be so multiple that the offense doesn't know who is coming and from where.

The first thing I'm going to show you is what we refer to as *Sam and Mike.* We are going to use the Sam and Mike linebackers to rush the passer. We slant our strong end, noseguard, and 3-technique tackle to the open side of the formation. The weakside end is going to drop into coverage. The alignment is the same as always. The corners are lined up in bump coverage, but are going to bail out and play deep outside zone coverage. They play outside leverage and force everything inside. The free safety is playing deep middle. The weakside end and strong safety are the outside defender to each side. They are playing seam coverage, with the Will linebacker in the middle seam. The strong safety and weakside end play what we call the *hot-two receiver* to his side. If the tight end comes down the middle seam, the strong safety collapses on him. The end does the same thing with the back out of the backfield.

The Will linebacker is playing hot to number three in the middle. That means he is finding the third receiver and covering him if he comes out on a hot route. When we overload on the rush, the ball will be thrown quickly. We want good spacing in our coverage people so we can react by changing up, and make the play for a short gain.

SAM AND MIKE

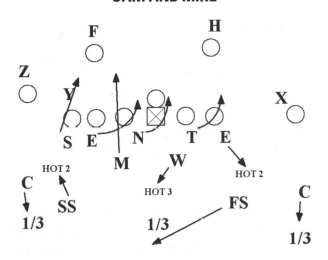

The formation doesn't matter. We have to find our hot receivers and identify them. Another advantage the defense has in these types of stunts is the charge of the line. The defensive line is slanting away from where they have been playing the entire game. That changes the landmark for the offensive lineman and gives the defensive lineman an advantage in his pass rush. The defense has to have counter moves to keep the offense off balance.

This stunt can also be used in run defense. To give us a change-up, we bring the Sam linebacker underneath the tight end's block. We can also let the Sam linebacker play under all blocks and bounce plays to the outside. Those are changes we add to the base defense to keep the offense off balance.

Another way to get five-man pressure on the quarterback is called *safety.* On this stunt we are bringing the free safety from the outside. The defensive line is slanting away from his blitz. The corners are playing their bail coverage and the strong safety is going to the deep middle. The Sam and Will linebackers have the hot-two receivers, and the Mike linebacker is playing hot three.

UNDER SAFETY

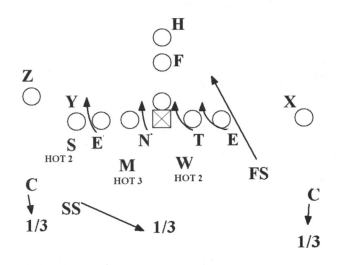

A very effective stunt from this defense is called *Sam and safety.* On this stunt we are blitzing with Sam linebacker and free safety. The defensive line slants to the free safety. The open-side end comes off in coverage, and everything else is the same. The Mike linebacker and the drop end have the hot-two receivers and the Will linebacker has the hot three.

UNDER SAM AND SAFETY

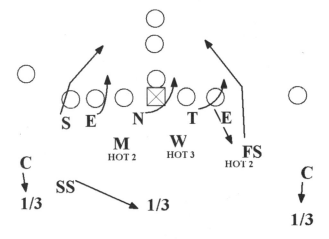

One of the problems we have when we drop the end in coverage is containment. When we drop the end, it means the 3-technique has to contain. That is not a good situation, but we work hard to make it work.

We like to bring defensive backs in the blitz scheme. If they can disguise the stunt, they can get there in a hurry. We like to bring the corner as a change-up. The corner aligns in his bump and run technique. On the snap of the ball, he comes hard off the corner. The free safety cheats back and covers the deep outside third. The strong safety is covering the middle third and the strongside corner is taking the outside third. The rush end and 3-technique blitz the A gap and the B gap. The corner comes off the edge.

The Sam, Mike, and Will linebackers play the hot zones. The Sam and Will take the hot-two receivers and the Mike takes hot three.

You can mix your blitzes up according to your needs. The simplistic blitz scheme lets you bring pressure from a number of different areas. You can game plan the matchups you want. The important point about this blitz pattern is we are not changing any teaching or basic schemes in the defense.

That's all the time I have. I hope I have given you something you can take with you today. It is extremely important to have a philosophy that can guide you to the success you are looking for. Men, I'll be back here tonight, and I'll answer any question you may have about any phase of our defense. Thank you. It's been a pleasure.

UNDER CORNER

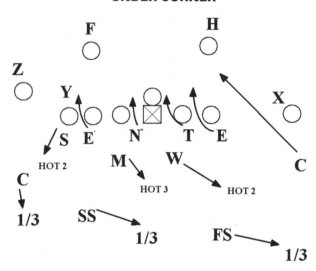

DEFENSIVE SECONDARY BLITZ PACKAGE

University of Illinois

Thank you. It's been 20 years since I've been to this clinic. When I graduated from the University of Kentucky in 1976, I took a job at Paducah High School in western Kentucky. I remember counting down the days until this clinic came around. This is an established clinic, and it is good to see the attendance at this session. I see a lot of familiar faces here today.

I spent some time last night with the University of Louisville and the University of Kentucky coaching staffs. You coaches need to know you have some tremendous assets in those two programs. I talked to Guy Morriss at Kentucky last week. They have some problems they have to work through, but with the coaching staff they have, they will be just fine. If you don't know John Goodner, you need to get to know him. He can teach you a lot about coaching football other than X's and O's.

If you go right down the road to Louisville, John L. Smith has done a wonderful job there. We played them this year, and they have a great group of players.

The message I'm trying to relay to you is to build some working relationships with your local colleges and universities. Those relationships can be such a valuable asset to you and your program. I want you to have that same attitude about our staff at Illinois. We have an open door.

I have been in coaching for 26 years. I've been at 11 universities. My roots are here in Kentucky. I played at Fort Campbell in high school. I played at the University of Kentucky in college. I coached at Paducah Tilghman, Kentucky, Morehead State, and Western Kentucky. There is a strong feeling in my heart for the state of Kentucky.

I did not know Ron Turner before I came to Illinois last year. When he came to Illinois five years ago, they went 0-11 in his first season. Within three years, they were 8-4. This year we were 10-1 and Big Ten Champions. It just didn't happen because Ron Turner came to Illinois. There are two things that we always talk about. They both begin with the letter A. They are attitude and attention to detail.

A person's attitude can influence another person's attitude positively or negatively. Attention to details is doing the little things. There is such a fine line between winning and losing. Five of our games this year went deep into the fourth quarter before the outcome of the game was decided. We won all five of those games.

Attention to details means that all 120 players put their hands behind the line, when the coach tells them to line down. They don't put it in front of the line, or on the line, they put it behind the line. Attention to details starts with the philosophy of the head coach.

I was hired last year to take over a defense that finished 113 out of 114 teams in the NCAA on defense. Coach Turner wanted a pressure style of defense.

The first day I took the job, I had a team meeting with my defensive players. I thanked them and told them I appreciated them letting me be their coach. I told them I would earn their respect. I think earning the respect of your players is tremendously important.

I believe in some principles, which relate to a pressure style of defense.

The first principle is an aggressive mentality. That starts with the head coach. I had been a shade-fifty defensive man at eight other universities. My defensive philosophy was that the defense should bend not break. We played a quarter-quarter-half scheme in the secondary. Men, there is a lot of value to that philosophy. But in today's football with the one-back attack and the west coast offense, that idea is not working.

The old adage of playing base defense and being sound does not work anymore. The people we play are too good to play that way. We used to think the offense wasn't patient enough to drive the ball down the field with a controlled passing game. That is the new trend in offensive football. They take what the defense gives them. They use the control passing game like a running attack. They take the short throw and control the time of possession.

To run this kind of defense, you must have assistant coaches that buy into what you are trying to do. The most important thing is to have players buy into that philosophy. We accomplished both of those things this year. Our players loved that type of defense. However, there are two things you have to do to run this type of defense: You have to get to the quarterback when you blitz, and you have to be able to cover people when the quarterback gets the ball off.

Playing an attacking defense allowed us to jump-start our defense. In practice, we practice with a very high tempo with a lot of repetitions. In college we have a 20-hour rule. That means we have only 20 hours for our meetings and practice time with our players on a weekly basis. We are limited to the amount of time we can spend on the field. We can't waste time in practice and cover everything we have to get done out there.

At the University of Illinois, we practice a maximum of an hour and 40 minutes daily. The time is usually less than the one hour and 40 minutes. You have to be extremely organized to get your practice work done.

We do a little drill every single day. We do this drill in spring practice, fall practice, or bowl preparation. I feel a lot of the success we had this year was due to this simple drill. The drill is called *orange pride*. It develops team tempo.

I went to Wal-Mart and bought five 55-gallon gray trash cans. I set them up to represent the five offensive linemen. We have a defensive meeting before we go on the field. I have four or five things outside of football that I want my players to improve on. We have a 15-minute walk-through, and I run the offense. I have a set of receivers and backs. We set up on defense and walk through our blitz package. We do that every day.

From there we go to our stretch program and into our "orange pride" drill. The offense goes to the other end of the field and goes through their team takeoff drill. I take the defense and put them on the sideline grouped into teams. The five trash cans are set up on the hash marks closest to that sideline. We are trying to accomplish a lot of things during this drill. We want to create turnovers, put out the fire, come out with a sense of urgency, create attitude, and pay attention to details.

I take my position on the field close to the trash cans, and call for the first, second, or third team. Whichever team I call is supposed to hustle onto the field and get in their defensive huddle. I let them almost get to me before I stop them and send them back to the sideline. I tell them they didn't come out like they wanted to play. I then demonstrate the way they should come out. As old as I am, I go to the sideline and sprint out on the field, yelling and screaming. I want them to show enthusiasm.

When I call them out this time, they sprint out on the field, screaming like a bunch of wild Indians, and get into the huddle. I know it is false enthusiasm when they do it initially. But it becomes real the more they do the drill. I have a stick with a football attached to the end of it. That is how I assimilate the snap.

When the defense gets into the huddle, they practice huddle discipline. Their eyes are focused on the Mike linebacker. The Mike linebacker gives a defensive call. He makes the call one time. We don't repeat the huddle call. On our huddle break we say, "Orange Crush!" We clap at the same time we say "crush." I hold up my right fist or my left fist. That represents the tight end. The defense makes their direction call and lines up on the five trash cans. The cornerbacks have to have imagination. They line up in positions where wide receivers would be. I don't put out cones or managers to mark those positions.

We have 11 guys in a great football stance. They have taken the field with great enthusiasm, had a great huddle break, made all their adjustment calls, and have gotten aligned.

I make the cadence call and try to get them to jump offsides. If anyone comes offsides, the whole defense has to do an up-down. If they don't do it perfectly, they do it again. We have four coaches spaced around the field. We have one on the numbers, down the field about 15 yards. We have one at the same position on the opposite numbers. We have one around the line of scrimmage, close to the sideline and the fourth coach opposite him on the other side of the field.

The perfect up-down requires the players to pop off the ground and pump their feet. As they come off the ground, I point to one of those four coaches. It had better be elbows and butt holes to get to that coach. I want them to sprint to the coach, get their shoulders square, be in a good football position, and chop their feet. I want a good base, with proper power angles in their knees and ankles. If it is not fast enough, they come back and repeat the drill.

The coach ends the drill by saying, "orange." The players respond with "crush," and sprint off the field. This takes about two-and-a-half minutes to do this drill. We don't compromise on any detail in this drill. We demand that our players do this drill perfectly every day. It is the player's job to raise their level of play to my expectations each day. That is the attitude I want so that it sets the tempo for practice.

This is not a pursuit drill. They simply sprint to the coach and break down on him. I usually take it easy on them, and send them to one of the other coaches close by. If it had been a bad day the day before, I point to one of the coaches further down the field.

We have been working through our film cutups. We are evaluating everything we did this season on defense. We played 900 snaps on defense at Illinois this year. On 600 of those snaps, we brought five-, six-, seven-, or eight-man pressure. We consider our base defense to be a four-man pressure package, with zone or man-free coverage.

As a defensive coordinator, I have spent countless hours working on adjustments to sets and formations. I want the offensive coordinator to go through the same thing to play us. I want them to know that we are bringing blitzes on two out of every three snaps. Our players know that also.

We give our players three to four blitzes a week. We rep them over and over again until they become second nature. Our kids want to blitz. They like it be-cause they know something is going to happen. The media called our defense a high-risk defense. I don't know what a high-risk defense is. On each defense we call, every gap is covered, and we have a man responsible for every zone in zone coverage or every man in man-free coverage. That doesn't sound high-risk to me.

If you give up big plays on defense, it is because of missed tackles or assignment, not because the defense is high-risk. It is easy for a coach to beat up his players emotionally every day. But he has to remember he is seeing what he is coaching. If his players are making mistakes, it is because of his teaching techniques or his willingness to accept substandard play. If what the coach is seeing from his player is not up to his expectations, he needs to change what he is doing.

At Illinois, we are very similar to you guys. If we have a guy who is not getting the job done, we can be hardheaded and continue to get beat or adapt our coaching. Players don't wake up in the morning and develop a scheme to make the coach mad. They want to please you as a coach. You are their role model. They are going to practice every day and are trying to do what you are coaching to the best of their ability.

If you continually see the same mistake over and over, it is one of two things that are causing it: The player doesn't understand your coaching, or you are asking him to do something he can't do. If you make a bad call on defense, have enough resolve in yourself to stand up in front of your defense and admit it. If you are always finger-pointing at the kids, they will see right through that. If that happens, they won't trust what you are telling them.

Coaching is earning the respect of your players. Treat them fair. If you tell them what you want to accomplish, and demand that it is done that way, everyone is on the same page.

The third principle of pressure defense is to create involvement. Players and fans alike like to see pressure defense. We play a lot of guys on defense. One player may not be as good as the other, but when the first player gets tired, the second player is better. Our defensive-line coach played 12 guys in those positions this year. Those 12 guys knew their role. One player may have played 20 reps, while the other one played 15. The players knew they were going to get to play going into the game. That meant they worked harder in practice all week long so they wouldn't let down their teammates during the game.

We name our blitzes for our players, strength coaches, trainers, or anyone associated with our team. Several years ago, I worked with a guy named Rob Ryan. His father was Buddy Ryan. Rob has a twin brother named Rex. Rob coached with me at Western Kentucky. His brother Rex coached at Eastern Kentucky at the same time. That game was a heck of a game. When the boys went home to see Buddy, Rob used to sit in the other room when they sat down to eat. Buddy had two Super Bowl rings and Rex had one. Rob was with the Patriots this year and won his Super Bowl ring. Now he can sit in the same room with them.

I learned the naming of blitzes from Rob at Oklahoma State. He found out if you called a corner blitz after the player running the stunt, they ran it better and came harder. I didn't buy into that initially, but it works. In our playbook, we call one of our blitzes *46-Buddy-Go*. The Buddy in the stunt comes from Buddy Ryan.

In coaching we should never lose sight of the simplicity of our defense. I work from the press box because I get a better view from that position. If I am late getting the defense into the game, it is a crime. There is nothing more disheartening to your defense, than the offense breaking the huddle before they have the defensive call. My philosophy is any call that is sound is better than a late call. Even if we are indecisive, we are going to make the call, so our defense can break the huddle before the offense does. We want to line up and wait for the offense to come out of the huddle.

We want to disrupt the offensive rhythm. I want the opponent's quarterback to feel uncomfortable. I want him to be aware we are coming after him. While the quarterback is in his cadence, we are going to stem to another defensive front. We stem 100 percent of the time. We want a relentless effort by our people to get to the quarterback. I want penetration by the defense into the backfield. The offense knows that two-thirds of the time we are bringing five, six, seven, or eight men.

If a team comes to the line of scrimmage and snaps the ball quickly, we slant to the defense for which we were going to stem. It is second nature because we do it every day in practice on those five trash cans. People have asked me when we stem the front or shift the secondary. We watch the quarterback. When he is walking toward the line of scrimmage, he is trying to find where your safety is aligned. Our front and secondary is in our disguise package.

Once the quarterback gets under the center, he will look to the right and then to the left. Once his head comes to balance, we move the defense. The secondary coverage has to move a little before the line stems. They have further to go in their alignment. That is a little thing, but it took me a lot of years to find it out.

In our defense, we want to create turnovers. We had 27 of them this year. I don't know whether that is good or bad. We talk to our defense every day about minus-yardage plays. If the offense is always in a first and ten, second and four, and third and one situation, we are not going to win. On the first play of the game I like to come with a maximum blitz. I don't want the offense to get into a rhythm or routine. We are going to work to get the offense into a second or third and long situation.

This year our defense created 90 minus-yardage plays. Most of them came from our defensive line and our twist game or five-man pressure scheme. We were second in the Big Ten Conference in number of sacks. We had 44 sacks by 18 different guys. As long as I've been coaching, I've never had that many different people make sacks. As I looked at our cutups, there were 15 other times we came absolutely clean and missed the sack.

I want to cover a coaching point right here. When we bring a player off the corner in a blitz scheme, we have a technique we like to coach into it. On occasion we blitz everyone off the corner except the noseguard. Any time we have a player coming off the corner, where he has to maintain leverage, we call it *hips*. If your kids can understand this concept, they won't lose containment as often.

As we run this technique, we key the fullback in the I formation. If the fullback comes at the outside blitz on an isolation track, the defender breaks off his containment and tackles the tailback on the isolation play. If the fullback comes at the blitz on a flat track, the defender plays toss-sweep or speed-option.

If the fullback goes away from the blitz, the defender plays a hips technique on the quarterback. The one game we lost in the Big Ten this year was to Michigan. They went five straight series in the first half where they ran three plays and punted the ball. They got on track with a trick play. It was totally my fault. It will never happen again. They ran a toss-sweep. Our defensive end came flat down the line of scrimmage in a good angle to make the tackle. The quarterback slid out the backside past the defensive end. The tailback stopped and threw the ball back to the quarterback for a touchdown.

When both backs go away, the backside blitz should redirect and hit the quarterback. We played Minnesota three weeks later. They had a great tailback and ran the same play Michigan ran. Their quarterback didn't know we had gone back and reinforced that technique. The quarterback is taught to take two steps, turn, and run. He took his two steps, turned, and took one big shot right under the chin. He didn't get up. That is the hips technique.

We alert the referee to make sure we don't get a penalty for roughness. We remind the referee that when the quarterback tosses the ball and runs out of the backside, he loses his protection as a quarterback. We applied that technique 131 times. It may not affect the quarterback in the first quarter, but by the fourth quarter, they are aware they are going to get hit. It wears on their minds and by the fourth quarter, it effects his execution. In 900 defensive snaps, with 600 of them pressure-type plays, we had one 15-yard penalty for roughing the quarterback.

That was one too many. We don't coach outside the rules of the game. When the quarterback is in motion or throwing the ball, we are going to light him up. We record how many times we hit the opposing quarterback.

We have cheer drills in the spring. The quarterback wears a yellow vest in the spring and is off-limits to the defense. I run the defense, but the head-man never allows me to hit his quarterback. We start our spring practice with a meeting just like we do in the fall. In those meetings we talk about our cheer drills, where we would have sacked or hit the quarterback. It goes back to attitude and attention to detail. I don't want a quarterback to feel comfortable.

We want the quarterback to hurry his throws. We want someone in the quarterback's face pressuring him at all times. If we can cause the quarterback to hurry and throw the ball into the ground, we have accomplished our goal. We give the player doing the pressuring bonus points on his rating sheet. We want the quarterback to throw off his back foot, throw the ball away, or simply throw incomplete passes. We keep relentless pressure on the quarterback.

When you play the type of defense we play, you force offensive coaches to prepare hard for us. The offensive coaches know what we are going to do. It causes them to cut down their offensive package to prepare for us. If they don't devise a scheme to handle the pressure, they will run out of quarterbacks. If the offense continues to line up in a four-wide receiver formation or empty formation, they won't have enough quarterbacks to finish the game.

We want to force the quarterback to hold the ball and not throw on time. We want him to see the rush coming instead of looking downfield. When the quarterback steps up into the pocket, he will be looking where he is going to throw the ball. We disguise our max coverage by making it look like a max blitz. That makes the quarterback double clutch the ball and confuses his reads.

We want to put doubt into the minds of the offensive linemen. We align in different fronts throughout the year. We stem from those fronts. On two-thirds of our snaps we slant, angle, and use two- and four-men twist schemes. We force the offensive linemen to block a moving target. It makes the offensive-line coaches restrict their schemes. We see almost totally zone schemes.

Our defense doesn't change from week to week, although it looks like we do. All we do is redraw the lines on our defense. Instead of the Mike linebacker running through the A gap, the Will linebacker will run the stunt. By teaching sound gap control, it allows us defensive freedom. Coach Turner told us that he had a lot of confidence in us. He is not in our defensive meetings hounding us about defense. He is a brilliant offensive mind. He ran the offense for the Chicago Bears and he runs our offense, which has broken every offensive record that existed here at Illinois. When you have been in 11 different schools, you learn how to read between the lines. You have to be good at that if you want to be a successful coach. There is one philosophy and that is the head coach's philosophy. Your job as an assistant is to be an extension of his philosophy.

Coach Turner only told me one thing concerning my defensive plan: He told me to make sure we were sound in our defensive scheme. Everything we do, we have gap integrity. My job as a coach is to make sure that 100 percent of the time we know who has what gap. I coach the corners. We play "cat coverage." One corner has "that cat" and the other corner has the "other cat." If they don't catch the ball, we win. Ninety-eight percent of the time we are going to have an eight-man front. And a lot of the time we will have nine guys in the front to stop the run. If the corners can't cover, it's my fault and the defense breaks down.

This kind of defense can complement your zone pressures. The offensive tendencies to pressure are to max protect or throw hot off your blitz. We play a coverage called "hot coverage." We blitz six defenders and play two defenders man-to-man on the offense's hot receivers. Behind the man coverage, we play a three-deep zone. We take the hot receivers away from the quarterback so he can't dump the ball. What we do in our zone and man coverage looks identical.

This defensive package allows you to max cover in the secondary. In the BCS Bowl we played LSU and it became a track meet in the first half. They were the sprinters and we were the guys trying to catch up. We dug too deep a hole to climb out. We didn't play well on either side of the ball. Three different times we dropped eight men in coverage, with five under and three deep. They hit three plays against the heart of what we were trying to accomplish.

These are my thoughts. Hear what I am saying because I think this can really help you. When you break down an offense, they are going to have their tendencies against a blitz. Against a blitz, the two-receiver side, you will run a stop by the outside receiver and a corner by the inside receiver. Or they will go to a post-corner and fade route. The offense thinks you are going to be in man coverage with inside leverage. When we call a max blitz, those are the routes we have to cover.

When we call a max coverage, we are selling to the quarterback that we are coming on a max blitz. I told the cornerbacks the quarterback was going to throw him a gift. All he had to do was drop back and intercept the ball. LSU did exactly as we expected, except it went for a 43-yard touchdown. They did everything that we expected, but we didn't execute.

Predict the offense's adjustments when they see blitz, and overplay them. Watch film to see where an offense or quarterback will go with the ball when they see blitz. Zero in on defense to stop those routes. Know the kinds of runs you will see versus the blitz. Offenses have a go-to route and it doesn't change. When you play pressure defense, you can count on the go-to route even more. We had a cornerback who intercepted a pass for a touchdown against Louisville and Purdue. All he did was overplay the route and made the reception.

Let's talk about types of pressure. The first one is a four-man pressure with zone, man-free, and man coverage. If an offense lines up in an I formation, we may be in four-man pressure scheme, but we will have eight or nine defenders in the box to stop the run.

The next type of pressure is five-man pressure. We are big on this type of pressure. When we run this pressure, we are going to bring the Sam, Mike, or Will linebackers on the rush. The coverage we run with this pressure is man-free.

We run a six-man pressure and play fire-zone coverage behind it. That means we are covering the two hot receivers man-to-man, with a three-deep zone.

When we run seven-man pressure, we are in man coverage in the secondary. The last type of pressure is an eight-man max blitz. The secondary coverage is man-peel coverage. When you bring an eight-man blitz, the corners and one of the safeties cover the wideouts and the tight end. But you have to account for the fullback and tailback in coverage. Whoever is coming off the corner in a hips technique takes the back and peels back on him. If the back releases inside, the inside blitz defender takes him.

Our four down linemen create our four-man pressure package. At Illinois we flip-flop our defensive linemen. We have a contain end, noseguard, tackle, and rush end. The contain end, noseguard, and the Sam and Mike linebackers travel together. They go to the side of the call. The tackle is a 3-technique tackle. The rush end is a 5-technique to the open side. The Will linebacker travels with them.

From our four-man pressure, we have straight-line rushes. We have a two-man and four-man twist game. We can play a two-deep zone, which is a five-under and two-deep zone. We can play a three-deep zone or a four-deep zone. In the three-deep zone, we have four under, and in the four-deep zone, we have three under. I don't want to get hung up on that because I have too much left to show you.

Our primary coverage in our secondary is a press man-free coverage. We play with a shallow-hole and deep-hole helper. Our man coverage is our run-stopper coverage. Both of our safeties will be down within 5 to 6 yards of the line of scrimmage to stop the run in this coverage. The corners are out on an island. We play off man coverage with our man coverage.

In our defense the Mike linebacker calls our directions. If he says, "rip," we declare right. If he says, "liz," we declare left. If we declare right, the contain end, noseguard, and the Sam and Mike linebackers move to the right side of the ball. The tackle, rush end, and Will linebacker go to the left side of the ball.

The noseguard is in a weakside shade technique on the center. The contain end is in a 5-technique. The Sam linebacker is on the line of scrimmage with his toe pointed directly at the quarterback. He is a disrupter. The quarterback has to guess if he is coming or not. The Mike linebacker is aligned in a 30-alignment on the offensive guard. The linebackers squirm away from the 3-technique tackle. The tackle is in a 3-technique. The rush end aligns in a 6-technique, but is responsible for the C gap. The strong safety is aligned outside of him. That gives us an eight-man front. The Will linebacker is in a 40-technique on the offensive tackle.

The straight-line rush lanes for the four-man pressure are through their technique gaps. The tackle has a three-way go he can use. The contain end and rush end have contain on the football.

BASE STRAIGHT-LINE RUSH

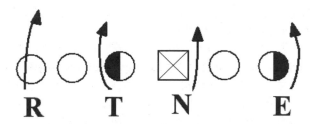

In our two-man twist game we have two variations. They are called *tan* and *nat*. They are the same stunt basically. The only difference is which man goes first. Tan means the tackle and the noseguard are going to twist, with the tackle penetrating and the noseguard looping around. We call the looping action a *flash* technique. The tackle slants hard across the face of the offensive guard. The noseguard starts upfield to draw the block of the center and flashes across the center's face. His charge is through the tackle's B gap.

Nat is the opposite stunt. The noseguard penetrates and the tackle flashes behind. The first letter in each stunt tells our players who goes first. I use these maneuvers to change up the rush lanes on the pass.

OVER TAN

OVER NAT

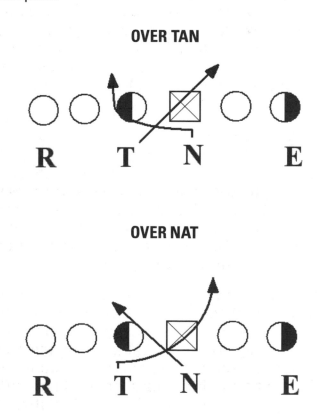

We also run a two-man twist to the other side. We call them *con* and *noc*. They are the same stunt as the other side. On the con, the contain end goes first and the noseguard second. This is a good first-and-10 run-stopper defense. The 5-technique slants hard through the hip of the offensive guard. We want at least 2 yards of penetration. With the noc, the noseguard goes first and the contain end second. If the offense were to sprint out toward this stunt, we would have a problem. I am not bringing the noseguard outside the offensive tackle. I would never call this stunt in a passing situation. The end tightens his alignment so he can be the flasher. These stunts are run stoppers.

OVER CON

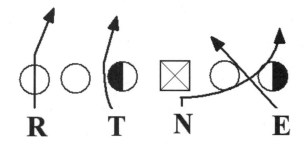

OVER NOC

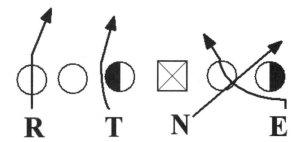

If we want to involve the rush end and tackle we call it *tar*. The tackle goes first and does the penetration. The rush end goes second and becomes the flasher.

OVER TAR

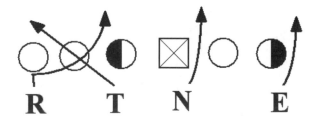

The companion stunt is called *rat*. The rush end goes first off the butt of the offensive tackle. The tackle drives upfield and flashes around to the outside.

OVER RAT

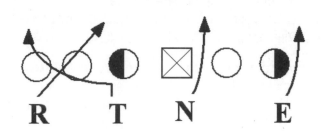

We run the two inside pressures a ton. I usually don't call the con, rat, or tar independently. But in teaching the concept we run them. What I do is combine the stunts. I like to run the con-rat. They become four-man twist games. I use them against the dropback passing game in particular. If a team rolls the pocket or sprints out, we won't use them much. The line stunts don't change our linebackers' fit in their pursuit and gap responsibilities. We use the con-rat as both a pass and run stopper.

OVER CON-RAT

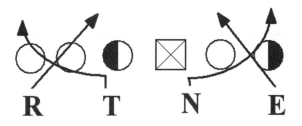

The last stunt is called a *noc-tar*. In this stunt the defenders that are to penetrate are working outside with the flashers coming inside. This was a good run stopper on the inside running game. We end up coming free inside on the penetration at times and cause fumbles.

OVER NOC-TAR

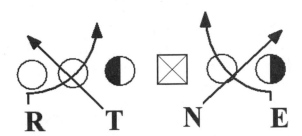

In the five-man pressure game, we are going to blitz five men. We are going to play man-free coverage, but we lose our shallow hole player because he is blitzing. The blitz comes from one of our three linebackers or our strong safety. The call is simple. We call *over*, which means we are overshifted toward the split end. *Single*, to us, means our man-free coverage. If we tag a name onto the call, it means the player that is going to blitz. With the call *over-single-sam*, the defense is an overshift to the split end, with man-free secondary coverage, and the Sam linebacker blitzing.

When I teach the blitzes to the linebacker, I use the terms *inside*, *shoot*, and *plug*. *Inside* means to blitz the A gap. *Shoot* means to fire through the B gap. *Plug* means a blitz through the C gap. If the Sam linebacker is aligned on the right side of the defense, he runs through the gap to his side. When he is on the right and we call inside Sam, the Sam linebacker runs through the A gap on the right side of the ball. The coverage is man-free. The corners have the wide receivers. The strong safety has the tight end and the two linebackers have the two remaining backs. The free safety is free.

OVER INSIDE SAM

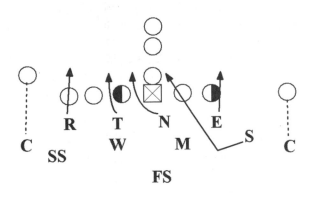

OVER SHOOT SAM

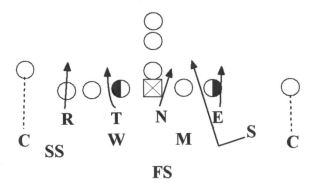

OVER PLUG SAM

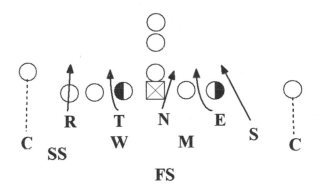

If the fullback moves into the strong halfback set, it puts the linebacker in a bind. Teams like to run the back out of the backfield into the flat and pick off your linebacker. If the back aligns in that position, the strong safety has two calls he can make with the linebacker. He either calls *lock* or *zebra*. *Lock* means the strong safety is locked on the tight end and the linebacker is locked on the back. If he calls *zebra*, they switch. If the tight end goes inside, the linebacker takes him. If he releases outside, the strong safety takes him. If the linebacker takes the tight end, the strong safety has the fullback.

In the I formation or in the weakside halfback set, the call will be *lock*. If the back is toward the tight end, the call will be *zebra*. We make the call every time.

I like the Sam plug best of all these stunts. We can run the same stunts with the Mike linebacker. The only ones I run are Mike inside and shoot. We move our Mike linebacker in and out of the line of scrimmage. I can move him up and get him out in coverage or move him up and blitz him. The Sam and Will linebackers take the pass coverage on the remaining backs.

OVER INSIDE MIKE

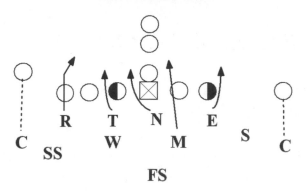

The last thing I want to cover before I get to the film is what we do with the Will linebacker. We can run the Will linebacker on the inside, shoot, and plug.

OVER INSIDE WILL

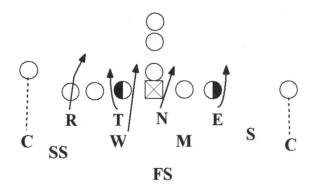

Twenty years ago, I was in the same place as you are today. You can get something from this clinic, if you ask questions.

In teaching the press coverage we start with the defensive back's stance. I want their feet closer than shoulder-width. I want the weight on the balls of their feet, with their toes cocked inside. I want their elbows up. I want a bend in the waist with the back flat. I want a little air under their heels.

We have two ways to play press coverage. On press coverage the corner has to know where his help is coming from. If the safety is inside, the corners have outside leverage on the receiver. If the receiver takes an inside release, the corner punches with his outside hand and opens his hips inside so he can run with the receiver.

If the receiver takes an outside release, the corner still uses his outside hand to punch. However, if he locks out with the outside hand, he gets his hip locked. He won't be able to get his hip open and has to trail the receiver. The corner has to use a double punch to get his hips open and get back on top of the receiver. That is one technique.

I like the second technique. The corner staggers his feet slightly. His feet get a little closer together. Receivers work on all kinds of release moves to get off the line of scrimmage. They learn the swim, rips, clubs, and all kinds of foot movement. When the ball is snapped, the defensive back does what we call baby step. He takes his baby steps back to get separation between himself and the receiver. We want about 2 yards of separation.

This allows the defensive back to get in good position to punch with his outside hand. When we get separation, the receiver is performing his escape moves on air. As he releases, the defensive back is waiting on him. If the receiver's hips are outside, the defensive back punches with the hand away from the way the receiver is going.

If you play an off-man technique in your man coverage, you may find this interesting. When playing off man, we focus on the quarterback. The ball is going to be thrown quickly when we bring a max blitz. We are keying the quarterback for a one- or three-step drop. Our defensive backs are 8 yards off the receivers. On the snap, our backs don't back up. We don't get in a hurry to get any depth. If the back starts to backpedal, he creates about 6 yards of separation on a quickly thrown ball.

If the defensive back reads a three-step drop, his focus turns to the receiver and he plays forward to the receiver. His leverage from his alignment helps him to cover the slant.

I appreciate the opportunity to come back home and have a chance to talk to you guys. You are welcome anytime at Illinois. Thank you very much.

PLANNING FOR A CHAMPIONSHIP TEAM

University of Miami

The run for the National Championship was a great thing. It was a great run for us. I would not trade it for anything. I have found out that you must not take yourself too serious with winning one National Championship. It has been 53 years since a rookie coach has won a National Championship in the NCAA. I have been a head coach one year, and we have won a National Championship. Some people would like to think we have it all figured out as far as winning is concerned. I was told another rookie coach won the NCAA Championship 53 years ago. His name was Bennie Oosterbaan, and he coached at Michigan. I understand he got fired the very next year. We have to put winning all in perspective. People tend to forget about the championships after awhile. Today, they are not very forgiving when it comes to winning and losing. The point is you cannot take yourself too seriously just because you won last year.

I appreciate the opportunity to be here. Coaching in the state of Florida, we have to feel very fortunate. In the last 18 years, schools from the state of Florida have won nine of the NCAA National Championships. Florida State, the University of Florida, and Miami University have been national champs in nine of those years. It all goes back to the players we are getting. We signed 16 players from the state of Florida this year. As long as the Florida schools have a chance to keep the Florida players at home, we will have a chance to win championships.

I want to talk with you about some of the things we did this last year that made us a better football team. I know a lot of you are not rookie coaches, but nevertheless, these things are important in building a winning football team.

Obliviously we had some talent on the team last year. The talent played very well, and that helped us win last year. There are some things we did that you can do that will help your team.

The first thing I want to discuss relates to the *"Great Expectations"* everyone had for our team before the season started last year. I had a chance to listen to a lecture by Lou Holtz last summer. He talked at length about the fact that the team he took over at South Carolina had not won many games before he took over. In fact, they lost all 11 games the first year he took over. While listening to Lou Holtz discuss the past record of South Carolina, it hit me. Coach Holtz took over a team that very few people expected to win a game. I took over a team at Miami, and everyone expected us to win all of our games, including the National Championship. I can assure you, everyone in Miami had us penciled in to play in the Rose Bowl back in August. Our Alumni were sky high. They should have been optimistic because we did have a good team coming back from the year before. We had ended up as second in the country the year before. We had only lost one half, and that was the first half to the University of Washington. We had an opportunity to play for a National Championship. That is what you want as a football team. You want to coach in a school where the expectations are high every year.

The first thing we decided when we started the season was to *make sure we had a plan.* We wanted to have an organized plan of how we were going to win and how we wanted to go about it. In discussing the plan, I wanted to stress to the coaches and players that I wanted them to have fun in planning our season. I wanted to make sure we worked hard, but I wanted everyone to enjoy what we were doing. Let's face it, sometimes football coaches take it too serious. It is important to win, and I hear this more and more from college coaches. I am sure the high school coaches feel the same way on this. You are expected to win to keep your job. So, we definitely wanted to have an organized plan.

Talent was not an issue for us. On our football team, we had enough talent to win every game. Not that we would win every game, but we had the talent to compete at a high level, and we could compete for the National Championship. We felt we had a chance to win every game we played in. We talked about talent not being an issue with our team. The media of Miami reminded us over and over that we had so much talent on our team. We tried to tell the media that some of the teams on our schedule also had some pretty good talent as well.

We did some research just as the season started. We felt the best team in pro football was the Washington Redskins. The Redskins had All-Pro players at several positions. Also, they had several first-round draft choices. As the season started, they lost the first two games by a total score of 63 to 7. We knew we had talent, but talent only gives you a chance to win. We wanted our players to know this. The talent is there, but it only gives you a chance. We stressed the important thing was what we were going to do with our talent. We stressed this was the thing that was going to make the difference for us.

One thing I did when I got the job at Miami was to *meet individually with each of the players.* This may have been the best thing I did right after I got the job. Even if you have been at a school for several years, I think it is still important to meet individually with the players. You will be surprised what you can learn from these players. You may find a player that you think will be an All-Conference player. But that player may be thinking, he will be lucky just to make the starting lineup. You may have to sit down with the players and set goals with each individual. You want to make sure the players are on the same page you are on.

We wanted to develop a role for each of our players. Not everyone on the team could be a star on the team. Not everyone could be the starting quarterback. Not everyone could be a Kim Dorsey. But there are a lot of players that are less talented that can fill a role on the football team. The beauty of football is that you can have a number of players who can fill a role, and everyone can feel successful. We have a backup long snapper that ended up as our starter after the first snapper got hurt. That was his role. It is an important role, especially when you don't have a long snapper.

At the present time, we are just finishing up with our 6:00 am workouts. Our position coaches have met with all of their players. After spring practice, I will meet with everyone on the football team. One of the things I will do different this year than what I did last year is this: I will listen more to the players in those meetings. Last year I did a lot of the talking in the individual meetings. I was telling them I was the head coach, and I had plans for the team. This year I will do a lot more listening and a little less talking.

One other thing we must not overlook in making out our plans for the season is to *meet with the support people around our program.* When I became the head coach, I was the CEO of all of the assistant coaches, the secretaries, the strength coaches, the equipment people, the grad assistants, and everyone who was involved with football, plus all of our players. You had better know who is working for you. I wanted to know what their thoughts were. I wanted to meet with anyone that touched the lives of our players. I wanted to make sure they were a positive influence for our players.

My secretary is absolutely great. She is the best in the world. If you polled our 100 players and asked them who would they rather lose, me or Myrna Snyder—my secretary, I will guarantee you they would say, "We can get a new head coach, but let's keep Myrna." When they come in to see me, she is waiting for them. She has candy for them. She has a friendly face for everyone. She was the secretary for Lou Saban, Howard Schnellenberger, Jimmy Johnson, and Butch Davis, and now she is my secretary. She is not that old. She is terrific. They come in the office, and she is there for them. The thing I think makes her special is the fact that she does not know if the players are first team, fourth team, or walk-ons. She treats every player the same regardless of their position or status on the team. She has a positive influence on our players.

We feel the trainers can also have a positive influence on the players. The players go into the training room to get their ankles taped before practice. A player may come into the training room complaining about being tired and not really excited about going out to practice. The trainer can go along with the player and show sympathy for him. Or he can make a positive influence with the player. He can tell him something like this: "I am sure you know not many players are in condition to go hard at this time of the season. But the good players find a way to pick it up a level and go out in the heat and get the job done."

The same is true with the equipment people when it comes to making a positive influence on the players. They can let the players know they have the finest equipment in the world that money can buy. They can assure them that when they take the field, they are well protected.

All of these people can have a strong influence on the players. It is important to know the people working around you and working for you. Another example is strength training. I am sure the high school coaches are aware of this fact. In high school, the coaches have more influence with the players than the college coaches have. We only have 15 days of spring practice. We cannot coach outside of those 15 days. In the summer, the practice field is off-limits for the college coaches. The strength and conditioning coaches can be around the players all of the time. They can watch the players run, and they can put the players through conditioning drills. They are very important at our level. I think our guys are the very best at working with our players.

The other thing we talked about in making our plans was *how we were going to win.* I think this was very important. What did we have to do as a staff for this football team to win? I think it is important for the team to know this important information. You must analyze your personnel. We get to recruit players. This allows us to do the things we like to do. We want to be a balanced offense. We want to be able to run the ball and pass the ball equally as well. You cannot always be a balanced team. You may not have the players who can do the things you would like to do with the offense or defense. The important thing is for you and your staff to decide how you are going to win games.

The one thing we wanted to do was to sell our team on one important issue: We want to take a lot of pride in playing for the team. We did not want to become selfish. We wanted to make sure we were unselfish in our approach to the team. We had a lot of good football players, but we wanted to make sure we did not end up developing a super star. If you want to come to our program and throw for one million yards, it probably will not happen for you. That is not

our style. Our quarterback this year was a candidate for the Heisman Trophy. The point here is that our players are never going to have the numbers to win national awards because that is not our goal. If you are a receiver, you may not be able to catch more passes than anyone in the NCAA. That is not our style. The point I am making is this. We took pride in being unselfish. This may be easy to say, but it is difficult to get this point across to a lot of players.

At the Rose Bowl game, we had former players come by to talk with the team the week of the game. Almost every one of the former players told our team about situations when they were on National Championship teams or played for a National Championship. They stressed the fact that it was more important to be unselfish and win the National Championship than it was to win individual awards.

I used this example in getting this point across to the team: I asked the team how many bowl games John Elway had played in? They guessed four, three, and two. The fact was that John Elway did not play in a single college bowl game. They never won enough games to qualify for a bowl game. Obviously, he was one of the best quarterbacks to ever play the game of football. I think that made an impression on our players.

Another important part of our planning was that *we did not want any excuses.* We had good talent. There was no reason for us not to be successful. We did not want to give a lot of reasons why we were not doing well. We had to play at Penn State. They had a legendary coach in Joe Paterno, and there would be 109,000 people watching the game in their stadium. We had to go to Florida State where they had not lost a game in their stadium in ten years. What the people did not tell you is the fact that Florida State has not lost many games in any other stadium either. All of these points were just reasons for us not to do well. We knew we had to go to Virginia Tech in December. We knew it could be 40 below zero or it could be snowing. The rap was out that we could not play in bad weather. It turned out to be a record warm day in Blacksburg, Virginia when we got there in December. We brought all of our cold weather equipment but did not get a chance to use any of it. But we will take the warm weather anytime. The point here is that we did not want to have any excuses for not winning. All we wanted to do was to win the game and play with enthusiasm. That was all we asked.

We wanted to *play with self-discipline.* The first thing you want to do is to avoid losing the game before you can win the game. I am talking about turnovers. We wanted to create turnovers, force turnovers, and protect the football ourselves, and we did not want to throw interceptions. Jimmy Johnson did a study in the NFL, and he found that a team that turns the ball over three times a game has a very slim chance of winning the game. If a team turns the ball over four times in an NFL game, they are going to lose. We led the nation in turnover margin this past year. That means we forced more turnovers than we gave up than anyone in college football. In one game this year, we did have four turnovers—the Boston College game. That was a game that many said we should have lost, or that we could have lost, but we did manage to win the game. The point here is to avoid losing first. Give yourself a chance to win, and play hard and things will take care of themselves.

The next point we discussed in our planning was our preparation. If you prepare to win, you can play with a lot of confidence. You cannot play with false confidence. We have had players at Miami that tried to play with false confidence. We have had players that liked to yell and scream and jump and carry on in the game, trying to trick themselves that they were confident in winning the game. We did not want any false confidence. We wanted to be prepared. Our assistant coaches did a great job in getting our players prepared each week. We felt if our players knew what they had to do, they could go out in the game and perform at full speed.

We had a very fast, fast, football team this year. It was one of the fastest teams I have ever been around. As an assistant coach, I had been fortunate to have been around some fast teams at Ohio State and Oklahoma. We had a lot of fast players at those two schools. However, those teams were not as fast as the players we had this past year at Miami.

If a player is not sure about his assignment, those 4.5 players become 4.9 players. The thing we stressed this year when we were on the practice field was to practice at game speed. If you get noth-

ing else from this talk, it is something I think you should think about. Practice at game speed. This is something we stressed a great deal with our players this year. The players really took this at heart.

I mentioned this earlier that *we wanted a balanced offense.* We are going to recruit each year so we can have a balanced offense. We are going to recruit running backs and receivers each year. We play with a tight end. A lot of teams do not do much with the tight end anymore. We use our tight end. If we have 100 plays, we want to run 50 plays and pass 50 plays. If you stop our run, we feel we are still good enough with the pass that we will have a chance to win. If you stop our passing game, we hope we are good enough to win with our running game.

We wanted our players to take ownership of the team. What I mean by this is that we want the players to feel it is their team. We want the players to take the responsibility of the team. We have a players council. It was something I started this year. The players actually selected players from different classes and by position that could have a voice for the team. They could come in the coach's office and talk with the staff about football issues. We did not allow them to come in and talk about playing time or come in with a personal agenda. We wanted them to come to us with football issues related to the team.

For example, we had some long trips on our schedule. Most of our flights from Miami are somewhat long. Our team council decided they wanted to be comfortable on the flights on the long trips. We were going to do this before they came to us as a group. As coaches, you must do what you have to do to win. But at the same time, if you can involve the players, it helps to make things go smoother. It is better if the players will take ownership of the team.

This past year, we had way too many penalties. This was especially true in the early part of the season. We had a lot of penalties that I call foolish penalties. We all know those things will beat us in the close games. On Thursdays, I talked with the travel squad, and this is one of the things I stressed. I wanted to know what we could do to cut down on the penalties. The players decided as a team that they were going to improve in that area of the game.

We all know we are going to get some penalties called. That is just part of the game. We know we are going to get holding penalties. But when one of our players grabs a player on the opposite team and shoves him down after the whistle, or jumps offsides, these are examples of what I call foolish penalties. The team decided to do something about our penalties, and they did a good job of reducing our penalties.

We always have the officials come to us before the game to check our equipment. They check the length of the socks, and check other equipment related to the rules. This year I decided I would talk to our players about this problem at the beginning of the season. Before I could address the team on this issue, our All-American safety came to me and told me not to worry about the problem. He said he would take care of it with the team. He talked to the team, and it worked very well. It is much better for the players to make those decisions without the coach stepping in and forcing the team to make the corrections. Why should the coach always have to be the bad guy? When the team takes ownership like that, it has a very positive effect.

We really wanted to stress focus. What I mean by focus is the fact that we wanted the focus to be on us as a team. We did not want them to worry about Penn State, Florida State, or the teams that we had to play. We could not control the teams we played. We wanted the team to be concerned about US. We could not control the thing the other teams do, but we could control the things we did. Our philosophy was to be as good as we could, but we wanted the focus to be on our team. If we could do that, we felt we had a chance to win every game. We lost one game the year before and did not get the chance to play for a National Championship. But we knew up front for us to have a chance for the National Championship, we had to win each game. To win each game, we had to be as good as we could be. If that was not good enough, that was too bad. The focus was going to be on us and not the other teams.

The thing we had as a goal going into the Rose Bowl was unique. I had never heard of this before. It was not original with me, as I got it from Bill Parcels. I just happened to read about it. When the New York Giants went to the Super Bowl, they set individual goals for each individual position. *"Dominate your po-sition."* I thought a lot about this. It really narrows it down. This means every player must play good. What is play good? We set our goals for each position to be dominant players. Our right guard set his goal to be a dominant player for that position. Now, you cannot be a dominant linebacker if you are a right guard. You cannot do it all. But each player can be a dominant player at his position. If we can dominate 22 positions in the game, chances are we will have a good chance of winning the game. In the Rose Bowl, I think we did a good job of dominating our share of positions.

Last year we were 12-0 and National Champions. Now, what can we do for an encore? My wife told me I should retire because I we could not do any better than what we did last year. I told her retiring was not a bad idea. There is a lot of stress, and we spend a lot of hours away from home. Then, my wife found out that the athletic director gave me a new contract and found out what they were going to pay me to continue to coach at Miami. She told me I should coach five more years, and she would not complain at all. "Just get it done." She was not as worried about my health after she found out I had a new contract. I do think she knows it is a lot of hard work and a lot of stress to stay on top.

Where do we go from here? I do think this is important. I think we must set some new goals. People ask me if we can repeat next year. Who knows? Who says we can't win it again. We have good players coming back. We have a tough schedule. We go to Florida and Tennessee. We have Florida State coming to play us. We have all of the Big East teams to play. We have a tough schedule. The strength of schedule is more involved now in football, and it is important whom you play.

I tell this story to our players to get the point across about preparing for next year. I tell them about the World Champion bull rider. He had won three World Championships in recent years. He was a lot like Tiger Woods or Joe Montana. He had won three National Championships in bull riding. A week after the last World Championship, he had returned home in Colorado and was working out. Some of his friends came to see him and suggested that he should take a break from the vigorous training. He replied, "I can't do that. The bulls don't know that I have won three World Championships." There is a lot of truth to that story.

As the season goes on, you can ask people who the National Champion was in football, and over half of them will not know the answer. If you asked me who was the National Champion three years ago, unless I sat down and thought about it for awhile... The teams on our schedule do not care if we were National Champs last year. All that does is to put a target on us.

Another thing we did in planning our season was to *select goals for our players.* We had them involved in selecting their goals. We wanted them to have visionary goals, and goals that were very lofty. By the same token, we wanted them to select goals that were achievable.

When we talk about setting goals, we like to tell our players what they can do. We want to stress the positive things, not the negative points. I was in the Big Eight Conference for 10 years at Oklahoma State and Oklahoma. Also, I coached at Tulsa several years. We played Kansas State 13 games and beat them 13 times. I had made up my mind that no coach could ever win at Kansas State. There was no way they could win and have a chance for national recognition at Kansas State. We all know what has happened since that time. Coach Bill Snyder has done a wonderful job at Kansas State. He has built the program up and has developed a great staff. At one time, they were only one win away from the National Championship game a few years ago. They have made it to a bowl game most every year since Coach Snyder has been at Kansas State. No one thought you could ever win at Kansas State. However, no one told Bill Snyder he could not win at Kansas State. He came in and went to work. He got the job done by working hard in the off-season and turned the program around.

Most jobs that are open in coaching are not like my job at Miami, where there are good players coming back the next year. Most jobs that are open are bad jobs that are open because the former coach is let go because of the lack of wins. It may be the school is out of players, and the head coach went to the NFL, or moved to another school. So when you take a job, there are going to be a lot of reasons why you can't win at that school.

We have talked about having a plan for winning. You must be committed to the plan. You need to visit with the players individually. You need to get to know the people that work for you. I was a high school coach for nine years, so I know where most of you are coming from. A lot of coaches do not give their best because they are at a small school. They keep thinking they are going to go all out when they get the "good" job at a larger school. They just pass the time waiting until things are better. That is not the way you get to the next level. The thing I have tried to do was to try to be the best high school head coach I could be, and to be the best assistant college coach I could be wherever I was coaching. You should not be planning ahead to the point that you neglect your job at the present school. You can plan your goals to be a better coach at the level you are coaching on, and still have goals to get that better job. Be the best you can be wherever you are.

We all face difficulties. If you have a chance to read a book by Scott Beck, you will find it is very good. If you do not read the entire book, you should read the first chapter. The thing he said on the first page in a profound statement is this: "Life is tough." I did not know this for a long time. I thought life should be easier. When you figure out that life is not easy and life is tough, the process is to grow with each challenge. We all have our ups and downs. It is that way in life, and it is that way in coaching. Once you figure that out and resolve the issue that life is tough, you have a chance to react accordingly.

The next issue we must deal with is this. *We are going to do things the right way.* "Is this the right way to do things?" We are not going to win by cheating. We do not need to cheat in the classroom or on the field. We want to treat our players the way we would want our son to be treated. This is what I mean that we are going to do things the right way.

The last point is simple. *"Don't give up!"* We ask the players to stay with us. I never thought about anything except football even when I was in high school. The same thing was true in college and when I started coaching. I would not know what to do if I were not in coaching. I have never thought about anything else. I have been around athletics and football a long time. Stay with football and do not give up on your dream.

Next, I want to talk about our passing game. Later, I will show you a video of our passing game. Our quarterback is a good athlete. Our philosophy on the passing game is this. Last year, our quarterback completed about 60 percent of his passes. Next year, our goal will be to have a 65-percent completion ratio with our quarterback. We have good receivers, but we did lose some good players at that position.

Our quarterback must know our philosophy. One, we are going to throw a lot of low-risk passes. We are going to stress possession passing. We are not going to throw interceptions. We are not going to force the football. On many of our passes, we can treat them as a run in our system. At the same time, we are going to take a shot at the long ball on certain match-ups. In watching the tapes on Nebraska before the Rose Bowl, we saw some mismatches, especially against our tight end. He caught the first TD in the Rose Bowl. So, we are going to take advantage of any mismatch in the passing game.

The good defensive teams will try to force the offense to run 12 to 15 plays in a drive to score. If the defense can do that, they know the chances are good that the offense will make a mistake and turn the ball over. If we get the mismatch, we will take advantage of the situation.

We feel it is important to throw deep to try to score. I do not want to throw deep just to scare teams. We work on throwing the ball deep. We have drills to develop the techniques in throwing the ball deep. Throwing the deep pass is not that easy. We have the quarterbacks throw the ball 22 yards deep, trying to drop the ball into the big trash cans at certain spots on the field. When you put the fans in the stands and put the defense across the line of scrimmage, it does not get any easier to throw the ball into the trash can. But, it forces the quarterback to focus on a small target.

We draw an orange line four yards inside the boundary. We have receivers that run vertical routes who do not give the quarterback enough room to throw the football. When the defense presses the receiver, they press them into the boundary. If the receiver does not give the quarterback room to throw the ball, it is very difficult to complete the pass. We are always going to have deep opportunities.

We want to win the FIRST DOWNS! If we can win the first downs, we will have a good chance to win the game. Against Florida State, we found out if we only made one yard on first down, we had a chance to be successful on the next two downs. To us, a win on first down is a gain of four yards.

We want the passing game designed for the quarterback. We will have different personnel groups and different alignments. We are going to have our reads, and we are going to use certain concepts. We are not going to try to screw up the quarterback with a lot of reads and concepts. We know we have to make some adjustments each week, but we do not want to confuse our quarterback. We want to allow our quarterback to be aggressive.

The *concept* of the play is more important than the play. We do not like to change the assignments of our players. Personnel groups do change. That has been a nice change that we have made, and it has worked well for us. We are going to run the basic passing routes, and we are going to run the screens and draw plays.

The last point is to run after the catch on a pass. Lou Holtz made a great point about this. He said, "You will never get beat by teams playing catch." How simple is that? You can watch Jerry Rice in the pros. He will catch a 6-yard slant pass and then go 60 yards after the catch. We stress this a great deal: "Run after the catch." This principle works both on offense and defense. Two years ago, when Oklahoma won the National Championship, the best thing they did was to tackle on defense after the pass was caught.

We are going to throw the check-off passes and the out routes. When kids are young, all they want to do is to throw the deep pass. That is all they want to do when throwing the ball. They do not think it counts unless they throw the ball 40 to 50 yards down the field. We want to stress making the completion. We are talented enough on offense to win if we can throw completions.

We work on the check-down and short routes in practice. We want to make our quarterbacks to make the check-off and dump the ball off to the short man and allow him to run with the ball after the completions. We are going to treat the high-percentage passes as a running play.

As we run our route, we think of man coverage first and then zone coverage. A lot of the time, teams will have a problem with communication in the passing game. The quarterback may throw the ball deep, but the receiver thought it was man coverage and cut the route short. If our receiver is not sure what the coverage is, he should think man coverage first, and then adjust if it is zone coverage. We try to take the guesswork out of the plays for our guys running the routes. That has been very good for us.

Going down the list, I have several things here that have helped us. We have handled the blitz by not running any double moves, bootlegs, waggles, or naked plays. A lot of teams run the zone blitz. We like to run the screen pass, we like to run the ball against zone blitzes, and we like to use our three-man sets against those defenses.

We want to eliminate penalties. Again, we are talking about foolish penalties. Also, we want to maintain tempo. We want to maintain rhythm and pace. We would like to have the perfect play called on every down against every defense. We all know this does not happen all of the time. The defense gets to change up and mix the defenses up to confuse the offense. We have several plays that we like to run against any defense we face. We want to have a rhythm to our offense. We want to get to the line of scrimmage and run eight or ten more plays per game. We do not like for the quarterback to spend a lot of time checking the play at the line. We do have our checks, but we like to get to the line and go. We want to have a rhythm, and we want to get in and out of the huddle. Once our quarterback gets his hands under the center, the defense will get to the position they are going to run instead of trying to disguise the defense.

We want to follow the game plan. We do not want to make things up as we go along in the game. We do not want to panic when things go wrong for us. We stay with our game plan. At times it may be tough. If you are down 17 points, it is hard not to panic. Stay with your game plan, and make things work according to the game plan.

We always want to protect the backside of the quarterback. This is very big for us. We had not done a great job on this in the past until we had the talent to protect the backside last year. We will do what we need to do to protect the quarterback on his backside. This past year, we gave up four sacks. We did a good job of protecting the quarterback. He does a good job, he knows the routes, and he knows when to get rid of the ball. We did a good job of protecting him.

We want to make sure we are all on the same page with our offense. We do not want a lot of calls at the line of scrimmage. We do not like a lot of "me" or "you" calls. We do not want the players saying, "I thought?" We do not want to change a lot on the plays. I do not care if it is the wrong play. If we run the same plays and run them right, we feel we have a chance. We realize playing on the road can be a problem for the offense, but we will deal with that aspect the best we can. It is always a problem playing away from home.

We do not want to check from a good play to a better play. If it is a good play, we want to stay with that play. It goes back to developing a rhythm and tempo. If it is a good play, we want to run that play. If we have a mismatch and the defense is stacked and we can't block them, and we have players that can execute, we will change the play and go outside.

I mentioned earlier that we do look for match-ups where we have an advantage. This year, we got our tight end matched up with a linebacker. He could accelerate, and he could run. We used him to get open on the pass route against the linebacker.

Against soft coverages, we like to use hitch and slant routes. If the defensive backs are off the receiver and lined up inside, we like to run the speed-out route against those coverages. Again, we treat this just like a run. We want to go to that play anytime just like a running play. We have combination routes off these plays where we have hitch-and-go routes. This gives us a chance for the deep pass.

We do not use sight adjustments. What I mean by sight adjustments is this: When the defense brings the extra player in the box that you cannot block. Some teams will have hot receivers adjust their route and break off the route when they see the defender rush. We have gotten away from this technique. We have several built-in quick throws to take care of this tactic. We have tried to go away from sight adjustments and use quick throws in this situation.

We do have hot routes. If we cannot block all of the defenders, the quarterback knows he must look for the hot receiver quickly to prevent the sack. He must know where to go with the football. This is a very important key for us.

To finish up, I want to go over one concept. It is a route that we call Texas. The routes are all built in the same. On the backside, we have what we call an alert route. Our tight end runs what we call a read route. Our flanker runs a pivot route. The back runs an angle route. The tailback runs the check-down route.

On the alert route, the receiver breaks at 12 yards. When the quarterback goes to the alert route, he is going deep to give us a chance to have a big play.

On the angle route, we want the receiver to get a 4-by-4 yards relationship. He goes four yards deep and four yards outside. On the read route, the receiver breaks the route at 8 to 10 yards deep. What is a read route? If we are facing a cover two with an open middle of the field, we are going to attack that area of the field. It may be hard to determine the coverage, but we can see if the middle is open or not. If there is no one in the middle of the deep area, we will attack that area. If the middle of the deep area is closed and they have a safety man in that area, we want the receiver to break the route off and come back down the stem of the route.

On the pivot route, we run it 14 yards deep and break it off and come back to 12 yards deep. We pivot away from the defensive back and come back to the boundary.

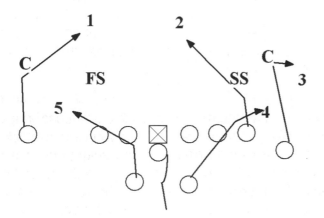

The progression on the route for the quarterback is this. We are always going to look for the angle. If the angle route is open, we want to hit that route. This is an easy throw for the quarterback. The read route comes into play when the defense is playing a two-deep secondary. It gives us a chance for a deep play. We need to know who the player is who runs this route. Some of these receivers can really stretch the defense on this route. On the pivot route, we use this against the defense that plays off the receiver, and we want to play catch against the defense. It is an easy play if the defense is playing off the receiver and to the inside.

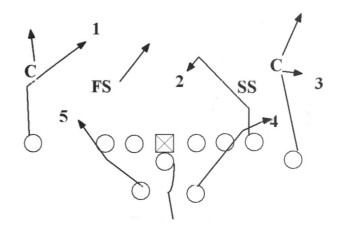

Another concept off this play is when we have two tight ends, two wide receivers, and a one-back set. We can motion the man over to the other side, and we have the same concept. We have the same routes, but we may have a different player running the different routes. You are running the same routes. The concept stays the same for the quarterback. It is a five-step drop for the quarterback.

You can run the same play with three wide receivers and one tight end and the one-back set. You can motion the man over or line him up on the opposite side, it does not matter. You have the same routes from this formation. We run the same routes but with different players running the same routes.

You can run the same play from several different formations, but the concept stays the same. There is a lot of flexibility with the concept, and there are a lot of things you can do with this one concept.

I have a tape of these routes that will give you a better idea of how the concept works. I do appreciate your attention.

SPECIAL TEAMS ARE SPECIAL

Ohio State University

Thank you. I appreciate the warm welcome. I want you young guys to understand that the people you are with will be the best people you will ever know. The fraternity of coaching is a very special group of people. Coming back to Cincinnati has a special place in my heart.

When I started coaching in junior high, I had a great player named "Hacksaw" Reynolds. We won every game, and people thought I was the greatest thing in coaching. I found out real early in life that you win with people. That was one of Woody Hayes's statements he kept framed and hanging on a wall in his office.

When "Hacksaw" moved on to the varsity, I didn't win too many games. I found out I would have to coach a lot better or get better players. The secret of coaching is to get your players in the right place.

I was a high school coach at Harrison High School. They were zero and forty-nine before I came. After my first year, we were zero and fifty-nine. That tells you a little about my tenure there. The next year, we were on a roll. We played a team that had the starting quarterback out with an injury. They lost their second quarterback before our game. They took a tight end who had never played quarterback before, taught him to take snaps before the game, and beat my butt with him.

That taught me another lesson. Their coach knew how to coach a lot better than I did. I knew I was going to have to work a lot harder.

Anyone who coaches in high school today, my heart goes out to them. I really appreciate what they are doing with young players. I love the job they are doing. I am more into kids these days than I am into football.

Coach Trestle and I were at Syracuse together under Dick McPherson. I went on to San Diego State because I wanted to get into coaching at the pro level. They fired us all after a few years, and I moved on.

I was talking to one of our kids the other day. He was really depressed because he didn't get a job for which he had applied. I told him to thank God for unanswered prayers. There was something better out there for him. I have a simple philosophy. The place where you are is the best place to be, because that is where you are.

Our players are the best players there are, because they are our players. I am coaching at Ohio State. I walk into that place each day and walk by so many All-Americans. There is a hall in St. John Arena that is lined with pictures of the great players and teams at Ohio State. It is very special to me. I went to St. John Arena when I was a high school coach and listened to Woody Hayes talk. I only met him twice in my life. I'm an Ohio guy and a Woody Hayes type of guy. I love being at Ohio State. The traditions are as deep as any place in the country.

I was in Wisconsin last year speaking at their high school clinic, representing Youngstown State. I went to the University of Wisconsin stadium. When I walked in, I found a whole wall dedicated to high school coaches. I went back to Ohio State and told Coach Trestle about it. Next year when you come into the rotunda at Ohio State Stadium, you are going to find a wall dedicated to the state of Ohio high school coaches. He is going to build that. He believes that without you guys, we can't do the job we need to do here. It will be awesome. The guys that deserve the respect will be where they belong. To me, that is special.

I was special-teams coordinator for 12 years at Youngstown State. I was the punt coach. The punt is the most important play in football. As you build your special teams in high school or college, try to make everyone on the teams accountable for what they do.

This year, I made a graph of the best and worst teams in special-team areas. I was trying to show our players where they fit as compared to other teams. We were above the average in some areas and at the top in others. I showed this graph to our players. Oklahoma was the best team in the country last year in net-punt yardage. I wanted to show our players where I wanted to go. I want to have the best special teams in the nation.

Whenever you talk about special teams, I believe you have to set the format for your talk. Special units win championships. There are some keys to greatness in special-teams coaching. Why special teams need special coaching is the first thing you should understand. Coaching special teams involves three important factors: momentum, field position, and solidarity. I have coached at the high school level. If you want to put the principal's son, who is 5-9 and 140 lbs, on your kickoff team, put him on the outside where he can contain. Don't put him in a position where he has to make a tackle. Don't put people on special teams to do them a favor. Momentum and field position come from the opening kickoff.

Coach Tressel told us the special teams would decide how good our season was going to be. He was right on with that assessment. If we had made two field goals and not gotten a punt blocked, we could have been 10-1. We were right in the middle of the pack in offensive statistics and better in our defensive stats. The difference was in our special teams. We won two or three games because of our special teams, and we lost a couple because of them.

When you start to coach the special teams, you have to develop a philosophy. Field position and where a team starts a drive is a big momentum builder. We kicked the ball out of bounds three times on kickoffs this year. When you do that, the opponent's drive starts at the 35-yard line. The opposition scored two out of the three times we kicked it out of bounds. You have to instill in your kicker how important it is to keep the ball inbounds.

When you have a philosophy, you have to set objectives. We have an objectives chart we post that lists 12 objectives.

1. No turnovers.
2. No penalties.
3. Score or set up a score.
4. Return all punts for a 5-yard gain.
5. No blocked or forced bad punts.
6. Net punt of 35 yards.
7. Hold all punt returns under 5 yards.
8. No blocked or forced bad field goals.
9. Make all PATs and FGAs inside the 25-yard line
10. Block or force at least one bad kick or punt a game.
11. Return all kickoffs past the 28-yard line, or return a kick 20 yards if the ball is caught outside 10 yards.
12. Hold kickoff returns inside 25-yard line, or under 20 yards when ball is fielded outside the 10-yard line.

Penalties and turnovers are at the top of our objectives chart. Those are the things that will kill you in the kicking game.

People want to know how much time we allot for teaching and coaching the special-teams game. Our head coach is the type of coach who is there every time we do anything related to special teams. He knows how important they are because he is involved. He doesn't give it lip service. The time that you practice special teams has to be quality time. You have to be enthusiastic and really into it when you coach special teams. I don't want anyone coaching special teams because they have been assigned to do it. The accountability and evaluation of our coaching are built into our objectives chart. That will tell you how your special-teams coach is doing.

The personnel used on your special teams must be the best people available on your teams. You have to have a way to substitute on each of these teams. Don't wait until someone gets hurt before you think about how to replace him. You need a depth chart at each position on each team.

I bought six G.I. dog tags for our six special teams. I have a set for each game we play. I gave one to the most outstanding player on each special unit for each game. I thought they might put them on their book bags or key chains. These guys are wearing them around their necks. They don't take them off. If a guy were to get three of them, it would be a great honor. I bought these things for 99 cents. It has the name of the special team and the opponent we are playing. It is a gimmick, but it tells them that the special teams are important.

The head coach wants our punters to work on the jugs machine. He wants them to be able to catch the ball. They work like a receiver. They have to work on their hands. Coach Tressel goes down with the holders on extra points and field goals. He does drills with them. He practices bad-snap drills with them.

He has the stopwatch on them when we are practicing kickoffs, and emphasizes the importance of everyone being at the same place on their coverage. He is always doing something with our special units.

When we lay out our practice schedule, our special periods are called "special Ts." The "special T" is a 10-minute drill. The specialists during this period will split their time during this period. They spend five minutes at each site. If a guy is a long snapper, he spends five minutes snapping to the punters and five minutes snapping for extra points and field goals.

On Tuesday, the punt blockers are in a special drill on blocking the kick. We do it with a volleyball because it's hard for a manager to kick a football and get the type of consistency we need in a kick. The kick blockers practice on getting the hands up, blocking the ball, and not hitting the punter.

On Wednesday, we do our "sniper drill." Our snipers are the guys who are aligned outside on our punting team. You can't do this drill twenty times. We do it two or three times and go on to something else. We don't want our snipers to squeeze the ball carrier. We want them to come down hard and force the punt-return man to bubble out. It is like a defensive end wrong arming a kick-out block. We want the return man to catch the ball and not be able to run the ball up the middle. If he is going to run the ball anywhere, it will to the outside. We align defenders on the snipers to make them fight their way down the field. The cen-

ter snaps the ball and covers also. This is a very competitive drill. We can get about four punts off in this seven-minute drill.

SNIPER DRILL

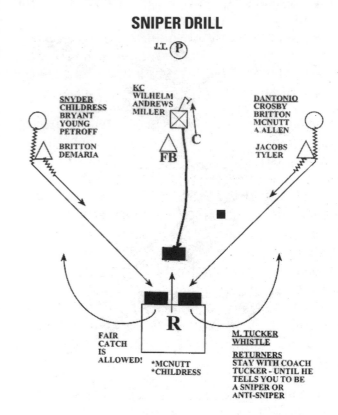

On Tuesday and Wednesday, our special T's involve mostly our specialists. The punt and kickoff return men, punters, and kicker are doing their thing on these days. Everyone else is with his teams going through a walk through.

On Friday, we have a script that we run through. We work against air for fifteen minutes. We cover all of the following things:

- Kick return right vs. squib
- Punt block
- +40 left punt in
- −5 middle tight punt
- −20 left fake punt pass
- Punt return (hold-up) middle
- Kick return middle
- Kickoff after safety
- Punt return, wall left

- −40 left punt vs. block

- Hands team

- +40 right punt return/fake alert

- X point block

- Punt out end zone/bad snap safety

- Run field team on/no time-outs/clock running

We go through these situations each Friday. We want them to focus on what they have to do and concentrate on their assignment.

At Ohio State, our punting stat is different from the NCAA's ratings. If a guy kicks the ball 50 yards and it goes in the end zone, he gets credit for a 50-yard kick with no return. If our punter kicks the ball into the end zone, the referee will bring the ball out to the 20-yard line for the next snap. The punter has his kick reduced by 20 yards. The NCAA gives him credit for a 50-yard kick. We give him credit for a 30-yard kick. We record net yardage on punts. That is the important stat for us.

Let me tell you a little story that happened to me this year. When we played Michigan this year in Ann Arbor, they were the leading punt-blocking team in the country. They also had the leading punt-return man in the country. We wanted to secure our punts. We used a formation that had two fullbacks in the protection scheme.

We were leading the game 23-0 in the fourth quarter. Coach Tressel had gone into a conservative mode on offense. He was running off-tackle and playing defense. He was not going to throw the ball. Michigan had even taken their safety out of the game and replaced him with a linebacker. He was still running the ball. But, he knew we could play defense. He knew if we started throwing the football, they would start celebrating.

We continued to run off-tackle and punt the ball. We punted the ball eleven times that game. On our ninth punt, we were leading 23-14. We had two fullbacks in the formation who allowed a guy to run right between them and block the punt. They scored on that possession.

We were playing our asses off. It came down to our next punt, but this time we were backed up. The score was 26-20, with about four minutes to go in the game. I asked Coach Tressel if he was going to take a safety. He asked me if I had talked to the two fullbacks. I told him I had. He told me to punt the ball and find out how good a coach I was. We punted the ball out to about their 40-yard line.

The defense held, and we got the ball back. We were trying to run out the clock. We were on our 45-yard line with 56 seconds to go in the game. I thought he would run the ball again and keep the clock running. He turned to me and told me we were going to punt the ball. He said, "The punt is the biggest play in football, right?" I told him it was and sent out the punt team. I told the punter on the way to the field to get it off. He took one step and kicked the ball. It came out, hit the ground, and rolled for seven seconds. That is like a lifetime in Michigan Stadium with a hundred and seven thousand fans in the stands.

After the game, Coach Tressel asked the team what is the most important play in football? They all answered, "THE PUNT!" They all believed that now. They couldn't remember much about the game. But, they could remember the game ended with a punt.

Every championship we won at Youngstown State was because we played good defense, had no turnovers, and had great special teams. We weren't great this year at Ohio State. We were average at best. But, Coach Tressel was behind us all the way. He kept encouraging us to keep working hard. He never changed what we were doing. He stayed the course. When we got to the end of the season at Michigan, our special teams won the game for us.

I'm going to put on the film now and show you all the phases of our kicking game. I'll give you some suggestions about what I think you should do.

The first team I'll show you is the punting game. The punt is the most important play in football. Bo Schembechler, the great Michigan coach, said that. Jim Tressel says that, and I believe it more than anyone. I know that you can look back at any game this season, and the punt has been the difference. It has either cost you or won a game for you.

When we punt the football, we kick the football away from the return man. We kick the ball anywhere except to the man returning the ball. Our punter has a 44-yard average, but he will give that up to keep the ball away from a great kick-return man.

The mechanics in the punting game are important. Our long snapper was a walk-on who won a scholarship because of his hard work at that position. The job of the snapper is to snap the ball and put it in the window. The window is an area around the belt line of the kicker. If the kicker has to catch the ball above his chin, you have a problem. That adds seven-tenths of a second to the time it takes to punt the ball. If the ball is on the ground, the punter can still make a play on it. He can pick it up and kick it. If the ball is over the punter's head, or so high that he has to leave his feet to retrieve it, you've got a blocked punt.

The next thing is protection. I don't care what kind of formation you use, it better be good. Whatever the protection, it has to take care of protecting the punter. The kick protection has to be a gap-control blocking scheme.

Our fullback in our protection calls the protection. We don't want him moving up and pointing to people. The defenders get a rhythm from what he is doing and can get a jump on the punt block. We want him to give his instructions from the stance. We want poise in the communication. The key is to get your punt team on the field quickly, communicate, and punt the ball. You have to put them under pressure in practice. On Tuesday, we teach them the protection, and on Wednesday, we run them on the field for timing. On Tuesday, when we are teaching, we have one tempo. On Wednesday when we are pressuring the punt, it is a faster tempo.

The things that we maximize in the punting game are protection, cover in lanes, tackling, and the halo area. We want to practice ball awareness and try to down the ball inside the 10-yard line whenever we get the chance.

We use the pro-style punt formation. We have two snipers out wide. If you have a right-footed punter, he is going to kick the ball to the left 90 percent of the time. If we have the ball on the right-hash mark, we put both our snipers to the wide side of the field. We simply call Louie for left, or Roger for right.

Both snipers align to the side of the call.

It also gives the defense something else to think about. If you step one sniper off the line and move the opposite wing back up onto the line, you have three eligible receivers to one side.

PUNT FORMATION

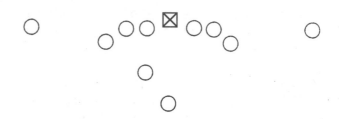

Special units build solidarity with your team. Our guys are called the "difference makers." We were 7-5 this year, and it could have been a hell of a lot better. If we had kicked the field goals we attempted against Penn State and not had a punt blocked against Illinois, we would have had a great season. I take responsibility for those shortcomings.

Players on these teams come from offensive and defensive teams. If you emphasize the special teams, you will get back what you believe in. You may have a great player, but if he is selfish or you can't trust him, don't put him on a special team. Don't put that great linebacker on the coverage team if all he wants to do is knock someone's head off. If you do, he will run down and get you a penalty.

Our punt-return unit is called the "Rangers." This name comes from a West Point graduate who actually was a ranger. His name is Mike Sullivan. He was coaching at Ohio University. He runs this unit, and our players really get into that. This unit could turn a game into insanity. We were less than average on our returns, but we blocked two punts. When we blocked the punt against UCLA, it broke their backs. In the Indiana game, they were playing great defense until we blocked the punt. That turned the game around. Guys who get on the ranger unit get a ranger patch. They are proud of them.

There are more punts blocked on what we call punt safe, than on a punt-block scheme. Punt safe is making sure the opponent punts the ball. It is not an all-out rush. The punting team has a tendency to relax when they see a no-rush scheme coming. That is when someone breaks clear and blocks the punt. The block wasn't designed; the punting team just lost their focus.

We have several things in mind when our return team comes out. If we are going to try to block a punt, we want to score off the block. We have to know the situation and stay off the punter if we can't get to the ball. We don't want to run into or rough the punter, which would give the offense another shot with the ball. We want to make sure all the blocks are high, and the screen blocks are made in front.

When they line up, they watch the ball to stop the fakes. They should expect fakes and try to talk the punting team out of a fake by calling out, "Watch the fake." On all short punts, the deep return man has to make a "poison" call. Poison means he can't get to the ball to catch it. When the blockers hear the poison call, they need to get away from the ball. A football will take some funny hops. All the return man has to do is catch the ball. He either returns the ball or fair catches it. Do not put the ball on the ground.

When we run back with a defender to block on the return, we teach our blockers to run on the defender's hip. We are really not trying to block them. We are trying to get in their way. Sometimes, when the blocker tries to block the defender, they forget to run and lose contact.

Our kickoff coverage was the best in the Big Ten Conference. We called them the "recon unit." I tell our team that covering a kick-off is like parachuting from a plane. They stand up, hook up, and shuffle to the door. They all have a number, and they count off as they get into the huddle. They get all revved up. They understand they are the first play of defense. They can get your crowd going like no one else. Our kicker kicked the ball for a touchback 21 times during the season. We want to kick the ball into the corners of the field and try to keep the return inside the 20-yard line.

As we cover, we want to sprint down and stay in our lanes. The interior-coverage players keep the ball inside and in front of them at all times. The outside man in coverage, as he approaches a blocker, attacks him differently, depending on who is attempting to

block him. If the blocker is a tight end or back, he wants to go under them and spill the ball outside. He knows if he goes under the block, someone else will make the play, scrapping over him like a linebacker.

If the outside man sees a fullback coming to kick him out, he wrong arms him and goes under the block. If he is a big lineman, he is going to squeeze and beat him with speed.

Our recon unit is comprised mainly of linebackers and a few defensive backs. They are guys who will run fast and tackle. Sometimes, we put offensive personnel on this team.

If the blocker is a lineman, he wants to squeeze the ball and keep it inside. We want to take away the running lane. We want to create the big play and make a tackle that causes a fumble. The seventh or eighth man away from the corner the ball is kicked into has to stay at home and cut off the field. He is playing for the reverse or long lateral on the kickoff.

The things we emphasize are staying in the lane, speed, and collision. We want the ball outside the hash mark and in the air for four seconds. If that happens, we can close and beat a block. If the ball stays in the air for four seconds, the coverage team should be at the 30-yard line when the ball is caught.

We don't let our kicking team stand around on the sidelines after they are finished with their kicking workouts in practice. We send them inside to break down films of the opponent's kickers. They use a yardage chart to chart all kicks. They record hang time, type of return, distance of kicks, and any other tendency they might find. They can tell us where the ball is going before it is kicked. We want ball awareness. We want to give our return men a chance to handle the ball.

We want to stay on our blocks and use high screens as a blocking technique. I don't know anyone in the country who can get square up on a coverage man and block him. I haven't seen it yet. We sprint back, turn, and make the coverage player pick a side. The blocker tilts his hips to the sideline. If the defender comes in front, we pin him and get on his hip. If the defender tries to go behind the blocker, the blocker wheels and blocks him because he has come out of his lane. You cannot give the coverage man two ways to go.

We run different returns. If the opponent's best coverage men come down the middle of the field, then that is where I want to return the ball. If we run a middle wedge, I have two fullbacks and two tight ends forming the middle wedge. When we start our count on the coverage team, we don't count the two guys on either side of the kicker. We start our count from outside them. We let them go, and they become the responsibility of the fullbacks and tight ends.

The wedge has to be 12 yards in front of the return man. When the wedge starts up the field, we want them to run as hard as they can. We don't want them slowing down to try to block anyone. They are going to level the two guys coming down the middle of the field or at least make them come out of their lanes.

Our front guys sprint back to set the return. We want our guys to turn at about the 40-yard line, depending on the kick. We time the kicks and know what they are doing. If they turn at the 40, they are in position to run with a defender. If a football team gets the ball outside the 35-yard line and it has a good field-goal kicker, they will score.

KICK OFF RETURN MIDDLE

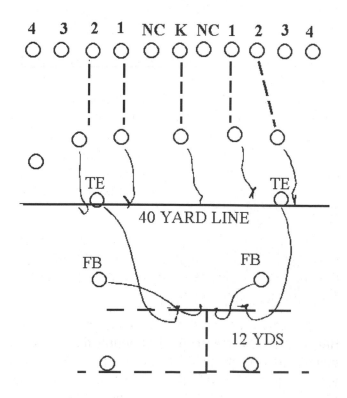

On our kickoff returns, we were in the middle of the pack in the Big Ten Conference. We use a standard 5-2-2-2 alignment. The most important thing in the kickoff return is speed. That goes for the return man and the guys in the wedge. They have to attack the coverage players. They have to make the coverage player move right or left. When the blocker breaks down to block someone, it cuts down the running lanes. The return man has to bring the ball into a seam and attack the coverage.

At Youngstown State, we had won four national championships. Twice, the teams we were losing to relaxed on an extra point and allowed us to block them. Every point in a game counts. There are more games won by one point than they are by 50.

There are a number of ways to play your line on a field goal or extra-point play. We get into a stance with our hands down. The key to defending on an extra point play is to always protect your inside gap. If a lineman's outside arm goes inside, there is a gap created. The linemen have to stay square and big.

The biggest factor in field goal protection and kicking is timing. It is snap, hold, and kick. The kicker can't see the rush or worry about it. We have a guy dive in front of the field goal kicker in practice.

On the tape I showed you, the field goal we blocked against Purdue was by the guy diving across in front of the kicker. The kicker saw the guy coming and pulled off.

What I tried to do today was to give you an overall picture of what we are doing at Ohio State. You can't win without great special teams and accountability.

If there's anything I can do for you, let me know. If you need forms or copies of things we do, please call. Our program at Ohio State is an open book. Coach Tressel wants to serve the high school coaches of Ohio in any way he can. The better you guys are, the better we are going to be. Coach McPherson used to say this is the greatest game of them all. I believe it. It was especially special for me to come back to Cincinnati and speak.

I am a guy representing you. I'm a high school guy at heart. I've been in your shoes and know where you're coming from. I know what a tough job you have. I'll keep trying to do a better job and make Ohio State a place that you will be proud of. God bless you. Thank you very much. Come see us.

INDIVIDUAL SECONDARY TECHNIQUES AND DRILLS

Cincinnati Bengals

Thank you. It is funny to hear that introduction with a list of the places I have coached. It seems as only yesterday I was coming right out of college to go to University of Cincinnati as a graduate assistant. There have been a lot of games between now and then. I have been fortunate to have had the opportunity to coach on almost every level of football. I coached in high school for one year and wished I had coached more at that level. I coached at small colleges, mid-major colleges, major colleges, and just finished my first year with the Bengals.

Tonight, I'm going to talk to you about defensive secondary play and some of the fundamentals that go along with it. Before I do that, I want to share some ideas with you from places that I've been, which will help you approach your players and give you a chance to be successful.

Coaching involves effort, and you have to demand great effort from your players. A great example of that are the St. Louis Rams. They play great defense, but it is one of the simplest defenses in the league. The reason their defense is so good is the intensity level at which they play the scheme. That is coaching. What you accept from an effort standpoint is going to determine how well you play as a team. You can make up for a lot of things when you have a team that is sound and playing with great effort. That means you can't allow people to loaf. As the coach, you have to do something about it when they do loaf. My last college job was at Fresno State. In spring practice, after every practice, we would watch the film and count the times that a defensive player loafed in practice. The next day before we did anything, the defense would get together and do up-downs for the number of times we loafed the previous day. The guys who were actually the ones who had loafed had to do extra gassers at the end of practice. These are things that you as a coach can control without a doubt.

I think your players have to understand the scheme. The one thing we did with the Bengals this year was cut down on some things. We made things a little simpler. We wanted our guys to go out and execute without thinking about it. It makes a difference in their performance level if they can. We have a long way to go to get to where we want to be. Defensively, this year we finished ninth in the league in total defense. We had forty-eight sacks this season, which set a club record and ranked fourth in the league. A lot of those things happened because we made it easier. We've always had some guys who were talented players, but this year they knew what they were doing, played with great effort, and executed the defensive scheme. Our scheme didn't change that much from week to week. The sacks we made in the last game against Tennessee were the same pressures we ran in the opening game against New England. That was a big-time key for us.

You have to be technique sound. We are going to spend the rest of this lecture on techniques in the secondary. I think whatever level you are at, you have to constantly look for edges to improve in the techniques you teach. Players want to learn. I found that out this year. I am dealing with guys who are making a heck of a lot of money. Yet, if they feel you can give them something that is going to make them better, they will listen to you.

Make players know that you care about them outside of football. That is true even with the guys I deal with every day. Be a part of their lives and give them the direction they need.

You have to reward and recognize great effort. Recognize the little things that people do. If you are going to demand great effort, make sure that the kids who are giving that kind of effort are recognized constantly. Be positive in your reinforcement as often as you can be. In our meeting rooms, we have all kinds of charts displayed to show the accomplishments of our players. We had a hit chart which was color-coded and by position for each game. We did the same thing with big plays and what we called drive stoppers.

We counted drive stops this year with the Bengals. We wanted to know how many guys were involved with getting off the field on third down. We had a chart for that. It was important to them, and it was quite competitive. They wanted to be the leader in drive stops.

Let me tell you a quick, funny story, and then we'll get into the lecture. I went to Maryland when Coach Duffner was the head coach there. We were terrible on defense. When we got there, we were 106th in the nation in defense. There are only 106 teams in our division. It wasn't even close. We were 106th by about eighty total yards. When we got there, we wanted to start building some new mindsets for our team. We were going to have a "black shirt" defense, but they were going to have to earn those shirts each week. It wasn't just the first team who got them. If anyone displayed a winning performance in Saturday's game, he got a black shirt on Monday in our defensive meeting. That didn't mean the team had to win, because we were trying to build from the ground up.

If you played your position and were worthy of a black shirt, we gave you one. But, you had to turn it in at the end of the week. That was a reminder that you had to earn the shirt again next week. You didn't earn a black shirt just because you were a starter. At our place, some guys were starting because they were the only ones left.

We did it at Fresno State, and it became a pride type of thing. Once a player wins a black shirt, they don't want to give it up. You can do some of the same things. Have some fun with your players. Football is a tough game. It is tough to practice, but there are a lot of things that are inherently funny if you make it that way.

At the Bengals, Coach Duffner gives out candy bars for our special awards in our defensive meeting. We give them a $100,000 candy bar for effort. If a guy makes a big hit, he gives him a Crunch bar. For extra effort, they get a PayDay candy bar. Here is an NFL player making more money then you can imagine sitting in a meeting waiting to be awarded a candy bar

for achievement on the football field. And if they don't get them, they come up and want to know why?

This is a stupid little thing, but guys enjoy being around it and look forward to it. They have fun with it and enjoy being around those guys.

Let's get into why I am here. After looking at tons of high school films over the years I have come up with four things that are critical areas that need to be addressed when you are coaching the secondary. The first thing is poor run/pass recognition. It doesn't matter at what level you coach, you are going to give up big plays because a defensive back didn't read the pass or run correctly. He is coming up when he should be dropping. He can't understand his keys and things like that. You have to drill it and coach it, and there are some simple ways to do it.

The second area is taking poor angles to the ball. This area involves backside angles going into pursuit. Poor leverage on the ball when it is on the perimeter is another example. Proper angles have to be taken to get into a proper tackling position. Big plays are created because improper pursuit angles are taken. The longest pass we had thrown against us this year was forty-seven yards. That's not good, but we were number one in the NFL with yardage per completion. A lot of that success comes from taking proper angles to the ball.

The next thing is kind of wordy. It is the inability to maintain proper leverage with cushion and poor transition versus the deep pass. I'm going to talk about a number of footwork drills that can teach players how to come out of a backpedal that will make a difference for them.

The fourth factor is poor judgment on the deep ball in flight. Some guys have great knacks for doing that, and some don't. You can drill those skills to improve that aspect of the game. Those are the areas that I am going to try to concentrate on. You can improve your techniques by drill work in each area.

I am going to have to fly through the rest on my lecture to get it all in. I hope you get something from it.

As you plan your practices there are some areas that you need to give attention to each day. Those areas include basic fundamental footwork, block protection, tackling, ball drills, and group drills.

We do some kind of footwork drills every day. There are three different ways that we do it. We do individual footwork drills, partner footwork drills, and warm-up drills on those days when we don't have a lot of time. But, we do footwork drills every day.

I think it is critical that you teach guys how to get off blocks. I don't think enough time is spent with that in the secondary. As a result, you have guys who are constantly getting blocked down field. You give up big plays because guys don't know how to disengage, maintain proper leverage, and make the tackle.

You have to work on tackling every day. There are some specific types of tackling drills that apply to defensive backs rather than other positions on the field. I'll show you those.

You need to practice ball skills whenever you can and incorporate them into your footwork drills. We do that daily.

The last area involves performing some group drills, which are predominantly recognition-type drills. I think they are important for all defensive backs.

That is our starting point from which we are going to go forward. I'm going to start with the backpedal and go into the drills we do on a daily basis. A lot of this stuff you may have heard before, so I'm going to go quickly.

When we get into the backpedal, the first thing we have to talk about is the stance. I want the defensive back's feet in a narrow, but comfortable, stance. If I am talking about corners, I want their feet inside their shoulders in width. I want a four to six inch stagger in their feet. I want their outside foot up and their inside foot back. Their weight should be resting predominantly on their upfield foot because we are going to rock back with a slow, controlled, read step initially.

I do this progression on the first day of mini-camps with our players. You have to coach these things the way you know it. The only way I know to coach is go back and coach the fundamentals like the players have never heard them before. I think you have to do that every year.

The stance is comfortable with a narrow base. The feet are a narrow width apart. The knees are bent, and the hips have to sink. The weight is on the front foot. The first step is the read step. It is a slow, controlled step. We want to read the course of the ball. We have to be alert for the three-step drop. Actually today, we are reading the one-step drop of the quarterback. They are rising up and throwing the ball so quickly on the quick screen, we have to read that first. What we are coaching is the three-step drop. We take two to three steps and react to what we see. By the third step, the back should recognize what is happening.

There are some keys on the three-step drop. When the quarterback comes out, the ball is in a high position in his carry. He has the ball already in a cocked-and-ready position. If the quarterback is going to a five-step drop, the ball is carried lower in most cases. The quarterback is more upright because he is getting ready to throw. Those are two keys to give the defensive back a quicker break on the ball.

As we work into the backpedal, we don't want to get over extended. We don't reach back as far as we used to teach. The stride length should be about the length of a comfortable walking stride. We want the feet close to the ground. We talk about skimming the grass. You should hear their feet moving over the top of the grass. If you stand behind the backs as they backpedal, you don't want to see their heels coming up. We push off the front foot, reach back, keep the shoulders in front of the hips, keep the feet close to the ground, skim the grass with a narrow base, and maintain good arm action.

In the arm action, the harder you pump the arms going back, the harder it is to stop. The majority of the game for a defensive back is played breaking back for the ball. You have to control the arm action going back. Keep the shoulders relaxed, and don't drive the arms like you were running a 40-yard dash. We want the arm action controlled on the backpedal and want a violent pumping of the arms coming forward back to the ball. The controlled action going back lends to a quicker momentum change coming forward.

There is a slight difference in zone coverage versus man coverage. When we are playing man coverage, the stride is shorter and quicker. We want the feet as close to the ground as possible, and we want to turn over the feet as quickly as we can. In zone coverage, the defensive back is in a nice rhythm in his backpedal. It is not a race. Rather, it should involve a good smooth rhythm to get into his zone.

I'm going to get into our individual footwork drills. I get four lines of players aligned on the sideline facing the middle of the field. We are going to work from the sidelines to the hash marks on the field. They are all on a yard line going across the field. I give the command, "break." With that command, they jump out on their line about three yards in front of me in a good stance. If someone is not in a good stance, I wait until they get it right. We do a number of things from that point. To start with, we do nothing but the read-step. I have them react to the action of the ball. I pull the ball to my stomach. That means the ball has been snapped. They take the two to three slow, controlled steps and react to the action of the ball.

If I pull the ball up, that means pass. If I push the ball out, that means run. When we teach the read-step, they take the two to three steps and react back to the sidelines.

The next thing we get into is the backward run to the hash marks. We do one drop in a zone-run and one in a man-drop. I tell them backward run zone. I pull the ball back to snap the ball. They go into the read-step to the backward run. They react to what they see from the ball. We come back and do our backward run in a man-drop, using those techniques.

FOOTWORK DRILLS ORGANIZATION

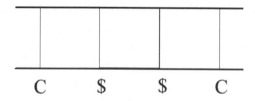

From the backward run, we go to the transition. This is going from a backpedal to a crossover run. These are components of what you have to do as a defensive back. I turn my shoulders, which means go into the transition run. They always tilt their hips toward me. The guys on the right tilt to me, and the guys on the left do the same thing. I want their eyes on me. They are not looking downfield. They keep their eyes on me, hop and tilt their hips, and get into a crossover run.

This next technique I want to take some time to explain. I think it is the most important technique you use to get turned in as few as steps as possible. This is what I call *plant the toe deep*. If you had only one drill to do every day, I would do this one. This lets you get from a backpedal to a full sprint down the field as smoothly as possible.

Here are the coaching points. If I am going to turn to my left out of the backpedal, I want to take my right foot and pigeon-toe it to the inside. Doing that enables me to get my left toe headed completely down the field in one step. Without doing this, most guys take at least four steps to get out of the backpedal and turned downfield. The right foot is turned inside, and the right toe is planted deep. The weight is placed on the right toe. The left elbow leads, and the hips spin. It is almost like a hop. A lot of it is psychological, because when you walked your defensive backs through their turn without planting the toe, it took them three steps to turn. Now, you are showing them something that gets them turned in one step.

If you are making a turn to the right, you simply do the opposite. Turn the left foot inside, and follow the same progression. That is a key drill that we do all the time. We do this drill down the line.

The next drill we do is a forty-five degree change of direction drill. We tilt and crossover step at a forty-five degree angle, plant, and go the opposite direction at a forty-five degree angle. We zigzag, gaining depth with each change of direction.

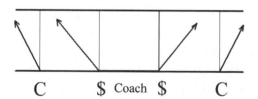

We also use the hip-flip drill. It is a loosening-up drill also. We go down the line with the hips turned left, and completely turn them to the right and back again. We do that in rapid succession.

We have a speed-turn drill off the forty-five degree drop. Instead of tilting the hips and opening up to turn, we snap our head and eyes around, turn our back to the quarterback, and get back on the receiver we are covering. That is the fastest, most efficient way to turn when your cushion has been broken down.

The key coaching point in teaching the speed turn is the angle of the break of the receiver. The defensive back has to determine the angle of the break of the receiver. If the receiver is running a post-corner route on the defender, the defender will drive on the post move. When the receiver breaks back to the corner, the first thing the defender has to do as he executes his speed turn is to think post route first. We want to react to the deep area first. If the pattern becomes a dig or come back, the defensive back has to react back down to the pattern. Too many times, defenders come out of the speed turn too flat. The receiver simply runs past them.

The last drill we do is what we call *angle backpedal*. A lot of people call this a weave back. What we are working on is backpedaling at an angle and keeping our shoulders and hip square to the line of scrimmage.

We do all these drills in that area of the sideline to the hash marks. And we do most of them every day. They may be done in the agility and loosening up period.

The next technique we work on is the different types of breaks to the ball. This term came from Holy Cross, when I coached there years ago. My players named this one. They called it a "roadrunner." It is basically keeping your feet alive on the break. When I was in high school, we were taught to plant and break on the ball. If it works for you, keep on doing it. We don't teach that. We like to plant, get our hips down, and keep our feet moving. Whichever foot you are breaking from, the next step has to get in the ground as fast as you can get it there. We want to keep the feet moving, and get the hips, knees, and feet pointed in the direction you want to go. Drive violently and forcefully with the arms. Get the weight forward and burn your eyes in on the target. We close to the contact. We don't look back for the ball until we have gotten to a position where we can actually touch the receiver. Then, we look back to the quarterback. The roadrunner break is coming off the toe.

We do another break we call a *"duck-foot plant."* That is a plant with more of the foot on the ground. Instead of coming off the toe as in the roadrunner, the duck foot opens the hips more and puts more of the foot on the ground. When we do these drills in practice, they look neat and sharp, but in the game situation, one type of break may not get the job done. That

is why we teach and drill both types of breaks. When we get in transition and the receiver stops, we have to duck-foot plant and come back. The rest of the techniques in the break are the same. It is simply the foot and weight placement that makes a difference.

We use the duck-foot plant when there is questionable footing. We want them to have all the cleats on the ground that they can possibly have. That keeps them from slipping when they come out of their break. Remember the three B's: break, balance, and burst.

There are some tips for breaks that I want to pass on to you. When a receiver is running a pattern, unless he is running a speed cut, his stride length will shorten as he approaches his break point. His hips start to drop to get him under control to make the cut, and his arm action will decrease.

The next thing we do is partner footwork. These drills involve two guys working together. We start out with the weave drill. One guy is the receiver, and the other is the defender. The defender assumes a position on the receiver. It could be inside or outside. He gets five yards off the receiver, and as the receiver works downfield, he will make moves and small breaks. The defender weaves his footwork and keeps his position and cushion on the receiver down the field. The defender may turn his butt slightly, but he wants to keep his shoulders as square as possible.

The next drill is a key drill to understand how to cut a receiver off. It is one of the biggest flaws I've seen over the years in high school players. Defensive backs are going to go against receivers who are faster than they are. It doesn't matter at what level you play, there is going to be someone who can run past you. The defender has to know when to turn and run, and what to do as he turns and runs.

For example, let's say the receiver is running a fade route. As he comes off the line of scrimmage, he breaks to the defender's outside shoulder and starts upfield. The defender doesn't let the receiver run upfield and then follow him. He wants to get in the receiver's lane and force him to get wider, but not deeper. The receiver has to get wider to get away from the defender, or he has to run up the defender back.

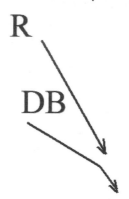

He could break back inside, but to do that, he has to stop and chop his feet. That cuts all his momentum. It is important to learn how to cut off the streak route. Remember to run in his lane and make him run wider to get away from you. The defender wants to feel the receiver by getting his hand down around the hip of the receiver.

We do this drill as a partner drill. The receiver breaks off the line, chokes his motor down, and restarts his move down field. He does this twice as he approaches the defender. On the third move, he tries to run past the defender. The defender has to react to each choke-down, and as the receiver tries to run past him, he has to cut off the receiver.

The next drill is called the *snake drill*. In this drill, the receiver and defender align five yards apart. The receiver is looking at the coach for directions. The defender is focusing on the lower body of the receiver and reacting to what he sees. The coach starts the receiver back in a backpedal and brings him forward. We work in forty-five degree angles from sideline to hash mark. They keep working on a zigzag pattern until they are called back. When that happens, we throw a ball for an interception or toss out a fumble for them to scoop and score. After that, we turn them sideways and do the same drill with them working off the outside of the foot.

The next drill is called *run even*. The indicators as to when a receiver is going to break his route are the hips. It is not the head and shoulders. The lower body tells you what a receiver is going to do. As the defender is running with the receiver, he should not be looking at him until he gets down the field where there is a threat for a vertical route. This is a mirror drill. The receiver chokes down after a couple of steps and restarts his momentum. The defender stays in position and mirrors the moves of the receiver. We do this from a trail position as well.

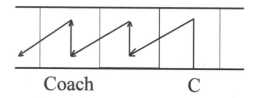

Coach   C

If you play a cover-2 in the secondary, it is necessary for defenders to funnel the receivers to certain areas of the field. The first thing I talk to my guys about is not to funnel with the upper body. You funnel with the feet and hips. The arms, hands, and helmet are a bonus. In order to use any of those things, you have to get your feet and hips in a position to reroute the receiver. Too often a young guy thinks he can reroute the receiver with his hands. It doesn't happen that way. It is like taking a charge in basketball. They can understand that. Get in position, take the charge, deliver the blow, and lock out.

You teach that with the mirror drill. Linemen do it in pass blocking, receivers do it in stalk blocking, and defensive backs do it in the funnel drill. Align two cones about five yards apart. Put the defender on the receiver. Let the receiver work laterally between the cones. The defender mirrors the moves of the receiver and stays in front of him. We start out with the defender's hands behind his back. All the defender is doing is sliding and shuffling to stay right down the middle of the receiver. We want the feet shoulder-width apart. I don't want them to crossover or click their heels. The second phase is to put the hands out as he does the drill, but not contact the receiver. In the third phase, the receiver moves laterally turning his hips. On the third move, he attacks one of the defender's shoulders. The defender mirrors until the receiver attacks. The defender jabs with his outside hand hoping to get to the outside shoulder of the receiver. If he doesn't, he is still in a position to open his hips and take away the fade ball. We do that same break two or three times.

In the funnel, after contact, the defender flips his hips and expands to the boundary. Get more width than you think you need to. That keeps the ball from coming into the boundary too early.

MIRROR DRILL

$$\longleftarrow \text{DB} \longrightarrow$$

*   *

DB

(Slide and Shuffle)

The last footwork drill we do is off lines that I have drawn in the end zone. The lines are five yards in depth and three yards apart. The second set of lines is two yards by two yards. The third set of lines is the same as the first. We start on the line backpedaling. At the end of the line, we run forward at a forty-five degree angle to the next line. We repeat the backpedal and sprint at a 45° angle to the next line.

When we get to the second group of lines, we either do all kinds of footwork movement, or we shuffle through them. At the last group of lines, we repeat what we did in the first group. It doesn't have to be all backpedal. It could be crossover runs, or plants and comebacks. You can mix it up. In two minutes, you can get everyone through there and go to the next drill. They have gotten a good warm-up with good tempo.

END ZONE DRILL

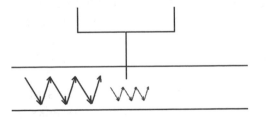

Let's shift gears and talk about block protection. I'm not going to spend much time on this, but I do think it is worthwhile to talk about. I think it is important to teach your guys in the secondary how to get off stalk, cut-off type, and kick-out blocks. I don't think enough time is spent on this area. The players don't like to do it.

We start with a quick hands drill. We also call it target practice. We line up across from one another. One guy is the dummy, and the other is playing the block. We do this in three drills. We have a block protection progression we go through. The first thing we do is shoot the hands. I call it shoot from the holster. We want the thumbs up and the palms out. The elbows are tight to the body and stay within the cylinder of the body. At the end, we grab cloth.

The first drill is a quick-reps movement on a whistle. I give them five quick whistles. They shoot their hands into the breastplate of the blocker on each whistle. In the next drill, we do the same quick reps, but on the last whistle, they grab cloth and lock out. I check their hands, eyes, and make sure their helmet is below the blocker's helmet in a good leverage position. The low man is going to win the fight.

In the next drill, we get in a fit position on the blocker in a locked-out position. The key to beating the stalk block is getting the blocker back on his heels. Once you get the blocker on his heels, we are in the advantage position. On the whistle, we are going to run the blocker back five yards. We want the eyes looking through the chin in a leverage position. We want control of the blocker, and we cannot pick a side.

After we get control of the block, we have to shed the block. The next drill is the shed movement. We use two whistles in this drill. On the first whistle, we are repeating the previous drill of running the blocker back. On the second whistle, we want to shed the blocker. If we get the blocker moving backward, it is easy to shed him. The blocker will sink and try to change the momentum. When he pushes forward, we use his momentum to rip, swim, or shrug off his block. It is like judo. We use his momentum to move him.

Another block that defensive backs have to play is the kick-out block. These can be brutal blocks. They are delivered by fullbacks, pulling guards, and tackles. The first thing we talk about in these types of blocks is getting the chest to the knee. We have to be that low. We want a toe-to-heel stagger with the feet. The back wants a solid base. If he gets his feet parallel, he is going down. He wants to hit the kick-out block on the rise with the point of his pads. We lift with the legs, shoulder, and forearm. We want to maintain our balance and keep the outside arm and leg free. If we can stay on our feet, we want to spin back inside and try to make a strip on the ball.

The next block the defensive back has to play is the crack-back block. That is a tough block to play because teams have been known to crack on the safety and run a pattern off that. That's why you have to really drill this, so the corner can tell the difference and not get fooled. If the safety gets cracked, the corner has to replace him in the force scheme.

The thing that helps the corner is the safety's reaction to his key. When the safety gets a block key and he is the force, he has to get on his horse and get to the line of scrimmage right now. That means if the wide receiver is going to crack him, he has to get flat and commit to his block, which makes an easy read for the corner. If the safety waits, the receiver can work downfield, and the corner doesn't know what to do.

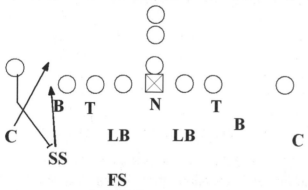

I'm going to talk a little about tackling. The first thing we do is a fit-and-lift drill. We start the tackler in a fit position. He rolls his tail, lifts, and gets the sensation of driving through the ball carrier from a low position to a high position.

We want the knee over the front foot with his hands on the ball carrier's hips. The head is up, and the eyes are going through the chin. We roll over the front foot, bring our hips underneath, extend, and lock out.

We have an angle tackling drill. We start off in the fit position. We want to strike with the same foot and shoulder. That gives you so much more momentum, it is unbelievable. We run through with the back leg. We practice hitting from low to high on the rise.

We teach the roll tackle. The first time I did this with the Bengals, they thought I was crazy. We cut-tackle a lot because we have to tackle a lot of big guys. Sometimes that is the only way you can get a guy down. We have to get low, pull the legs toward us, dip the shoulder to the ground, and get the eyes to the sky as quickly as possible. We actually leave our feet and lay out to make the tackle. We drill that now.

One of the most important tackles the defensive back ever makes is on a hitch pattern. How many times have you seen a hitch pattern being thrown that goes the distance because the defensive back missed the tackle? On the hitch tackle, the defensive back has to be aggressive. He can't wait to come up. He has to come hard. He can gather a bit just before contact, but he has to be aggressive. If he fails to make the tackle, he has to miss to the outside. He cannot let the ball get to the sideline. If he doesn't make the tackle, the ball has to come back to the field, not the sideline.

The other type of tackling we do is called vice tackling. That is a 2-on-1 tackle. The defenders put the ball carrier in a vice. We want both tacklers keeping their head gear on the outside of the ball carrier. It could be a corner and strong safety. The corner gets there first; his helmet goes on the outside of the ball carrier. The strong safety applies the vice hit, but his head gear goes to the outside also. If the corner misses him, the ball carrier is turned back inside to the strong safety that comes with his hat on the outside. That turns the ballcarrier back into the pursuit. We want to force the ballcarrier to the other guy if we don't make the tackle.

VICE TACKLING

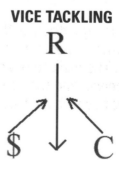

Defensive backs have to catch the ball. Therefore, we have to do ball drills to improve their ability to catch. The first one we use is the defensive back coming straight on the ball. We start them out 15 yards away. I want to find out who will catch the ball on a run with the ball coming straight at them. I throw the ball hard and right at their nose. I want to see the guys who don't slow down or flinch when they catch the ball. I want them to never break stride. I want them to catch the ball and keep on running. You can evaluate some players real quickly doing this drill.

The next drill we use is an over-the-top drill. We run the defensive back down the line, and I am going to throw the ball right over the top. What I am trying to do is throw the ball right over his head. It may come over one shoulder or the other, but I'm trying to get it directly over their head.

This next drill is like a warm up drill for the receivers and quarterbacks. We call it *post-streak-fade*. We have two lines of receivers. We line the corners up in one line and the safeties up in the other. They switch lines after they go. We run a post, streak, or fade pattern. The only difference is they start off in the backpedal to a transition or a turn-and-run. This helps the defensive back with his judgment on the deep ball. They love to catch the ball anyway, but they don't get enough work on catching a deep ball. This is what this drill is supposed to do. You can also use it as a conditioning drill. Instead of running a gasser, run this drill.

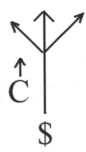

The dog fight is a good competitive drill. Put two defensive backs in a backpedal, and break them to one side or the other. The back to the side of the break becomes the receiver, and the other guy is the defender. They fight to catch the ball.

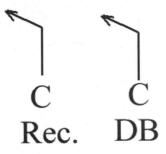

Another drill is called *end of the route*. Oftentimes, a defensive back doesn't know how to play the ball. He doesn't know whether to knock it down or try to intercept it. In this drill, we put the receiver at the end of their route. The defensive back is put in position at the end of his coverage. Instead of running the entire route, we run only the end of it. I throw the ball and make the defensive back make decisions of how to play the ball. Some balls I'll throw where he has no play on the ball. In that case, he has to make the tackle. I'll throw some that he can intercept, and some that he has to knock down. We increase the reps he gets because we are doing everything at the end of the route.

The last thing that I'm going to cover before I put on the tape and show you some of the things we do is what I call *quick read*. We have done this forever. I take the whole secondary out to the practice field and put them into a small area. All you need is a 5-yard box. The coach tells them the formation and situation. He makes the players visualize the offensive set. He simulates the ball being on or off the line of scrimmage. He gives them boundary calls and snaps the ball. In that small area, the defensive backs go through their pre-snap communication, calls, and alignments. When the ball is snapped, they take two or three quick steps in the direction of their designated responsibility.

By doing this, the defensive backs have gotten multiple reps, a chance to ask questions, and the opportunity to hone their communication skills. It is well worth your while to get into this drill. You are teaching, and they are learning to communicate with each other. The mental aspects of the game are hard enough. We want to make them comfortable and get a lot of teaching in a limited amount of time.

Let's turn on the film and watch some of the things I've been talking about. Thank you very much for your attention.

THE BYU PASSING GAME

Brigham Young University

It is a real pleasure to be here in sunny Hawaii, although the last time I was here I wasn't treated very well. The Rainbows had a heck of a football team.

This year was a great year for us. I wish we had finished the season better, but we played hard all year. I would like to thank Earl Browning and the Coach of the Year Clinic for inviting me to speak.

My topic today is the BYU passing game. We threw the ball quite a bit this year, but we also ran the ball. I believe that you must run the ball effectively when you run it. We had a real good running back and an inside receiver. Our quarterback was mobile and a good passer. We had a group of hardworking, good-blocking receivers on the outside.

We had three tight ends who were very athletic. We had two big tight ends and one not so big. With that kind of personnel, we felt we had to do a good job with the inside receivers and run the ball effectively. Along with that offensive plan, we wanted to run some options.

I don't do the same things that BYU has done in the past. When I sat down with the previous offensive staff, we made adjustments to the offense. I put in the offense I wanted to run first, and then I listened to the other coaches from the previous staff. They had a lot of good input, and we added what they wanted to do afterwards. We ended up helping each other, and our coaches did a great job. We ended up number one in the country in total offense. We averaged 540 yards a game in total offense. We had 220 yards a game rushing and 320 yards a game passing. We scored 82 touchdowns, which led the nation in that category. We also led the nation in scoring, averaging 47 points a game.

We had a good year with our offense is what I'm trying to tell you. If you have questions, don't be afraid to ask them.

At BYU, we didn't have a great amount of speed in our wide receivers. We had some guys with average speed for a wide receiver. But, they were hard working. We did have a very elusive slot receiver with good hands. His name was Reno Mahe.

Our receivers knew that they had to *block first if they wanted to play.* If they couldn't block, they were not going to get on the field. We ran a number of wide-receiver screens and bubble screens. For those types of plays to work, the wide receivers have to block.

Knowing their *splits and depth of their routes* was the second thing they had to do if they wanted to play. In our offense, the splits are crucial. As the ball moves from hash mark to hash mark, we are trying to create some little islands. That means we are trying to get the inside receiver in a 1-on-1 situation with a nickel back or linebacker. If the spacing between the receivers is too tight, the next receiver overlaps the previous receiver's zone. It is easier to double the receivers, and cuts down on the throwing lanes. The splits are very important.

If the depth of the route is too high or too shallow, it hurts the route and the idea of what we are doing in that area. We want them to know what we are trying to accomplish. We want them to understand the concept of the route, so they can adjust and adapt to the defense they are facing.

We want our wide receivers to *be aggressive.* We don't want them thinking too much when they play. If we felt like they were thinking too much, we would slow down on our installation of our offense. If a player showed great ability in drills but was slow in the game situation, we felt he was thinking too much. We slow down the installation and add the offense when we think they are ready to accept it.

Some guys didn't get the concepts as fast as others. We gave them a limited amount of things to do.

We made sure he had those things down while we were moving the offense forward with the other receivers. We didn't stop the installation for everyone else. We were patient with him and let him progress at his own speed. Once he knew what we had given him to learn, we went forward with the next part of his learning.

I had to do that with Troy Edwards. He plays for the Pittsburgh Steelers. He was a great athlete. We had a veteran receiving corps there that already knew the offense. I went too fast with him the first year. He started making mistakes in his reads and patterns. That affected the throws the quarterback was making. Troy was getting frustrated, so we slowed him down. Rather than play him every play, we played him every other play. When he went into the game, we called a play we knew he had confidence in. After he got the offense down, he became a big time receiver. He had a big game against Nebraska a few years ago. He had 425 yards receiving on 22 catches.

When a receiver catches a ball, we want him to *think score*. We want him to catch the ball, turn, and get up the field. He is thinking score when he turns up. If the defense misses the tackle, that can lead to big gains on the play.

We want our receivers who don't catch the ball to be the *escorts to the end zone*. In our team drill or any drill where there is more than one receiver, when a receiver catches the ball, the other receiver has to run to him. They run to that receiver and escort him to the end zone. If the receiver fumbles the ball, he has help recovering it. We want them coming to block for the receiver who caught the ball. We never block behind a receiver. If everyone is working to get in front of the receiver, you can turn an 8- or 9-yard gain into a touchdown.

We want our receivers to *know all positions*. I don't have the running backs know the wide receivers' route the first year. After he has the running back position down, we get him to work with the receivers. That allows you to create an island for the running back, like Marshall Faulk with the Rams. We did

it with Luke Staley this year.

Our receiver coach gets our receivers comfortable in a position. As soon as they know that position, he changes them to another position. He doesn't change all of them at once. He changes one at a time. The X receiver moves to the Z-receiver position. The second X receiver gets all the reps at the X end and gets better, while the first X is learning the Z position. The next day, he may take the starting Z receiver and move him to the second X position. He continues to alternate the receivers around until they know all positions. That gives you flexibility in case of injury. If you have a great receiver and the rest of your receivers are average, it is easy to find your best receiver if he is in one position all the time. If you don't want the defense to take your best receiver out of the game, you have to move him around.

The receiver has to *make the catch first* and add to the run after that. We don't want them to think score until they catch the ball. Make the catch first, and everything else is gravy. If the receiver runs the perfect pattern and drops the ball, that is like working all week and forgetting to pick up your pay check. I want them to understand if they just make the catch, the play is successful.

The last thing we talk to our receivers about is *play to win*. You have to find out what it takes to win. It may be something different every game. Whatever it takes, find a way to do something to help win the game. That is the mindset we start out with in the passing game.

At the beginning of practice, we don't team stretch. We have cones set up in a zigzag pattern across the width of the field. We have two sets of them. All our receivers, tight ends, and backs get in a line at the first cone. On the whistle, the first guy in line starts to the first cone at half speed. At the cone, he does a three-step break. He steps with his outside foot, then his inside foot, and plants on his outside foot the second time it hits the ground. He kicks out to the next cone and does the same thing all the way across the field. We are teaching the receiver that we have three steps in and out of our breaks. This is called the *zag drill*.

ZAG DRILL

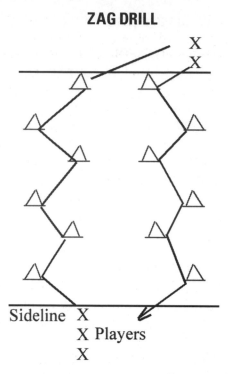

Sideline X
X Players
X

After we finish the zag drill, we go to a pitch-and-catch warm-up for the receivers, backs, and quarterbacks called the *settle drill*. We place eight large stand-up dummies across the end of the field. That gives us four stations of receivers and quarterbacks. We have four lines of receivers and backs and four quarterbacks with a center each. The receiver breaks into the area between two of the stand-up dummies. He hits the dummies and settles closer to one of the dummies than the other one. The quarterback throws the ball to the number on his jersey away from the dummy. The receiver catches the ball, turns, and gets upfield. This is all done at half speed. The quarterback is taking a snap, retreating in a five-step drop, and throwing the ball. He is not throwing hard. He is warming up. We do this for five minutes.

SETTLE DRILL

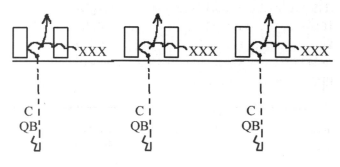

From there, we go to a *pat-and-go drill*. We have two lines of receivers on opposite sides of the field. There is a quarterback with each group. The quarterback pats the ball, and the receivers run down the field and receive the ball. After they catch the ball, they get in the other line on the opposite side of the field. The drill is oval-looking in shape with the receivers running from one sideline to the other catching the ball. The drill starts out as a three-quarter-speed drill and ends up as a full-speed drill. As they catch the ball, they return it to a manager who is standing by the quarterbacks. While the receivers are waiting in line, they continue to stretch and get loose.

PAT AND GO

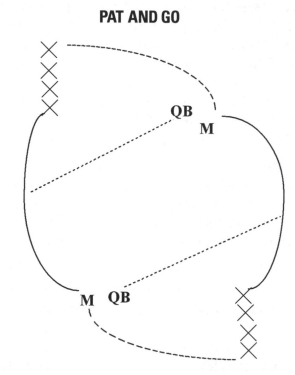

The zag, the settle, and the pat-and-go drills take about 12 minutes to get through. That is our stretching period. I don't like to sit everyone down and stretch the hamstrings and everything else in a team stretch period. You are stretching a cold muscle. After they finish stretching, they still have to warm up the muscles with some running. I start off with the running and let them stretch on their own in between their running reps.

We have four base plays. It is important to have a good base. If you have a good solid base in what you are doing, you can always go back to that. You can disguise your base by changing formations. We use our base plays as part of our automatic system. Let me give you an example. One of our base plays is called *79 Z option cross*. On this play, the slot or Z receiver runs an option pattern. He runs up the field 8 to 10 yards and turns either inside or outside. The X end runs a go up the field, and the tight end or Y receiver runs a cross. The W receiver runs a post route. That is one of our base plays, and I'll get to the mechanics of this play later.

If we are running a run play, we call *package 36-open*. The *package* call tells us if we have to check the play, we are going to the base play from that set. The base play from this set is the *79-Z option cross*. The 36-open is a zone play to the open side of the formation. We tell the quarterback to count the people to that side. If there are three defenders to that side, we can run the play. If there is a fourth player in the area, the quarterback has the option to automatic out of the play. We can automatic in two different ways. All our base plays are named. This particular play is called dragon. So the quarterback can call dragon or simply call the play. That allows you to call a lot more runs and check them to passes.

We have a different base play out of each formation we have. The word package means there are two plays in the call. We started out by calling both plays in the huddle. As the team gets comfortable with the package call and the two plays, we only call package. That really cuts down on the communication in the huddle.

I learned this automatic from my high school coach. I used to go to his house on Wednesday night before the Friday game. He told me we were going to run the zone play to the split-end side. He told me as long as they had three defenders on that side of the ball, we could run the play. Then, he asked me what my favorite pass was. I told him it was the 79-cross. I liked that play because we had a big tight end with good hands, and I could complete that pass most of the time. He told me if they had more than three defenders to the split-end side to run the 79-cross. It was simple then, and it is simple now.

I'm going to talk about that play. If you have a good play like that, you need some kind of complimentary play. The option route by the slot back is a good route for us. However, the defense will start to play the route and start sitting on your slot receivers, which makes it hard to complete.

Sometimes I get confused on the call of this play. I've had this offense in about five different languages because I've been all over the place. When I was with the Chicago Bears, we called it 76-Z; at Georgia Tech, it was called 74-Z; and with BYU, it is called 79-Z. The reason for the different calls in the play is the protection scheme.

The complimentary play runs the slot receiver on the vertical, and the X receiver sits down and runs the option. Instead of the Y receiver coming on a high-cross route, he comes on a shallow cross.

The quarterback has four reads. The first read is a *progression read*. The quarterback reads 1, 2, and 3 to a side. The quarterback reads the receivers in the progression that they come open. Try to keep the progression to three reads. The quarterback can probably get through the second read before he has to move in the pocket to find the third read. He very seldom gets to a fourth read in a progression.

The second read is called an *object receiver read*. That is a good read to have if you have a stud player. This read is an option route by the receiver. He is running his pattern off the defense with multiple options in his route. The quarterback is looking to throw the ball to the object receiver.

The third read is called an *area read*. An area read is a high/low scheme. The quarterback is looking into a certain area with multiple receivers at different depths in that area or coming into that area.

The fourth read is called *direction read*. If we are in a double formation, the defense will generally give us a two-shell coverage to each side. If we flood a back one way or the other, the Mike linebacker will generally take him. Whichever way the Mike linebacker goes, we throw the opposite direction. The defense will tell us which direction to throw the ball. It is a full-field read. Once the defense gives the quarterback the direction, the read becomes a progression read. He has two receivers to that side, and he reads a primary receiver to a secondary one. He reads one to two in his progression.

Those are all the reads we have, and everything we tie in is done off those four reads. I'll go into those in greater detail if you want to talk later on.

The call for this play is *7-Right 79 Z option cross*. It is a very good play if you have a good slot receiver. The Z receiver gets 8 to 10 yards in depth. While that is the ideal depth of the pattern, sometimes, he can only get five yards deep. This is an object-receiver read by the quarterback. That means the slot back is the object receiver. He has to get open, because the quarterback is going to throw the ball to him first. If he can't get open, we build complimentary routes around the receiver.

The X end clears the pattern out with a go route. The tight end or Y is going to climb up over the top of the Z receiver. The W receiver on the backside runs a post to hold the safety. The back has a check down in his protection. If no one comes, he releases to the flat.

The tight end releases inside and runs three steps vertical. That gives him height to get over the option route of the Z receiver. If the tight end is too close to the option route, he is not going vertical enough.

79 Z OPTION CROSS

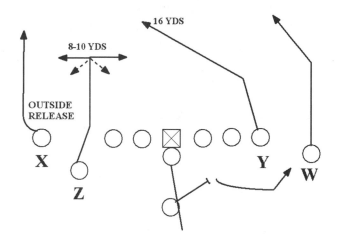

The protection on this play is called *sub*. If the back is going left, the uncovered lineman on the line of scrimmage has a duel read. In this case, the center is uncovered and reads the Mike linebacker from the outside to the weakside. If there is a threat to the weakside, the center comes out for the threat, and the back reads middle linebacker to left linebacker. Two blitzes to one side means the quarterbacks have to throw hot. The hot routes we run are a quick out and a slant over the top. Of course, we can adjust that from week to week.

SUB PROTECTION

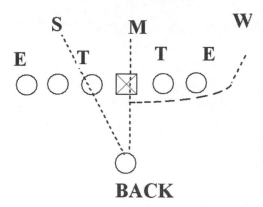

If there is a double threat of the Mike linebacker and Will linebacker both coming, the center would call *gun*. That means the back is taking the Mike linebacker, and the center is stepping out on the Will linebacker. If the quarterback is not in the shotgun, the center would call *help*. That tells the quarterback to wait until the back moves up into position to block the Mike linebacker.

BACK ADJUSTMENT

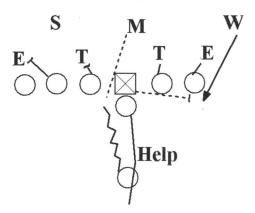

We can also slide the protection toward the Will linebacker by calling *slide*. In that situation, the center, guard, and tackle will slide to the weakside. When we start out, we simply tell the uncovered lineman they have to double read to one side, while the back double reads to the other side.

That play just reminded me of something else. In the silent count, there are some things the center can do. The quarterback develops a signal with the center to let him know he is ready for the ball to be snapped. He can leg kick, or flash a fingers sign to the center, which means he is ready for the ball. The center from that point is in charge of when the ball is snapped.

Generally, the center takes one last look to see where the quarterback is and snaps the ball. The defense will time their moves off the center when he lifts his head. To combat the defense from timing the snap, have the center look between his legs, raise his head, and then look again. That generally draws the defense offsides. We have an early call and a late call. On the early call, the center looks between his legs, counts one second, and snaps the ball. On the late call, he looks twice between his legs and snaps the ball in about three seconds.

The thing I like about the option is you can run the play over and over, and you always have a chance for a completion because Reno was so good at getting open. When he was healthy, we were really good. When he was hurt, we were very average. In the bowl game, he couldn't play because he was beat up so bad from the Hawaii game. In the Hawaii game, he tore a cartilage in his knee and had a hip pointer. He was in a wheelchair for two weeks after the Hawaii game. How he finished the game was amazing to me. He is just a tough kid. He is hard to tackle because he runs low and can cut on a dime. He caught 92 balls this year.

This next route is a complimentary route. This route is called *79-streak Y shallow*. The X receiver runs a go route. If the defensive back bails out of his coverage and runs deep, the X receiver sits down. If the receiver can't win the race for the touchdown, he should choke his route off and sit down. If the defensive back is off him, he plants and runs a deep hook at 10 to 12 yards. If the back is on the X receiver close, the receiver bends a little outside, like he is going deep, and stops. The quarterback should throw the ball because the defensive back will run right by the receiver. If the X receiver gets to the defensive back and gets on top of him, he goes for the score. We didn't have any good ones that could do that this year, but we will next year.

Some people think this route is too hard to teach in high school. My suggestion is to take the read out of the pattern and run an out route at 12 yards or a deep hook at 10 yards. That way there is no reading involved.

The Z receiver has to get by the first defender. After he gets by that defender, he threatens the safety. He breaks his pattern off at 14 to 16 yards and comes over the middle. This is a Y shallow, so the Y receiver is running a 6-yard cross coming across.

The W receiver to the backside is running a go with the option to go to the post. The back is running his check-down and drifting wide into the flare area. This is our second base play out of this formation. This is the complimentary play to the first play.

79 STREAK Y SHALLOW

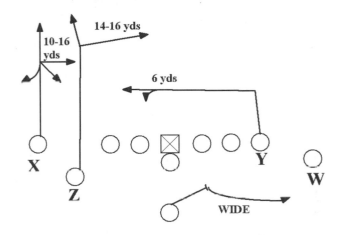

I do have another play off this play. I just put it in last year. The patterns are the same as the Y shallow. We would go to a five-man protection scheme and free release the back on an option route down the seam, trailing the release of the tight end. Luke made a lot of catches on that this year. I tagged it with dodge. The *dodge* call told the tight end to drag.

79 STREAK Y DODGE

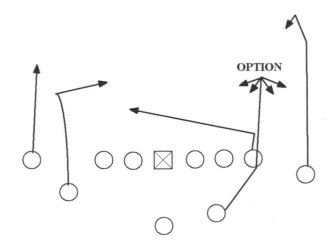

These plays work together. One without the other is not very good. You can run this play out of two tight ends also. You can run it out of the trips set also. Let me show you that quickly without talking about what we do. You can see that all the patterns end up in the same place regardless of the set.

I'm running out of time, so let me show you some of the things we do from the trips formation. If you have a stud receiver, put him on the backside of a trips formation. We have choice routes that we can throw to the X receiver because he is always on an island. We give the choice to one side and call the scheme to the other side. If I had Troy Edwards one-on-one with the corner, it wouldn't matter who the corner was. He was too good to be covered 1-on-1. The quarterback could call a hitch, out, curl, in, or a comeback. I don't necessarily like the inside routes and probably would take them out of our game plan. The quarterback could go to the choice side if there was single coverage on the X receiver. If he didn't like the coverage, he could come back to the concept side and go through his reads.

The tight end runs the option route. The Z receiver runs a "go" or skinny post. The W receiver runs a comeback at 14 to 16 yards. The running back runs a weakside option route off the outside linebacker.

Our quarterback didn't throw many interceptions this year. He threw over 30 touchdowns and only nine interceptions. That is pretty good.

69 CHOICE Y OPTION COBB

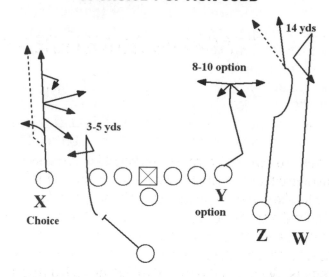

I like what we are doing. There are a lot of ways to do what we are doing. You don't have to run the same offense to use the patterns I've discussed. There are a lot of ways to run this offense. If we can give you any kind of help, let us know. We are always looking for new things too. I have our coaches out studying to see if they can come up with some new ideas. The game is always changing. It means a lot that you guys are here working. Thanks so much for your time. Good luck to you all.

TEACHING QUARTERBACKS TO ATTACK DEFENSES

University of Maryland

I want to take you through the teaching process we involve our quarterbacks with in attacking defenses. I will take you through the whole concept of defense that we want to get across to our quarterbacks. We have been doing this since I have been working with quarterbacks. We concentrate on learning about defenses. We teach them how to recognize fronts and how to recognize coverages. We teach them how those things relate and what they can learn about the defense in general.

Quarterback play is about how fast you can react and how accurate your decision can be. In order to do this, you must be able to anticipate certain things the defense will do. We teach the quarterbacks how to recognize certain aspects of the defense so they can anticipate and react and make the proper decision quickly.

When I went to San Diego of the NFL in 1991, I went as the H-back and tight end coach. I was also the running-game coordinator. We also had a passing game coordinator on the team. Now in my opinion, if you have two offensive coordinators on the team, you are probably going to get them both fired. I think you should go with one coordinator. In 1994, I was elevated to the coordinator position. I did not coach a position then, but I did work directly with the quarterback coach. I was with Coach Bobby Ross and I had the opportunity to hire the quarterback coach, so philosophically we were on the same page.

In February, we brought in the quarterbacks to meet with the coaches. We had Stan Humphries, John Friesz, and Trent Green. We started teaching them the same things I had taught the quarterbacks when I coached in college. I did not know any better and that is the way I wanted to do it. If you know me, you know I always go back to the fundamentals every year to start out. Those three quarterbacks were not real happy campers to start out with in February.

We worked three to four hours a day for three or four days a week. In the middle of this quarterback fundamentals review, John Friesz was traded to Washington. He was a free agent and signed a nice contract with a bonus. He told me he was going to go with the Redskins. He said, "I really appreciate all the help you have given me. The thing you are doing right now, no one has ever sat me down and taught me those things. It is amazing what I have learned."

Now, those guys did gripe about the meetings, but what he said really opened my eyes. At first, I was a little concerned about the meetings, and I was a little intimidated. Stan Humphries had run the offense for the Redskins for nine years, and I had only been working with the quarterbacks for two years. We did go on to the Super Bowl that year. Stan went on to have his best year and was named all-pro quarterback. So, I am convinced now more than ever that the program I am going to go over with you can help at all levels.

Depending on how much time we have, I will tell you how we train quarterbacks on vision. Vision is a big part of playing quarterback. We will start off being very basic, and then we will get more complicated. I will teach you just like I would teach our quarterbacks. You are going to get in one lecture what the quarterbacks get in a month.

First, I want to talk about our offensive philosophy. We want to be able to run and pass the football. Let me talk about balance in the two areas. When I came back to the college game from the pros, I could have gone to Detroit, but my family did not want to move to that area. I had some property in South Carolina and some in Atlanta. Coach George O'Leary was at Georgia Tech. He is a good friend of mine. He offered me a job. I talked with George and he said, "Ralph, we are going to be 60-40, right?" I asked what he meant by that statement. He said, "That is our philosophy. We run the ball 60 percent of the time and pass it 40 percent of the time." I told him to get himself another coach. I told him I was not going to get tied down to percentages. I told him the game would dictate how much we run the ball or pass the ball. He agreed to this, and so I stayed with him.

I think you have to do run and pass equally well. You can do both averagely and still be successful. The thing you are going to learn here is how to make the right play at the right time. I believe you train your quarterback, and the moment of truth comes when the ball is snapped. No matter how hard our coaches prepare, the opponent's coaches are preparing as well. You have good coaches on both sides of the ball. If your quarterback can get you in a good play or get you out of a bad play, you are one up on the defense.

You hear coaches make the statement that they are not going to put their job in the hands of a 17- or 18-year-old kid. I am not afraid to do that. It is not because I am a great play caller. It is because about 60 percent of the time our quarterback is going to put us in the right play. That is what I want to cover with you here tonight. So, we want a balance between the run and pass, and I want to have the ability to do both.

In the last six years, I have had four teams that have run the ball for 200 yards per game and have passed for 200 yards per game. This past year, we were only seven yards apart on the average. In some games, we have 300-plus yards passing, and in some games, we have 300-plus yards running the ball. At the end of the year, it always comes out that way. Each of those teams won nine or 10 games in those four years where we had such a great balanced offense. I think it is a good philosophy to have.

Multiple formations, personnel groups, shifting, and motion are ways we use to create problems for the defense. Formations to me are like weapons. Every formation attacks the defense in a different way. I will tell you how we use these formations to attack defenses. I will tell you what the defense has to do to defend us.

I learned in the NFL that matchups are a big part of winning. If you can get the right matchup, you have a chance to win. Let me give you an example. A few years ago at Georgia Tech, we had two running backs hurt, so we had to go to a spread formation with four wideouts. I put the offense into a tight slot and we were getting nickel-and-dime coverage. We were running the wishbone to the tight slot with four wideouts. That was fun. We could still run the triple option with Joe Hamilton, and yet we could throw the pass too.

I like to look for players who are dual players. I like players who can play either tight end or fullback. I look for players who can play running back or play slot back. If we have these types on the field, we can change the personnel groups and not have to change players on the field. I get some matchups that way.

Sometimes when we use shifting and motion, it is to create movement on the defense. I do not want the defense to sit there and tee off on us when the ball is snapped. I do not want them to line up with all the blood out of their fingers and here they come. I want them to have to think, and I want them to adjust. This takes some of the aggressiveness out of them.

The line coaches will say that it is a headache when our offense is moving around. "We do not know who to block." I will show you how to cover that situation. I will show you how simple it can be.

We prepare for every situation that may arise in a game. We have our four-minute offense when we are ahead. We have a four-minute offense when we are behind. We have a four-minute defense when we are ahead, and when we are behind. We try to cover every situation at least by Friday in the walk-through, but also during the week.

Now, I want to talk about training the quarterback. This is very basic, so hang with me for a while. When we start game planning, the first thing we do is determine what kind of animal we are going against. Defenses to me are different animals. You have the seven-man front with four secondary players. We declare the defense as a seven-man front or an eight-man front. If they have four secondary players, we know they have seven up-front players. Now, does the defense play with four down linemen, or do they play with three down linemen? If they have four down linemen, then they have three linebackers. If they have three down linemen, they have four linebackers.

If it is an eight-man front, it means they only have three secondary people. We see two kinds of eight-man fronts. We see the four down linemen with four linebackers. In high school, you may see five down linemen and three linebackers. That depends on how the ends play. Are they linebackers or are they down linemen?

We do this in determining matchups. "Nickel" to us indicates the defense has five secondary players. You can have a 40 nickel, which is four down linemen with two linebackers. You can have a 30 nickel, which is three down linemen, three linebackers, and five defensive backs. I tell our staff that when we see a 30 nickel defense, a loud siren should go off in their heads. We have problems with this defense. The 30 nickel defense creates problems for us. We have problems in the areas of protection and identification. You must be sound against this defense.

If you see the dime defense, you have six defensive backs. You could have a 40 dime. You have four down linemen and one linebacker. You could have a 30 dime with three down linemen and two linebackers.

Next, I want to talk about naming the defenders. This is very elementary. If we face a four-down-linemen scheme, the two inside men are called tackles and the two outside defenders are ends. If we have a three-down-linemen scheme, the middle man is the nose man, and the two outside men are the two tackles. If we face a five-down-linemen scheme, we have a nose man, two tackles, and two ends. We do this so everyone is on the same page.

If we have a three-linebacker scheme, the Sam linebacker is to the tight-end side, Mike is the middle linebacker, and the Will linebacker is the split end. If we have a four-linebacker scheme, Sam is to the tight-end side, Mike is the inside linebacker, Buck is the weakside inside linebacker, and Will is to the split-end side.

If the defense is in a nickel, you have two linebackers inside Mike and Will. Again, Mike is to the nickel side, and Will is away.

Let me get into reading defenses. What does a quarterback look for in reading a defense? First, let me tell you that we run all of our plays with a 25-second clock. When the quarterback breaks the huddle, that is the first thing he should look for. He should look to see how much time he has to deal with. I want our quarterbacks to the line of scrimmage with 18 seconds to go on the clock. This is because we shift, because we motion, and because we "check off." The quarterback must have time to get all of this action

called. If the quarterback is still calling the plays out at 10 seconds and we are still shifting or in motion, he has a call he makes, and everyone lines up where they are going to end up.

The next thing the quarterback does is to look at the free safety. I am going to tell you how we read coverages. He looks at the free safety and determines where he is. You will hear me use the term "open" or "closed." "Closed" means there is a defender in the deep middle of the field. "Open" means there is no defender in the middle of the field deep. The quarterback looks to see where the free safety is lined up. He looks to see the depth of the free safety. If he is at 12 yards, he is a deep back. It could be deep one-half or deep one-third of the field coverage. If the man is lined up less than 10 yards away, the quarterback should be alert because that free safety probably is in a blitz mode.

The second thing the quarterback wants to know about the free safety is where the safety is in relation to the hash mark. If the ball is on that hash mark, where is the free safety in relation to that hash mark?

The next thing the quarterback looks at is the strong safety. Where the strong safety is lined up verifies what the quarterback read in regards to where the free safety is lined up. The quarterback looks at the strong safety and determines if the defense is man or zone by the way the strongside safety is playing.

Next, the quarterback looks at the front. He determines if the front and secondary are coordinated. So, this is what he looks for. He reads the free safety first, the strong safety second, and the front third.

One year, I had a quarterback that refused, flat refused, to look at the free safety. You know how quarterbacks are when they come out of the huddle. They are thinking of all the pass patterns they have, what the snap count is on, and what the defense is playing. Now, everyone thinks we have the answer to attacking defenses. The closest thing I can give you on this is to read the free safety. This kid I had playing quarterback that one year would never look at the free safety. He would throw the ball into double cover more than a few times. So one day I started calling him "Ray." "Ray, you have to get the ball to the tight end. "He said, "Coach, my name is not Ray. Why do you call me Ray?" I said, "Well, you play quarter-back like Ray Charles."

Another day, we came out and we were getting ready to scrimmage. I had a red bandana. I took it to "Ray" and told him I wanted him to wear it over his eyes in the scrimmage. "Coach, how can I play quarterback with that bandana over my eyes?" I said, "You do not use your eyes anyway, so what difference does it make?"

This is how I finally got the kid to read the free safety. I had him come to the line of scrimmage, and I had him call out the coverage to me as he pre-read the coverage. He would come up to the line of scrimmage and call out "one," "two," or "three." Now, the defensive secondary was really getting nervous. I did not care if the quarterback was wrong on his call, because I was trying to train him to read the free safety first. That is the first man he needed to look at. It all starts from there.

We look at the play clock, the free safety, the strong safety, and then the front. I will tell you how to identify defensive fronts. To the offensive line coaches, this is the simplest method I know. In high school and sometimes in college, the fronts do not always line up where they are supposed to line up. Those are the worst fronts to work against. You get these bastard fronts. A defender lines up in the gap between the guard and tackle. The guard thinks he is in a 4-technique. The tackle thinks he is in a 3-technique. Neither of the blockers picks him up, and he comes free and makes the tackle. The guard tells the coach, "I thought the tackle had him." The tackle responds, "I thought the guard had him." We all have been down that road. So to prevent that, we have what we call "identifying characteristics." I make everyone on the team learn these characteristics. If there is no one over the guard or if a linebacker is over the guard, it is a 50 defense to us. It is not if the defense has a nose guard. If our guard is uncovered, we call it a 50 defense. Now, everyone should be on the same page. If there is not a playside linebacker over the guard or tackle, it is a 60 defense to us. If we are going to the three-man side and there is a linebacker on the outside of the tackle, it is a 70 defense to us. An 80 defense is four defenders to that three-man side. On a 90 defense, the linebacker is over the guard, or he is in the A gap.

Here is how we call them out: 50—linebacker over the guard. 60—no playside linebacker. 70—three-man side with a linebacker over the tackle. 80—four defenders to the three-man side. 90—to the three-man side with a linebacker inside over the guard. So, we are talking about the 50 defense, the 60 defense, the 70 defense, the 80 defense, and the 90 defense.

We have a couple of other terms to clarify these fronts. If it is a 50 stack front, then the linebackers have slid one man toward the tight-end side. If it is a solid defense, it means the center is covered, and the two offensive guards are covered. If we called "wide-70 solid," it means the three-man side is solid and the linebacker is over the tackle.

A bear defense is when you have that 46 bear look, where you have a linebacker inside the tight end and another cover man outside the tight end. A plus front is when the nose guard is shading the center to the tight-end side. A minus front is when the nose guard is shading to the split-end side. You can have a 50 minus or a 50 plus front. A wide front means there is no down lineman over the tackle. If we are going to the three-man side and we have a linebacker over the tackle, it would be a 70 wide front. If the linebacker aligned on the tackle, it would be a 70 tight. It is the same call on an 80 or 90. If the tackle is covered it is tight; if he is uncovered, it is a wide front.

With that in mind, this is how we call our fronts. We call the tight end first, and the split-end side second. If we call a combination, it is a call to each side. For example, we could call "plus 57-tight." We could call "wide 70-wide solid." We could call "tight 89-tight." We use this system in breaking down film and in communicating.

Here is where we tie it all together. When the center comes out of the huddle, he is going to make one of four calls. If he calls "odd," he is telling the quarterback, the guards, and the tackles that the defensive man is shading him. That is "odd." If there is a linebacker over the center, he calls it "even." If there is no one over the center, he calls out "clear." If he is covered and the two guards are covered, he calls out "solid."

This is how it all works. The center calls the separation first. Each side calls out the defender to his side. We are communicating with each other. We may not block it right, but we are all on the same page blocking the defense. The right side will come out and call the front: "odd-50." They do not need to hear the plus or minus calls. On the backside, we may call out "90." We know the frontside called an odd defense.

Let me talk about coverage. There are four types of zone coverage. That is all God created. You have a three-deep coverage, a two-deep coverage, quarter coverage, and rotation coverage. I love the word rotation. Ask your quarterbacks what rotation means. They will surprise you. They do not know what you are talking about. What is rotation? Rotation is when a secondary man lines up deep but ends up playing an underneath coverage. He ends up playing one of those short zones.

If we see three-deep zone coverage, we see a free safety 12 yards deep. In our league, he can disguise his position at about two yards off the hash mark. If he gets three yards off the hash mark, he cannot make it back to the other side. On his first step, we expect him to go back to the middle of the coverage. The strong safety is usually lined up outside the tight end in a five-by-five area looking into the backfield. This is a strong rotation because the strongside safety is playing the flat to strongside. If I know it is cover three, I also know my rush-pass ratio. We know there are four deep defenders and seven rush defenders.

Another thing I know about cover three: The strong safety has the flat, the Sam linebacker has the inside hook, the Mike linebacker is going to go weakside, and the Will linebacker has the weakside flat. Why is this important? If I tell the quarterback to read the weakside flat, he needs to know what the coverage is.

We call a cover six a weakside, three-deep coverage. "Fox" means the weak safety rotates to the flat, and "cloud" means the corner comes up and takes the flat. If we say the coverage is a "6 Cloud," it means the rotation has occurred to the weakside corner playing in the weakside flat. Now, the safety is going to be created 12 yards off the hash mark. On the first movement, he is going to get width. Anytime the safety gains depth, I know the cornerback is going to roll up. I do not have to see that corner roll up; I know he is going to roll up. Otherwise, they would have two men in the deep-third area. The free safety

is giving you the answer. You do not have to look at the corner to tell what he is going to do. The corners lie. They are deceptive. The free safety is a truth seeker.

Another thing we will see is that the strong safety is a little deeper, and he is going to the middle. Now, when I see the weak safety go to the weakside, I know who has the strong flat. I know the Sam linebacker has to get out covering that strong flat. I like that Sam linebacker covering backs in the strong flat if I have a quarterback that can throw the strong flat route.

The defense still has a three-deep coverage. They have three deep and four underneath. One side is strong rotation, and one side is weak rotation. The Mike linebacker goes strong, and the Will linebacker has the weakside hook area.

Here is what I preach to the quarterback against three deep: "You should never throw a possession pass for an incompletion against three-deep zone coverage. That is an aggressive statement. The defense had four men underneath on the coverage. Every possession pass route I know has three receivers coming to one side. That gives us a 3-on-2 option against the coverage. The offense should win. It is a fast break. The defense only has two men on each side underneath, so we should win on either side of the ball. It is our three receivers on two of their defenders. We like to throw the ball against three deep.

Now, we take a look at a two-deep zone coverage called "cover two." Now, we have a bigger challenge on our hands. The rush-pass ratio is this: They are going to rush four men and defend with five men underneath and two deep.

There are a lot of different types of cover two. You must decide which type of cover two you are facing. Is it going to be a cover two that sinks, or is it going to be a collision-type sinking offense? Now, teams are playing the two deep backs closer to the sideline and sending the Mike linebacker down the middle.

There are a lot of variations of cover two. They are in the cover two family. You must attack each type of cover two differently. There are some phony cover twos. You see the two deep, and you release two vertical receivers. They drop with the receivers, and it becomes a cover four. They do not end up in cover three. If you high-low them, it becomes a cover two.

In cover two, here is what we look for: The safety is three yards off our hash mark. He could be on the hash mark in high school. He is 12 yards deep. Where is the strong safety going to be? He is going to be 12 yards deep too, and depending on what the split of the wideout is, he could be on the hash mark or inside the hash mark. But he is deep. He is not down low where the strong safety was before. His first movement is backwards. He is going to back up as soon as the ball is snapped. What do we know when that safety starts backing up as soon as the ball is snapped? What do we know? If we are smart, we will not throw the out route if the quarterback read the free safety backing up. We are not going to read the corner. We are not going to fall into that trap. We are going to read the safety. Don't read the corner because he lies. That is a weakside cover two.

We also have a strongside cover two. Most of the time, the strongside cover two is played against a slot formation. The weak safety will come all the way across the formation, and the safeties will roll up on the slot. The corners will play half coverage. The safeties' depth will be determined on how good the tight end is. The front is kicked over, but we still have the same ratio of five defenders underneath, with two deep and four men rushing. That would be cover five for us now.

The next coverage we have is quarter coverage. This is the "in" coverage. Woo baby! Teams think they have the world by the tail with this coverage. They have two safeties on run support. They come down on the run. They have four players defending the deep pass. Now, what is the cover ratio on this defense? You have four men rushing. How many underneath men do you have? They have three linebackers underneath. If the offense was good against the defense in four underneath, you should be great against three underneath. This is where we run the possession pass offense.

In cover two, we wanted to attack the deep thirds. You do not want to attack the underneath with four defenders underneath. In the four-deep look, we want to attack the flat. The defense has Sam and Will covering the flat on the four-deep alignments. If Sam and Will cannot cover the flats, we want to attack the flat. We must know the strengths and weaknesses of the coverage.

We have strongside quarter coverage. We call this "cover seven." The strongside safety is going to be the strongside flat defender. The safeties are lined up about 11 yards deep. If the corners roll up, the safety will cover deep.

Let me tell you how those quarter-coverage people play safety. They play flat-footed. When the ball is snapped, they are hanging in that position, looking at the number two receiver. If the play is a run, the safeties want to come up to support. When they do that, we can throw over their heads. So, if the safety is backing up, it is cover two. If the safety goes into the deep one–third, that indicates cover three; and if he is standing flat-footed at 10 yards deep, it indicates cover six. Those are all zone coverages.

Let me talk about man coverage next. First is man free. We call it cover one. It is a strongside coverage. It is like our cover three. Now, I look at the strong safety, and he is sitting *inside* of our number two receiver. He is not outside anymore. He is inside and he is eyeballing the second receiver, who could be a tight end or a slot man. He is not looking at the quarterback. I can confirm this by looking to see how the corners are playing. They are lined up inside the wide receivers, and they are not looking at the quarterback. They may be pressed up on the widest receivers. On cover one, I always assume we are going to get a five-man run. If you run hot routes, the quarterback has to be alert for the six-man rush. If Sam is coming, the quarterback has to dump the ball to the hot receiver. You can tell when Sam is coming on the blitz. How? He lines up like he is on the hood of a car. Right! The quarterback reads the free safety, then the strong safety, and then he looks at Sam. Oh, Sam, how are you doing? The quarterback is anticipating what is coming on the play. He can see if Sam is up on his toes.

Let's say Sam does blitz, and the defense only rushes four men. Now, the quarterback knows they have a free linebacker inside. That means we must watch our crossing routes. If Sam does not come, it is still five underneath, but one of those defenders is free to play ins and outs.

If we go the other way on cover one, it becomes cover eight. Now, the weak safety comes over and takes the second receiver. The strong safety goes back to the middle. Everyone else plays the same, but I know the pressure is coming from the weakside now. Another thing I know is that I have Sam lined up on our second receiver on the other side. It could be a tight end, and it could be a wideout. I like that situation. I like that matchup. When you get a wideout or the tight end covered by the Sam linebacker, you should light the wind. I also know I am one-on-one on the strongside. Those are man-free coverages.

Next is pressure man coverage. We have two of those coverages. If the safeties are lined up less than 10 yards back, but playing over the number two or number three receivers, you are going to get linebacker pressure, and it is going to be a six-man dog. Here they come. How do you tell if they are coming on the blitz? If the safeties are lined up less than 10 yards deep, the linebackers are coming. They are telling you to be alert for your hot receivers. That is cover zero to us. When we see this defense, the Mike linebacker lines up in some really unusual positions to line up on number three.

Next, we have what we call "cover nine." Cover nine is three secondary players lined up less than 10 yards deep. When that happens, it means we are going to see the safety blitz. If the free safety is all the way over to the strongside, we get the strong safety blitz. If that free safety is all the way over to the weakside, you get a corner blitz. If the free safety is cheating down on his alignment, and the corner and strong safety are on the same side, you are going to the weakside corner blitz. I will not get into zone blitzes. Those are all of your coverages.

Let me get into formations and how they affect defense. The big thing you want to know is this: Is the middle of the field open, or is it closed? If the middle is open and the defense is playing cover two, we have a running situation. If the middle is closed and the cover three defense is called or you have cover three man coverage, you have a passing situation. When we talk about a right or left formation, we are talking about two wideouts, a tight end, and two backs in the backfield. Most defenses are going to play you with eight defenders in the box. If the middle of the field is closed, they are going to play cover four and bring the safety down. You cannot run the ball. You will see at least eight men in the box. If you are really good at running the ball, the defense will bring nine in the box. If the defense plays cover two here, you have a good chance to run the ball.

It all depends on where they are playing you. The number of men in the box will be determined by the way the defense plays you. It is a numbers game as to whether you run the weakside or the strongside against the seven- or eight-man fronts. It will depend on where the ball is in the middle of the field, and if the middle of the field is open or closed. In our open-slot formation, we do not have a tight end. We have two wide receivers and two backs. Now, you look to see if you have a six-man box or a seven-man box. If the defense lines up with the middle of the field open and a two-deep look with six men inside the box and another man outside, where you cannot block him, you have to take advantage of the alignment and throw the football.

The more you spread the offense or reduce the defense, the more they come out of the box. Let's look at a one-back formation with two tight ends, one back, and two wide receivers. Is this a running formation, or is it a passing formation? What would you think? It is a passing formation. How does that stretch the defense? It stretches the defense because you have added another gap. If you have one tight end in the game, you have seven gaps to defend. You have the A, B, C, and the D gap to the tight end. When you put the end on the other side, you force the defense to defend that other gap. You have the same four gaps to both sides. You are going to see cover four where the defense can cut the gaps down or where they can support on either side of the gaps.

The other look you will see is cover one with four defenders to both sides. If you get any coverage other than cover four or cover one, you should *run* the ball. Run it! If you get cover one and cover four, you are one-on-one on the outside. Throw the ball!

George O'Leary used to get after me about throwing the ball. "Why are we throwing the ball when we have two big slugs at tight end?" Every Monday, we went in and did our self-scout. Every week, the most productive formation was the two tight ends and two wideouts. The reason for this was that those two slugs at tight end ate up those two safeties. It left our two wide receivers one-on-one on the outside against their corners. We were not throwing the ball to the slug ends. We were throwing the ball to the wide receivers. When the defense came outside to double those wide receivers, we ran the football. We would come out and call "alert-quick-hitch." If the defense was in cover two, the quarterback would check the play, and we would run the ball.

On doubles, this is what we do: We have three wide receivers and one back. If the middle of the field is open, you have a six-man box. If the middle of the field is closed, you have a seven-man box. In our spread formation, we have four wide receivers. It is a fun formation. You can run the ball with four wide receivers. When the middle of the field is open, the defense cheats the Will linebacker halfway into the boundary, where he can still help on the run. You can run play-action and get the receiver down the middle. You can crack-block on the Will linebacker, and you can run the option. You can do a lot of things and still run the ball. But when the defense closes the middle, you are one-on-one with four wide receivers. Now, you can go to your three-man side, and you should win all of the time on that play.

Next is a three-back formation. We run the double slot. I love that formation. We see how the defense is going to play us, and take what they give us. I just went through our cutups. Every year the defense plays this formation differently. When I was at Georgia Tech, we ran the formation with four wide receivers. We would see quarter coverage. They played a 60 defense with the man in the middle pretty much balanced. This year, we did it with a running back and a wideout in the two slots, with our fullback deep in the middle. The defenses played us with an eight-man front. The coaches thought they did that because of the particular personnel we had at the slots. But, we got eight-man fronts almost the whole year. We use a couple of checks with it, and it has always been good for us.

We have not gotten to the no-backs formation at Maryland yet. But when we get in no-backs, you want to look for linebackers and displace them. If you have a quarterback that can run, you can use all of your one-back plays with the quarterback running the ball. But, you must be ready to handle pressure.

Next, we want to look at understanding how fronts and coverages are coordinated. We talked about rotation. We said that is a secondary defender with underneath coverage. You can have strongside or weakside rotation. We talked about rush-coverage ratio. We said that related to the number of defenders that rushed and the number of defenders deep.

We identify the flat defender. The quarterback should know the flat defender, both strong and weak, by reading coverage. He must be able to anticipate pressure by reading the coverages and fronts. It is important to identify the front and coverage and to coordinate them. What do I mean by this? If we have weakside zone coverage, such as cover two—let's say it is a 4-3 defense—the quarterback should know that the Mike linebacker is going to be to the strongside. Against the 4-3, Mike tells you if the defense is undershifted or overshifted.

If we had cover three with the strong safety rotated down, the Mike linebackers should be to the weakside. If we see a 3-4 defense and we have a weakside coverage, the nose man is going to tell you which side is strong or weak.

On cover three with a 4-3 defense, where is Mike? He is weak. That is balanced. You have two rush defenders on each side of the center. Mike has the weakside hook. Will has the weakside flat. Sam has the strongside hook. The strong safety has the strongside flat.

On cover two, you have a 59 defense. In pro football, the coaches would see this defense and tell me the front is undershifted. That is because they see the line is undershifted. If you count the defense, you have three-and-a-half men to the tight end and only three men to the split end. The strength is where Mike is lined up. Now, the safeties are lined up less than 10 yards deep. Here comes the pressure. When you get man coverage, this does not always hold up. Now look at the 3-4 defensive alignment. The problem with the 3-4 alignment is that you do not know which outside linebacker is going to rush. If we have a weakside coverage, who is going to rush? It will be Will or Buck. If we have a strongside coverage, Sam or Mike is going to rush. It will be one of those two on the rush.

Another thing about the weakside coverage is the nose man should be kicked to the strongside. This is so they are balanced up.

How to understand where to run the football is our next coaching point for the quarterback. We number the defense. This is our two-back set running rules. Everyone can run the ball to the tight-end side. But, we do not want to run the ball over there if they have five defenders there. If there are five people to the tight-end side, here is what is happening: The front and the coverage are together. I will guarantee you the weakside flat is open. We have a general rule for the quarterbacks. If the middle of the field is closed and the Will is over the tackle—man or zone coverage, the receiver is one-on-one to the weakside. He can check off and go there anytime he wants. If we get the one-on-one to the weakside, we will take it. We will throw the ball to that side. If you see the five-man side to the tight end, that is what is happening. We are not going to run the ball to the tight-end side if that is what the defense is going to do. We are going to throw the ball to the split-end side, or we are going to run it over there.

You must be able to run the ball to the split-end side. The defense is going to make you run the ball to the weakside. If you want to be able to run the ball to both sides, you must be able to run the ball to the split-end side first. You must know how to do that.

We have a two-backs-with-a-split-end formation rule. When we have two backs and a split-end formation and we want to run the ball to the split-end side, this is how we do it: Each week we group plays, but the rules do not change. If we tell the quarterback we are going to run the sprint draw weak or strong this week, we are going to run it off the two-backs-split-end rule. He knows right now if there are three defenders or less to the split-end side, we are running the play to the split-end side. If there are three-and-a-half or more to the split-end side, we are going to run the play to the tight-end side.

It is simple, right? Let's look at it. How would we attack that defense? The tackle is one-half, the Mike is one, the end is two, and the Will linebacker is three. So we have three-and-a-half defenders to that split-end side. Where would we run the football? We run it to the tight-end side.

Over on the tight-end side, we have a shade to the other side. We do not count that man. He is zero. If we have three or more to that side, we run the ball to the split-end side. The safety man is up close. Why would we want to run the ball? Let's throw the ball. Why run it into pressure? You could run the ball to either side, but the quarterback can throw the ball outside anytime.

Here is a rule you can use with your countergame. It is a rule where you do not want to run the ball to the split-end side if two defenders are hanging over the outside. I call this the split-end-reduction rule. Remember what the 70 defense was? If the defense is in a 70-90 look to the two-man side, we are going to run the ball to the split end. On any other defensive look, we are going to run the ball to the tight end. We are going to run the ball to the split-end side against a 70 defense, a 90 defense, and the stack defense. If we have a 50, 60, or 80 defense, we run the ball to the tight end.

We are going to run counter gap weak, or we are going to run toss strong. Let me take you through that situation. Is the defense in a 70 or 90 look to the two-man side? No! It is a 50 on the two-man side. So we sweep to the strongside. We do not want to run the two plays into that look on the split-end side. Why do we not want to run the plays into that look? If we block down and kick out, I still do not know if our tackle can get the Will linebacker.

I would prefer to run the sweep to the tight-end side and put the three down linemen on the inside down blocks and use the fullback to kick out at the point of attack. But, when we get a 70 look on the split-end side, we can get a double-team block on the 3-technique. We can kick out or log the end. We can put the tackle or the back on the Will linebacker. I like to run the weakside counter against that look.

We may want to run some of our option game to the split-end side against that defense. That is a reduction defense with three men.

Let me talk about two backs with three wide receivers. Say we have called the spring draw to either side. I tell them if the middle of the field is open, we are going to see a six-man box. We must determine if the Y end can block the Sam linebacker. If he can't make that block, then we have to run the play to the weakside. If the Y end can block Sam, then we only have a two-man side over there, and that is a better way to go. We have a split-end rule, but we have to be careful to see where the reduction takes place.

On a one-back set, we have a rule. On the tight-end side, we never run to the four-man side. We do not like to run into a four-man look. Some teams do run into four men. On the split-end side, we count the men in the box. If the middle of the field is open and it is a six-man box, we run the ball. If you can block the defenders, you do not count them. If you can't block them, you count the numbers. You must look at the depth and the width of the safeties. We split the receivers wide enough to force the safeties to declare. If they are going to cover deep, they must get depth and width.

It is easy to count the number of people in the box. You want to be able to run the ball from the one-back set even though the defense has seven men in the box. We apply the one-back-split-end rule that allows you to run to the split end when there are seven men in the box. Here is the rule: If the center is covered and there are two men to the split-end side, we want to run the ball to the split end. If the center is uncovered and there are three men to the split-end side, run the ball to the split-end side.

If the center is covered and there are three men to the split-end side, run the ball to the tight end or throw the ball. If the center is uncovered and there are four defenders to the split-end side, you have to run the ball to the tight end or throw the ball. That is another rule that can work for you. If we are in a one-back set with four wide receivers and it is strictly a five- or six-man box, we block it straight up.

Let me hit on the spread formation. If the middle is closed and there are six men in the box, we are going to throw the ball. If we get cover two, we are going to run the football.

It is the same thing against quarter coverage. If the safeties are 10 yards deep and flat-footed, you throw the ball, but you can still run it because you have a five-man box.

Let me review the topic of understanding where to throw the football. Know how to read the coverage on a pre-snap look. Know the position of the free safety. We talked about the hash mark and depth they line up. Identify the flat defenders.

I bet a lot of you read progression. I did it for a long time myself. What I mean by progression is this: Say you are running a curl-flat-hook with three receivers. The quarterback comes back and sets up. He reads the receivers in the order we gave him: curl, flat, and hook. We do not read the play that way now. We read the flat defender now.

I identify the flat defender by reading the coverage. Against a cover three, I am going to look at the strong safety. If he runs to the flat, I am going to look for that linebacker. I am throwing either the curl or the hook route. The strong safety took the flat out of the equation. If the safety went back and played the curl, we do not need to go any further. We go to the flat right now.

When you read the defenders, your decisions are more accurate, and they are faster. The reason for this is that you read the body language of the defender. If that man has his shoulders turned and he is running, and you are looking at a receiver, you do not see that. You throw to the receiver, thinking he is open. But, the defender comes out of nowhere and picks off the pass. If you can see the body of the defender, you can make a better decision.

When the quarterback gets really good, he can start making the defender do what you want him to do. I do not do this with the kids until I feel they are confident. I have the kid take the ball back on the drop and look at the flat. But, he still sees the flat defender. If the safety jumps the flat, he comes back to the curl route. He can look the defender off, but he has to be pretty good before he can do that.

We talked about recognizing man coverage. We talked about all of these things. For example, look at the depth of the secondary. If you see the safety is in the middle of the field, the strong safety is lined up inside, and the corner is pressed up, we are looking for the Sam blitz. If we have a "hot" on and we have called what we refer to as "press-no deep help," and I have an X receiver that I think is a good receiver, and the safety is in the middle of the field, we can run the conversion route to the split end anytime we want. If we have a "hot" called, we will throw the ball to him. But, I would rather take a shot throwing the ball up the field than throwing the "hot."

In man coverage, the defenders are going to look at the receivers and not the quarterback. The alignment of the corners and the body of the linebackers indicate man coverage. The quarterback must know when he is one-on-one and take the first open receiver.

I talk to the kids in terms of field zones. I tell them how accurate we should be in each field zone. The first zone we talk about is the "no cover zone." We should be 90 percent in that no cover zone. The no cover zones are routes such as swings, screens, check downs, and any pattern that is behind or on the line of scrimmage.

On the short game, we should be successful on 60 percent of the passes. I would change this based on the last few years. We are closer to 70 percent now on completions in the short game. If you have the middle of the field close and you are reading the defenders, you should make those completions. They are a pitch-and-catch for us. If we see quarter coverage and we have the hitch and flat routes wide open, we are going to take them. We do not want to turn down a six- to eight-yard gain if it is there. Be patient, and take it. Take it, and then the defense will try to jump the play. When they do, then hit the big play up on top.

The next zone is the intermediate zone. It is about 50 percent for us. These are the play-action passes on normal downs, the third down and seven yards plus. Now, we are going to high-low the safety man. It can be against a two deep or a three deep. If we are throwing a post with a dig route, I want to read the safety. If the safety is going back and we are close and the shoulders of the safety are square, we want to throw to the post. If it is close, we want to throw to the post. If the shoulders of the safety are not square, I tell the quarterback to throw the dig route. So, the body language is involved in the read.

The last zone is the deep zone. I think you have to go deep at least four times per game to let them know you have a chance to hit the long ball. This may be the most underpracticed, yet the most important, skill we do.

At Maryland, we have dotted lines three yards from our sideline on the field. That is for the wideouts to allow for a cushion for the quarterbacks to throw the ball. We run a simple pat-and-go drill. We let them throw the long ball down the sideline. Then we put the defensive backs running with the receivers and make them catch the ball by looking it in. Throwing the deep ball is an art. You need to know where the safety is on the deep throw. If the safety is in the middle of the field, I can put some arc on the ball down the sideline on the deep ball. If the safety is playing too deep, I have to drill the long ball to keep the safety

from getting to the ball. Knowing how much air to put under the ball is very important.

I have a test that I give the quarterbacks. I think most of them can pass the test without any problems. I will review some of the items on the test with you. I am going to give you my slide show. At Georgia Tech, I took file-folder-type cards and on the back of the card, I put a formation, a front, and a coverage. On the other side, I listed all of the plays we would run from that formation. Then, I laminated the card. I would make up 10 plays in a set of cards. I used them as my "flash cards." I would hold up a card and the quarterback would respond to my questions. "What is the coverage? What is the front?" I would call out a pass route. "Who is your read?" Then, I would do another card. The kids were getting good at the end. I was trying to teach them to make quick decisions.

Then, I went to see an eye doctor, and he showed me some interesting things to do with the players. Then, I got PowerPoint on the computer. I emailed the same type of cards to the quarterbacks. They had to complete the cards and email them back to me to let me know they completed the test. I would do this on Sunday night. They were getting part of the game plan then.

I made up the cards and sent the quarterbacks questions that I wanted them to be aware of concerning the plays we selected. We ended up putting the plays in a manual. It is a fun thing to do because you are training the kids to know the routes and the situation, and they have to do this under pressure.

Now, what I am working on is virtual reality, where we put the system into a video where the quarterback can make the same decisions. The difference is that we are seeing it in video. We are getting close to that position and hopefully that will be even better.

I hope you have gotten something out of this tonight. I think there are some values in this for high school coaches. I realize some of this material is not possible for high schools.

In closing, I encourage you to teach your quarterbacks to read the defenders and check the depth of the safeties. Life will be a lot easier on you. Thank you very much.

PASS PROTECTION AND THE SPREAD OFFENSE

Georgia Tech

I hope you can see the overhead, because I'll be using that a lot this morning. The title of my talk this morning is "The Georgia Tech Offense." We haven't even had a spring practice yet. So, we don't know exactly what a Georgia Tech offense is. It should be an interesting time down there. For those who have followed Georgia Tech, you know they used Ralph Friedgen's offense. They have been successful using all the multiple looks he has with the option and the passing game.

I have been an offensive coach for the last 20 years. The first 10 years of my career I was on the defensive side of the ball. I was the defensive coordinator at the Air Force Academy and moved on to special-teams coach for the Denver Broncos.

The question has already been asked if I am going to change the offense at Georgia Tech and run the things that I have always run. I'm not the smartest sucker that has ever rolled down the pike. But, they have been averaging 31 points a game, and I'm not going to change a thing right now. We are going to keep on doing what they were doing. Billy O'Bryan is a great young offensive mind. He will continue to run things on the offensive side of the ball.

What I want to talk to you about this morning is where we are headed with our four and five wide receiver package. I am going to talk about our protection scheme that goes with the four and five receiver package and our best passes off those sets. I want to make sure we get to answer your questions. I do not want to be so formal that I can't get your questions answered.

You have unique situations at every one of your schools. We have unique problems and things that come up at Georgia Tech. Your job is to take the talent you have and move the football with it. Very few of us are fortunate enough to have a system that we can force people to play 100 percent within that sys-

tem. If you have been able to do that through the years, you are a very fortunate person.

In high school, your talent changes on a yearly basis. In our situation and at the pro level, it happens to us. Even though we can recruit in college and draft in the NFL for certain needs, we recruit or draft the best athlete and find a way to use him. That is what we are doing with our four- and five-wide receiver package. We are trying to get our four or five best athletes on the field and use them. If your best athlete is a tight end, you need to find a way to incorporate him into the offense so you can use him.

Any offensive passing game has to start out with the protection scheme. I'll start with our four wide-out protection. We call the number of down linemen and linebackers in the game. When we call 41, we are talking about four down linemen and one linebacker in the game. When we talk about this situation, we are talking about personnel not alignment. I'll talk about 42, 32, and 33. If there is something else you want to see, just ask.

I'll talk about a *slide, a five down, and a pack* protection. I'll talk about what all three of those terms mean. I'll go through all those protections in our four-wide receivers scheme.

In our shotgun set with four wide receivers, we usually see one linebacker with a nickel and dime back in the game. This protection is a *slide* protection. Our tackles are in a two-point stance, and the guards are in a three-point stance. Our back is set in the weak halfback position, and the center is sliding away from him. The center does not always slide away from the back, but in base-slide protection, he does. If he played the protection the same way every time, the guys playing defense would figure that out. At times, he will slide toward the back, run him across to the other side, and protect from there. The center, guard, and tackle to the right are sliding to the right.

We use what we call a *sort* technique to the slide side. We block the first rusher who comes to that side. It doesn't matter if it is a lineman, linebacker, or secondary player. We block the first rusher coming from that side. We don't man up. We block whoever comes on the rush. If defensive brings the nickel back, they could bring him from the outside or inside in a stunt with the defensive end. The offensive tackle sorts the first man coming from the outside as his man.

The thing the offensive line assumes is the defense is going to rush in lanes. If the defense screws up and has two rushers in the same lane, you have to block that. We assume if the nickel comes from the outside, the end and tackle will be slanting one gap inside. If the nickel rushed in the B-Gap, we assume the defensive end is coming outside. We assume the defense is going to be sound in their techniques.

On the backside, we are locked up man-to-man with our guard and tackle. The tailback is double reading from the inside to the outside. He is checking the linebacker for a blitz first and then checking the dime back for a blitz.

Our quarterback is in the shotgun set. I believe that is the best way to go to keep the rush from getting to the quarterback too quickly. We tell the quarterback if he gets two defenders blitzing from either side, he has to throw hot to one of the receiver on that side. The receivers are reading the defense. If they see two blitzers coming from their side, they break to their hot routes. We call our slide protection toward or away from the back in the huddle.

One of the problems the defense can create for the slide protection is to walk the linebacker up on the line of scrimmage over the center. The defense wants to draw the block from the center. They like to bail the linebacker out into coverage and bring a blitz from the outside. The back is responsible for the linebacker if he comes. The center is going to slide his protection, and the back will block the linebacker if he comes. If the quarterback is under the center, this protection will not work. The quarterback can't get away from the center without being tackled by the linebacker. The back can block the linebacker if the quarterback is in the shotgun.

SLIDE AWAY

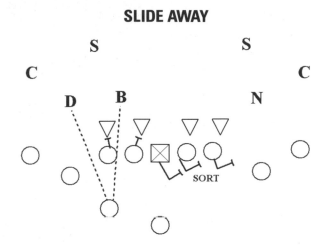

We have a call that we can go to if we see an overload blitz coming. We can call *ringo* and get the center and back to the same side

The next protection is called *five-man-down*. I'll give you the same defensive alignment to start with, and then we will go to something different. This is a catch-all protection. If there is a lot of confusion on the defensive side, this is the protection you want to be in. Let's say the linebacker's jersey number is 51. The quarterback comes to the line of scrimmage and calls; "five-down/51." If there are two linebackers in the middle, we call the number of the linebacker who blitzes the most. That means the center is taking the number 51 if he blitzes. The running back is on a *search* technique. The left side of the line is blocking a sort technique. If the linebacker walked outside and blitzed, the line would slide to the left, and the tackle would end up blocking the blitzing linebacker. The center and guard block their area gaps.

FIVE DOWN

#51

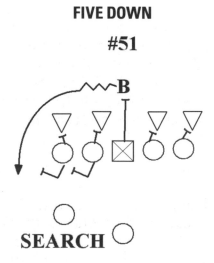

The beauty of this protection is we slide the protection to the side that number 51 aligns. If they stack the right defensive end and the linebacker walked up on the right side, the protection would slide right. If the defense is trying to confuse the offense as to where they are going to bring the fifth rusher, there is no gray area with this protection.

FIVE DOWN SHIFT

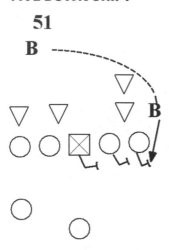

The running back is using the search technique. He is watching middle first, left, and right. If anyone other than the number 51 linebacker blitzes up the middle, that is the man he is taking. If the defense only brings one blitzer from the left other than number 51, the running back blocks him. If the defense brings one from the right other than number 51, the running back blocks him. He searches out the blitz other than the linebacker. He checks middle, left, and right, because of the hot reads. We tell our receivers on the five-down protection if there is a safety in the middle of the field, there are no hot routes.

As long as there is a safety in the middle of the field, the defense can only rush six defenders and still cover all the receivers. If that happens, we can block all six defenders. If the linebacker blitzes, the line blocks him. If one of the safeties blitzes, the running back blocks him. That accounts for all defenders. Those are easy reads for the quarterback and receivers. The receivers don't have to worry about how many blitzes came from their side. We are sound in that protection.

SEARCH TECHNIQUE

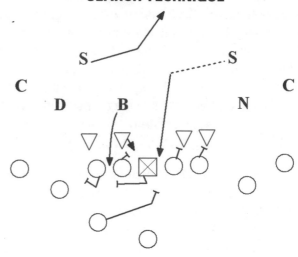

The defense can spoil this protection if they know what they are doing. There are entirely too many defensive coaches in this meeting. I'll show you what they can do, and let them try it.

The defense can rush your quarterback by using a zone blitz. They take both defensive ends and rush under the tackles into the B gaps. The nickel and dime backs both come outside from the secondary. The corners squat in the outside zones, the linebacker sinks into the middle hole, and the defensive tackles run for the curl area. That is how the defense gets to the quarterback.

DOWN FIVE BREAKER

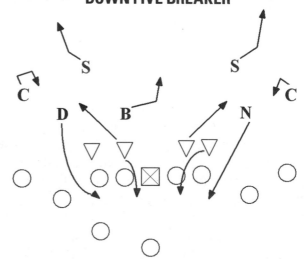

But, remember one thing defensive coaches: This only works if we are in our five-down protection scheme. If we have called a slide protection, the defense loses because a slide protection will pick up that stunt. If the defense brings two from a side and we are in down-five protection, the offense wins. If we are in slide protection, the defense wins, and the offense has to throw hot. The two protections compliment each other. If you can slide and use five-down, you've got the defense guessing about which one you are using. We try to use one of these protections a week.

The reason for that is to stay ahead of the defense. If the defense has prepared to attack your five-down scheme and you use slide protection, it keeps you ahead. If they can't get to your quarterback, they will quit running the blitz. That is the fun part about this game. When we call a protection in the huddle, that is what we run when we come to the line. We feel like the responsibility of playing the guessing game should be on the shoulders of the coach not the player.

Let's go to what we call *pack* protection. The defense I am drawing up is what we see most of the time. If you want to see something different, I'll show you that in a minute. For the example, let's use the term *five-pack*. That means that everyone is stepping into their right gap and away from the five-hole. The back is taking the first defender that comes off the outside from the left.

We are assuming that the defense is going to rush people in gaps. If they do that, the protection is okay. If you are playing against a good sound defense, this protection is fine. If the defense is unsound and runs two guys outside the tackle, the protection could be in a bind. There are two reasons to run this protection. In our other protections, we are in a man-on-man situation away from the linebacker. If the defense has a man-beater stunt called to your man side, this protection eliminates that stunt.

PACK PROTECTION

The problem this protection has is the back blocking the first threat to the backside. Coaches don't like to match a back up on a defensive end. Well, I'll tell

you something fellows: That running back doesn't like the match-up either. The key to this protection is the technique of the defensive end. When a defensive end is coached, he is told if the tackle blocks down, there are a number of things he has to play. If the tackle blocks down, the first thing the end is thinking is trap, off tackle, or shovel pass. He is not thinking pass rush. All those other situations will slow down the defensive end, so he isn't coming off the corner like a runaway freight train.

If the defensive end is ignoring the down block of the tackle and attacking on the pass rush, run the trap at him. If the nickel and dime backs blitz, this protection should hold up. If the dime comes off the back's side, the defensive end's charge should be inside the offensive tackle to stay sound on defense. That means the right tackle takes the nickel coming from one side, and the back takes the dime coming the other way.

PACK VS. DIME AND NICKEL

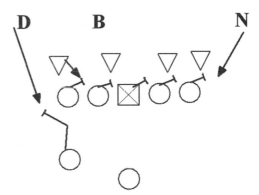

That is the thought process of using the three protections. The slide, 5-man, and pack protections all tie together to give us a very workable pass-protection scheme. Defenses will figure out that we are only packing away from the back. That is why we are toying with the idea of cheating his alignment and letting him come to the other side and running the pass protection toward him. That doesn't give the defense much credit about catching the adjusted position of the running back to get him across to the other side. They will pick that adjustment up, but we will do something else to disguise it.

The second thing that fits into the protection is the running game. You can't do the pass protection and never run off tackle or throw the shovel pass. You can't think the defense will respect the down block of the tackle if all you do is pass block off of it. You have to threaten the defensive end to make him respect the down block. If you don't, you will get exactly what you were afraid of. You'll get the complete mismatch of that defensive end on your running back.

Let me quickly go through our protection versus the 42 defense. The first thing the defense has to figure out is how they are going to play your four-wide receiver set and keep four down linemen and two linebackers in the game. The first thing the defense is telling you is they have a great deal of respect for your running game. That means you have a quarterback who is also a running threat in your offense. That is an advantage for the offense because that means the defense is one-on-one with your receivers. The defense has a hard time rolling up in coverage from the four-two if they are going to keep two linebackers in the box.

SLIDES VS. 42

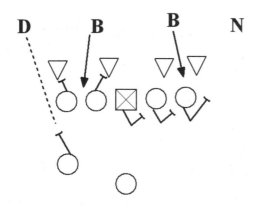

If the defense backs the dime back up into the safety spot and moves the linebacker out to the position of the dime back, that is just like the four-one defense we just talked about. The slide protection works just fine against that scheme. If they bring one from the outside, we block him. If they bring two from the outside, we throw hot. It is hard to disguise anything in the secondary with one safety back there. The quarterback can watch his movement and figure out where the blitz is coming from. If the safety is moving right, the quarterback knows he has to be alert to his right. The safety is moving over to pick up the blitzing man's coverage.

The quarterback can tell who is in the box. We have gone to great lengths to define the box. It is 2.3 yards outside the tackles. Don't get carried away with that it is not hard to see. There are players who

are going to align in what we call the gray area. The gray area is not in the box or not on the receiver. It is a player that is in the box one moment and out of it the next. He is on the receiver one second and somewhere inside of him the next. It is the coach's job to figure out the gray areas.

If the quarterback is under the center and the one-back is behind him, that is an advantage for the offense because the defense doesn't know which way the protection is sliding. Also, with the quarterback under the center, the running game is a little better. Those are two advantages to being under the center. In the shotgun with the back offset, the defense has a better idea which way the line will slide. However, the reason we are in four wideouts is to throw the football, not run it.

If we go to our *five-down* protection, we designate one of the linebackers to be blocked. If the linebacker's jersey numbers are 51 and 53, we call the one who blitzes the most. That means the center is on number 51 if he blitzes up the middle. If the linebacker wearing number 53 blitzes, he is blocked by the running back. The running back is searching middle first on any blitz besides number 51. From that point, he goes left and finally across to the right. If the middle linebacker comes inside the offensive tackles, that is a middle blitz for the running back. If the linebacker doesn't come, he looks at the dime back and then the nickel. Both the four-one and the four-two have the same reads for the search by the running back.

DOWN VS. 42

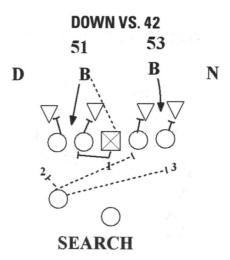

SEARCH

The receivers know there is a safety in the middle of the field, so there are no hot routes. If the safety moves over toward the right-slot receiver, the quarterback should begin to think he is going to have to throw hot. The safety is moving over to take the slot, so the nickel can blitz. If he moves the other way, the quarterback can easily see that and be ready for the blitz from that side. The defense could easily bring linebackers and either the nickel or dime. If they bring the nickel or dime, the safety has to take one of the receivers. The quarterback should be ready to throw hot on movement by the safety. Anytime there is no safety in the middle of the field, both slots run hot routes.

DOWN HOT READ

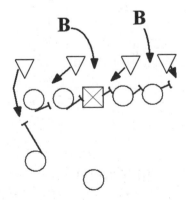

On our pass protection, nothing has changed. Running this protection allows us to pick up four defenders to one side. But, there is basically no change for this protection.

PACK VS. FOUR-MAN SIDE

Let's move on and talk about three-man fronts. When we go to slide protection in a three-man front, the backside guard blocks over the center. We have

an extra guy to the slide side. The back reads linebacker to dime back. On a three-man front, the defense cannot make you hot to the slide side without going to great lengths. When the quarterback calls the three-man front, the receivers know there are no hot routes to the slide side. Away from the slide, it takes two blitzes to make us throw hot. That keeps it consistent for the receivers. They are breaking hot on any two-man blitz to their side in a four- or three-man front.

We don't throw the hot slant anymore. Too many teams are using the zone blitz and dropping the defensive lineman into the slant route. When we throw hot, it is the quick out, hitch, or fade. To the dual-receiver side, we change up our hot routes each week. One week, we will run a fade-and-out pattern, the next week, we may run double hitches. It changes from week to week. If there are some gray areas in the coverage, we may tell the outside receiver to run his route, and the inside receiver will handle the hot route.

SLIDE VS. 3-MAN FRONT

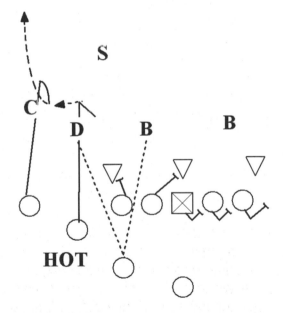

In the three-man front we designate the three down linemen and the linebackers as the responsibility of the five interior linemen. We are not blocking man-on-man. We never block man-on-man when we have people off the line of scrimmage. We pass the linebacker-line stunt off from one man to another. We will lock up man-to-man with men on the line of scrimmage, but never with men off the line of scrimmage. If you get a team that does a lot of line and linebacker cross stunts, the five-down scheme handles it all. The search back stays the same. He is checking middle, left, and right.

The five-down protection is the same for every front. As soon as you designate the five guys the offense line is responsible for, nothing else changes. If there is a safety in the middle of the field, no one breaks hot. If there are two safeties in the middle, the only one who breaks hot is the receiver away from the back.

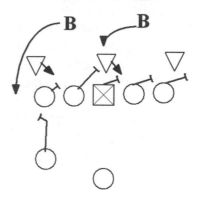

FIVE DOWN VS 3-MAN

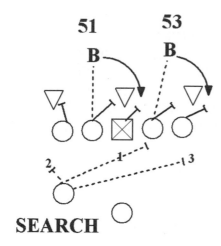

SEARCH

The pack scheme versus the three-man front is the same as it was earlier. Everyone is blocking away from the back. The back is picking up the first threat outside of the offensive tackle. The left tackle picks up air sometimes. But, we don't want him to ever turn back and block. If the defense ran a crossing stunt involving the nose guard, both linebackers, and the backside tackle, everyone would block their gaps. The back would take the linebacker as he came around to the outside. If the defensive end slanted across the offensive tackle's face, he blocks him down.

We can't run the pass protection every down in a football game, but it will take care of a stunting football team. Teams like Mississippi State that align in a three-three type defense and stunt like crazy is what the pack scheme was designed to handle.

You can't go into a football game with one protection. The guys on the other side of the ball are too good. We feel like we need three protections. We may only use two of them in a game, but for the course of the year, we need three protections. The pass protection is easy. The decision you have to make is which of the other two you want to keep in the offense. In some cases, having three is the way to go. That is a decision for you to make based on your personnel. The pass protection is designed to handle all the junk a defense can throw at you. There has to be a reason that you are doing these things. If you have a team that takes the linebacker, walks him to the end, and shifts everyone down, the five-down protection can handle that. If the defense plays base defense, the slide handles it.

Let's talk about the 33 defense. This is a defense people play when they think they have a better chance by putting linebackers in the game instead of defensive backs. If the defense moves the outside linebacker down over the tackle, and moves the defensive end inside, it gives them a 42 defensive spacing look. That is the way we treat it. The alignment of their personnel looks likes a four-two defense even though they have three-three personnel in the game. We designate one of the three linebackers as a down lineman. After we do that, we apply our rules like it was a 42-defense. The protection rules hold up for the slide, five down, and pass protection against the three-three. If the linebacker's jersey numbers were 51, 53, and 56, we would designate 56 as a defensive lineman. He is the linebacker they like to align on the end of the line or stack him in the middle to run stunts.

THREE-THREE

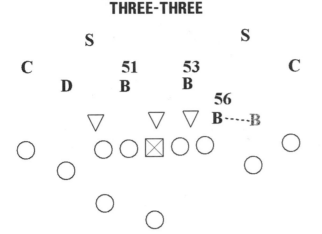

SLIDE

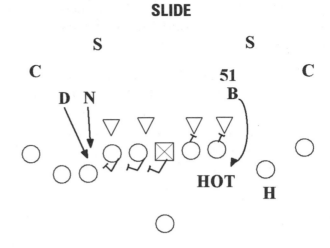

FIVE DOWN

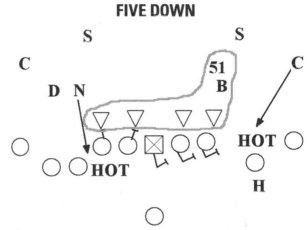

When you are in a spread offense, you have to have a protection for a five-wideout scheme. The five-wide receiver set is commonly called the empty set. When we get into this formation, we have a three-by-two wide receiver formation. I believe the defense would put the dime and nickel together on your slot receivers in the trips set. The running back would be the slot receiver to the other side with the split end. I believe the linebacker will adjust toward the running back in the slot. We don't try to change anything with our protection. If we slide protect, we will slide away from the running back. In this case, the line is sliding to the left, since the back is aligned in the right slot.

The key to this scheme is we never read hot with our wideouts. Every route we run with our five wideouts has a built in hot route. If you get into that set, you don't want to put the burden on the receiver or a back that is not used to reading hot routes. Because of that, we build the hot route into our five-wideout scheme. What it does is give you some freedom to move your receivers in motion without asking them to read hot routes. That is an advantage because the quarterback is the only one who has to know anything.

The quarterback knows the protection is sliding to the left. His hot reads are any two blitzes from the left and any blitz from the right. That is his thought process.

If we call the five-down protection, it would be a slide protection toward number 51. The quarterback knows that if anyone blitzes besides the four down linemen and the linebacker, he has to throw hot. We put a lot of pressure on the quarterback to know all these reads.

Some people think they gain protection by playing with a tight end. I don't disagree with that. The only thing I am saying is using four wideouts gives the quarterback a better chance to read the blitz. The safeties have a harder time disguising what they are doing. The quarterback can see it coming. Having receivers detached from the formation lets the quarterback see the blitz. The defense has to give it away to get to where they are supposed to be before the ball is snapped.

When you have a tight end aligned in a tight formation, they can cover him with the defensive end aligned on him and bring a linebacker. That is hard for the quarterback to see developing. That could be a well-disguised coverage. You can't do that when the defenders are aligned in space. The quarterback can see all their movements. They can't hide where they are going.

We have to handle the 32 defense from the empty set. We have a decision to make on the type of protection to use. We can use the slide or five-down protection. If we use the slide protection, we could get a quick blitz from one of the linebackers. If we get two blitzes from the left or one blitz from the right, the quarterback has to throw hot.

If we ran the five-down protection, the five inside people match up in an area zone-blocking scheme on the three-two look. If anyone outside of the three-two package comes on a blitz, the quarterback has to throw hot. In that case, all he has to do is watch the safety for movement to get the alert for the blitz. If the safety goes right, the blitz is coming from that side. If he goes left, that is the side he has to watch.

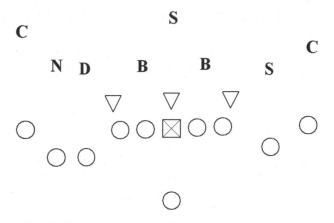

I'm going to go to some of our favorite routes in this offense. Our number one route is a double slant on the short side and the takeoff quick out on the wide side. The back has an option read, depending on his blocking responsibility to the widest receiver to the field lined up three yards outside of the numbers. The widest receiver to the short side aligns the same way. The slot receivers split the difference between the widest receiver and the offensive tackle.

Let's talk about where our thought processes were. I like slant patterns against everything except cover three. In cover three, the nickel and low safety, have an inside-out coverage on the slant routes. Both corners are going to the deep outside third. The free safety is going to the deep middle. You think the outside slant is open, and end up hitting the nickel back right in the chest with the ball. He is falling off on the outside slant, and the strong safety is coming under the inside slant. If we see cover three, we tell our quarterback to forget the slants and throw the ball to the other side. We look for the go route, to the out pattern, and to the dump off to the running back. We will throw the slant on every other coverage except cover three.

DOUBLE SLANT

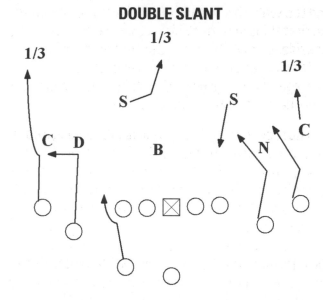

We tell our inside receiver if he is getting a bump-and-run cover, he gets inside and slants right now. If the defender is off him, he comes off hard for three steps and breaks his pattern off into the crease between the defenders. All cuts have to be made at forty-five degree angles. The outside receiver has to win on his route. He gets off the line any way he can. If he has to come under the defender, it is all right. If he pushes up the field when he runs his slant, we want it flat. That keeps him away from the corner.

If the coverage is not cover three, we throw the inside receiver first and the outside receiver second. If we know it is cover two, the defender is doing everything he can to keep the inside receiver out of the middle. When that happens, the outside receiver is open. The quick passing game comes from what we call a quick five-step drop. We don't throw any three-step passes. The corners are coached to watch the quarterback on his third step. If he stops on the third step, the corners are taught to break on the receiver. We want to take the drop past the third step to get the corner off balance as to what is coming. The timing is not that different for the pattern, but it looks different to the corner.

To the wide side of the field, we sit the inside receiver down if he see zone defense. If it is man coverage, he is running outside on the out. We always bring the back away from the slant routes in case it is man coverage. If it is man cover, that pulls the linebacker from underneath the slant routes.

The trips formation is the easiest way to teach a young quarterback. If he is a great athlete but can't read too well, this formation is the way to teach him. The first thing you teach him is the one-on-one to the backside. Most of the time, the best receiver is to the single receiver side. If that receiver has one-on-one coverage, throw the ball to him. If he is not single coverage, he goes to the trips side.

The receivers on the trips side are running a combination pattern. The inside slot is running a 12- yard to 14-yard in route and continues to run across the field. We don't want him to stop in the middle in a hole. The outside slot is running a shallow crossing pattern and comes across on the snap of the ball. The depth of the pattern is two to three yards over the line of scrimmage. The outside receiver is running a 6-yard to 8-yard in route. We want him to square off the cut and settle down in zone coverage if he finds a hole. The single receiver is running a 15-yard comeback pattern. The running back is running a swing route to the trips side.

We call this route *all in*, because all the patterns are going in except the swing pattern of the back. If it is man coverage, the shallow cross could rub off the defender covering the running back. Defenses don't switch coverage on those kinds of routes. If there is any contact between the receiver and either the defender covering the receiver or the linebacker, it could pop the running back free.

Our progression for this pattern is the split end if he is single covered. In the trip set, we throw the shallow cross first, the deep in route second, and the outside in route third.

flare the back to clear out under the curl. To the trips side, we run a go route by the outside receiver. Don't make the mistake of calling it a clear-out route. This is the pattern you have to throw. You don't have to complete it, but you have to throw it to keep the defense honest. This is the home-run throw, and you will hit it sometimes. Don't think it is a wasted pattern. The outside slot starts his pattern just like the shallow cross he ran on the *all-in* pattern. He takes three steps and breaks the pattern outside at a depth of two to three yards.

The inside slots pattern is the one we have to talk about. We spent more time running this route in the last eight years than any other route we have. I'm sure we'll do the same thing at Georgia Tech. We try to read coverages with this route. If the coverage is any kind of man coverage, the receiver breaks the pattern out at 10 to 12 yards. If it is any kind of zone coverage, he works his way up to 15 yards and bends it out and settles in the hole at 18, 3 yards outside the numbers.

The dime back keeping the inside slot out of the middle of the field is running to the deep middle. The receiver settles in the hole at 18 yards and stays out of the corner's zone. The nickel locks on the outside slot to keep him out of the middle and drifts with him outside. He is so preoccupied with the slot that he can't get back under the inside slot at 18-yards deep. This has been our number one route for the last eight years.

ZONE BEATER

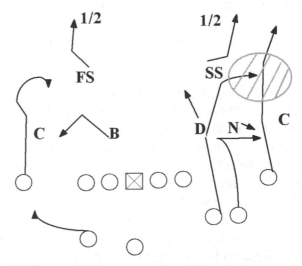

ALL IN

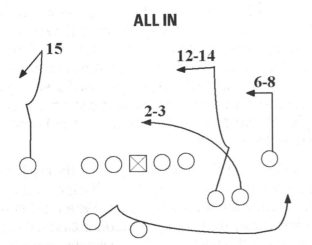

This next play is the counter to the previous play. If the split end is single covered, we go to him as the first choice. If he has two defenders to that side, we

Well, we didn't get to the offensive game planning or the no-huddle offense, but if you would like to talk about those things come see us at Georgia Tech. Thank you very much.

THE ANGLE AND SLANT DEFENSE

Wake Forest University

It is a pleasure to be here this evening. I want to thank Nike and the Coach of the Year Clinics for having me here to speak.

When I went to Ohio University, they had a reputation of not winning too many games. I spoke at an alumni gathering a day after I accepted the job at Ohio University. I told them about the success we were looking forward to, and said I would appreciate their support. I jokingly asked anyone who had any suggestions for how we could keep from losing so many games to let me know. A lady stood up in the back of the room and asked had we ever thought about playing only 10 games.

In my first year at Ohio University, we were 2-8-1. We played Toledo in the last game of the year. They had a good football team and went to a bowl game that year. We were close at halftime. I signed a five-year contract when I took the job at Ohio University. My offensive line coach was Mike Sewak, who is the new head coach at Georgia Southern. I had known Mike for a long time. He was coaching at Hawaii when I was coaching at Air Force. My assistant head coach was a guy named Billy Mitchell.

Mitch coaches the special teams and uses a stopwatch to time the hang time on kicks. He also keeps time while we are in at halftime so we can stay on time and get things done. It was halftime at the Toledo game, and I was getting ready to talk to the team before we went back out for the second half. I turned to Mitch and asked him how much time we had. Coach Sewak replied, "Four more years." That got me motivated to go back out.

When I went to Wake Forest, I wasn't quite as worried. I knew we had done some good things at Ohio, and I thought we could do the same things at Wake Forest. The thing I found at Wake Forest that was a real blessing to us was great kids.

I am going to talk to you today about how we evolved into a slant-and-angle team on defense. I coached for 11 years at the Air Force Academy. They have a lot of traditions, and I learned something about personal qualities. We are going to build our program at Wake Forest on discipline and character. However, we are going to talk X's and O's today.

I want to give you some rationale as to why we ended up in this defense. We do not get the biggest or the fastest kids at Wake. That was the same story at Air Force. Sometimes, the field would tilt the wrong way because we weren't the biggest, most talented team. A friend of mine by the name of Bruce Johnson, who is crazy as a bedbug, got the defensive coordinator's job at Air Force and asked me to come out and help him. At the time, I was the defensive coordinator at Marshall. I went out there to coach linebackers.

When I was at Marshall, we put in the shade-eagle package. When I went to Air Force, we did the same thing. We had what we called a "junk side" and an "open side." You can put these things down if you want, but I am going to work my way into how we evolved into the slant-and-angle defense. We called the tackle to that side a "junk tackle," and he played a 3-technique or a 2-technique. The backer was called a "junk backer," and he played on the tight end. The Okie side had a shade nose guard, a 5-technique tackle, a walked-off linebacker, and a 3-technique linebacker.

We prerotated our secondary to the strongside and called it "red coverage." We took great pride in being a sound technique defense. We were a gap control football team.

If we wanted to go the other way with the call, we put the junk side into the boundary and played the Okie side to the formation. To the boundary on the Okie side, we aligned in a 3-technique, a 5-technique, and a 10-technique for the Will linebacker. On the junk side, we were shade, 5-technique, 9-technique, and a 30-technique for the Sam linebacker.

OKIE-EAGLE

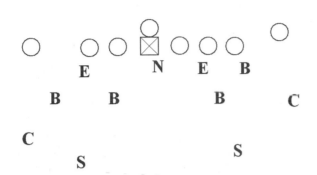

Basically, all we were doing was showing the eagle into the field or the boundary. For a long time, we played pretty good defense. We had kids that were easy to coach at the Academy. If we said, "Step with the left foot," they stepped with their left foot. I thought we played good defense at Air Force.

That is what we started out doing, and we did that for a couple of years at the Academy. We thought we were a good defensive team. We had a good offense, and we ran the ball up and down the field. We were in the wishbone and the offense controlled the ball for 35 or 40 minutes a game. We were standing on the sideline drinking Gatorade and thinking our defense was really good. We ended the year 12-1, and finished fifth in the nation. We lost a lot of kids to graduation and had an inexperienced quarterback the next year. The team we brought back on offense was young and inexperienced.

Our defense had always been a "bend-but-don't-break" defense. That was fine as long as you had the offense dominating the play of the game, controlling the ball, scoring points, and we were off the field. In the third season, we were spending too much time on the field. We ran into some problems with our defense.

Our junk linebacker was always the rush man. The Okie linebacker was always the drop man. When the free safety rotated up, everyone knew where the junk side had aligned. We were giving the junk side away. At that time, we were in the WAC conference. They didn't call the conference the "wacky WAC" for nothing. The teams in that conference were throw-ing the ball all over the lot.

The problems we were running into with our shade-eagle package were numerous. First of all, we were sitting ducks. We were coaching the heck out of our players, but we were easy to read. The offense knew where everyone was on the defense and what they were going to do.

The other thing we found out about our defense was that we were soft. We were reading hats and not getting penetration up the field. We weren't causing any problems for the offense, except when we shot our linebackers. Even then, we were giving things away.

In the third year, we found out how nice it was to be great on offense, when the defense is a reading defense. We had to do something. We decided to line up in the shade-eagle defense and bend the defense back to the other side. The problem we ended up with was that our players weren't very good at playing techniques. That adjustment helped a little.

The inside zone play was giving us fits. Marshall Faulk was playing at San Diego State at the time. Several other good backs in the league were killing us on the inside zone play. We went to a split-defensive look. We had two 3-technique linemen and two 7-techniques on the outside. The defense looked like a 44 defense. The only time we played this defense was against a two-tight-end set. If the offense tried to run the inside zone, we held the two guards with our 3-techniques. When the center came off on the Sam linebacker, our Will linebacker was screaming to the ball unblocked.

We were having trouble with the I formation team running the ball at us. We were getting ready to play Ohio State in a bowl game, and they were good at running the ball to the tight-end side. What we decided to do was play our 5-technique tackle in a 4i alignment and the 9-technique in a 6-technique. We slid our linebackers over to the tight-end side and adjusted our secondary to the other side. We got so concerned about the physical mismatch we were going to have, that we slid the linebackers toward the tight end and then slanted everyone that way.

Willie Shaw was the defensive coordinator at Stanford back then. Everyone was talking about the bear package he was running. He had gotten it from Buddy Ryan, who was with the Bears at that time. We were having trouble pressuring the quarterback out of our front, and we needed something to help us. We played this defense, and while it did help us pressure the quarterback, it forced us into more man-free coverage then we had ever played. That put us in a bind because we didn't have a group of man-coverage players. But, it gave us something that we could jump into, and it helped us some.

What happened to us is we became the jack-of-all-trades and the master of none. We didn't realize we were doing that, but it happened to us. What we began to find out was we were making a ton of mistakes. We were playing with rocket scientists and engineers and making a ton of mistakes. We had too many defensive schemes, and we weren't really good at any of them. We didn't just line up in these defenses, we checked to them. We were giving up too many big plays because our kids were on their heels and full of indecision.

We looked at what we were doing and felt we were doing too many things. We needed to settle on something. We felt the bear package was out because of the man-coverage aspect of that defense.

We decided to go with the old slant-and-angle defense. We put everyone in a head-up position and slanted from there. We could align our secondary at seven yards in a four-across alignment. We could have gone to a cover-two look and done the same thing, but we settled on a four-across look. We could make all the same calls that we did on our eagle package. The only difference was we would move on the snap of the ball.

At Air Force, we had too many things in our scheme. We have smart kids at Wake Forest now, but if the kids at Air Force got confused, there is no one in the country that could handle what we were doing.

We went into spring football to find out if we could be a shade-eagle defense out of a 50 defense. We were going to continue to draw a line down the middle of the formation and play two sides. We were going to slant our players on either side to the Okie and the eagle on the snap of the ball. We were going to do the same thing in the secondary. We were going to make offenses read us when the ball was snapped. The offensive linemen and quarterback were going to have to read the defense on the run and figure out what we were doing after the snap of the ball. That is the way we got to the slant-and-angle package.

For our defensive ends, we went to two Okie linebackers. They were guys that could drop into coverage, and they could speed rush the passer. We felt if we were going to reduce our front, we weren't going to be able to bull rush the offensive tackle, but we felt we might be quick enough to beat him back to the quarterback. That is the kind of guys we were looking for as defensive ends.

We changed our thinking about the free safety and strong safety. We wanted two free safeties in the game. We wanted to be able to play cover two or roll the coverage and not worry about our coverage. The strong safeties ended up being our outside linebackers.

We weren't looking for big physical linemen to play the junk tackle. We wanted guys who could move their feet and make people have trouble cutting them off. One of the advantages we found about the slant-and-angle defense is the way offensive linemen viewed the techniques. It put them back on their heels. It made the offensive linemen more cautious as they came off the ball. They weren't sure what the defense was going to do. They couldn't just roar off the ball and block you. The thing it did for us was give us a chance to play on their side of the ball and play with undersized players. Probably the number one thing it did for us was give us a disguise.

The defensive call for the old defense was 3-Okie-red. The new defensive call now became angle-Okie-red. We still had an Okie side, but we played left and right positions on the defensive line and did not flip-flop personnel. Since angle was called first, the angle is into the field. If we had called Okie-angle-purple, the Okie would have been the field call. Our players got comfortable playing the left or right side, and we didn't have to move them around.

To our angle side, we were going to angle the defensive end and outside linebacker inside. Their landmark was the hip of the offensive guard and tackle. We told the end and linebacker not to worry about reading. We wanted them to get about a yard of penetration.

ANGLE

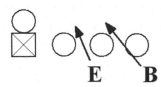

We started out being a field defense. If the ball was on the hash mark and we called Okie-angle-purple, Okie was to the field, and angle was to the boundary. It didn't matter what formation the offense came out in; we played the defense according to the boundary and the field. The players knew when they broke the huddle where they were going to line up. We weren't going to line up in that defense, but the players knew where they were going to be.

To the Okie side, the end and outside linebacker lined up in a 4- and 6-technique and slanted to a 5- and 9-technique. The nose guard was aligned in a 0-technique and slanted to a 1-technique strong. We didn't want them to get too much penetration. We were going to attack, but we didn't want to get reached if we could possibly avoid it.

OKIE

The mentality is still a gap-control defense. The nose guard has the A gap strong, the inside linebacker has the B gap strong, the defensive end has the C gap, and the outside linebacker has the D gap.

The reasons we wanted to go to the slant-and-angle defense are simple. First, we wanted to disguise what we were doing on defense. The second thing was the defense made it simple for the players. The defense maximizes quick football players. It is an attack-oriented defense. On the snap of the football, we are moving. The thing our players like about this defense is we read on the run.

We didn't quit coaching. We are still working on all the things we have always coached. In our individual periods, we worked on not getting cut off, redirect skills, contain, seeing the pass, and seeing the run. We worked in half-line situations and inside drills, but we were doing it on the run. We asked the players to take off and, while they were running, to make some decisions. The thing that gave us the biggest problem was getting our players to go full speed. They were so afraid of making a mistake, they didn't run full-out.

We told them to pin their ears back and go hit somebody. If it was the wrong person, we would straighten him out.

ANGLE-OKIE-PURPLE

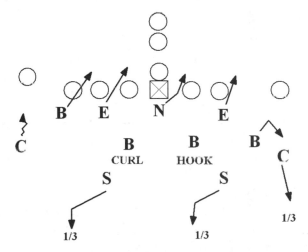

Once we got good at angling, we did some different things with our front. Remember, with a combination of all these calls, there is an Okie side involved. We are going to have a shade 5-technique and a 9-technique side whether it is strong or weak. To change up what we were doing, we called "four." All that meant was instead of the end and outside linebacker slanting down into the B and C gaps, they would step with their covered foot into a 4-technique and 6-technique with inside responsibilities. We were afraid our end and backer were not going to be strong enough to hold their own in these techniques. If we lined up in a 4-technique and a 6-technique the whole game, that tackle and tight end would knock our headgear off. But we are angling so much, when the end and backer don't angle, it catches the offensive linemen by surprise and we can push them back.

4

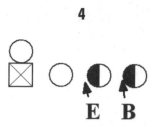

At times, we felt that angle was not enough. We felt like we needed to spill the play, particularly if we played a team that was running a lot of isolations. You can run this movement to either side. We called this movement the "A stunt." When we called the A stunt, it was like the angle movement, except the landmark changed. Instead of using the hip of the guard and tackle as the aiming point, the neck became the landmark. The end and linebacker went as flat as they could across the face of the guard and tackle. We had to tell the inside linebacker his scrape was going to be wider, because the A stunt is spilling everything outside.

The defenders as they run the A stunt are crossing all out blocks. If someone steps outside to block, they cross face. The center is going to the guard's neck. He is crossing anything that tries to down block on him. Teams that had scouted us decided the way to control the angle was to out block on the angles. This stunt either puts us across the face of the out blocks or we end up going under them. This helped us on the inside zone play and with option teams. If the offense ran a play away from the A stunt, we could chase them down from behind.

A STUNT

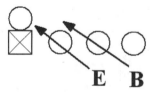

Because we were effective in running the angle, one-back teams began to tighten up their splits in the offensive line. They were running the inside and outside zone plays, and the offensive line was gaining ground almost as a single unit. That was somewhat of a problem for us because our angle and A stunt were too flat. We added a stunt called "ram." Instead of angling down the line, we take our steps inside and penetrate the gap into the backfield. We were actually trying to skin and split the offensive linemen. The zone teams give ground in the offensive line to get width on the play. What happens is the tackle overblocks so much that the end comes free underneath him. The end gets into the backfield and hits the zone play.

RAM

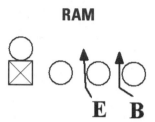

About the last thing we try to do out of our angle scheme is slant. The defensive end angles through the hip of the offensive guard. The outside linebacker plays a 6-technique on the tight end.

SLANT

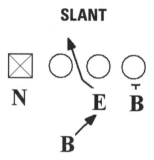

The thing we play the least of all our movements is the A stunt. I really like to run this stunt, but we don't have many I formation football teams in the ACC.

We are not a big two-deep football team. If we get a team that is running a lot of inside zone isolation or inside cuts, we angle from both sides. We go to two deep and give up a zone. If we run angle from both sides, we think you are going to run the ball inside. We call 44-double-angle. That means we are going to angle off both sides. We can still play purple coverage, but we give up the strongside flat if we do. The nose guard is going to play the backdoor of the center. He will allow the center to reach him. He hangs on to the center and plays the cutback. That allows the inside linebackers to fast flow and not worry about the cutback.

44-DOUBLE-SLANT

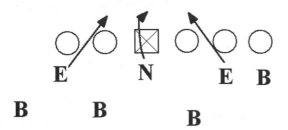

We got out of the mentality of a defense that can stop everything all the time. We know we are going to get beat some times running these defensive schemes. What we want is our share of successes. You are going to get us sometimes, and we are going to get you sometimes. If we can disguise what we are doing until the ball is snapped, we have a better chance.

If we can reduce both sides like we do in the double-angle scheme, we can play 5-techniques to both sides. If we play a team that runs outside the tackle from the one-back set, this is a good adjustment. The center is working backdoor on the center's reach block. This also is a good adjustment for a passing down. We can rush three and drop eight into coverage. This defense is called our "55 look."

55

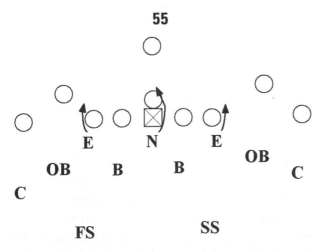

Let me give you some coaching points on some of these things. I think this year we aligned to formation strength more than anything we did. Anytime things started to go wrong for us on defense, we called field defenses to settle our kids down. Our huddle call would be split-angle. The side to the open set is running the angle. The side away from the open side is the Okie side. We can call our coverage to the split side or recall it when they see the formation. We

could call strong angle just as easy. On that defense, the angle side would be to the tight end and the Okie side would be to the split-end side.

Let's look at some of the defenses with our secondary calls. The first one is called "Okie-angle-purple." The Okie is to the strongside, and the angle is to the weakside. The purple is a three-deep coverage rolled to the weakside. On this call, the left linebacker and end are angling inside. The nose guard, right defensive end, and linebacker are aligned in their 0-, 4-, and 6-techniques and slanting outside.

OKIE-ANGLE-PURPLE

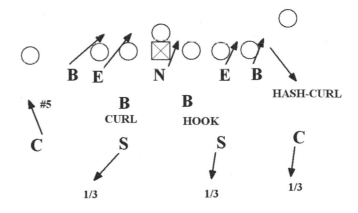

If the call is angle-Okie-red, the angle side is the strongside. The Okie is the weakside and we are in red coverage. The strong safety is down for run support to the strongside. Everyone is slanting away from the tight end. The red coverage is a three-deep zone rolled strong.

ANGLE-OKIE-RED

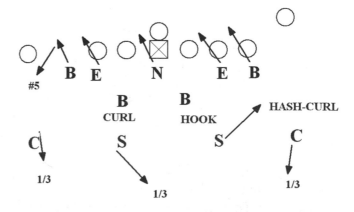

The next defense is an Okie-A-stunt-purple. The Okie is to the strongside and slanting out. The A stunt is run to the other side with the linebacker, end, and nose guard angling for the neck of the offensive linemen.

OKIE-A-STUNT-PURPLE

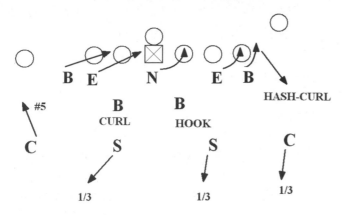

The last example I will show you is the Okie-ram-purple. The Okie is the strongside, and the ram side is weak. Everyone runs a ram stunt in this defense.

OKIE-RAM-PURPLE

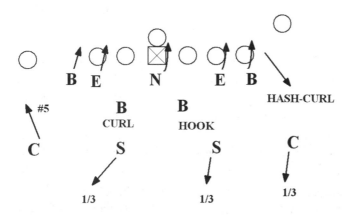

We have on occasion talked to opposing team coaches after we have played them. The thing they can't figure out is why we slant certain ways. They can't figure out why we are not slanting the same way against certain sets. The reason is we make an awful lot of field calls. In that case, it doesn't matter how the offense lines up. We are running the stunt and aligning to the field. That is a little disconcerting as a coach, because we are not really sure what we are going to get formation-wise. Being a natural mixer is the nice thing about the field call.

The 50 slant-and-angle defense can be disguised very well. When we come in on Sunday, that is the first thought our coaches have. How are we giving away our disguise?

When we were in the WAC, so many of the opposing quarterbacks were hitting on that fifth step and delivering the ball. The quarterback knew where he was going with the ball before he snapped it. I think we have corrected that problem.

Probably the best thing we have done is get away from giving a percentage grade to our players. When I was at Air Force, I had two good defensive ends. They were great technicians at their position. They always stepped with the right foot and dropped to the proper areas. They did all the techniques right. Every time I graded them, they were in the ninety percentages. We had a third-team end who didn't grade out well at all. But after the scrimmages, when we looked at the statistic sheet, my ninety-percent scorers were making one tackle and maybe one assist. The third-team end was making sacks, hurrying the quarterback, recovering fumbles, and making tackles in less playing time than the starters. He was making plays. He was not a great player, but had great production.

That is when we changed our thinking about grading players. When our guys come in on Monday, they are looking to see who got the bonus points. We tell them if they are not making plays, they are not playing on the defense. There are lots of different ways you can get bonus points. People do different things with their production charts, and you can too. We give points for production. Tackles, fumble recoveries, and interceptions are where the player gets his bonus points. But, if the player is not getting any of the points, he is not going to play. We do the same thing with the special teams.

We still grade our kids individually. If their grade is low, we bring them in and talk to them about it, but we don't make a big deal about the percentage grade. We want playmakers.

I hope you got something from this lecture that you can use in your system. We are working hard at Wake Forest to try to become competitive with all the good teams in our league. Thank you for your attention.

DEFENSIVE LINE TECHNIQUES AND STUNTS

University of Nebraska

It is always great to come to the great state of Hawaii. I called my secretary back in Nebraska, and they are expecting a blizzard. She almost hung up on me when she heard that ocean breeze in the background.

I have a lot of respect for the coaches out here. We see a lot of tape of your kids. We are really impressed with the way your kids play. The biggest thing I notice is how hard the players play. We have been fortunate to have four players from Hawaii play at Nebraska the past five years. We had Toniu Foniti, Dominic Riela, Tony Tata, and Is Tagoi. The bad part about that is we had two players that left early for the NFL draft. We hated to see that happen, but we certainly understand. Coach George Darlington does a lot of recruiting over here and loves to visit. Now I know why.

If you can get one thing from my talk tonight, it will be worth it. It doesn't matter how old you are, you can still learn something new about football.

This past year, we were 11-2 and played for the national title. Unfortunately, at the University of Nebraska that is a disappointing season when you don't win the national championship. In the 1990's to the present, Nebraska has won three national titles and played for three more. Nebraska has won nine or more football games in thirty-four straight football seasons.

Last week, I spoke in Los Angeles, and our chancellor was there. We were talking about our winning streak, and I mentioned what has happened to North Carolina in basketball this year. He told me, "Don't ever let that happen to our program while I'm chancellor." That gives you some idea about the pressure that comes with the program at Nebraska. Everyone expect us to compete for the national title every year. Everyone is so aware of our success.

It is great for me to represent Coach Frank Solich and our defensive staff at this clinic. Everything we do at Nebraska comes back to a simple philosophy.

We want to stop the run. We want the offense to throw the ball and throw it in a hurry. Everything we do in our drills, whether it is with linebackers, defensive line, or defensive backs, is predicated on that philosophy. I emphasize stopping the run in all my drills.

The thing we never want to happen to us is to have someone run the ball. It is the worst thing that can happen to you. I know because it happened to us this year. All eleven of our players came to the sideline feeling bad. If you get beat in the passing game, it is not as bad.

I hope I can give you some tips about drill work that will help you. I have gone to other colleges and pro teams to get ideas that I can use. We are not a unique program, and we don't have a lot of original ideas, but we adapt what we have learned. We have studied other schemes and made them fit what we are doing at Nebraska. What works for us may not fit what you are doing. We have a lot of people come to our campus to see what we are doing.

As far as drills go, as a coach you need to explain to your players why you are doing a particular drill. We do all our explanations in meetings and not on the field. We never want to waste time on the football field.

We always use movement to initiate any drill. Use a football or your foot to make players react to movement. Never run a defensive drill on cadence.

It is very important to expect and demand effort from your offensive linemen in individual drill work. I have coached the front seven, and it never seems like you have enough individual time. Coaching the defensive line at Nebraska, I have the most individual time of anyone. However, that seems like it is never enough. The thing I stress to our offensive players is to give our defense a good look. It is important for pad levels in drills to carry over to team drills and ultimately to the game.

It is important to get as many reps as possible. We are fortunate at Nebraska to have a large squad. We have 155 players on our team. When we go to team drills, it is a big advantage for us. We are able to get reps for our first, second, and third team players.

We believe in coaching on the run. The practice field is not the place for a walk-through. Do it before practice or after practice. Don't waste time in practice. Don't stop a drill to correct a mistake. You should keep the drill going while you are coaching an individual.

Have your drills set up and ready to go. Know what you want to do in the drill and what you want to get out of the drill. Get your managers or injured players to help set up the drills. I don't want people standing around while I set up the drill.

Go full speed in the drills, so you get a good look at what is supposed to happen. You don't want to get people hurt because someone is going full speed and the other guy is not.

Always grade the film and show it to your players. We stole this idea from Florida State. They film and grade all their winter conditioning drills. It is important to have a plan year round for your players. When our new players report to Nebraska, we have about three days before the varsity comes in. We take time to expose all our players to the drills we are going to be using. We walk through the drills and go through them slowly. When the upper classman report and we start practice, everyone knows what is expected of them.

We use a green football in our drills. I got this idea from the Tampa Bay defensive line coach. The whole idea is stimulus-response. The clearer a stimulus a player has, the quicker response you will get. The green football blends into the green grass or Astroturf. On Friday night when the brown football is used, it looks crystal clear. Your players will have a clear stimulus and a clear response. That response translates to getting off the ball. That is one thing we want to have as a defensive lineman.

It is important to not trick your defensive players early. Start out slowly telling them what blocks they are going to see and how to play them. We teach them the base, reach, cut off, and trap blocks. We teach them the pass set up and what it looks like. After that we work on each phase of those blocks before we get into the combination blocks, double teams, and down-G schemes.

Always start your defensive linemen on a line. We want to crowd the ball as much as we can. We start our young players off the ball a bit until they get some experience. The better they get with their footwork and get-off, the closer they can get up on the ball.

I like to incorporate two or more skills into a drill. For instance in their shuffle over the bags drill, I'll put a pop-up bag at the end of the shuffle. They shuffle over the bags, club or rip the pop-up bag, and sprint past the quarterback. You could do the same shuffle drill and finish with an angle tackle.

Another example would be the cut-block drill. In this drill, the defensive end learns how to play cut blocks. We have three tube dummies lying on the ground. The defensive end comes down the front of those bags and punches down on them as if he were playing a series of cut blocks. As he comes off the last dummy, we could throw a ball on the ground and have him work on fumble recovery or scoop and score skill.

We want our defensive linemen to have great peripheral vision. We send them over the bag and make them look for number cards the coach holds up. That keeps them from looking at their feet and lets them feel the bags.

You can't take for granted that players have speed and quickness. You need to work on body coordination and foot quickness all the time. You need a daily plan and checklist for things you want to get done. I have some advice I would like to pass along to you. Every drill that you do should be written up with a checklist for that drill. After you list all the drills you do, I would put a column on the left of the drills as to when you are going to do them. That way you don't forget to do a drill or de-emphasize a drill that doesn't need to be done often.

I firmly believe you get from your players what you emphasize. If your players do your drills well, you will see a correlation on game day.

I never want to teach blocking schemes until I completely cover defeating the 1-on-1 block. There are four blocks a defensive lineman has to play. He has to play the base, reach, cut-off, and high-hat blocks. Before we go any further, we are going to be able to whip our man 1-on-1. We flip-flop our defensive linemen so they have to learn a right-handed stance as well as a left-handed stance. When we start in the 1-on-1 drill, we do it from both stances.

I think it is important to praise your players when they do a good job. Keep encouraging them to work hard, and praise them when they do. Too many times, the only thing a coach does is to point out the negative things a player does. You need to praise your players when they do things right and try to motivate them in a positive way.

It is important for the defensive linemen to be prepared for things they are going to see on game day. We were trapped once last year. I feel the reason for that is the way we work in practice. We work on trap block at sometime in our drill each day. Even if the trap is not in the game plan, we work on it during that week. If a team does not trap in the scouting films, it does not mean they won't put something in for us if they feel we have a weakness for that type of scheme. We want to be prepared to play trap every week, even though it may not occur.

In your game planning, make sure you work on the schemes you are going to see in the game on Saturday. We have a list of skills we are going to ask our players to do. We will have different drills to teach those things. Our defensive linemen are no different than yours. All linemen must have great get-off ability. They must have great agility and be able to change direction. All defensive linemen have to take on blockers. All defensive linemen must have great hands. That is one of the prerequisites for all great defensive linemen. We do a lot of drills starting out in a six-point stance on a sled. We learn how to shoot the hands on ball movement. From the six-point stance, we go to a three-point stance, shooting the hands, but not taking a step. After we have done that, we get in the three-point stance, shoot the hands and take the first step.

You need drills that teach the stunting game. The more stunts a defense runs, the more they need to practice them.

You need pass-rush drills. You have to teach pass-rush moves and counter moves. We try to get all our defensive lineman to learn and become good at one pass-rush move and one counter off that move.

We have zone blitzes as part of our defensive schemes. We don't do it very often, but it has to be taught. You need drills to teach that skill. We have a drill for dropping our defensive linemen into coverage. We don't rep that drill a lot because we don't use that scheme a lot in the game situation.

We have second-effort drills we work on, as well as pursuit drills. Pursuit is nothing more than effort and desire. A person chases the ball because he wants to make every tackle.

Tackling is the last thing in our drill work. Some defensive-line coaches don't work on this skill as much as the linebackers and defensive back coaches. But, tackling is an important skill in the defensive game plan. It is hard to get backs in a defensive-line tackling drill. We end up tackling each other, but that is not too realistic because of the size of the defensive linemen, although there are some huge fullbacks in our league.

It is important to do drills. This drill is called the line drill. It is a drill where the player does not know what you are going to do, and his reactions become tremendously important. Reaction is what football is all about. One of the drills that is done in any pro combine practice is a line drill. The player starts out and sprints five yards in one direction, touches a line, sprints 10 yards in the other direction, touches that line, and sprints back to the original point. It is a reaction drill that is timed. We have some players playing at Nebraska who have fabulous times in that drill, but on a football field, they have poor agility.

There are players at Nebraska who test out great in that drill who will not see the football field. We also have had players that don't test out at all that become great football players because they know how to react.

I want to show you a *get-off drill.* I am four yards from two defensive linemen. I tell them the down and distance, because it affects the stance they will get into. If it is a run situation, they will be in a more balanced stance. If it is a pass situation, they will be in an elongated stance with a narrower base.

They get in their stance, and I drop my hand. They are getting off as fast as they can and come straight ahead. There are a number of things I can do. If I move my hand right or left, they plant, turn flat, and sprint down the line of scrimmage.

The next thing I do is drop my hands and start backpedaling. They should think pass rush and make a quick pass-rush move. If I continue to drop, they sprint by me in a good vertical pass rush.

If I start backpedaling for a couple of steps and come forward, that is the draw. They get off, plant, and retrace their steps to the original position.

I can drop my hands and point flat to the line. That means the flanker or jailbreak screen. They sprint back in an angle to get to the screen play. If I point at an angle, they assume quick pass downfield and pursue downfield. I got this quote from an NFL coach that I really like: "*It is the tedious repetitions of the simplest movement that produces the greatest results.*" Players sometimes get bored with the drills we do. I show them drill films from pro camps and combines. They find the same drills there that we do, and it leaves an impression that the drill may be important.

The next thing I want to cover is our base front and alignments. After that I will talk about some inline stunts and movements. We have one-, two-, three-, and four-man games, which could be adaptable to your scheme. I have them on film that I will show you later. Some of these stunts have been good to us at Nebraska.

The front that we have considered our base front is called *even-strong.* We flip-flop our nose and tackle. The nose will go to the running strength of the formation. He lines up in a 2-technique, which is head up the offensive guard. The tackle will also be in a 2-technique on the guard to the weakside. The rush end to the strongside is in a loose 9-technique, and the rush end to the weakside is in a loose 5-technique.

We are playing with a three-linebacker scheme. The Sam linebacker is off the line in a 60-technique. The Mike linebacker is head up on the center in a 0-technique off the ball, and the Will linebacker is in a 40-technique head up on the weak offensive tackle.

In our coverage, we roll down one of our safeties to be in our eight-man scheme. The corners are usually manned up on the wide receivers, with the free safety in the middle. The Sam linebacker has the tight end. The Mike and Will linebackers have the tailback—whichever way he comes.

EVEN STRONG

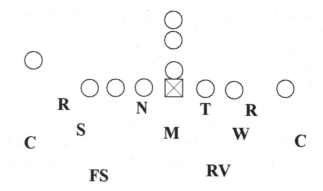

We are a gap-responsibility team. The nose is stepping with his outside foot into the B-gap strong. He is in a right-handed stance, with his inside hand down and his inside foot back. The tackle would be in a left-handed stance, with his inside hand down and his inside foot back playing the A-gap weak.

In this front, our Mike linebacker overlaps a lot. If we get a wide-reach block by the guard on the nose, the Mike linebacker runs backdoor on a lot of plays from his head-up alignment. We get fast flow by or Mike and Will linebacker, with the rover coming down to the cut-back side.

The next front is called *even.* All that basically does is move the strong rush end into a 67 alignment on the tight end. That technique is head up on the tight end. The nose and tackle are still in their 2-technique alignments, and the weakside rush end is still in a 5-technique.

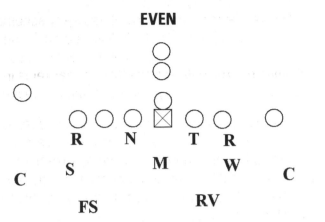

EVEN

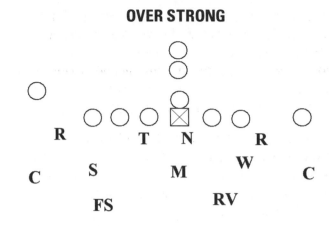

OVER STRONG

The next front is called *over*. The tackle moves to the 3-technique to the strongside. We secure him in the B-gap to the strongside. His right foot is splitting the crouch of the offensive guard. The more experience he has at that technique, the tighter he can align. Obviously on passing downs, he will get in a wider alignment. We play his technique a little differently than most people because we step with our outside foot with a short power step on our first step. The nose is playing a shade to the weakside of the center. He has the A-gap weak. He is stepping with his inside foot aiming for the neck of the center.

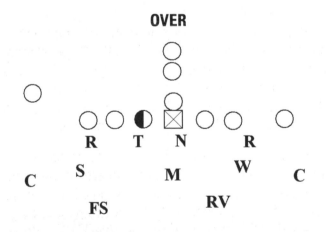

OVER

If we call *over strong,* it is the same defense except the strong rush end is kicked out into a wide 9-technique alignment. The word "strong" indicates that point to the defense end.

This next front has been a very popular front. It is a form of the double-eagle defense. We took this idea from Arizona back in the 90's when they had their "Desert Storm defense." We adapted it and played it a little bit different than they did. There are a number of ways you can get into this front. One way we do it is called *bubble over.* It is an over defense for the nose and tackle. The Mike linebacker is lined up in the weakside B-gap at the heels of the defensive linemen. He is a B-gap player versus the run. If the guard pulls in front of him, he flows over the top.

The tackle in the 3-technique plays a loose 3, and a lot of times we will slide-tilt him inside. He steps with his inside foot to protect against the zone-blocking scheme. We push hard on the guard and get in the crack in the B-gap.

BUBBLE OVER

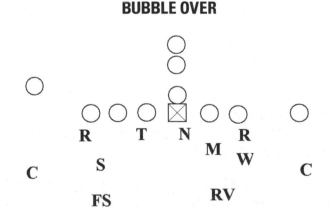

We can call *bubble under* and change the defense. We bring down the free safety. We play cover 0, which tells the free safety he has the tight end. The Sam, Mike, and Will linebackers are on the two backs in the backfield. If both backs went toward the Sam and Mike linebackers, the Will linebacker would be a short-hole defender in the middle of the field. The rover will be in the deep middle, and the corners are locked up on the wideouts. The nose is in a strongside shade of the center. The tackle is in a weakside, loose 3-technique with a slight tilt inside. The Mike linebacker is playing the B-gap to the strongside at the heels of the defensive linemen.

BUBBLE UNDER

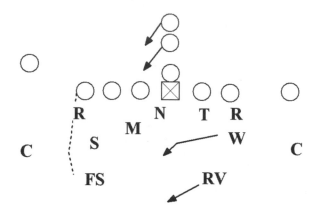

If we call *bubble over Mike,* we are blitzing. That tells the Sam and Will linebackers they have the two backs, the free safety has the tight end, and the rover is in the middle of the field. If we call "*bubble under Mike,*" it is also a stunting defense. I'll show you the stunts in a minute.

The last front I'm going to talk about is what we call *single front.* We walk the Mike linebacker up over the center. The coverage for the Sam and Will linebackers and the defensive backs stays the same. We can play a three-man game with our nose, tackle, and Mike linebacker. In one game this year, we replaced the Mike linebacker with another down lineman.

SINGLE

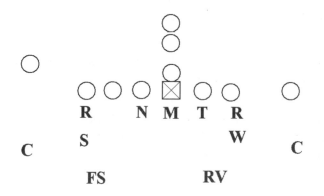

A lot of people want to know why we run defensive-line stunts. Stunts are very good versus inside zone plays because they free up the defender and get penetration. They are good against teams that like to pull linemen. If you mix up your stunts, it confuses the offensive linemen. It is hard for the offensive linemen to make great body contact on a stunting defensive lineman.

Stunts are effective when people try to down block on defenders. It frees up the defensive line, and keeps them from having to go 1-on-1 all day. It causes indecision in the offensive line. Anytime you can get an offensive lineman to redirect his original charge, we think we have the advantage. It breaks up their aiming points and breaks down their footwork. I tell our players they are better than the offensive linemen they are playing against. I tell them if they get too big or out of shape, their next stop is the offensive line. I tell them they are the best athletes on the football field.

By being a multiple-packaged defense, we feel like the opponents have to spend additional practice preparing for us. They have to limit the amount of things they may do, so they can be more prepared for what we do. At Nebraska, we have enough players that we can get four teams working at the same time. That increases the number of reps you get.

Stunting can muddy up rush lanes and lets you play the draw better. As much man coverage as we play, it scares me when the quarterback takes off and runs the ball from a pass drop. We feel like stunting helps us free up on the pass rush.

There are some pass protection schemes that stunts work well against. I'll show you some of those.

Obviously, there are some disadvantages, but we feel like the advantages out-weigh the disadvantages. Stunts are not particularly good against the outside zone play. If you guess wrong on a stunt, it could hurt you. When you stunt, you create gaps for linebackers and secondary players to fill.

The first stunt is an individual stunt called a go stunt. We line up head up, but we want to penetrate our gap responsibility. The nose is a B-gap player on the right side. He wants to step with his left foot on a 45-degree angle and rip with the right arm. He tries to skim the guard as he rips with the right arm.

The tackle is an A-gap player. He steps with his left foot and rips with his right arm into his gap. We want vertical penetration and change the line of scrimmage. We react to blocking schemes on the run. The nose is skimming the guard, but is keying the guard and tackle. They will give him his reads.

The tackle skims the guard, but is keying the center. We always skim the man on which we are aligned, but we also key the man on the other side of our gap. We like the *go stunt*. These are one-man stunts. It is hard to rip up field from a 2-technique, but we like this stunt.

GO

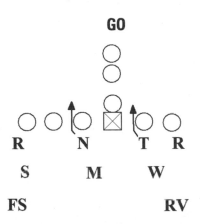

The down side to this stunt is it allows offensive linemen to get up on linebackers too easily. Our guys like the go stunt as a change up.

Another one-man stunt we run is called *nun*. This is for the shade nose. I think to be effective playing a shade technique on the center, you must allow your nose to play across the center's face. It can give you a big play sometimes. Usually we blitz the Mike linebacker in the B-gap. If you don't, it makes you a little soft in the B-gap.

NUN

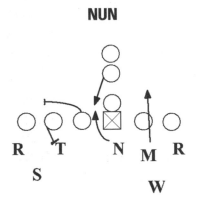

On the next stunt, we run out of a shade front at times. The stunt is call *whip*. This is a two-man game for the defensive line. We are going to fast flow our linebackers weak. The free safety rolls down to the strongside. The nose goes to the A-gap, and the tackle goes to the B-gap. That gives you weakside movement in your front.

WHIP

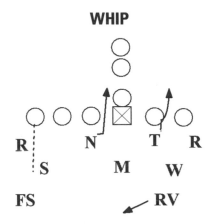

On the whip stunt, we have taken a shade nose and given him B-gap responsibility. What we have done is aligned him as a shade on the center, run him under the block of the guard, and gotten him into the B-gap. It works great if it is a zone play that way. The nose is running away from the center who is supposed to block him.

The next stunt is good against the run and the pass. This is a two-man stunt. The first lineman's movement is critical. The man who goes first must gain penetration into the B-gap. If he doesn't get the gap, the stunt won't work. These stunts are TE and ET stunts. The first man has to penetrate to the back of the blocker. The second man has to sell vertical rush upfield first. If he just slants, the stunt will break down. The guy who goes second is the "loop" man on this stunt. This is a delay stunt. We want to come around tight on the defensive tackle and be ready to make a move on another blocker.

We don't grab and pick people as we go through the stunt. We want the mindset that the nose thinks he is going to make the tackle or sack, and the end does too. We don't want one of these guys to think that he is giving himself up so his buddy can be the hero. We want the mentality that both players are thinking sack.

This stunt is called the *jet stunt*. The tackle is the first guy to go. He is the man that penetrates, and the rush end is the man that loops. We want to run this stunt when the center is turning away to the other side in protection. If the penetrating tackle can get the gap, we are going to be successful. The key is the rush end not changing his alignment or cheating in any way. He has to sell his vertical pass rush so the offensive tackle kicks out on his pass-blocking scheme. We don't tell the end to take any particular amount of steps. It is a feel type of thing. When he feels the tackle has gotten the B-gap, he breaks off his upfield rush and comes inside as tight to the tackle as he can.

JET STUNT

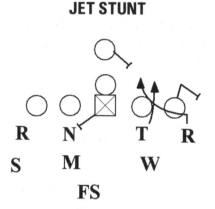

We like this stunt because it can be used on running downs as well as passing downs. The only thing that is different is the end. He is going to read the offensive tackle as he starts up field. If it is a reach block by the tackle, he doesn't complete the stunt. He plays the reach block and gets into his C-gap contain responsibility. The tackle on the penetration becomes the containment on a pass play.

If we call *twist,* that becomes a four-man game. The stunt is basically a double jet run to both sides.

TWIST

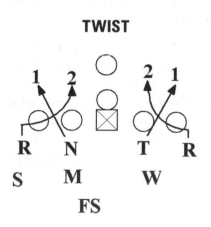

The next stunt we run is called *stab*. This is an ET stunt. That means the end goes first and is the man that penetrates, and the tackle comes second as the man that loops. This stunt has all the techniques of the jet stunt, but reversed. The end is the man that *penetrates* and must get the B-gap for the stunt to work. The tackle has to sell his inside rush and feel the rush end getting the gap. He comes off the hip of the rush end and outside rushes. This is an excellent stunt if the center turns toward the tackle. It is also good on run downs.

STAB

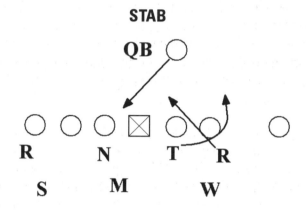

This stunt is really good against teams such as Northwestern, and teams who are in the shotgun offset-back look. They run their zone play, but tell the quarterback if the end is closing hard, to pull the ball and run a bootleg out the backside. This play works well against that type of running game.

This stunt is a great stunt out of the bubble over front. We call it *bubble over Mike stab.* We rush the nose hard in the A-gap and run the stab stunt with the Mike linebacker and rush end. The rush end goes first and is the penetrating end. The Mike linebacker comes second off the end's butt and is the *loop man.* This is a great stunt. We have the end chasing and making plays on the running back, and the Mike linebacker coming around for the bootleg by the quarterback.

MIKE STAB

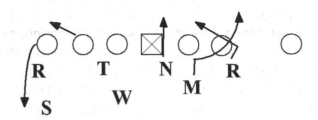

MIKE SWITCH JET

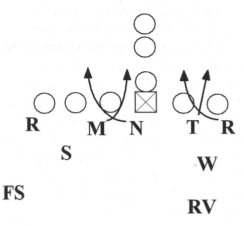

The next stunt we put in to change up our rush ends. This stunt is called Detroit. It is a four-man game. The rush ends start upfield on their vertical pass-rush lanes. This is not a stab stunt. The rush ends are four or five steps up the field before they comes inside. We want him to collapse the pocket, so the quarterback can't step up to throw. They plant and do a late counter inside.

For the second part of the stunt, we game plan which man is to go first. If it is a right-handed quarterback, we tell the tackle to go first, and he is contain to that side. The nose goes second the opposite way and is contain on that side. We like this stunt because the coverage has everyone manned up. When the quarterback sees the ends go inside, he thinks he can escape outside. We have had some slow tackles come on the delayed rush and make the tackle out there. This has been an excellent stunt for us.

DETROIT 4 MAN GAME

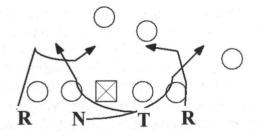

If we get in the under front, we have a four-man game we like to run. It is called *Mike switch*. We run the Mike switch with the *jet* call. The Mike linebacker attacks the center, and the nose loops off his butt and behind through the B-gap. To the open side, the tackle and end run a jet stunt. The downside to this stunt is there is no short hole-player in the middle.

If we got into a single front and called *single switch,* it would be like the Mike-switch call. The only difference would be that Mike would read before he ran the stunt. If it were pass or run flow to the nose, the Mike linebacker blitzed the B-gap. If it were a run flow away from the nose, the Mike linebacker flowed and played run to the weakside.

SINGLE SWITCH

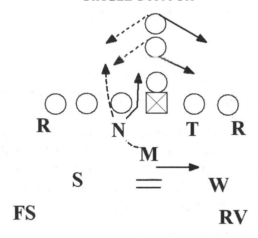

Those are some stunts that we have run at Nebraska that have been good for us.

There are some blocking schemes that we always go over to prepare for a game. There are only so many things that an offensive lineman can do to you. We give handouts every week as part of our scouting report that tells them the blocks they are going to see. We rep those blocks in practice and study their cut-ups of blocking scheme from film.

The first things I talk to them about are the basic "1-on-1" blocks. They are the base, reach, and cut-off blocks. Some people are really into cut blocks as a cut-off block. They don't cut you too much on the playside, but they could on some reach blocks.

From there, we go into the 2-on-1 blocking schemes. We work on double teams, power scrape, and scoop blocks. We get a lot of down-G blocks. We have a base rule of thumb for the down-G block. If the blocker's head is in front of us, we are going to wipe across the blocker's face. If the blocker's head goes behind the defender, we are going to flip our hips, backdoor the block, and get flat down the line. Most offensive line coaches don't want the cross face escape.

The veer release trap is the most common one you will see. That is when the man the defender is aligned on will block down inside. The good guards will head fake outside before they go inside. When we play the trapper, we spill everything outside. We take our outside shoulder and rip through the trapper's inside shoulder and try to make a play.

The toughest ones to read are the pass influence and pull influences. That goes back to reading the player inside and outside your gap of responsibility. If the guard pass-blocks, and the tackle is run blocking, it is an influence trap.

The last thing I'm going to talk about before I show the film is pre-snap reads. The first one is down and distance. The second thing to consider is time and score. A lot of coaches in their game planning break down an opponent's films. They plan their defensive scheme by down and distance, personnel grouping, and things like that. At Nebraska, we do the same thing, but we do it with the opponents whether they are ahead or behind in the game. If you are using a computer to give you offensive tendencies, remember this point: When you put your numbers into the computer on the opponent, if they were ahead, the results will be totally different than when you put in the number when they were behind. When we evaluate this situation, we look at 0-0 or a tie score as being behind.

The next thing we look at is the stance of the offensive linemen. We look for heavy or light stances. We look at the pressure on the hand, the level of the back, and the distance from the elbow to the knee. All of those things will tell you if the lineman is going to pull, pass block, or fire straight ahead. If he has pressure on his hand and his tail is high, he is going to roar off the ball. If the distance between the elbow and knee is great, he has weight forward; if the distance is really small, that means he is going to pull or pass block.

We call our light and heavy stances on our defensive line. If both the guard and tackle are in light stances on one side and the guard and tackle on the other are in a heavy stance, we know the counter trey is coming.

We watch the split of the offensive lineman and the depth they are off the ball. Offensive linemen like to split wider if they are trying to open a hole inside the defender. They like to get off the ball to get a better angle inside or outside.

Offensive linemen have to know whom they are going to block. They have to use their eyes to find him. Watch the eyes of the offensive linemen. They peek and glance around; watch what they are looking at.

The personnel grouping, formation, and backfield set, are all keys for the offensive tendencies.

Let's go to the film and show some of these things I've been talking about. Is that it? Fellows, I appreciate your time, and it is nice to be here. Mahalo!

Brad Lawing

DEFENSIVE FRONT CONCEPTS VS. SPREAD OFFENSE

Michigan State University

It is good to be here today. I was talking to some guys in the lobby today while I was getting ready to come in here to speak. Those guys couldn't believe I was from Michigan. I told them I made my home in southern Michigan.

I chose this topic because of what is happening in college football these days. People are spreading people all over the field and playing basketball. They are throwing the ball all over the place. What it amounts to is throwing the ball up and going to rebound it.

Schools have been successful with the passing game and have made us kind of switch gears on defense. It has made us look at some of the things we are doing that may not be conventional. Two years ago, when we played Northwestern, we were not attuned to what was going on with that offense. We did a very poor job against them. They ran the football up and down the field on us.

We spent a lot of time in the off-season studying that offense. We visited some people and got a number of great ideas about how to slow down those types of offenses. We are not where we need to be with our scheme, but we have improved a great deal over last season.

There is a tight fraternity of spread offense teams in college football. It is like the teams that run the wing-T. There are two types of spread offenses. There is one like Purdue, which is in the spread offense to throw the ball. Teams like Northwestern are in the spread offense because they want to run the football. What I'm going to talk about is both types of offenses.

When you defend the spread offense, you have to determine what their objectives are. If the offense is throwing the ball on every snap, your mindset is different in how you are going to defend it. If they are trying to run the ball, your mindset is different.

I talked to Brad Scott, who is the offensive coordinator at Clemson. He told me their fans couldn't understand how they were lining up with three and four wide receivers and breaking all the rushing records. The Clemson teams used to be two tight ends and two backs in the backfield. The spread offense is a very successful offense.

What I am going to talk about first is understanding the spread offense. I believe it is critical that you understand what the spread teams are trying to do before you can defend it. In the spread offense, there are three main plays that you have to defend.

The first play you have to defend is what I call the *dart*. I am going to draw these plays up with a four-wide receiver, one-back set and a three-wide receiver, one-back set. The mentality and thought processes of those two offensive sets are entirely different. It is different when you have a tight end in the game. When a tight end comes into the game, the defensive keys can change. I really believe that can help your players. I am going to put everything up against a four-man front as we go through this. After that, I'll show it to you with a three-man look. That is what we are getting to. We are playing with a nose guard and a pair of 5-techniques.

The dart is nothing more than a lead play. The offense aligns in the shotgun with its running back in a weak set. We put our 3-technique to the side of the halfback. They try to influence the defensive 5-technique to come upfield with a high-hat release by the offensive tackle. The offensive tackle fakes the pass set. He influences the 5-technique to come upfield, then latches the 5-technique and blocks him outside. The guard and center will combination block on the shade tackle playing in the A-gap. One of them will come off that block and block the Mike linebacker. The backside guard turns out on the 3-technique to his side. The backside tackle pulls through the offside

B-gap to isolate the linebacker. That block is like a fullback isolation block. The quarterback hands the ball off and fakes the bootleg.

DART

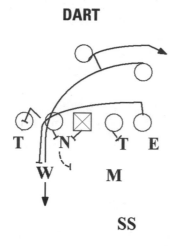

In conventional thinking when you look at the set, you can only see five blockers. Your thinking is to put six defenders in the box. That is what we did two years ago against Northwestern, and we were dead wrong. The quarterback with his play action blocked the defensive end. You have to count the quarterback as an extra blocker. Therefore, you have to have seven defenders in the box. When you see four wideouts and one back, you don't have to put seven in the box to stop the run.

When we teach our players this offense, we teach them that the pulling tackle is nothing more than a fullback. We teach them that the quarterback is an offensive tackle. With his bootleg faking, he is basically high-walling your backside end.

The *dart* versus four wideouts will be run to the bubble. The bubble is where the noseguard, 5-technique, and linebacker are aligned. That is where the offense wants to run the ball. If there is no tight end in the game, the bubble linebacker needs to read through the guard. The linebacker away from the bubble needs to key his offensive tackle. The *dart* will not be run toward the 3-technique.

The next play the offense will run is the *trap*. The trap play will always be run toward your 3-technique tackle. The onside guard uses an influence pull to the outside. The center blocks back on the shade tackle. The backside guard pulls and traps the 3-technique. The onside tackle comes off on the linebacker. The

backside tackle comes up on the inside linebacker. The quarterback fakes the bootleg away to hold the defensive end. The influence pull by the guard turns up on the onside defensive end.

TRAP

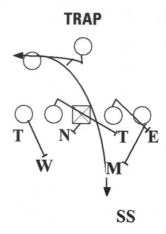

The quarterback is an extra blocker with his play action. That is the whole key to defending this offense. The bubble linebacker is keying the guard. When the guard pulls, that is the trap. He has to fill right now. The linebacker away from the bubble is keying the tackle. When the tackle releases through him, it means the play is the trap. He has to fill right now.

The *zone* play is the next play you have to play from this offense. If the four-wideouts, one-back offense, the zone will always be run to the bubble. The offensive guard and tackle to the backside work a combination block on the 3-technique tackle and Mike linebacker. The center and onside guard work their combination block on the shade tackle and bubble linebacker. The offensive tackle goes for a reach block on the 5-technique end. The quarterback hands the ball off and bootlegs outside.

ZONE

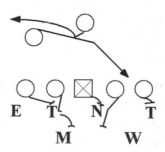

The term we use for four wideouts and one back is *red*. To the bubble side, they can run the dart and zone. To the 3-technique side, they run the trap. The linebackers are the ones who get confused on these plays. The down linemen make contact, leverage their gap, and play football.

The bubble linebacker keys the guard. If the guard blocks down, it is the dart. He has to fill right now. If the guard pulls, it is the trap. He has to play over the top. If the guard comes out on him, it is the zone, and he fills immediately.

The linebacker away from the bubble positions himself so he has vision on the offensive tackle. He is the man who is going to take him to where the ball is going. If the tackle pulls, it is the dart. If the tackle scoops inside, it is the zone play. If he releases through him, it is the trap. That helps your kids.

If you are going to play a four-man front versus the spread, you can key your linebackers in on those linemen. They can key the guard and tackle and know what the play is right away.

The next formation spread teams like to run utilizes three wide receivers, one tight end, and one back. We call this formation *blue*. We are going to set our 3-technique toward the tight end. That means our bubble is on the two-man blocking side regardless of where the back aligns. With three wideouts and one back, the *dart* play is run to the bubble side of the defense. If they set the back to the tight-end side, he is still going to run toward the bubble. The play is blocked the same way as it was with four wide receivers and one back. The quarterback holds the defensive end with a bootleg fake.

The *trap* play is run toward the 3-technique just like the four-wide receivers set. There is no change from the four-wide receivers set or the three-wide receivers set in the dart and trap plays. They are blocked the same in both sets.

The play that is different is the *zone* play. The zone play is run to the 3-technique in the three-wide receivers and one-back set. When the linebacker identifies the formation he knows with the tight end in the game, the zone play will be run toward the tight end or the 3-technique. The center and backside

guard combination block on the nose tackle and Will linebacker. The backside tackle releases through the Will linebacker. The onside guard blocks the 3-technique. The on-side tackle and tight end are combination blocking on the defensive end and Mike linebacker.

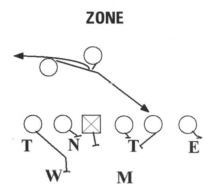

ZONE

I'm going to show you some film of these plays. I want you to watch the keys for the linebacker. The film will show you how the keys hold up in this offense.

Spread teams can run the dart play with the quarterback carrying the ball. They block it the same with the tackle pulling. The difference is the quarterback fakes to the back going across on the zone play and keeps the ball following the tackle into the bubble area. If the set is four wide receivers and one back, the offense will not run the zone play to the 3-technique. If you see the tailback running the zone play to the 3-technique, it is a quarterback dart play in the bubble area. They are faking the zone to set up the quarterback dart play.

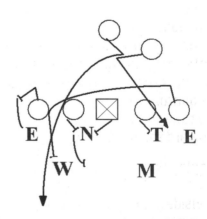

The offense in four-wide receivers and one-back set will run the dart and zone plays to the bubble side. They will run the trap to the 3-technique.

OFFENSE WITH FOUR WIDEOUTS

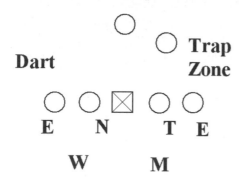

However, when the offense goes to three wide receivers, one tight end, and one back, their play distribution changes. To the bubble side, they run the dart play only. To the 3-technique side, they run the zone and trap plays. You have to coach your kids to understand the difference between the *red* and *blue* sets and what plays go which way.

OFFENSE WITH THREE WIDEOUTS

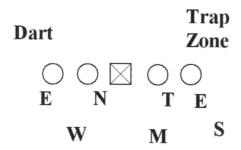

That is how we play the spread with a four-man defensive front. When we use a three-man defensive front, things are different for the offense. The defense has two bubble areas instead of one. The offense is going to count the defenders starting from the center over. Toward the least amount of people is where they want to run the ball. That goes for the zone, dart, and trap

With a three-man defensive front, you have eliminated the influence trap. But, you get a lot of quarterback trap against this defense. In the three-man front, the guards do the pulling instead of the tackle. They are the uncovered linemen. The linebackers should focus all their vision on the guards, because that will tell the linebacker where to go. The offense wants the veer release by the tackle on the line-

backer. If for some reason they can't pull the guard, the center will pull.

I know you didn't come in here to hear an offensive talk. But, it is critical when you put together a defense, that you understand what the offense is trying to do to you.

Let's look at the four-wide receivers set first. We like to set our 3-technique to the side of the running back. We need seven people in the box. We take a defender and align him to the side of the tailback. He ends up outside, and we call him the *thief*. He is going to allow our defensive end to turn it loose. The defensive end doesn't have to worry about the quarterback.

The first thing we have to stop is the trap. In the four-wide receivers set, the offense runs the trap at the 3-technique. We are going to take our 3-technique and slant him inside every time. We are not going to let the trap beat us. That is the first part of building this defense.

Since they run the zone and dart play toward the bubble, we are going to gap our nose guard. He is coming off the shade and moving into the gap to try to expand the bubble.

The defense end aligned to the side of the running back is in a *chase technique*. That means he is disregarding the quarterback. The offense is depending on the quarterback fake to hold that defensive end. We tell him to forget the quarterback and chase the back. He is coming flat down the line.

The play the spread offense runs when the defensive end is coming inside is the bootleg. The quarterback will look at the defensive end. If the defensive end is coming down, the quarterback pulls the ball back and runs the bootleg. That becomes the thief's job. He is keying on the quarterback. If the quarterback pulls the ball and runs the bootleg, the thief is closing hard on the quarterback.

If the bubble is to the short side of the field, the defensive end to that side can jam to the inside. What that does is bounce the dart and zone play to the outside into the sideline. That is what you want the play to do. Don't sit in there and let people beat you north and south. Make them go east and west into the sideline. The sideline can act as another defender.

ADJUSTMENTS

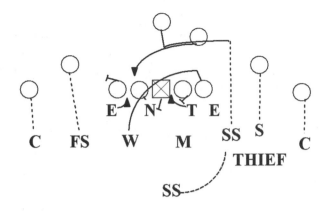

From the three-wide receivers and one-back set, we have adjustments also. When the offense brings a tight end into the game, they have seven blockers counting the quarterback's fake. We play the *thief* to the running back's side. With the tight end in the game, the offense runs the trap and zone play to the 3-technique and the dart to the bubble. We still want to stop the trap, so we slant the 3-technique inside hard. Instead of gapping the nose guard into the bubble every time, we read him on block recognition. If he gets a reach block from the center, he will play the reach. If he gets anything inside of him, he is working over the top. I call that a *spike technique*. It is a read out for the noseguard. It is not that hard.

The 3-technique is coming down hard inside. If the offense is running to the tight-end side, the center will be working up to the second level. He is going to get the crap kicked out of him. The slanting 3-technique is going to blow up the center on his slant. The noseguard is going to play right over the top of the center and slanting 3-technique. The defensive end to the tight-end side can't be a chase end.

The 5-technique end to the two-man side is aligned on an offensive tackle. When the offense runs the dart play, they like to soft set the offensive tackle instead of high-wall blocking on the defensive end. A soft set means the tackle is showing a pass-blocking set. If the defensive end jumps inside, the tackle will drive him down the line. We have a technique we use called a *false jam*. The defensive end fakes an inside move and steps back outside. The offensive tackle who doesn't have the best feet in the world will fall all over himself trying to recover. The defensive end becomes a chase player if the back is

set toward him. If the back is set away from him, he fakes inside and steps back outside.

We disguise the thief. He may line up in the middle of the field or in the secondary. But, on the snap of the ball, he gets into position to play the quarterback on the bootleg.

ADUSTMENTS VS. TIGHT END

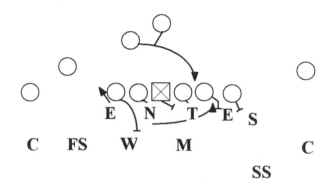

Teams that use the spread as a running offense are not very good at throwing the ball. The same thing is true about teams that use the spread offense as a pass set. They don't run the football very well. If you are committed to the run, you have to spend so much time developing the run that there is very little time to develop the passing game. The same thing is true of the passing team. They spend the majority of their time trying to develop their passing game. The running game is something they seldom do.

What we have gotten into to stop the spread offense is the three-man front. Teams that run the spread offense hate this type of defense. In the three-man front, the offense has to make some decisions. It is not cut and dry for them.

If you play a spread team that throws the ball, they hate eight men in coverage. I was at a school years ago that had to play Florida every year. We did not have the personnel that they had. We had a coach who left Florida and came to work at our school. He was an offensive coach, but he came into our defensive meeting and told us that Coach Spurrier hated to play against eight men in the secondary. The extra man in the secondary screws up the offensive team's reads. We started playing eight men in the secondary against Florida and held them to less than three touchdowns a game.

In 1999, we had a great football team at Michigan State. We were 10-2 that year. One of the games we lost was to Purdue. We went to Purdue to play them. They were undefeated. We had a blitz package that would make you cry because it was so damn good. Purdue's quarterback was Drew Brees. He was only sacked nine times that season. We sacked him five times in that game. We beat him to death and got our lunch handed to us. They beat us to death. We sacked him, knocked him down, hurried him, and he completed passes all over the place.

The next year, we played them at home with a very average team. Our personnel were not nearly as good as it was the year before. They had primarily the same offense unit. We only rushed three that night. We held Purdue to 10 points and beat them 35-10. We never got close to the quarterback that night. That was our philosophy that night, and it screwed up Drew Brees.

The three-man front does the same thing to a team that is trying to run the ball out of the spread offense. When you have two bubbles, the offense has to make a decision on which bubble to attack. They have to count your defensive personnel on each side of the ball. As a defensive coach, it is not good to stay in two bubbles against a team that is running the ball. You have to be far superior to the offense to do that. What we like to do is *jam* the bubble from the outside. By slanting the 5-techniques inside, we stop the dart, zone, and trap plays. We have forced the ball to bounce east and west.

The linebackers are scrapping outside of the slanting 5-techniques. We have two outside rushers coming from the outside in.

When we are in the four-man front, we are in a lot of man-to-man coverage. However, when we go to the three-man front, we can bring five-man pressure and play some kind of zone behind it. We feel a lot better calling the three-man front on first down because we can play zone behind it.

Our noseguard is a two-gap noseguard if the center comes off straight at him. If the center moves one way or the other, the noseguard is playing the back

half of the block. He is not reading and playing soft. He is playing aggressively on the backside of the block. In a pass-rush situation, the noseguard, in some situations, simply pops the center and looks for the back. We can use him to spy on the back or the quarterback. The linebackers know he is playing the back half of the block and fast flow over the top.

THREE-MAN FRONT

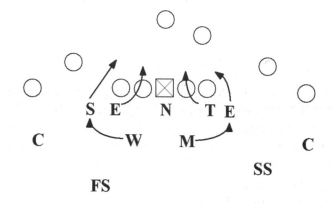

Against some teams, instead of jamming the bubble immediately, we jab step upfield to draw the block and slant underneath the offensive tackle. Sometimes, that will free a 5-technique up for a big hit.

The outside rushers are like chase linebackers. If the back is toward the outside rusher, he comes flat to the line of scrimmage and tries to run the play down from the backside. Since we are in zone coverage, we have protection against the quarterback on the bootleg. Our zone coverage is like the thief in relationship to the quarterback. You have to account for the quarterback every time.

The way to blitz this offense is to overload to the side of the running back. We try to get the end upfield and bring someone underneath him. That gives us a man coming free on the back.

However, if the offense reads the blitz coming, they like to run the Utah pass away from the blitz. The Utah pass is a shovel pass to the running back coming under the drop of the quarterback. If you are going to blitz to the side of the running back, you have to play the shovel pass away from the blitz. That is the main check by the offense in that situation.

UTAH PASS VS. BLITZ

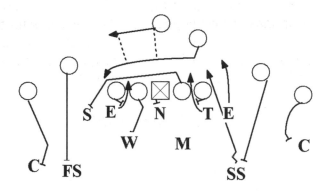

If we want to really come after the quarterback, we blitz one or two safeties. We jam the B-gap with the 3-technique. The noseguard grabs the center. We bring our safeties down and blitz the A-gaps. This blitz is designed to be run against one-back formations. We played Florida in the bowl game. Coach Spurrier brought a wide receiver back in motion and stopped him in the backfield to try to help with the protection. It didn't work very well. That is another way of attacking the spread offense. When we do that, we are in man coverage.

SAFETY BLITZ

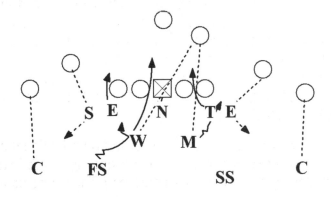

Another blitz we use is to twist with the noseguard and linebackers. We are dropping the outside rushers in the three-man front and bringing both linebackers inside. They have as many blockers as we have defenders, but we want offensive linemen to have to move their feet against quicker players.

TWIST BLITZ

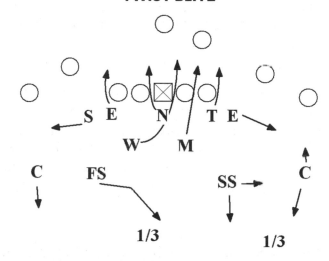

The last thing I want to talk about is how we feel about Michigan high school coaches. We appreciate the support of the coaches in this state. We appreciate what you do. I've been in Michigan for three years. I am extremely impressed with the coaching up here in Michigan. It is damn good. You guys do a great job. When we get your kids on campus, they are well schooled in fundamentals and know how to play. That tells me you guys are doing a heck of a job. We appreciate it, and anytime you want to come on our campus to visit, you are welcome. Come on up — we would love to have you. Thanks for letting me speak here today.

DEVELOPING AN OFFENSE

University of Arizona

It is great to be back in the heartland of America. I spent a little time in this area at the University of Illinois. I have been a lot of places, and they all have been good. It's impressive to see coaches who care enough about what they do and how they do it to come to a clinic. You see the same people who are interested in being around football at these clinics all the time. That is why they win.

When I was 23 years old, I was a young coach in high school at my hometown school, Barberton, Ohio. My coaches were the kind who would coach a game on Friday night, jump into a car, and drive to Iowa City to see the Hawkeyes the next day. The next week, they would coach the game, and get into a car, and drive to Knoxville, Tennessee. That's what kind of people they were; they loved football. They would be around it all the time.

One time we went to this clinic in Wooster, Ohio. The attraction was Ara Parseghian who was going to be a featured speaker. Ara spoke on Saturday morning. The room was packed with people. Ara Parseghian talked about the 4-second interval, the length of a play. He talked in great detail about how he coached it, and what it meant. I remember that as we were coming out of the room afterwards, some of the coaches remarked that Ara's talk was one of the worst talks they ever heard. They were disgusted that he didn't draw any plays on the board. They felt that anyone could have talked about "stuff like that." I remember coming out of that room feeling that was the best talk I ever heard. The concept of the 4-second play is something I still use today. If you think about it, if you can get a player to play four seconds as hard as he can play, you have quite a player. This is particularly true about offensive and defensive linemen. I promise you only one out of ten linemen play for four seconds on every play. If you could get every player to play for four seconds, what a difference you will make on your team.

The point is that Ara had an impact on my life. I really do not remember another thing about that clinic. My hope for each of you is that you can get one thing from me or someone else at this clinic.

I was at the American Football Coaches Association clinic this winter. They had all these Coaches of the Year there, including Larry Coker, Ralph Friedgen, and some others. There was an old guy sitting next to me who was about my age. As we listened to each of these guys talk about their walk through the season and how great the year was, the old guy turned to me. He asked me, "Why don't they draw up the X's and O's anymore. I remember going to the old clinics to hear coaches talk about their best plays. Now, they want to talk about their philosophy." So, tonight I am going to talk about a career in coaching, and then I will talk about the plays.

Why would you want to be a coach? First of all, many of you read in the paper that Steve Spurrier just signed a five-year contract for 25 million dollars. This is not a good reason to be a coach. You could make money a lot easier if you took a job in the business world. If you are in it for the big bucks, you will probably be disappointed. There is a small percentage that gets to a certain level that do really well. At the college level, there are a lot of assistants who are paid comparably to university professors. It has not been like that for a long time. What we do not have, however, is security or tenure. The only thing that we do have is what shows up on Saturday afternoon. I don't know a coach who doesn't earn what he is paid.

Second, you must love your location. Someone might think that he would love to be in Arizona. Some coaches think, "If I only could coach in Arizona, I would be the happiest guy. The weather is wonderful; I could sit out in the evening in my short sleeves. It would be the greatest place to coach." But what if it is a lousy job? Coaching has nothing to do with the location; it has to do with the quality of the situation. I may be the exception and not the rule, but I have coached in all four corners of the country. I have learned that you cannot fall in love with the location, unless it fits you. Too many people limit themselves to location, and cannot get the type of job they want. There was one guy who played in the NFL from Texas. When he retired from playing, he told me there is only one place he would coach. It was right there at the University of Texas. I told him that may not work out or be possible. He had no experience, and we had no position. He felt because he played in the NFL, he could coach there with us. I told him he had to go out and coach somewhere else, and learn how to coach. He is at Nashville, Tennessee right now, moving up the ladder.

Next, career coaching is learning how. That is where these clinics come in. Years ago I was doing a clinic in Burlingame, California. I looked down, and right there, sitting in the front row, was John Ralston. At 72 years old, he was taking notes on the clinic talk. I was a child when John Ralston was a household name coaching college football. He loved the game even at that age. Tom Osborne is another person who demonstrates this. In 1995, I went to the clinic at the national convention. During his talk, I was sitting in the very back row. I just wanted to listen to him; we didn't even play them at that time. They were two-time defending national champion. I thought to myself that we might play them someday, so I just listened to his talk. He was talking about his team. When he put on his film, I wasn't listening to his plays; I was watching his line splits. That was important because I have a philosophy about splits between linemen. His team uses 1-foot splits, just like we do. They run the ball well. It was a confirmation for me of what we were teaching. When I returned from the convention, I told my coaches that we were using the same splits as the Huskers. They weren't going out with three feet between linemen; that was the national trend. The bigger line splits were in. However, it was to the point where double teams, slide blocks, and reach schemes had changed significantly, that shorter splits were needed. Nebraska recognized this, and they brought their splits in. They came off on their double teams, and knocked their opponents off the ball. The next year we played Nebraska in the first Big 12 championship game. We used the same things against them that I saw the year before at the clinic.

Networking is important in coaching. You have to be willing to start at the bottom with flunky jobs. Do what has to be done — drive the car, get the coffee. But, get to know the coaches you are working for. Ken Hatfield, the coach at Rice, started with me at Army. Al Groh, who is with the New York Jets, was also with me at West Point. Ray Handley, who followed Parcells with the Giants, was with me at West Point. Bill Parcells was our defensive line coach at Army. All five of us were head coaches at one time, and we worked together at the Academy. Get to know the people around you.

Next, in a career, be known for something. In 1972, I was an assistant coach at Arizona. We had a tremendous offense. We were split-back veer, triple option, and drop-back pass. We were good, but I felt uneasy about our team. When I came to Illinois, I remember speaking at the State High School Coaches Clinic. My talk was, "Be Known For Something." In 1975, I decided I would be known as a passing coach. So I changed everything in my career, as I did everything I could to learn about the passing game. My focus changed. It was no longer a matter about learning offense, but learning the passing game. I wanted to learn from the best.

When I went to Wake Forest, I decided to use the Wilson football. This was before Nike existed; the standard ball was the Spalding J5V. The Spalding rep came to me and said, "Let's sign you up." I told him I wanted to use the Wilson NFL ball. He told me that nobody played with that ball. My thoughts were that we were going to be a passing team. I wanted to tell players that this was the same ball that they would use when they got to the NFL.

Establish your work ethic. Come early and stay late. Try not to take your work home. You have to be able to work hard and work long. However, it is not just a matter of working hard, but working smart. Study the game and opponents. Find something that others do not see. One of the key values of someone on our staff is when he says: "I have been watching these guys. Every time their tailback lines up here, this is going to happen. Every time they take this type of split, they are going to run this play. Every time the back comes through the hole, he doesn't cover the ball. Each time the guard is pulling, he tips his hand with his stance." Be well prepared for your players.

Give them more. If you are well prepared, you can have a great practice.

We tell our coaches, if we have a bad practice, it is our fault. We are the ones who set the tempo, set the schedule, and establish the routine. If we do not have a good practice, it is our fault for letting them have a bad practice.

As a coach, you determine your values and ethics. Everyone is not shading the rules. When I was at Illinois, I was also athletic director. Once at a meeting of athletic directors, I told another A.D. that he had an assistant who was violating the "bump" rule. He was "bumping" into a high-school athlete the day of a competition. As coaches, we know that is a strict "NO-NO." After he met with that assistant, he came back to me and told me that while the coach was violating the rule, "Everybody does that." I replied to him "No! Everybody doesn't do that."

Sometimes, as you set your ethics and values, you find others shading the rules. You can't follow their lead. They may get ahead of us, but I can promise you one of two things will happen. One, they will fall with disgrace. Two, they will go to their graves knowing that they did not play within the rules. You ought to be able to put your head on your pillow every night knowing you did it the way it should be done. If you can do that, you can feel great because you did it the right way, whatever happens.

Establish your reputation one way or the other. People will look at you, knowing you are a coach, and identify something about you. "If someone were to say something bad about you, live your life so that no one would believe them." If you can do that, you can stand tall. It is hard to teach integrity, and then go out and break the rules. Coaches should be role models. How can they teach as role models, and then go out and break rules?

You must set your goals. I had a coach in college, Bill Tate, who played fullback at Illinois. I told him I wanted to be a head football coach. He answered, "Good. Set your goals, and if you don't get them, get out. Coaching is too hard a profession." If you don't reach what you want to reach, get out and do something else. I have career goals and life goals. If your only career goals are life goals, you are missing out. I

have two life goals, and I have already achieved one after 22 years. I will get the other. You must believe in yourself.

A good coach must have patience. It is not how you come into the world, but how you go out. Vince Lombardi did not become a head coach until he was 45 years old. All his friends seemed to go past him and get jobs earlier in their lives. They always passed over him. Yet, who do they use as a standard, to equate all other coaches to as being one of the best? Joe Torre, the great manager of the New York Yankees, was fired three times. Now look at him. These men show that you just have to have patience.

It is important that you have a career of significance, not just success. You should attempt to mean something to your family, friends, players, community, and school. Have a life of significance.

All these things, men, are part of what it takes to make coaching a career. Now, I would like to talk about developing an offense. Some coaches come to a clinic such as this and play "follow the leader." They hear John Mackovic speak, and they copy what he showed them, and they put it in their program. They decide to start all over again. They change everything they do and decide to run the wishbone or the run-and-shoot offense. Others will stay flexible. They decide that they will change their offense every year to adjust to the personnel they have. That is okay, but the problem is every year you may have to make changes. Teams that win and win consistently are teams that don't change offenses, but change personnel within their offense.

What you want to establish is based on a decision of what you want. When you go to a clinic, study and learn with a reason. If you came here to listen to me speak about defensive-line techniques, you will be very much disappointed. You must develop your passion for excellence. If you are a passing coach, you have to believe in that 100%. You must take the attitude that if your opponent does not stop your passing game, you will beat them. You will train and develop your quarterbacks to beat the opposition. You need a passion for excellence.

I feel you must adapt your system to the players. If you want to be a passing coach, you need to stay with that idea regardless of your players' strengths and weaknesses. If your quarterback is a sprint-out passer, then maybe you can't run a drop-back game. However, you still can remain a passing coach. If you have an option team, and your quarterback is not a very good runner, you can still run the option. Load the option; do something else. Don't abandon it. "Stick to your knitting." You must say, "This is what we are, and this is what we do!" And if you are going to play us, be ready to stop what we do. And we will do it.

In our offense, the Arizona offense, we establish the passing attack. You are going to have to stop that. This year, we returned one quarterback who had 25 snaps the year before. He was in a system that was in last place in the PAC 10. We had one player who played two plays, and two other redshirts who did not play. We had no tight ends who had caught passes, and an offensive line that just fired out and blocked. They did some play-action passes. That was it.

When we came in, we told them that they had to play football our way. Initially, it didn't go well. The last five games of the season we averaged 296 passing yards a game. We also averaged 449 yards a game total offense our last half of the year. It took us half a year to get going. Just think if we would have said after the first five games, "Maybe we should just do what these players do." We had also a 1200-yard rusher who was the number one rusher in the PAC 10. Too many people asked, "Why don't you do what everyone else does?" Well, first, I am hardheaded. Second, we are going to do what I know best.

Now, we return the top passer in the PAC 10. We just signed one of the top drop-back quarterbacks in the country. We signed two top six-foot-four-inch wide receivers. We signed five offensive linemen who average 300 pounds, and also two good running backs. This is because we stuck to what we do. You may say that is fine for college, but I am in high school. I take what I get. It doesn't work that way. My answer for that is that it does. If you create the excitement for some of these things, you will find kids in your school. You recruit that basketball kid who only plays basketball because he sees the excitement. When that ninth-grader comes through your door not sure if he wants to play, the excitement will make a difference.

We will use all the eligible receivers on the field. We will spread the field, and throw to everyone. We will show many looks. We have many formations, shifts, and motions. We will attack with a one- or two-back offense. Our receivers will play a lot of positions.

We have a great receiver. If you have to cover him, you better be able to cover him at different positions. He will play at the flanker, in the slot, or on the weakside of the four-receiver set. If you are going to cover him, you may need to assign someone to him. That will give us a mismatch somewhere else, or someone else will have to cover him, giving us a mismatch there.

Our number one priority in the passing game is to protect the passer. That is why we teach our offense with a two-back system first. If we cannot block you, we will use maximum protection and keep our backs in. We will use several different protections every game. Our quarterback will practice on the clock. Everyone is responsible for pass protection. The line, tight end, quarterback, backs, and wide receivers are all responsible. The wide receivers need to know when they are hot. The backs need to check first before they release. We grade the sacks and the hurries for evaluation. Two years ago, they gave up 44 sacks. Because of that emphasis, we reduced sacks 25% this year while throwing more passes. One out of nineteen is an acceptable ratio of sacks per play.

We threaten the defense all the time with our long and short passing game. You need good play action to compliment the running game. We will use double-team blocking for the run. We try to create angles for blocking in our run game. We demand a sound, solid, and simple running attack. We want excellence. We build something for every runner. If we have a power back, we will build something for him. If we have an inside runner, we will develop something for him. We will try to connect every one of our players with our offense. This will get more kids into the flow of the game.

We do our strategic play calling for advantages. This is especially true with our check-with-me plays. We don't check out of plays. We protect our best plays. We use variations with the same concepts. We use complementary plays consistently. Sometimes, we give our best plays a rest. Sometimes, we won't run a play during a week. If you keep running the same play over and over, and coaches watch your films and do all that studying, people can stop it if they want. So, at times, we just give a play a break.

Develop a strategic game plan. Have a plan to run or pass first. Study other opponents for ideas, but create your own design for the game. Coaches are guilty of this all the time. This is an observation of the national championship game. Virginia Tech was proficient at running the option. They ran well against Miami with a load option. Coming into the game, Nebraska saw what Tech did. They tried to utilize a similar option early, but Miami stuffed it. They changed their coverage. Even though the play worked for Tech, Nebraska could not get it going. The moral is that a play or idea may be good for someone else,

but it won't always work for you. We just don't put in what everyone else does, because we do not always know the history of what was done the previous week.

We teach our game plan with strategic situations. We build our game plan first and ten, second and long, third and three-to-five, third and long, short yardage, goal line, and two-minute situations. We then teach the blocks in our practices according to how we plan to attack the various strategic situations. We teach all of our offense that way.

We build our offense around four plays: the counter trey, the toss sweep, the power off-tackle, and the quick trap. These go well with passing the ball. We then teach our play-action package. With our drop-back package, we have a complete plan. We keep it simple. That is how we develop our offense. Thank you.

PASS PROTECTION IN THE FIVE-STEP DROP GAME

Marshall University

When I go to clinics, I like a lot of mini-clinics like this one because you can learn in this setting. If I am searching for something I am interested in, I try to find the best person in the field for that particular phase of the game. I try to set up an appointment and meet with that person. This year, I will visit four or five coaches. These are not only NFL coaches, but also college coaches. Also, I visit high school coaches during the recruiting season. I ask them what they are doing in some area of the game I am interested in. If they work our camp, it is the same thing. I want to know what they are doing. If it is a junior high school coach, I ask them what they are working on. Football is an area where you can always learn. There is a wide scope as far as learning football is concerned. If someone knows something that I do not know about the subject I am working on, I want to know about it.

I took the opportunity to listen to Steve Stripling of the University of Louisville speak here today. If you are coaching the offensive line, you can learn how to coach them better if you know what the defensive line is doing. Steve gave an excellent lecture. It is important for the offensive line coach to know what the defensive players they have to block are being taught. My point is, you must learn from the best because modeling is important. I want to learn how the defense is taught so we can teach our linemen how to block them.

I think it is very important to understand what the speaker is going to talk about. I am going to talk about the five-step drop passing game pass protection. If I were coaching in high school, would I use the five-step drop passing game? You bet I would. There are two reasons why. One reason is because everybody is playing the box game. Steve Stripling started his talk discussing six or seven men in the box. You may have five or six men in the box. You can do the numbers any way you want. The defense is set up to stop the run first with the numbers in the box. The second reason is this: If you have trouble running the ball, it

is your job to get them out of the box. To do that, you must be able to throw the football.

We have a high school coach in the state of West Virginia who won his fifth state championship with the five-step drop passing game. He comes to visit us every year. He uses a lot of what we do in high school. Can you use this system in high school? We think you can. I have used this passing game at the high school level. I have coached at a lot of places. I have visited with a lot of good coaches over the years. I think I have something very good to share with you. You can take it or leave it as you go out the door. But, I have something I believe in. I will make an effort to get it across to you. It is hard to give all of this to you in one hour and 25 minutes. I will try to get this across to you as best I can. I will talk to you just like I would talk to the players I am coaching at Marshall University. That is the way I will approach this lecture.

Last year, statistically, we threw for 4,200 yards in the regular season. We did have an extra game in the MAC. In the GMAC Bowl in Mobile, we threw for 570 yards. In order to do that, the quarterback cannot get sacked, pressured, or hurried. My job is to protect the quarterback so we can throw the ball.

We use the passing game on first down, on long-yardage plays, short-yardage plays, and other situations to mix up the plays. We approach the game with the idea that we are going to run the ball first. We will do that. If you are not going to try to stop the run by numbers in the box, we will run the ball until you do stop us. That is our philosophy.

In the GMAC bowl game, we had 108 plays on offense. How many of you saw the GMAC bowl game? How many of you saw the first half and turned the game off? A lot of others did the same thing. The score at halftime was 38 to 8 in favor of East Carolina. We scored 56 points in the second half. We ran

108 plays and threw the ball 70 times. On 90 percent of the times we threw the ball, it was the five-step drop passing game. I am going to cover the pass protection we use on our passing game scheme.

Steve Stripling talked about the University of Louisville defense leading the nation in sacks with 48. If I gave up 48 sacks, Bob Pruett, the head coach, would fire me. It is the responsibility of the offensive line to pick up the stunts, hot blitzes, and all of those things. In the regular season, our offensive line gave up *eight sacks*. We are very proud of that record.

A lot of that record is due to the fact that the offensive line coach got with the rest of the offensive staff and coordinated the passing game. It is very important, as a line coach, to get with the other coaches, and decide how we want to work out the protection schemes. We must be very involved in the running game. We must meet with the running back coach, the quarterback coach, and the tight end coach. You have to get together with all of the coaches and everyone has to be together as a one set mind. You must be cohesive with the staff. You must visit as a staff in discussing techniques. You need to meet with the coaches on individual techniques.

I went down to visit with Florida State this past month. They want to put in the five-step drop game. I could not teach the Florida State staff by drawing up a play and showing them where everyone goes on the play. I have a playbook that our offensive line uses. How many of you have a bible? I call it my bible. I use the bible for basic fundamentals in life. If I want to find out something about the basic fundamentals of life, I can find it in that bible. We tell our linemen their playbook is their bible. If they want to know something about the passing game we are covering, they have a book. This week, our players are picking up their booklet, getting ready for spring training. They turned it in after the bowl game. We have been working on it all winter, to get ready for the spring. I am going to teach you in the same manner as I teach the players.

When I visited at Florida State, the entire offensive staff was in the meetings. The entire offensive staff must be on the same page. They must understand the terms used in the passing game that will be utilized. They need to know what we are talking about when we talk about buckets, angle buckets, numbers, clusters, timing of the backs, and the entire terminology used with the offense. It is important for the line coach, if you are not the head coach, to understand the total picture of the plays. You must be on the same page.

You may have some questions as I move through the lecture. That happened at Florida State. I told them to be patient. When I put the next overhead on, the questions were answered. We should get to your answer. When I finish, it may be someone asking me to review one of the points.

In a nutshell, I am going to talk to you about the things an offensive lineman has to do fundamentally in the five-step drop passing game. I will try to get it across to you how the coach gets this across to the players to protect the quarterback. First, it is with fundamentals with a coach and the players. We must be able to communicate. As fast as we can, I want everyone in here to raise their right hand on my command. Hut! Good. We communicated. I already knew that you knew which hand was your right hand. If some raised the left hand, we would have a problem. But, everyone here was able to communicate. Football is the same way. To be a coach or a teacher, you must be able to communicate and get all of the players to do the simple things. You must have a system so you can talk to the players. When you leave here, you should be able to say that you know the four major pass rushes by a defense, and you should know how to count them.

Coach Steve Stripling talked about the things he liked to teach in a one-on-one pass drill. I am going to do just the opposite. I am going to show you how to counter the moves the defensive linemen use. This will enable you to have a fewer number of sacks and pressures when you go to throw the football. I have a drill tape that I use to teach the moves to defeat the four basic moves by the defensive lineman. I will show you how to set the drill up so you can work on it in practice. Then, I will show you that the drill applies in the game. What you teach the players in practice, they are going to do in the game.

I learned a lot from Joe Bugel when he was coaching with the Washington Redskins. He had a lot of coaches visit the Redskins because they were winning a lot of games, and they had won a Super Bowl. He asked me to show him what we taught our linemen. He said, "Mark, I have a lot of coaches come in and use the chalkboard to tell me what they teach their linemen. But, when they get the films on the linemen, they are not doing what the coach said they did on the chalkboard." He told me the players are not taking the steps in the game that the coaches said they took.

You are a coach. "Coach" means you are a teacher. If you are a teacher, you must communicate and get your worst players to execute as well as your best players. If I can get the worst player to execute as well as the best player, I am a good teacher. I have five positions that I must work with. I have to rank them one through five. You have your worst one and the best one. That worst player had better be doing what you are teaching the best player to do.

Everything must tie in with what you teach. For example, I will go over one simple thing — line splits. Everyone has a rule. Basically, we teach two-foot splits. Those are horizontal splits. I go one step beyond this and talk about vertical splits. Vertical splits are like this: If you bought a ticket to see us play and you were sitting on the 50 yard line looking down on us on offense, you would see that there is a space between the offensive and defensive line. You can see how our linemen are lined up.

You should know how long the football is if you are a line coach. The center will tilt the ball somewhat. But, the space is still between the two lines. The little space that no one can enter except the center is called the neutral zone. No one can be in that area except the center's hat. No one on offense can have their helmet break the imaginary line of the belt line of the center, or they will be considered in the backfield. If they are lined up with their hat beyond that belt line, they are illegal. I am talking to you to teach you about vertical splits.

We are talking about being *on* or *off* the ball. If we want our line *on* the ball, we are as close to the ball as we can be without being offsides with our fingertips. That is level one for us. If we are *off* the ball, we are as far off the ball as we can be. We have the helmet back toward the center's belt. To us, that is level three. The area between level one and level three is level two.

If I have one lineman who is 6'6" and another lineman who is 6'2", I can't tell those two players to have their feet in the same spot on the center. It has to be the headgear of each player on the center's belt or number. That is the level for them. On some occasions, the guard may be at level one, and the tackle could be on level three. We could have that type of alignment. This is called the spine or line posture to us.

I have what I call a tool bag. I use the tool bag to coach the offensive line. One of my tools is used on line splits. If the defense is rushing us to get us out of position, we want to line up at level three. We want to gain as much time as we can to pick up that defensive lineman or linebacker on the stunt. If I have a slower man, he is deeper to the line. If I have a man who is faster, he is closer to the line.

If we are down on the goal line, we want to line up at level one. If we are in short-yardage situations, we are on level one. If we are running the quarterback sneak, we are on level one. If we want to jump a bull rusher, we get up on level one. There are some tools you can use to help those big linemen who may not have good feet.

Again, as a base, we split our guards two feet, our tackles two feet, and the tight end three feet. On the goal line, we are split two feet. We are on level two for base teaching. When we zone block, we are at level two. We do not want contact on the first step. We want to use the second step down to beat the defensive lineman.

Let me get into the meat of the lecture. I am going to give you the pass protection techniques for the five-step drop passing game.

- Our dropback passes consist mainly of the quarterback taking a five-step drop straight back from the center or in the shotgun.
- The quarterback's depth is seven yards.
- Our job is to give him a pocket where he can set, step up, and throw.
- Our routes are timing routes, and if the quarterback has to move, then the timing is off.
- A "hurry" is just as bad as a sack.
- Take pride in having a perfect pocket every time.

I was from the old school. I used to teach pass protection by telling the line they had two yards wide of real estate and a depth of five yards. We do not teach it that way anymore. We have introduced a new term in our protection. I talk about the "dish" in pass protection for the linemen.

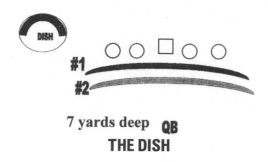

7 yards deep **QB**

THE DISH

- A dish is just what it says: a plate you eat off of.
- In the diagram above, you are looking at the shape of part of the dish.
- The #1 dish is where you take the defender on at contact.
- The #2 dish is two yards behind dish #1. This is where you work a defender if he gets inside of you or outside of you after contact (i.e., a right guard drops his post foot vs. a 3 position, and he has to catch up to him).
- **RULE FOR PASS PROTECTION:** You attempt to work the #1 dish every time, but if you can't, then you cannot get past the #2 dish.

The phrase "work the dish, work the dish" will be used a lot by your coach. This is what he is referring to when he says this.

Now, I can communicate with the offensive line. How do we work the dish? We talk to them in terms of sets. We talk to them about taking a "set." If we are zone blocking, I talk about the first step and then the second step. It does not matter if it is a square zone or an angle zone. I do the same thing in pass protection. You must have a *set* foot and a *post* foot.

Now, we look at the fundamentals and techniques that will help you maintain the dish. We said we must have a set for the linemen. When they are set, they must know where the defender is lining up on them. We said the key to the passing game is protection. The key to protection is the set. This is the way we communicate to our players about the defender who lines up in his area.

SETS - LEFT SIDE - RIGHT SIDE

The diagram on the left side is for a left guard or left tackle. The center is a left guard or tackle, depending on which way he works.

- L-3 = loose 3 position (in the gap to his outside)
- 3 = 3 position (outside shade)
- 2 = 2 position (head up)
- 1 = 1 position (inside shade)
- G-1 = gap 1 position (in the gap to his inside)

The diagram on the right side is for a right guard, or tackle. The center is a right guard or tackle, depending on which way he works.

- L-3 = loose 3 position (in the gap to his outside)
- 3 = 3 position (outside shade)
- 2 = 2 position (head up)
- 1 = 1 position (inside shade)
- G-1 = gap 1 position (in the gap to his inside)
- These are the positions that a defender can line up on the line of scrimmage for a pass rush.
- His position will determine which set you will take in order to best protect the quarterback.
- Sets will change from this theory if you have help.

SET FOOT - LEFT AND RIGHT SIDE

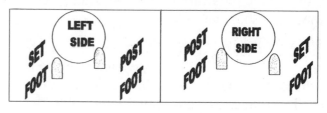

- We use numbers to define our sets.
- Sets will start with the post foot or set foot.
- Sets are determined by what "position" the defender is in.
- Always know if you have "help" (i.e., another blocker or body presence or not).

BASIC SETS, 2-SET

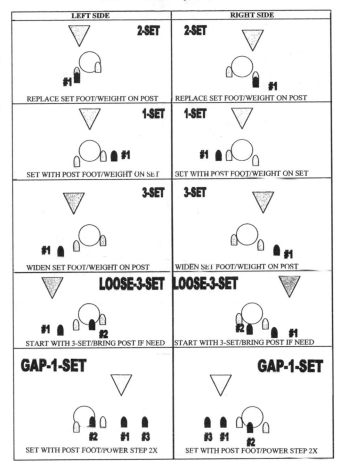

TACKLE SETS

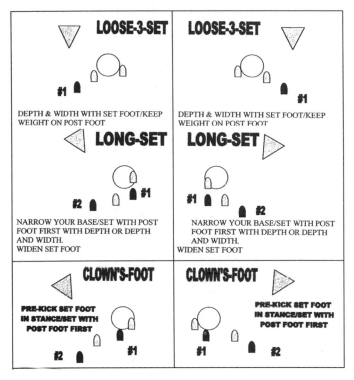

A clown's foot is a player who feels comfortable versus a long set. It is a pre-kick, and they lose the 3-set. You will see this on the film.

Now, I have a tool bag. I can communicate to them where the dish is, tell them what level to get on. I know their stance, and I can communicate post foot or set foot. I can communicate with them in working in practice. I can tell them how I want them to start the drill or the play in practice. I must be able to communicate with them somehow. This is the best method of communicating for me. You may call it something else. I researched the situation, and this is the best for me.

If we use play-action protection, we call it a jump set. A jump set involves the following actions:

- Use an angle-bucket with the set foot.
- Advance at the same angle with the post foot.
- Bring the set foot again and get under control.

JUMP SET

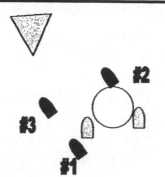
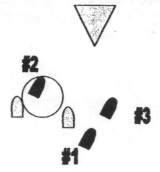

> ➤ USE AN **ANGLE-BUCKET** WITH THE SET FOOT
> ➤ ADVANCE AT THE SAME ANGLE WITH THE POST FOOT
> ➤ BRING THE SET FOOT AGAIN AND GET UNDER CONTROL

> ➤ USE AN **ANGLE-BUCKET** WITH THE SET FOOT
> ➤ ADVANCE AT THE SAME ANGLE WITH THE POST FOOT
> ➤ BRING THE SET FOOT AGAIN AND GET UNDER CONTROL

SPIDER SET

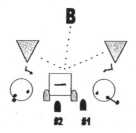

GUARD AND TACKLE SPIDER SETS

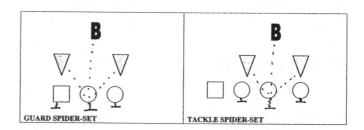

A spider set can be used by the center, guard, or tackle. He is uncovered. A spider set involves the following actions:

- The left guard takes a 2-set.
- The right guard takes a 3-set.
- The center sets off the ball with depth, starting with the foot that will put him in the midpoint between the guards.
- This invites the two down defenders to rush inside where the center now can help. All three eye the linebacker to bump off a dog.
- The center also looks for the T-T twist.

Spider sets are also used by guards and tackles when they are uncovered and have the linebacker over them. The same set is used.

We have dual-read sets. A dual-read set is similar to the spider set. The uncovered man must read two defenders. We use terms with these sets to indicate what we want them to do. We call Polly for the center, Molly for the guard, and Trolly for the tackle. It tells the man to check the linebacker and then to check outside. He may or may not do that. We may just get a piece of the man, but that is all we need to keep him from getting the quarterback.

Then, we use tandem sets. We may have three offensive men responsible for two down linemen and a linebacker on defense. The three blockers watch for any games coming from the three defenders.

TANDEM SETS

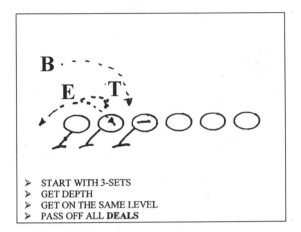

➤ START WITH 3-SETS
➤ GET DEPTH
➤ GET ON THE SAME LEVEL
➤ PASS OFF ALL **DEALS**

The three blockers start with 3-sets. They must get depth. We want them to get off on the same level. They pass off all deals by the defenders.

We use the term *sifting* to describe safety blitzes. We get all kinds of blitzes in the A gap by defenders trying to get to our quarterback. We check for those stunts and pick those up by the linemen. The key is to get the head up and get it out of the defender and look for those blitzing secondary men.

You must have rules to handle zone blitzes. We call them "zone fires." Again, the key is to look for the stunts. We talk about three zone blitzes. We set to block and look for the blitz.

Let me get into the fundamentals and techniques of blocking in pass protection. We said the key to the passing game is protection. The key to protection is the set. Now that we have gone over the various sets, we must cover the techniques once the proper set has been taken. This is the tool that I teach all of the time. *What is a target?* If you are going to make a successful block, you must have a pre-snap bull's-eye target. It is one of the most critical points of pass blocking.

The following guidelines apply concerning targeting:

- On the dropback pass protection, you must have a "target" on the defender you are blocking.
- The target will tell you the direction he is always going.
- Most linemen get beat by watching the defender's head, and they get faked out.
- In the diagram illustrating the bull's-eye target, the inside tip of the number 5 would be the target for a right guard who has a defender in a 3 position, or it could be a right tackle who is blocking a defensive end.
- You must know the defender's jersey number and have a target pre-snap.
- A left guard or left tackle would use the inside tip of the number 7.
- The center uses the same target concept on his defender.

Here are the coaching points. The target (bull's-eye) is one of the most critical fundamentals of pass blocking. Here is a tip. The faster the athlete is, the tighter the target. The slower the athlete, the wider the target. Look at your target when you are in your stance. It is hard to get a target if you are looking straight ahead in your stance and have to find the target on your set.

Next, we look at the invisible line. There is a line that represents the closest path for the defender to get to the quarterback on a dropback pass. The objective of the offensive linemen is to take a proper pass set that will have you straddle this line. You must get to this set point as fast as you can. Setting on this line will allow you to dictate to the defender that he has a limited pass rush.

BULL'S-EYE TARGET

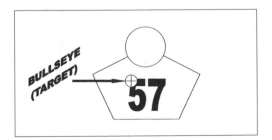

THE INVISIBLE LINE

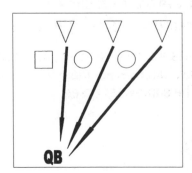

- You must know your line pre-snap. Take the proper set that allows you to straddle the line.
- As a rule, your outside knee should be in the defender's crotch.
- Your shoulders should be square to the line of scrimmage when you straddle the line.
- You must get depth and width to get to the line.

Here are the coaching points. There are generally two mistakes that all linemen make dealing with the line. First, they turn their body and shoulders to the sideline on the set. Subconsciously, they think they can block them better this way. Second, they lean into the set, thinking that this will get them to the line faster. In reality, it makes it easier for the defender to come underneath.

Now that we have covered set and the line, we must talk about your pass posture. It is just like teaching the power play. You must have proper posture. Let me show you what we mean by pass-blocking posture. These points are critical.

PASS-BLOCKING POSTURE

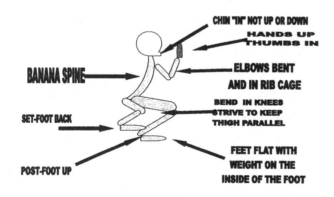

You must keep the chin in as you roll to the target. We all know what a banana is. That is what we want. You will get some players that God built just the opposite of what we want. They may be humpbacked. We have to teach them to power-cling to a banana spine. That is what we are talking about for power and pass blocking. We talk about the elbows being bent when we set. You must have a bend in the knees. The feet must be set flat with the weight on the inside of the foot. We always want to keep our stagger. That is what you have to teach for power. You must have power to pass block. This is what I teach over and over.

When the defender gives us his chest, we are going to take it. The jersey is made so the numbers will be on his chest. We want our thumbs up, and we take on the defender. When we take the chest, it is over for that defender. The important part of the block is the jam to the chest. It is the punch or the jam. You can call it what you want. They have to learn how to jam the man and lock out.

PUNCH OR JAM

WHEN THE HANDS GRAB THE "ARMPITS" OR PUNCH THE "SHOULDER," THE ELBOW JOINT SHOULD BE IN A 1/4 LOCKOUT POSITION

- You have maximum power in the punch at the one-fourth lockout position.
- You have to time the jam. It can only be done through repetitions.
- You have your strongest bench press the last one-fourth of your lift.
- This also keeps the defender off you. So, you can see your target and look for dogs, freaks, zone fires, and twist.

When I finish with that section, I give the players a quiz. At the end of the playbook, they have a copy of the quiz. We call it our "Pass Pro Time-Out Quiz." Now, I realize those players do not carry that playbook to class with them, and I know they do not look at it all the time. This is what I tell them. If they are used to taking a magazine to read while they are in the bathroom, I want them to substitute the playbook for that magazine. That is when I want them to read that playbook. They will tell me, "Coach, I read the playbook this morning when I went to the bathroom." So, I know this works. I want them to be ready to take that quiz.

This is just a sample of what we have on the quiz. We go on and on with questions that make them aware of their assignments and the techniques they must use to be an effective pass protector.

Most defenders rise up out of their stance when they pass rush and, in doing so, they will give you their chest. When that happens, we want to take the chest every time.

TAKING THE CHEST

Taking the chest involves the following factors:

- After taking your set, shoot the hands for the armpits.
- Time the jam with the one-fourth lockout.
- Keep the thumbs in and grab cloth.
- The only place where there is loose cloth on a game jersey is right in the armpits so a player is able to raise his arms.
- Squeeze the hands and grab cloth, locking out as you do.
- This will enable you to control the defender wherever he goes, and you can also control all of his moves, such as "spinning."
- If you miss the grab, you can re-punch.

When a defender does not give you his chest, then he will come at you turning his shoulders. When he does this, you must treat him like he is a cylinder. You can now place one or two hands on his shoulder. With him coming at you with a shoulder, that means he plans on using several moves. We must be alert for these moves when we get the shoulder: hand smack on your hands to knock them down, rip, and swim.

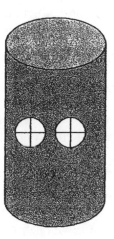

Let me cover the different rushes. The first rush we see is the bull rush. The defender can bull rush us and get the blocker off balance. So, we have a counter to the bull rush.

Bull rush— When the defender runs through you, attempting to knock you back to the quarterback (to disrupt his timing or flush him from the pocket), if you can take him on with your jam and keep your head out, that is great. Most of the time, it does not happen that way. You will most likely get your head into him. Get it out as soon as you can.

Hop-hop— Drop both feet back at the same time. This will slow his hop-hop.

Hop-hop-drive— When a defender bull rushes you and you slow him down or stop him, his next move will be to grab you and pull you forward. To counter his move, use the hop-hop-drive technique. As you feel the defender pull you forward after you have used the hop-hop, then counter it by going with him. You will use a drive technique by widening your feet and following him in the pull direction. As you follow him with a wide base, make sure you are under control and grab him with your hands.

Spinner — One of the moves a defender will use when he gives you a shoulder is the spin move. He will generally give you a quick bull move and spin to one side or the other. To counter the spin, use your hands as though you were rolling a barrel. Roll him in the direction he is spinning, while placing your hands on his shoulder. You may have to give ground and match him in the direction he is spinning. His objective is to get by your shoulders on the initial spin so you end up trailing him.

Rip — The defender grabs one of your shoulders and rips underneath to the opposite shoulder. When the defender lowers his shoulder to rip, then punch him forcefully on the rip shoulder. Follow him in that direction. Keep your base as you match him.

Swim — Another move is for the defender to grab one of your shoulders and swim his other arm over the top of that same shoulder. When the defender's arm is in the air on the swim, shoot your hand for his armpit. When your hand gets to the armpit, grab all of the hair in his armpit. Press and bring your body with you in the direction of his armpit. This will knock him to the ground.

KICK-SLIDE

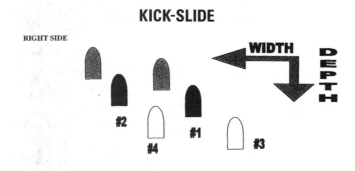

A kick-slide is the movement you make when going to your set-foot side (your outside). There are two kinds of kick slides: one, when you are setting to the defender, and two, when you have engaged with the defender.

- When you kick, you get width and depth, keeping the toe and knee straight to the line of scrimmage.

- When you slide, you keep most of your weight on your post leg, which will keep you from leaning to the outside and better prepare you for an inside move.

- The second kick and slide (#3 and #4) distance depends on your target. You kick-slide if the

target gets wider. You are trying to gain width and depth.

- If your target comes toward you, you settle with a shorter kick-slide.

Here is a coaching point. Adjust your kick-slide to the side of the original alignment of the defender (the imaginary line), and to his path to the quarterback.

The kick-slide when engaged is the next point we must look at. We must teach the linemen how to react now that we have the defender engaged.

KICK-SLIDE WHEN ENGAGED

You are a right-handed stance player, and you have jammed your defender. He has worked to your outside. The following points apply:

- You will be using a kick-slide step, but you will be forcing power with your set foot and outside arm.

- You will gain some width and depth. As you do so, you are not concentrating on slowing the defender down when he rushes to your outside.

- This is different than the kick-slide used for setting on a line.

The power steps are used when a defender is rushing to your inside (i.e., the post-foot side). You take lateral steps with the post foot to the inside, attempting to step on an imaginary line. You force the post foot over and up as you force with your inside arm.

The coaching point is this: Once you keep the defender on the dish to your inside, he has no choice but to try to spin to your outside. You counter this by either grabbing his jersey with your inside hand, or rolling the barrel while giving some ground to the outside.

POWER STEP

I will now review the dropback protection techniques. Let me list them for you:

- Take a pre-snap look.
- Work your stance (weight shift).
- Look at your target.
- Take the proper set quickly.
- Time your jam.
- Take the chest or place your hands on his shoulder.
- Keep your head out.
- Power-kick-slide to the outside.
- Power-step to the inside.
- Work the dish or second dish.
- Counter all moves.

The hand slapper — You have a defender who likes to knock your hands down when you take your set and start to throw your jam. First, use your outside hand only. Second, jab it forward just one inch and bring it back. The defender will react immediately to the short jab and smack at the hand that took the short jab. He will miss (if you keep the jab short and quick). When he misses, then take the chest. This works every time.

Now that we have covered the dropback fundamentals, we must cover what we are looking for when we get our head out of the defender. We look for the following: twists (like stunts); dogs (linebackers shooting gaps); blitzes (defensive backs shooting gaps); combos (line stunts plus dogs plus blitzes); and fire zones.

The following factors give away twists and the man who penetrates (he goes first) and who the looper is (he goes second).

- Take a pre-snap look.
- Many defensive linemen change up their stagger when they are going to stunt or twist. The foot that is staggered back usually tells the direction he is going. He will go to the back-foot side.
- The two adjacent defensive linemen will work different levels. One will be deeper than the other.
- Sometimes, they will give it away with their calls.
- Some defensive tackles only twist when they get in a loose 3 position on the guard.
- Some defensive ends only run an E-T twist when they get in a 3 position on the tackle.

Always take a pre-snap look. Communicate to your buddy.

TRAPPING THE TWIST

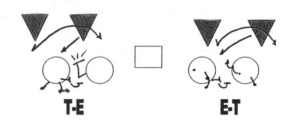

Left Guard: "Snap" the DT	Right Guard: "Trap" the DE
Left Tackle: "Trap" the DT	Right Tackle: "Press" the DE

Here are our rules for trapping the twist. The guard must snap the defensive tackle on a T-E in order to help the tackle from being picked. The trapper must get his head in front of the man penetrating and knock the "dog stew" out of him. He must immediately square up on him. The tackle on an E-T must power-step up into the man penetrating to help the guard. You must do this to avoid getting on different levels and getting picked.

TECHNIQUE VS. THE LOOPER

LEFT SIDE

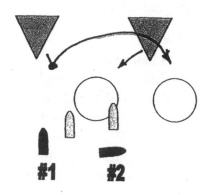

#1   #2

Take your normal set (leaving your weight on your post foot). When you see the looper, follow him with your head, drop your post foot, and air your foot to get your head in front of him. Follow up with your set foot and knock the "dog stew" out of him. Once you trap him with your head in front, square up immediately and get your head out. Getting your head out will allow you to look for a super twist or a linebacker dog coming off the edge.

When you recognize the twist, then verbally communicate to your buddy by yelling "switch, switch." He will now know to expect the twist stunt.

MAN BLOCKING THE TWIST

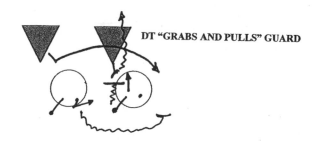

DT "GRABS AND PULLS" GUARD

This seldom happens in a game. But it might, with us using the hop-hop-drive technique against pullers. It happens more in a 2-on-2 drill against our defense.

Centers: Take warning of this twist. This is a twist stunt. It can hurt you.

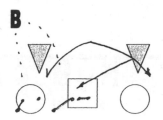

Your assignment calls for you to set to your left with the guard. You are concentrating on the linebacker. The defensive tackle from your right rams you right in the ribs to execute a T-T twist. Coaching point: Keep your head on a swivel. Look, look, look."

Here is the super twist. This is why you must get your head up and *look*.

SUPER TWIST

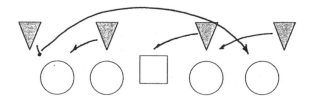

ALIGNMENT

Let me cover the linebacker blitz. For communication purposes, we talk about linebackers dogging in a gap. These are the gaps they can come through. We could also refer to strong A, B, C, and D gaps, and weak A, B, C, and D gaps by formation strength.

With a four-down and three-linebacker defense, we refer to the linebackers with the following names:

S = Sam — the linebacker to the strongside.
M = Mike — the linebacker to the middle.
W = Will — the linebacker to the weakside.

The following dogs are illustrated below:

Sam strong - B
Mike strong - A
Will weak - B

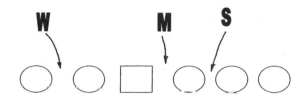

In a three-down and four-linebacker defense, we have Sam linebacker strong, Mike linebacker strong, PEG linebacker weak, and Will linebacker weak.

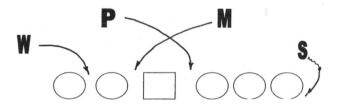

DEFENSE STEMS FROM A FOUR-DOWN DEFENSE TO A THREE-DOWN DEFENSE

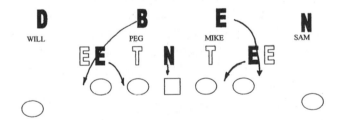

We will still have the same names for the four linebackers even though one is a nickel back, one a dime back, and one a defensive end.

This would be a combo (line stunts and dogs combined). For the most part in pass protection, the quarterback will identify who we will treat as the Mike linebacker anyway. But for communication purposes, like in the running game, we will use these names.

You block linebackers the same way you block down linemen with regard to techniques. You may have to lead with the head on a linebacker who is charging from four or five yards depth, but again, you must get your head out of there to look. You may have to keep switching even after you pick up your linebacker. The key is to look, look, look!

THREE-STEP DROP TECHNIQUE

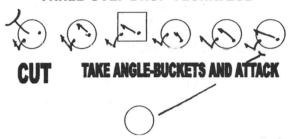

The quarterback takes three steps. This is a gap protection. Your technique is an aggressive technique. You attack the defender who shows or ends up in your gap. You break down into a pass-pro posture after making contact with the defender. The lineman blocking the end man on the line of scrimmage cuts his man. All other linemen can cut, but there are many dogs, combos, etc. with this protection when we check to it. It is used a lot against the blitz look.

This is how we would block on sprint protection.

SPRINT PROTECTION TECHNIQUE

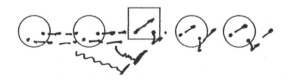

The backside guard and tackle take gap-1 sets and backpedal. They are making a swinging gate. They must be on the same plane. The center and frontside use the jump technique. They must check the backside.

THE WING-T JET-SWEEP SERIES

Cumberland University

I look at being on the clinic last in two ways. First, they have saved the best until the last. Second, if you have a speaker talking about the wing-T at 12 midnight the wing-T coaches will be there. It is like a religion to them. I think I have some information that will help your offense. We call it the jet series. It is the best thing we do on offense. If you are not running this series I think you are missing the boat. Over half of our offense now is out of the jet-sweep series.

I have a book that I sell for $20. I do not want to make a lot of money on the book because it will put me in a higher income bracket. I am the only college coach that is on Social Security, and I have to be careful how much money I make. I am going to send a copy of my 500-page book to each of the teams we play next year. If that does not screw them up, nothing will. We play in the Mid-South Conference, which is really good football.

I will cover a few other things before I get into the jet series. We are a multiple formation wing-T team. We use all of the formations you can imagine. We have 12 ways we can unbalance and not have to do a lot of teaching. When we get in different formations, we get the numbers and we get mismatches. We want to create the "Oh S_ _ _" syndrome. This means we are going to give you so much bull s _ _ _ you are going to throw up your hands and say the hell with it and switch to another defense. The more formations we use the more the defense has to adjust. The better the defensive coaching staff is we face, the better our offense works.

Let me give you our philosophy on the offensive game plan. If you do something different, you are not sure what you will see. Years ago I was a single wing coach. I ran the single wing in the 1970s. I used to run the single wing from an unbalanced line. I was never sure what defense I would see. We are in the same scenario now. We are never sure what we are going to see on defense. For us to script the first 15 plays of the game, it is not the thing to do.

We have two coaches that work with the offense during the game. I have one coach up in the press box. I can tell what is happening from the tackle outside. From the tackle to the inside it is hard to determine what is going on. What we do is this. We base our offense to run outside first and inside second.

I do not want to run inside just to be on your highlight tape. I know what I will see. I can tell what is happening on the outside. We want to have a reverse play off each play that we run. We have a misdirection play off everything we do. The buck series to me is not misdirection. After the fullback hits up the middle, everything is going in the same direction. To me that is not misdirection. Our buck series is the offense that we are having the least success with now. The best offensive series we run is the jet-sweep series. We run all options. We are not a great option team. But if you do not defend the option we can run it good enough to hurt the defense. The first series is the belly series. It has always been a reliable play. The next series is our buck sweep.

To run the buck sweep, you sort of have to nail people on the blocks. You can run the jet sweep and get three or four blocks and then run away from the rest of the defense. Then you have a chance. That is what we do.

The lost art in football is *deception*. How do you get your backs to fake? I will tell you how. You make them fake. We have a drill where we have everyone faking on the play. If only one back does not carry out his fake, we punish everyone in the drill. If they do not carry out the fakes in this drill, they stay and run the fakes after practice. Backs will only fake if you make them do it. If you punish everyone in the drill they get the point.

The worst player on carrying out his fake is the quarterback. He wants to turn and look at the running back after he hands the ball off on the jet sweep. The quarterback must carry out his fake to the outside. There is a team out on the West Coast that runs what they call the fly offense. They are the best faking team I have seen.

We are going to do a lot of things good on offense, but nothing great. If our players are better than your players, we do not have to do much. But if we are even in talent and it comes down to the nut-cutting time, the jet sweep and option is our best offensive attack.

First, I want to show you how we call our blocks at the line of scrimmage. This will help you understand what we are doing. I have studied the wing-T people and picked out the things I like best. We have done this for years. It is the best thing we are doing. It is how we call our blocks. All of our blocking calls are in by the first game. They never change. We are not a big check-off team. If we call something, we are going to run it most of the time.

Here is our blocking scheme. We letter the linemen that pull on plays. We can trap any defensive man that lines up on the line of scrimmage, regardless of where he lines up. If he is a down lineman, we can trap him. Now, if we are playing another team that never runs a trap, it thrills me to death. I watch some teams that line up the defensive linemen and turn them loose hell-bent for leather toward the quarterback. If they do that against us, we are going to trap their butt. We do not see too much upfield stuff like we used to see. We see the defenses that sit back and read. They have two choices. They can be blocked, or they can watch the backs. If they watch our backs they are screwed.

We never want to pull the same people. Some teams will say they are going to key the guard. That is bull. We never pull the guard on a misdirection play. We always pull someone else. We pull the tackle and tight end. We pull the tackle, the guard, center, and the tight end on all of our plays. We teach them all the same techniques.

Here is how we call our blocks. Again, we letter the people that pull. We take the onside with the tight end. If we are going to pull the *right guard* or onside guard, he is lettered with a *G.* If we pull the *onside tackle,* he is lettered with a *T.* If we pull the *tight end,* he is an *E.* If we pull the *tackle and the guard,* we call it *TAG.* If we pull the *end and tackle,* it is called *EAT.*

If we pull the backside players, we use different letters. We use W, X, Y, and Z. If we pull the backside tackle, it is called W. The backside guard is called X. The Z block is our counter tray block. We can pull two men from either side of the line. On the Y block our fullback or some other back blocks out at the hole. If we pull the frontside guard and backside guard, it is a G-X block. It is a G block on the frontside and an X block on the backside. If I want the fullback to block out at the hole, and pull the backside guard, we call it Y-X. If something is in front of your letter, you do not block out at the hole, you block through the hole. We have done this for years.

We can change our blocking at the half. We can call our blocks at the line of scrimmage. The defense does not know what we are calling. They know what trap it is, but they do not know who is going to do the trapping.

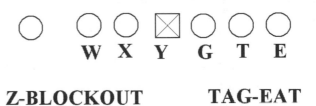

Z-BLOCKOUT   **TAG-EAT**

Here is something we do that I really like. I show this to other coaches, and they do not like it as much as I do. If we want the guard to block on a 1-, 2-, or 3-technique, we letter the man A. Instead of telling him to block 1, 2, or 3, we tell him to block A. That is anyone that is covering him in the 1, 2, or 3 position. If there is not an A-defender he blocks the linebacker. We tell the tackle to block the man from the tackle outside as B. In our pass protection, our guard blocks A, and the tackle blocks B. That is how we teach it, and we think it is simple. Anyone over the center is an 8 to us. That means a 0-technique or a shade technique. The rule for our guard on the inside veer is to block A to 8. It is easy to communicate. We have been doing these things for years.

Next is our line splits. We never split the same. We do have a base split. Our base split is two feet, two feet, and three feet. However, sometimes we split one foot. If we are going to run the midline veer, we split three feet. It is never the same. Our best inside play is our midline veer against a 3-technique. We over-split on the midline play.

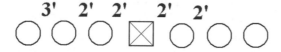

I want to go over our snap count. I will show you what we used to do, and then go over what we changed it to. We used to call out "Red-Set-Go." That was the traditional first sound. What we are working on this spring is this: "Set-Number-Set-Go." That is what we call "short go." Why do we call this short go? I did it because we have always done it that way. There is nothing short about it. It is simple. "Set-88-Set-Go." I left the second "set" in the count because the linemen said it helped them to get off on the count. That is the short go.

The long count is this. "Set-88-Set-Go-Go." That is our snap count. Our jet series is better for us if we go on the first sound. The quarterback lifts his heel and turns and watches the back coming toward him. "Set-88-Set-Go." The quarterback calls it on first sound, and the running back goes on the lift of the heel. This is how we teach it. We tell the quarterback to turn and watch the back coming toward him. Every quarterback wants to snap the ball too early. I had one quarterback that played for us three years. If I did not stay on him he would call the count early every time. He did that because he could hand off better. All the pressure is on the quarterback on the play. We tell the wingback to haul ass when the quarterback raises his heel. It is the job of the quarterback to get him the ball. If there is a fumble it is the fault of the quarterback.

We have two exchanges for the quarterback. If we are going backwards, we want the hands down. If we are going into the line, we do not care how the hands are positioned. We ask the running back to place his hands down on his stomach. We get the bubbles when the back starts reaching for the football on the handoff. We do not think you can take the ball in the arms on the handoff. We want them to take the ball with the open hands down.

I want to go over the quarterback's techniques on the jet sweep. If the midline is to the right of the center and the quarterback hands the ball off on the midline, I think it is too slow. This play is big in Georgia and Tennessee. We want the quarterback to pivot on the backside foot as fast as he can and not move that backside foot. We want the quarterback with his back to the line of scrimmage in the A gap. We want him off that midline. We want to hand the ball off as close to the midline as possible or just a little on the outside of the midline.

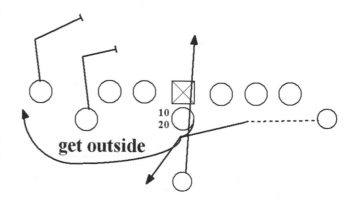

The ball disappears for just a second. We cannot hide the ball forever. We want the quarterback to snap the ball when the man in motion gets to the outside leg of the right guard. When the back passes the tackle line and enters the A gap, we want the ball snapped. We want the quarterback to take the snap and pivot all the way around before he hands the ball off. The running back is what we call "one big step" away from the quarterback on the handoff. The quarterback pivots away from the motion back.

We tell our quarterback this. If he can't get the ball to the back in motion he is to give the ball to the fullback. This alerts the fullback that he may get the ball even if we have called the play to go outside.

The fullback has the midline. He goes right up the midline. The quarterback is getting off the midline away from the direction the fullback is running. I tell the fullback if the quarterback is not off the midline, to run over him. The fullback goes over the midline, and the quarterback pivots off the midline. There is no daylight between the fullback and quarterback. The faker becomes a blocker in that the defense must respect the fake. If the fullback fakes on the play and no one hits him he automatically becomes a blocker on the backside linebacker. This is not a fumble play. It is a safe play for us.

This is how I look at the play. When you were a small kid, you learned to ride a bicycle. You tried to ride the bike and you fell down. You got up and tried it again. You get up and try it again and the first thing you know you can ride the bicycle. That is how this play is. It looks bad, looks bad, looks bad, and then all of a sudden they get the play right. We work on the play every day in practice. You have to work on it every day. We may work five minutes or 10 minutes on the play every day. If we have a group period we run the jet series. If it's the outside plays we are working on we work on the jet series.

This is what we teach the backs. When the back gets the ball — let me have that football. This ball reminds me of something else. See, I am in great shape other than no cartilage in my knees, two cataracts, two hearing aids, and a dead bird that is having a hard time getting out of its nest. Other than those problems I will live forever.

When the back gets the ball, we want him to have it covered when he comes out of the exchange with the quarterback. We want the back to take the ball on the exchange and cover the ball with the top of the arm. We want him to keep the ball there for two or three steps. We are not coaching this because we know that some things just happen. We tell the back to lose about a yard when he gets the ball on the exchange. Sometimes he may lose two yards. Sometimes he will not lose any yards. I do not want to screw them up by telling them what to do on this technique. It depends on the penetration by the defense. We just tell the back to lose a little ground when he gets the handoff.

Here is the secret on the play. I learned this the hard way. We tell the back we want him to take that ball and go to the hash mark, then to the numbers, and then to the sideline. We tell him not to cut the ball back inside unless he has to. If he does cut back inside, we want him to get back outside as soon as he can. Now, why do we want him to do that? We are not blocking the people on the backside. We want him to get his butt outside. We do have some exceptions when he cut back against the grain and scored. But we want him to get outside away from the defense.

This is what I hear at clinics. "I do not have any fast backs to get outside on that play." My answer is this. "Who is the fastest? The man in the starting blocks, or the man that has a running start?" We know the man that has a running start is faster.

Let me show you how we number the defense on the play. We number the defense from the tackle outside. On the defenders' inside, we harass them. That means we just try to get in their way. We run the play from a number of formations. We had to have a blocking scheme that covered everything. We cannot line up and run it just one way. If we got in that double wing with a split end and ran the ball to the split end, we could run the ball on some plays but not on all plays. We have numbers to describe blocking on all plays. How do we number the defense? If we are running a play to the split-end side, we number from the tackle to the outside. We do not number past the number four. If we go to anything past four, it screws our guys up.

G-STRETCH

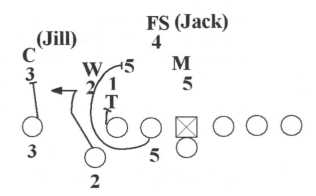

The first man inside is number 1. That is the tackle. The next man outside the tackle is number 2. The next man outside is number 3. Whoever is in the middle of the field is the number 4 man. The linebacker in the middle is number 5. Our players can understand this. We used to call this cloud and sky and all of that stuff. That did not mean much to them.

We call the defensive man on the deep outside level Jill. The deep man in the middle is Jack. If Jack is on a sky, we say that Jack is coming. If he is not coming, we call it Jack - off. If Jack is coming, then the deep man is Jill. We all know if Jack is coming, then Jill is on top. That is the rotation of the backs. The players understand this. If Jack is coming and Jill is on top, we have pass plays to take care of that situation. If Jack is coming and Jill stays deep outside, we have a good play. The tackle blocks number 1. The wingback blocks number 2. We call that G-stretch. It tells our wingback to block the number 2 man. The split end blocks number 3. If the middle linebacker sits inside and looks at the play, he ends up chasing the play if you keep the play outside. He will not make the tackles. If the Mike linebacker goes on the snap with the back, it becomes a foot race. He has a chance to get the back. We want the guard to pull and turn up on the first daylight he sees. As he turns up, he looks inside. He looks for the first opposite jersey to show. If the first man is the linebacker, then that is whom he blocks. The defense has us outnumbered. We have four blockers, and the defense has five players. I have to outrun someone. That is why we call the play the speed sweep.

We do not want penetration at the defensive tackle position. If the 4-technique or 5-technique penetrates our pulling guard, he will have to run the bubble, and he will not have a chance to get the man inside. At times, if we do not get the guard outside, we still can have a decent play. We coach our offensive tackle to cut the defensive man on the line.

We tell our tackle to rip through a defensive 5-technique. If the defensive man goes inside, we let him go. We are going outside. He will not make the play by going inside. I can prove this on tapes. We may not block a single defender and still make six yards. That is a darn good play. It is a play you can run and not be very good on blocking.

We do not want the man the tackle is blocking to penetrate. If he does penetrate it is not the end of the world for the play. It means the pulling guard has a hard time getting out making his block. This is what we have learned by trial and error. When the tackle pulls, he wants to look inside as soon as possible. You look at pulling linemen. Some of them pull and never look inside. They look toward the sideline. We want him to look inside. Football players must use their eyes. When we run a handoff drill we say hand off with your eyes. That means he looks the ball into the pocket. We want the pulling tackle to use his eyes and look inside and pick out the defender that is coming. That is our G-stretch.

We want our slot man to hook the number 2 man. If he can't hook the man, we tell him to trip him. He is what we call a hooker. We teach the hooker block to everyone on our team. What does a hooker do? She uses her tail, right. That is what blocks people. We want the blocker to get into the defender, and then we want him to work his tail around the defender and hook him. If he can do that, he has him. That is the hooker block. We like the block so much, we teach it to everyone. When the blocker fits into the defender, he works his tail around the man. We teach this block on the sleds. If the 5-technique tackle is stretching, we want our tackle to cut him.

What happens when the defense plays an eight-man front? They take the second man and put him outside. We tell the tackle to try to hook number 1. Anytime the second man is on the line of scrimmage, the slot man has to block him. If the defense sends both number 4 and 5, we have to outrun one of them. It is an open-field tackle and we have to beat one man.

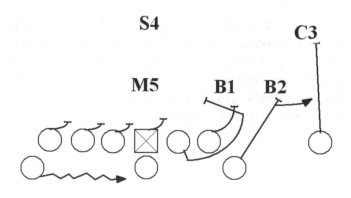

150

We do not need to block anyone back inside. Delaware does not even block the man over the guard. We tell the pulling guard if the defender gets on his train, he cuts him. If the defender goes behind the pulling guard, he lets him go because he will not make the play. We never block anyone coming off the blocker's tail. If he crosses the blocker's face, he cuts him.

What we really like to do on the play is to pull the tackle. If we see a 50-look, we run the tackle stretch. It tells the wingback the tackle is stretching on the outside. This helps the wingback with his block. He knows whom the tackle is blocking. I had one wingback that was so dumb he thought Moby Dick was a venereal disease. This lets the wingback know that he has the number 2 man, and the tackle is stretching outside. The guard has number 1, the wingback has number 2, and the tackle runs his stretch block.

TACKLE STRETCH

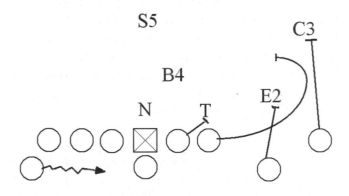

The guard had the tackle on the line of scrimmage. Does he have to block him with a clean block? Absolutely not! He just has to get into his way. That is our tackle stretch.

Now we want to run the play with our fullback offset to the playside. We bring the wideout down inside and seal inside and send the fullback outside and kick the outside man out. It is called our K-G for kick-out block. The fullback is kicking out and the guard is pulling on the stretch.

K - G STRETCH

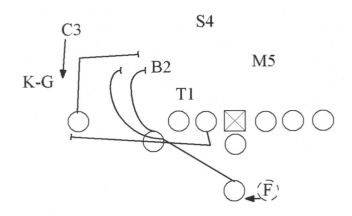

Against the 4-3 defense this is how it looks. If you have a play and you only block it one way, I do not think you have much. We like to block a play a lot of different ways. I am going to throw them all at you. We run the plays from a lot of different formations. If you stop the play one way, we will run it another way. We are going to find a way to run the play successfully.

How many times have you asked the question why a play did not work? You look at the tapes and you see that it did not work because of something you did and not because of something the defense did. Why did the play not work? It may have been because someone missed a block.

There is a coach in Nashville that runs the trap play better than any one play I have ever seen. I went to talk with him to find out why he was so successful on the play. This is what he told me when I asked him why they were so successful on the play. He said, "We run the play over and over until we get it right." How many times have you run a play and because it was not successful the first time, you quit running the play? Do you not know what they call that? They call it "sorry coaching." Why did the play not go? On this play, I can see outside and I know what is going on. If the coach is in the press box, he can tell you why the play did not work.

TAG DOWN VS. 4-3

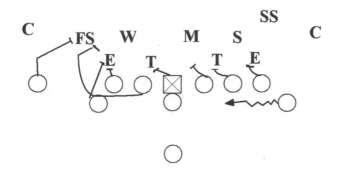

FORMATION - HAT ON HAT

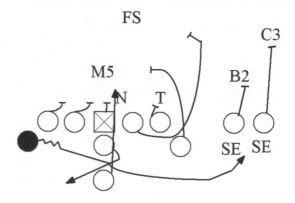

We see a lot of 4-3 defenses. Not many teams play both guards in 3-techniques. Jim Kennedy did that, and he was the best coach I ever knew. What we see is a 3-technique to the tight-end side, and a 1-technique to the split-end side. We put the tight end on the wing side to make you put the 3-technique on that side. The midline is a good play for us. We run the midline veer to the 3-technique and the inside veer to the 1-technique. If we get into two tight ends, I do not know how the defense will line up with the inside defenders.

If we call "down," we are going to block down on the defense. We may cut back. We would call the play "jet 21 - tag down." The 21 is the back and the hole. That is all our line listens for. The tackle blocks number 1. The slot blocks down on the inside. The guard pulls and tries to turn up and get the number 4 man.

Now I am going to get into a formation where I can get a hat on a hat. I can block everyone then. If we can get a hat on every hat then we have a play. If you are not using formations to gain advantages, you are missing the boat. It is not hard to teach. The more formations you use, the more the defense has to look at you. The better the coaching staff, the more they worry about it. If you get some coach that does not know what is going on, he doesn't have a clue what he is going to do.

Here is one of the formations we use. We take both split ends and put them on the same side. Now I outnumber the defense. I do not care what the defense is. I have them where I want them. I have as many men to block as they have defenders. We name everyone. The defender that covers the flat is the cover-down man. If you have a 3-deep corner, he is deep. We call him a Dick. On the outside we have two blockers to block two defenders.

We have a call here where the slot man blocks down inside on the linebacker. We have the second inside man block the number 2 man, and the slot man blocks down inside on the linebacker. We know the inside end is not an eligible pass receiver. We know that. Now, the defensive coaches also know this. But the darn outside linebacker does not know this. They will line up on them and cover them every time. I know how to make him eligible. The defense had better cover him. The slot looks outside and tells the inside end to take the number 2 man, and he will take the number 5 man. If the defense forces the back to cut the play back, he will, but he wants to get to the fence.

Here is the same play from our double-eagle right. Double means two. I know that because I looked it up in the dictionary. We call it "jet-22-G-stretch." The fullback can run the 1 or 2 traps now. He can fake the trap on one side or the option on the other side of the center. The quarterback can fake the trap, isolation, or the option play. The quarterback tells the fullback what play to fake.

DOUBLE EAGLE - G-STRETCH

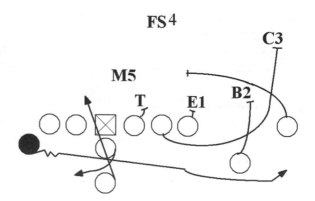

Now we have changed the eligible receivers on the line of scrimmage. If we want the slot up on the line, we would call it white eagle. If we move the other back and the slot moves up, we call it black eagle. Now we know we are limited on the backside.

If we look over on the strongside and see we do not have a good play, we can check off and run a play back to the backside. This is where we have an "either-or" call. We call it a "bunch" if the defense is loaded to the strongside. This is how we came up with the "bunch" term. We had a young quarterback that had a hard time counting the number of defenders in the box. We were in a game and he made several play changes at the line of scrimmage. I was on the sideline feeling good. My feel was that the young quarterback had finally gotten what we were trying to get across to him. He came out of the game and before I could say much to him he said to me, "Coach, there was a whole *bunch* of defenders over on that one side so I checked the play off to the other side." So we tell our quarterback if he looks to one side and sees a bunch of defenders, to change the play to the other side. We do not change the play much; we just change the direction we are going.

When we first started running the play to the split-end side, it was our split-end attack. Our tight-end attack was our traditional wing-T plays. It still is, but this has become a big play for us.

We put the wing on the right side outside the tight end. We call that north. If we want him to move outside wider, we call it northern. Now, the opposite of north is south. The opposite of northern is southern. We take one word and expand on it.

If we want our wingback to block the end, we call it bend. If we call Bob, it is back on the backer. This play has enabled us to take mediocre players and run this play against superior people. We played several Division I-AA teams and had success running this play. We could not run the other wing-T plays. We could run the jet series. We have played Western Kentucky and South Florida and we ran this offense. We played Jacksonville State last year and gained 260 yards rushing. We held the ball 40 minutes. All of the runs were the jet plays.

Most teams do not adjust when we run from the unbalanced line. We see the 3-technique, and they have a 9-technique on the outside. Everything else that is done unbalanced, you can do with the secondary. We want the coach that coaches the offensive line to earn his money. We have two tackles on the same side. We have a regular tackle and an outside tackle. We pull both tackles on the play. We call it O-T stretch.

O-T STRETCH

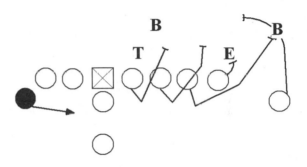

We do not take big splits on the strongside. We are in tight. We call those splits "V splits." They are tight splits. They are split one foot. A virgin split is the same thing. If we big split, it is called Gertie. Old Gertie would split for everyone. That is a big split.

Our best buck sweep is one hole tighter. It is not outside. If we call G-X, the outside tackle shows pass and then goes for the outside linebacker. That has made the play. We used to send the tackle across the face of the defender, and we did not have much. Now we have him set for a pass and then go, and it has helped the play. We fake the trap on the play and run the sweep. It is a great play. It is the buck sweep one hole tighter.

G-X BUCK SWEEP

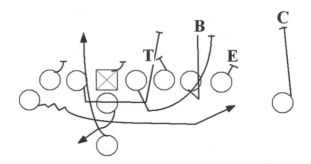

If our fullback is faking the trap then the quarterback fakes the bootleg. What do teams do when you run the bootleg? They key the ball. When the quarterback comes out on the bootleg, we want him to keep the ball down on the back hip until he gets ready to throw the pass. We do not want him to bring the ball up under his chin. The defense can see the ball if he does that. We want the quarterback to keep the off hand down after the handoff or the fake.

We run a jeep formation where we take two ends and stand them up on the unbalanced sides. We have one end inside. He is the tight end. We tell him to stand up like a split end even though he is inside. We tell the outside man on the line to stand up like a split end. This really blows the defense's mind. They do not know what is going on. It looks funny but we have four blockers on that side. We have the wingback outside the end. That's our jeep formation. It is an eagle and we call it jeep because young people can relate to that call.

Last year our best athlete was our split end. He ran a 4.5 for the 40-yard dash. We put him in the wing position on the short side. We took our fullback and offset him to the short side. The last time we offset the fullback, we ran to his side. This time we are going to run to the strongside. If we go to the tight-end side, we like to pull the tackle because he can get in front of the play better. We can get a hat on a hat. We may not block them very well, but we have a man assigned to each man. We call it jeep right.

JEEP RIGHT

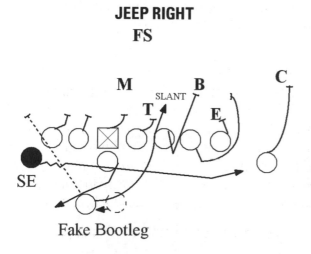

Fake Bootleg

We want that split end to take it to the barn. He wants to get outside and down the field. When the

fullback is offset, we can do one or two things. He can run the slant on the strongside or he can run the bootleg on the short side.

You may say you cannot do all of this. You can too if you have a system. You are welcome to come to our place at anytime. All you have to do is to call me and let me know you are coming. I will spend as much time with you as you want to spend. We have tapes you can see and we will cover anything we do. We have no secrets. If you are interested in anything we are doing come see us. Every year I have a staff of high school coaches from Michigan that comes down. They spend three days with me. I have a staff from Washington that spends two days with us. I have coaches from North Carolina that come to visit us. My time is your time. My time is running out. I am 75 years old from the waist down. I am going fast. But if you want to talk football, I am here for you.

I will tell you one thing. With all of the modern pills such as Viagra and that stuff, I might be immortal. I am only gone from the waist down. You know what is funny? I am never around anyone that is my age. Most of the people my age are dead. All of my coaches are young. I am used to young people. I have lost most of my equipment. I forget from time to time that I cannot do certain things anymore. My knees are gone. But you are welcome to visit us.

We are working on something new this spring. We are going to run the bunch look on one side and slot look on the other side. We are going to run this from an empty set. I can get any of the backs to the deep position with motion. If we motion them back, we can run the jet sweep from that set. But you will have to defend three receivers. It is E-bunch right and we are going to run the same play.

EMPTY - BUNCH RIGHT

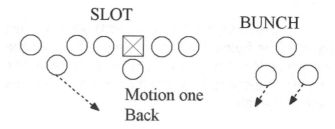

If we start a man in motion and then have him stop and go back the same way, we call it joker. This is joker trap. Here it is against the 50 defense. It helps if we start the wingback in one direction and bring him back to where he started. The tackle on that side is the man we are going to trap. It is a good play.

JOKER TRAP

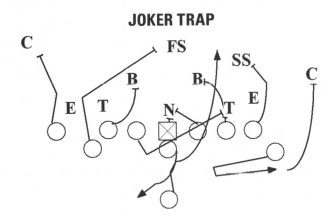

For some reason the bootleg play is not as good from the jet sweep as it is from the buck sweep. The buck sweep is not a play we have to hang our hats on. We still run it. We have run that play for 40 years. It is like having a child. If you have him for 40 years you love him. I am going to run it but we do not have to have it.

Next we are going to look at a double handoff. Let me show it against the 4-3 defense. We block down away from the direction we are going to run the ball. The fullback and pulling tackle block out. I looked in the dictionary and found this. If someone is "down and out" they are blue. This is our blue play. We do not want to pull a guard on a misdirection play. We pull the tackle. You must decide on whom you want to block. We want everyone on the defense to see the quarterback hand the ball to the wingback. Now we snap the ball early so they can see the handoff to the wingback. We want to hand the ball off on the midline.

On the reverse, the slot back pivots and then goes back to the fullback position. He goes behind the wingback. He starts out three yards outside the tackle and one yard off the ball. He pivots and comes back to the ball.

The fullback hits up over the guard and blocks out on the end. The tackle pulls and leads the play. As he pulls he turns up if he sees a defender's number. Then he bounces to the outside

As the quarterback hands off to the wingback he continues outside. He blocks the outside defender. How do you get the quarterback to block? If he does not block, I play the other quarterback. Our quarterbacks block. How many quarterbacks have you gotten hurt blocking? None!

BLUE - REVERSE

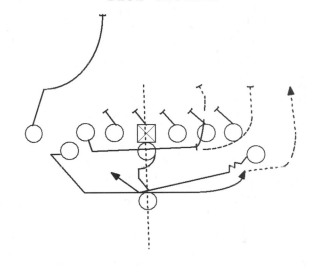

We can run the play inside or we can bounce it outside. It is a good misdirection play.

Now let me take some questions. I have a lot of books on what we do. I have tapes of the plays cut up. You can take them as well.

Let me tell you what we do not like. We do not like the *good ole buddy talk*. Do you remember when we used to meet a coach before the kickoff and we told the opposing coach "Good luck"? I do not do that anymore. I do not want that coach and his team to have good luck. I want them to have bad luck. I want all of the good luck. "I hope you fumble every damn play, coach." We do not tell them, "Good luck, coach!" Bull crap. We really mean, "Bad luck, coach."

I appreciate your time, men. Thank you.

KICKING GAME SCHEMES AND RETURNS

University of Kentucky

It is a pleasure and honor for me to represent the University of Kentucky and Coach Guy Morriss. I want you to know that we appreciate high school coaches. We have an open-door policy, and you are more than welcome to come down to visit with us anytime.

The thing about coaching is the fact that it is a continuous learning process. I learned something last night at the sessions and I have learned something today. I am going to tell you everything I know. I do not know a whole lot. I was fortunate enough to play in the Canadian Football League. I was later hired to coach in the NFL. Other people have helped me to learn about special teams. So I have no problems telling you what I know about special teams. If you get better, it is going to make me get better. In football, usually what we know is something we have stolen from someone else. Now what we have to do is to improve what we have taken from others. That is what I am going to try to do today.

In high school coaching, I believe you should win three games a year with the special teams. I really believe this will happen if you spend a little time working on it. We all know you can outcoach some teams, but in most situations the other team is going to be just as good as you are. So we have to beat them on special teams. That is where the "winning edge" is in football. You have to spend a little more time on special teams to be good. You cannot just talk about the kicking game. We spend time in the classroom and we spend time on the field working on the kicking game. We involve all of our staff in some phase of the kicking. They either work with us or they get the scouting team ready to go against us.

Over the years, the kicking game has been a deciding factor in many football games. It may be the part of a football game that can create the greatest number of momentum changes. Consider these elements of special team play:

- Each play usually covers at least 40 yards of field position. Let's be realistic and say about 35 yards in high school.

- Each play normally involves a change of possession.

- Plays that do not fall into the first two categories involve direct scoring opportunities.

To me those three things are more important than the average plays. An average offensive play is 3 or 4 yards. The average defensive play gives up 3 or 4 yards. More yards gained or lost is determined in the kicking game than on the average offensive or defensive play.

Here are some special team goals that we want to obtain:

- Score a touchdown or set up 6 points.

- Create a turnover; either a blocked kick or a fumble.

- Have a net of 35 yards punting.

- Have no returns over 25 yards.

- Never start an offensive series inside our 20 yards.

The kicking game gains importance when you realize how important a role it plays in determining offensive scoring ability. We already know that the farther away an offense starts from its goal line, the more difficult it is to score. Conversely, the closer the offense starts to its goal line the easier it is to score. The following chart clearly shows this difference.

20	1 out of 30	3% chance to score
40	1 out of 8	12% chance to score
50	1 out of 5	20% chance to score
40	1 out of 3	33% chance to score
20	1 out of 2	50% chance to score
10	2 out of 3	66% chance to score

Here are some other important points to note about the kicking game.

- One out of every five plays, or about 18-24 plays per game (20%), is a kick of some kind.

- 25% of all scoring is attributed to kicking downs.

- A sizable amount of yardage is involved (40 yards).

- There is a change of possession involved.

- A vast majority of all close games are decided by kicking game plays (often in pressure-filled final moments).

I have a tape on the kicking game drills we use. I want to show the tape and let you ask questions at the end.

Next I want to talk about our kicking game schemes. To start out, I want to remind you that it takes a lot of players with a lot of pride to play on the special teams. This is what we tell our players to get them to believe in the special teams.

Champions take *pride* in making things happen positively. Our kicking game is considered an "offensive" phase of our approach to the game of football. We plan to *win* in every phase of our special teams. Our schemes are designed to keep constant pressure on our opponent. The key to success will be *consistency* and *efficiency* executed with your intensity, effort, discipline, concentration, and unequaled enthusiasm.

We have three kicking game strategies. They are the way to beat your opponent. We want to use all of them in an effort to win the kicking game.

OUTWORK THEM

UK will give great effort, physical conditioning, and attention to detail, and practice the results we want in the game.

OUTSMART THEM

UK will not beat UK! We must be fundamentally sound. We must make wise use of personnel and attack our opponent's weakness.

We are not saying we are smarter than other coaches that we play. But what we mean by that is we are not going to beat ourselves. We are smart enough to know that we cannot do a lot of different things and do them well. We are more concerned about reps on what we do. We want to do a few things well. We will change a few things to get better but we are not going to add a whole lot of new things.

We worked real hard this past year. However, we did not beat anyone with the kicking game. I thought we executed well and we played with confidence. We played with intensity but we will have to turn up the dial to get better next year.

You must have a good attitude to play on the special teams. I tell you how you get a team with a good attitude. You are going to have a core of players on the team. Those players are going to be the backup linebackers, running backs, defensive ends, and defensive backs.

If we had a perfect world, this is how I would pick the players for special teams. I would pick all the starters in this manner. If you are a starter that can run, you would start on two special teams. It would be one cover team and one return team. I think it is asking too much to play on all four defensive special teams if you are a defensive starter.

I know in high school you have players that never get off the field. I am saying this is how we would select them if we were in a perfect world. We would have the linebackers on two teams, one cover and one return. If we cannot have the perfect world we are still going to have a core of players that are going to be on our special teams. We will have about seven or eight of those players involved. It could be 10 or 12 players that play on two or three teams. One or two of those players will play on all four of those teams. I want to take that unit and develop pride in that unit. When they go out on the field on one of the four special teams and they see their buddies on the field as a unit, they take pride in doing a good job. I have to do a better job of developing this unit and the pride in those individuals.

INTIMIDATE THEM

UK will *hit* you! Perfect execution! Play with confidence. Play with intensity.

By employing these strategies, we truly believe we can line up against anyone on any given day and win the kicking game.

I want to cover our schemes. I will talk about punt returns, and then I will show some cutups. I have six punts, six punt returns, six kickoffs, and six kickoff returns.

I think we were respectful in the kicking game this past year. We are going to do more next year. I know we have a lot of improvement to do.

That is the name of the game. We must improve. That means we must do a better job of coaching.

I like to involve the entire staff in the kicking game. Some teams give all the kicking game to one coach. I put our material together, but I get help from all of our coaches. I ask for their input and use them in any way we need them. There are a lot of different ways to attack the game.

I want to start off with punt returns. First I want to talk about the philosophy behind all of this.

The most important single factor in a punt return or punt block is your belief that it will succeed. If you believe it, you will find a way to make it work. If you can't find a way, *make a way!* It is our belief that the punt return/block is our first offensive play in a series. We are gong to make at least one first down with our punt return. This in turn eliminates at least one first down the offense has to get to score. We want to eliminate all of the first downs and score on the punt return/block. *Score on special teams.* Make your effort count. To do this we must eliminate costly penalties.

GENERAL

We have three general types of plays on punt returns:

- Returns.

- Safe returns (windy or expecting a fake).

- Blocks and pressures.

We try to combine our return and pressure on the punt teams. If you just have an all-out hold-them-at-the-line-return-the-punt team, they will scout you, and they will release quick and cover the punt. We want to pressure the punter.

COMMUNICATION

We will usually have a changeover in personnel when we go into a return or block punt. We must hustle onto the field and get the call to those not coming off the field. We will designate individuals going on the field to get the call to our players remaining on the field. We will use key words or signals to communicate our calls. Many teams will not huddle when punting the ball, so it is important to get the call in and get lined up as quickly as possible.

We feel it is very important to catch the football on the punts. If you cannot catch the ball with one back deep, put two backs deep to make sure you catch the ball. In certain situations, we will put two backs deep to catch the punt.

I want to cover a few things before I get to the schemes. First I want to talk about assignments. In order for us to be successful on our punt return team, we must all know and carry out our assignments. Again, we have some goals that we want to achieve related to our assignments.

- On all returns, catch the ball first so we can have great field position.

- No turnovers.

- No penalties.

- Do not give up a fake punt. We must be alert.

- We want to average at least first down on every return.

- Have a momentum changer each game. Examples of momentum changers are: blocked kick, great return that crosses into the opponent's territory.

- No blown assignments. We want execution.

Here are the keys to blocking a punt:

- Get a great get-off. React to the snap and not the sound. Do not be offside.

- The landmark for blocking a punt is five yards in front of the punter to the punter's foot. It is not at the punter.

- Never leave your feet to block the punt. Catch the punt with your hands. See the ball hit your hand. Aim for the sweet spot.

- A blocked punt can be advanced. We want to scoop it up and score.

- Partially blocked punts that cross the LOS belong to us. Make a "Peter" call and get away from the ball. Peter is the safe call to get away from the punt.

- Believe you will block the punt. We call the block for a reason. *Make it happen.*

We believe there are several keys to a good punt return.

- No turnovers. The return men must handle the punt clean.

- No penalties—block high and in front of the man.

- We want a great get-off. Key the ball and react to the snap.

- We want great hold-up at the line of scrimmage.

- We must get to the wall or get the blocks.

Here are our alignments. First is against the spread punt. We are in outside shades. We want to create leverage for our rushers. We want to force the punt team to get depth to block us. We want to be wide enough to stretch the wide punt-coverage people. If the punt team breaks formation, we are going to lock up man-to-man with them. Our outside rushers are defensive backs, and we just play them man-to-man. We have one man off the ball, and his eyes are scanning.

SPREAD PUNT RUSH

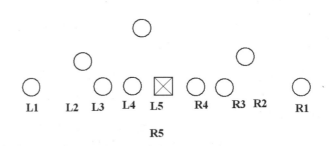

RETURN

If the punt team lines up in a tight punt, we drop the number 1 rushers on the outside back in the linebacker position between our 2 and 3 rushers. We do not want to change a lot on this formation.

TIGHT PUNT RUSH

P

RETURN

If the punt team is in an open formation with two slots, we move our two outside defenders outside to cover them.

OPEN PUNT RUSH

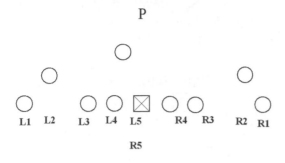

P

L1 L2   L3 L4 L5   R4 R3   R2 R1

R5

RETURN

We use three punt returns. First is Jesse James left.

L1 - Align inside shoulder of the bullet. Bump and run. Do not allow the bullet to get inside.

L2 - Align outside of wing. Key the snap. Burst upfield. Attack wing and force him away from the return. Bump and run downfield.

L3 - Align inside shoulder of wing. Key the snap. Burst upfield and attack the tackle and force him away from the return. Bump and run downfield.

L4 - Align inside shoulder of tackle. Key the snap. Burst upfield and attack the guard and force him away from the return. Bump and run downfield.

L5 - Align head-up on center. Key the snap. Burst upfield opposite the call side to the block point. Block the punt. If you do not block the punt, get to the wall.

R5 - Alignment on movement. Key the snap. Check for the fake on the wing opposite the call side. Make sure the ball is punted. Sprint back and get the return man to the wall.

R4 - Align inside shoulder of tackle. Key the snap. Burst upfield 3 to 4 yards, then to block point. Block the punt. If you do not block the punt, get to the wall.

R3 - Align inside shoulder of the wing. Key the snap. Burst upfield 3 to 4 yards, then to block point. Block the punt. If you do not block the punt, get to the wall.

R2 - Align outside wing. Key the snap. Burst upfield 3 to 4 yards, then to block point. Block the punt. If you do not block the punt get to the wall.

R1 - Align inside shoulder of bullet. Bump and run with him. Do not allow the bullet inside.

Return man - We will have a wall set to the left. If we do not block the punt, catch the ball and get to the wall. *Score!*

PUNT RETURN - JESSE JAMES LEFT

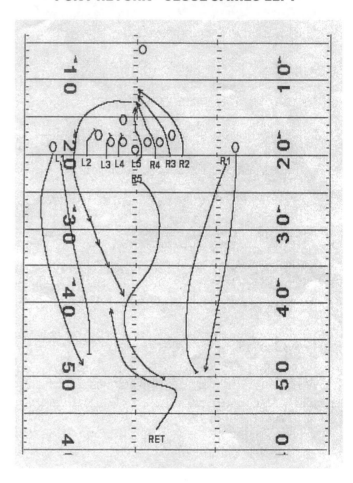

Next is the middle return. We call it Jesse James middle return.

L1 - Align inside shoulder of bullet. Bump and run against the bullet. Do not allow the bullet inside.

L2 - Align outside of the wing. Key the snap. Burst upfield 3 to 4 yards. Force the punt and then block the punter.

L3 - Align inside shoulder of wing. Key the snap. Burst upfield 3 to 4 yards. Attack the wing man. Force him away from return. Bump and run downfield.

L4 - Align inside shoulder of their tackle. Key the snap. Burst upfield 3 to 4 yards. Attack the tackle, and force him away from the return. Bump and run downfield.

L5 - Align head up on their center. Key the snap. Burst upfield to your left. Attack the guard, and force him away from the return. Bump and run downfield.

R5 - Alignment is on movement. Key the snap. Burst upfield to your right. Attack the guard, and force him away from the return. Bump and run downfield.

R4 - Align inside shoulder of tackle. Key the snap. Burst upfield 3 to 4 yards. Attack the tackle, and force him away from the return. Bump and run downfield.

R3 - Align inside shoulder of wing. Key the snap. Burst upfield 3 to 4 yards. Attack the wing, and force him away from the return. Bump and run downfield.

R2 - Align outside of wing. Key the snap. Burst upfield 2 to 3 yards. Stop and check the fake punt. Fall back inside for the fullback. Bump and run downfield.

R1 - Align inside shoulder of bullet. Bump and run against the bullet. Do not allow the bullet inside.

Punt return man - Catch the ball. You must beat the center on your own. Middle return and *score!*

JESSE JAMES MIDDLE

We run a return to the right side and it is just the opposite of the left return.

L1 - Align inside shoulder of bullet. Bump and run against the bullet. Do not allow the bullet inside.

L2 - Align outside of wing. Key the snap. Burst upfield 3 to 4 yards, and get to the block point. Block the punt if possible. If you do not block the punt, get to the wall.

L3 - Align inside shoulder of the wing. Key the snap. Burst upfield 3 to 4 yards, and get to the block point. Block the punt if possible. If you do not block the punt, get to the wall.

L4 - Align inside shoulder of the tackle. Key the snap. Burst upfield 3 to 4 yards to the block point. Block the punt if possible. If you do not block the punt, get to the wall.

L5 - Align head-up on the center. Key the snap. Burst upfield opposite the call side to the block point. Block the punt. If you do not block the punt, get to the wall.

R5 - Alignment is on movement. Key the snap. Check for the fake punt if you are the wing opposite the call side. Make sure the ball is punted. Sprint back and get the return man to the wall.

R4 - Align inside shoulder of tackle. Key the snap. Burst upfield. Attack the guard, and force him away from the return. Bump and run downfield.

R3 - Align inside shoulder of wing. Key the snap. Burst upfield. Attack the tackle, and force him away from the return. Bump and run downfield.

R2 - Align outside wing. Key the snap. Burst upfield. Attack the wing and force him away from the return.

R1 - Align inside shoulder to the bullet. Bump and run downfield. Do not allow the bullet inside.

Return man - We will have a wall set to the right. If we do not block the punt, catch the ball and get to the wall. *Score!*

JESSE JAMES RIGHT

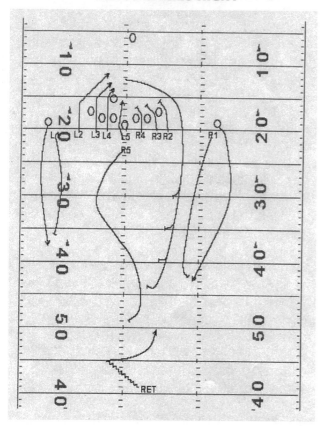

Let me get to the kickoff coverage. I will cover three kickoffs. Most of the time we are gong to kick from the hash mark to the short side of the field. I will show you how we cover on a deep kick to the left and to the right. Also, I will show you one of our onside kicks.

KICKOFF DEEP RIGHT

L1 - Middle safety.

L2 - Hard contain - squeeze the outside in to the ball. (9 yards)

L3 - Feather contain between the L-5 and R-5.

L4 - Attack lane - squeeze outside in to the ball. (6 yards)

L5 - Attack lane - squeeze outside in to the ball. (3 yards)

K - Short-side safety.

R5 - Arrow to the ball - inside shoulder.

R4 - Feather contain between the R-3 and R-2.

R3 - Attack lane - squeeze outside in to the ball. (3 yards)

R2 - Attack lane - squeeze outside in to the ball. (6 yards)

R1 - Hard contain - squeeze outside in to the ball. (9 yards)

KICKOFF DEEP RIGHT

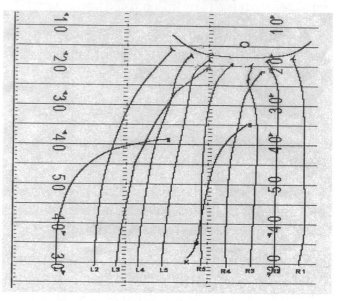

The kickoff to the deep left is just the opposite of the kickoff right. We can always switch the players around on the alignment if we want. The L3 and L4 and R3 and R4 can change places, but L3 and R4 are always the feathers.

KICKOFF DEEP LEFT

L1 - Hard contain - squeeze outside in to the ball. (9 yards)

L2 - Attack lane - squeeze outside in to the ball. (6 yards)

L3 - Attack lane - squeeze outside in to the ball. (3 yards)

L4 - Feather contain between the L2 and L3.

L5 - Arrow to the ball - inside shoulder.

K - Short-side safety.

R5 - Attack lane - squeeze outside in to the ball. (3 yards)

R4 - Attack lane - squeeze outside in to the ball. (6 yards)

R3 - Feather contain between R5 and the L5.

R2 - Hard contain - squeeze outside in to the ball. (9 yards)

R1 - Middle safety.

KICKOFF DEEP LEFT

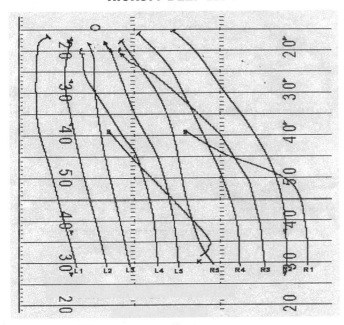

I want to show you one onside kick. We line up the same way. We call it surprise onside kick right.

L1 - Middle safety - cross the 35-yard line, and then sprint back to the deep middle.

L2 - Hard contain - squeeze outside in to the ball.

L3 - Feather contain between the L4 and the R5.

L4 - Attack the lane - squeeze outside in to the ball.

L5 - Feather contain between the R4 and R3.

K - Short-side safety.

R5 - Attack lane - squeeze outside in to the ball.

R4 - Arrow lane to the ball.

R3 - Arrow lane to the ball.

R2 - Attack lane - squeeze outside in to the ball.

R1 - Attack lane - squeeze outside in to the ball.

SURPRISE ONSIDE KICK RIGHT

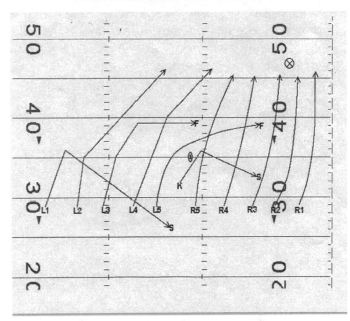

Next I want to show you a kickoff return to the right and one to the left. The first return is our kickoff return-23 trap left. First I will cover the assignments for each man.

Center - Locate the kickoff landmark. Line up on the opponent's 47-yard line, and offset the ball. On the kick, drop a full sprint to around the 30-yard line, depending on depth of the kick. Your man is the L5. Acquire a good angle, and block him inside.

Left guard - Locate the hash mark as your landmark. Adjust to the center's offset call. Line up on the opponent's 47-yard line. On the kick, drop at full-sprint speed to around the 30-yard line, depending on depth of the kick. Your man is the L4. Acquire a good angle, and block him inside.

Left tackle - Split the difference between the guard and the sideline on the opponent's 47-yard line. Exact position will depend on the offset of the center. On the kick, drop at full-sprint speed to around the 35-yard line. Attack the L3, blocking him inside. (Double-team the L3 with the left guard.)

Right guard - Locate the hash mark as your landmark. Adjust to the center's offset call. Align on the opponent's 47-yard line. On the kick, drop at full speed to around the 30-yard line, depending on the depth of kick. Get inside-out leverage on R5, and block him outside.

Right tackle - Split the difference between guard and sideline on opponent's 47-yard line. Exact position will depend upon the offset of the center. On the kick, drop at full-sprint speed to around the 30-yard line depending on the depth of the kick. Get inside-out leverage on R4 and block him out. Be prepared for R4 and the R3 cross. If this happens block the inside cover man.

Left end - Line up on the 35-yard line splitting the difference between the hash and the sideline. On the kick, drop and move to an outside position on L3. Double-team him with the left tackle.

Right end - Line up on the 35-yard line splitting the difference between the hash and the sideline. On the kick, drop and move to an inside-out leverage position on MDM, and block him out.

Left and right fullbacks - Line up inside the hash on the 20-yard line. On the kick, drop together to a distance of 12 yards in front of the return man that is catching the ball. Listen for the "go" call. Start forward toward the middle of the field before breaking to your left. Double-team L2 blocking him inside out.

Left and right return men - Line up on the goal line 4 yards outside the hash mark. Return man catching the ball calls out "ME, Me, me." Catch the ball and look it in and secure the ball. Start for the middle of the field initially, and then break hard for the alley between L2 and L3. Always find the crease going full speed. The return man not catching the ball calls out "YOU, You, you." He is to be 5 yards in front and to the return side of the return man. Make sure the ball is caught before you give the "go" call to the fullbacks. Start for the middle initially and then break hard looking to block L1 inside out.

Here is a coaching point for the man catching the ball. We want him to catch the ball on the run moving forward.

KICKOFF RETURN - 23 TRAP LEFT

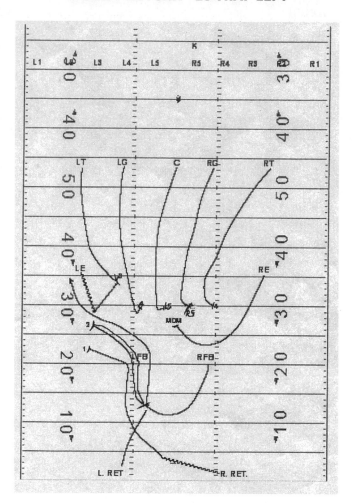

Here is the same play to the right side. It is "kickoff return - 23 trap right" to us.

Center - Same alignment; check for offset. Sprint back when the ball is kicked, and get outside-in leverage on R5 and block him inside.

Left guard - Same alignment; listen for the offset call. Sprint back when the ball is kicked and get inside-outside leverage on L5 and block him outside.

Left tackle - Same alignment; listen for the offset call. Sprint back when the ball is kicked, and get inside-outside leverage on L4 and block him outside.

Right guard - Same alignment; listen for the offset call. Sprint back when the ball is kicked, and get outside-in leverage on R4 and block him inside.

Right tackle - Same alignment; listen for the offset call. Sprint back when the ball is kicked, and get outside-in leverage on R3 and block him inside. You have a double-team block with the right end.

Left end - It is the same alignment as on the left return. On the kick, drop back and move to get inside-out leverage on MDM. Block them outside.

Right end - It is the same alignment as on the left return. On the kick, drop back and keep outside-in leverage on R3, and block him inside. You must double-team with the right tackle creating a crease in the gap between R2 and R3.

Left and right fullbacks - It is the same alignment as on the left return. On the kick, drop back 12 yards in front on the return man catching the ball. Listen for the "go" call. Start toward the middle of the field before breaking to your right. You are to double-team R2 blocking him inside.

Left and right return men - It is the same alignment as on the left return. Line up on the goal line 4 yards outside the hash mark. Return man catching the ball calls out "ME, Me, me." Catch the ball, and look it in and secure the ball. Start for the middle of the field initially, and then break hard for the alley between R2 and R3. Always find the crease going full speed. The return man not catching the ball calls out "YOU, You, you." He is to be 5 yards in front and to the return side of the return man. Make sure the ball is caught before you give the "go" call to the fullbacks. Start for the middle initially and then break hard looking to block R1 inside out.

We pick the best players the kicking team has, and we are going to double them. We do not want to ask one of our players to go 1-on-1 against their best players. We are going to give them some help. We will let the far outside people go and double in the middle. We tell them to double the MDM (most dangerous man).

We tell the deep man not returning the ball that he becomes a blocker when he is not returning the ball. We have had some good blocks out of our deep backs on the kickoff returns.

One thing we must do a better job on with the kickoff is timing. If the blockers have to hold their block longer than two seconds, our timing is not good. That is an area where we can improve on. That is something we can work on in the spring.

What we do on special teams is not a lot of different things. What we try to do is to give them enough for them to be successful. We ask our players to do things they can do. We want to help them at the point of attack. If we can do that, I think we have a chance to be successful. This past year we were not good in the kicking game, but we did not hurt ourselves. Now we must take the big step and start winning games with the special teams. We want to block punts, have a punt return for a touchdown, and run a kickoff back for a touchdown. The thing we want to do is to avoid putting our defense back out on the field.

You are welcome to come to see us practice. If we can help you, feel free to contact us or come to visit us. Thank you.

KICKOFF RETURN - 23 TRAP RIGHT

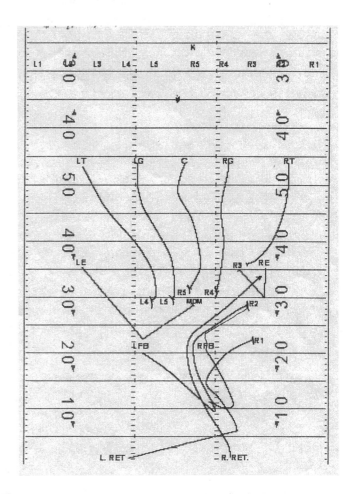

LINEBACKER DRILLS AND TECHNIQUES

University of Oregon

I appreciate the opportunity to speak at this clinic and visit the state of Hawaii. I would like to congratulate the University of Hawaii on the season they just had. I had a chance to watch a couple of their games, and they really got after people. Congratulations to Kahuku High School for winning the state playoffs here.

I recruit the Los Angeles area, and I have also recruited Florida and Texas. One thing I know about the football here in the islands: No one plays with more intensity than they do here. That is a tribute to your kids and to the coaches who coach them. I love watching your kids play.

I came to the University of Oregon in 1992. I coached the linebackers in a 3-4 scheme and in a 4-3 scheme. I coached the defensive line for a year. That was the best thing I could have done for myself. It helped me understand how the linebacker fits with the defensive line in their responsibility. I coached the safeties for a year, and now I'm back with the linebackers.

I have one thing to say before I get started with my presentation. I am blessed to be on the staff at the University of Oregon. We have been together for a long time. Our defensive line coach does such a good job with his players. They get up the field and play really aggressively. However, they are so well coached when they feel pressure, they do a good job of staying in their gaps. We are not a great defense, but we are solid. We force people to do things they don't want to do if they plan on beating us. Our gap control is really solid, and as the year goes on, we get better at it.

My linebackers can read and they can run. I coach the crap out of them, and I never want them to slow down. I don't want to see a linebacker locked up on a block. We want to read and run. We are able to do that because the defensive line is so good in their gap con-

trol that they occupy a lot of attention. All the coaches on the defensive staff at Oregon do a great job of coaching their players. Put the talent level with the coaching and you can have a good defense.

Today I want to share some of my experience, our drill work, and the defensive scheme itself. I think a large part of the success we've had at the linebacker position is because of our drills.

In 1997 I had a sophomore linebacker, Peter Sirmon, who led the conference in tackles. In 1998 I had two guys in the top 20 in the conference in tackles. In 1999 I went to the defensive line, and in 2000 I had two guys in the top 12 in tackles. I am excited about that. I am not bragging, I am just telling you what our kids have accomplished. I think it is the system they play in that leads to their success. This year we had three guys in the top eight in the tackles in the PAC-10. In the top 18, we had five guys. In the top 10, we had three linebackers and a strong safety.

I want to force leadership on the linebackers. When the linebacker is calling the defensive signals, he is the leader in the defensive huddle. I am going to force our entire linebacker corps to lead everywhere. If you have a kid come to the University of Oregon, he is going to be kicking butt on the field, in the classroom, and everywhere. I hold them to high accountability on their role as leaders.

We have mentors with our young linebackers. We want to be a great group of linebackers. The veterans are in charge of the young guys. The young guys don't have to listen to the older players, but if they make a mistake, I'm coming down on them hard. If the veterans are not helping the younger players, I will be on them hard also. That is our system.

I have our entire group of linebackers over to my house for dinner. The seniors are in charge of all the duties at the dinner. They decide who peels a potato, who makes the Kool-Aid, who cleans up, and everything that goes on at the dinner. They are seniors and have earned that right.

When it comes to the football field, the best players play. If the senior is not the best guy, he can't expect to start. I encourage our guys to come in and do extra things to work on their skill level or increase their knowledge. During the off-season, we can't meet with our kids. But I can guarantee that twice a week my linebackers will come into the coaches' office on their own to watch film.

I want all the linebackers on the same page. When they come off the field, I want to be able to talk to them about what is happening on the field. I can't always tell what play is being run from the sideline. When I bring a linebacker off the field and ask him what happened, he can tell me. He can say, "Coach, that was a 24 power play. It didn't come outside; it broke off in the A gap." From there we can talk, and each of us knows what the other one is saying. If he tells me, "I saw the guard pull, and I missed the scrape, I really don't know what happened." Now I have got problems communicating because I don't think he understands what went on.

They don't have to come in. There are a bunch of random things they can do. If you don't know what to do at Oregon, you will never play. If the kid is on scholarship he has a right to be on the team. Playing is a privilege. If the linebacker wants to play and compete at this level, there are some extra things he is going to have to do. They are here to do two things. They are here to play football and go to school. The social issues will take care of themselves. If the young linebacker can't meet with the rest of the linebackers because he doesn't have time, he is not managing his time very well.

We run three fronts and I will talk to you specifically about one of them. What I would like to do now is go over our general alignments and reads in that front. Afterward I'll put on the drill tape and show you some of our drills. I brought some game tapes so you can see the scheme at work. At the end, if we have time, I'll put on our blitz tape.

Our base front is the *over front,* which we run about 75 percent of the time. We are a base 4-3 de-

fense, which is overshifted toward the tight-end side. The Sam linebacker is aligned three to five yards outside the tight end and off the ball. His key comes from logical thinking. The person that can block the Sam linebacker first is the tight end. Therefore, the tight end becomes the Sam linebacker's key. He is keying the tight end to the near back. We never want to get more than a yard and a half deep in the backfield. If a sweep play comes toward the Sam linebacker, he wants to meet the blockers a yard-and-a-half deep behind where the tight end was aligned.

If the fullback is in the heavy set or strong halfback position, the Sam linebacker tightens his alignment to the line of scrimmage. When the blocker moves closer to the force point, the Sam linebacker has to do that also. If the set is a light set and the fullback is on the other side, the Sam linebacker can get more depth off the ball and get ready for the cutback.

We want to beat the fullback to the force spot, which is a yard-and-a-half behind the tight end. We don't want to get any deeper. If the Sam linebacker does, he will get kicked out, and everything gets inside of him. We want to force the play to bounce outside. We want to force the back to do something he doesn't want to do.

If the Sam linebacker sees the ball go inside with a full flow from the backfield, he starts to shuffle laterally. He does not want to capture the line of scrimmage. He wants to stay off the line of scrimmage about one-and-a-half yards and play the bootleg pass at him. If it is bootleg toward him, he has the tight end going to the flat. When he sees the full flow of the backs going away from him, he plays the bootleg by the quarterback.

If the tight end slams into the tackle and releases flat, the Sam linebacker won't see him unless he is off the line of scrimmage. If the Sam linebacker shuffles off the line, the tight end will run right into the linebacker. Now the Sam linebacker has a chance to cover him. If there is action totally away, the Sam linebacker becomes the fold and cutback player.

We play defense in the *battlefield.* The battlefield for us is two yards behind the line of scrimmage and three yards on our side of the line. We want to defeat blocks and attack everything that is in that area.

THE BATTLEFIELD

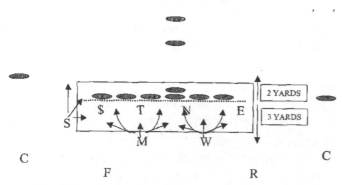

The Mike linebacker aligns in a 30- to 40-technique. He is four to five yards off the line of scrimmage. We want him deep. His alignment depends on the alignment of the fullback. The Mike linebacker is totally responsible for the A gap to his side. On any vertical play toward him, that is where he is going to attack. The Mike linebacker reads the nearest threat to block him. The offensive guard is the first threat to the Mike linebacker. The linemen are a consistent read for the linebackers. If the Mike linebacker sees the guard fan out on the 2-technique and both backs full flow to him, he attacks them as deep in the backfield as he can.

In our defense we always have what we call a *free hitter*. It is either the free safety or the rover. We play a lot of man-to-man coverage in the secondary. Sometimes both the free safety and rover are in the box.

The Will linebacker is in a 20-alignment to the open side. Again that is depending on where the fullback aligns. He is reading through the guard to the backs. On flow toward him, he is filling the B gap. Our Will linebacker this year was a small kid. He was 5'10" and 210 pounds. You will see him in the film. I had trouble getting him to be patient. He was always getting too tight to the line of scrimmage and getting blocked. He was hell on wheels when he got moving.

BASE OVER DEFENSE

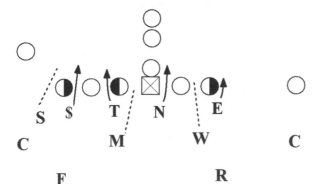

With two backs in the backfield we will play quarter coverage, cover two, and a fair amount of man coverage. We disguise what we are doing, but you can expect to get a heavy dose of man coverage. We blitz a lot out of that set also.

I lost three seniors last year to graduation. The group that played this year really played well for us. They had never really played a lot before this year. We don't have any big-name guys playing on our defense. Our Sam linebacker is 6'1" and about 215. He was a corner but was so reckless the defensive secondary coach gave up on him. They didn't want him, so I took him. He has never run anything higher than a 4.45. The Mike linebacker is 6'1" and 235. He is the strongest linebacker I have ever had. He runs about 4.6 in the 40-yard sprint. The Will linebacker is 5'10" and 210. He is a tiny little guy who is all heart.

If the offense runs a power play to the tight-end side, they will pull the backside guard for the Mike linebacker. They double-team down with the tackle and guard on the 3-technique. The tight end blocks down on the 7-technique. The fullback is kicking out on the Sam linebacker with the backside guard pulling through the hole for the Mike linebacker. The center blocks back on the shade tackle.

The Mike linebacker is tracking on the fullback. He takes a lateral step when the double team comes down on the defensive tackle. He sees the fullback heading for the off-tackle hole. He has to beat the fullback to that point.

The Will linebacker sees the guard pull. The first thing he thinks is trap. He plays downhill right now and finds the back. If he sees the back coming inside, he has to take him. The guy to stop the trap is the guy that sees the pull. He is looking to get right off the butt of the tackle. He is playing over the top of the center's block on a trap. If it continues on, he scrapes outside.

OVER DEFENSE AND READS

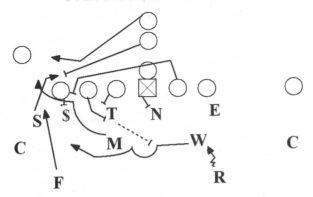

When a linebacker is reading a play, he has to find out who is going to block him. If you want to make plays as a linebacker you have to know who is going to block you and beat the block. Playing linebacker is not like playing safety. On every play someone is trying to block you. Once you beat the block it is only a matter of running to the ball.

I felt like to beat those blocks, we had to get better using our hands. Before practice we go out and do a series of drills. Eight to 10 minutes before practice, we go out and do these drills. The linebackers do them on their own most of the time with the seniors in charge. I check on them from time to time to make sure they keep up their intensity and don't play too much.

I'll go through the drills and tell you what we are trying to do, and then I'll show you some drill tape so you can see them. In my drill, I try to fatigue them. There is never a long line in any of my drills. I want to condition as well as work on skills. I break them into two groups so I can get quick 10- to 15-second bursts, with one group going for 10 to 15 seconds, and the other group going for 10 to 15 seconds. I also want to give them a focus point. In the hands drill, there are two guys paired up working together. One of the drills is a hand-slap drill. The first player puts his hands up, and the other player will slap them down and do a swim move. Some of these drills are boring. To keep them focused, I'll tell them that today they are playing a team that only punch out with the hands, but they don't try to hold. In that drill, we only break the elbow down before we swim.

The next day I'll tell them we are playing a team that does a lot of holding when they block. In this drill, we have to slap the hands down, grab the elbow, and swim. That gives them a focus and breaks up the monotony of the drill.

I was at an NFL camp a couple of years ago watching practice. I was standing with a group of other coaches watching some drill work. I overheard a comment from one of the coaches. He said the drill they were doing was a worthless drill. I didn't say anything, but in the back of my mind I thought there is no drill that is really worthless. It is what you are trying to get out of the drill that is important. We don't know what the focus of the drill really is. We may be working on the hands in a drill, but the purpose of the drill is to gain footwork. If you are on the outside, you don't know what the focus of the drill is.

Most of the drills I do, you guys probably have done. We are big on fundamentals. The drill may look simple, but these are the drills we do. If you have an old speed-punching bag, I would put that sucker up and have everyone work on it. I would use it year-round. There is no substitute for a linebacker with quick hands. Linebackers are playing in a five-yard box, which is like a small tunnel against any offensive lineman. They are going against a lineman that knows where he is going and knows the play. He knows the snap count which gives them the advantage.

We want to give our kids some artillery to counter what they are doing. Part of that artillery is the drill work, and part of it is changing up the attack. Sometimes when we take on an isolation block, we take them high, and sometimes we cut them. We are going to take the fight to the blocker and slow him down.

The first thing on the tape is a sled drill. I found an old sled that the offensive linemen weren't using. I painted numbers on the sled dummies. I painted five numbers on the dummies. I painted one in each corner section of the dummy and one number in the middle. When the players are doing the drill I stand behind them. The first two days we did the drill, they didn't want to do it because they were tired and didn't want to stay in the ready position that long.

SLED DRILL

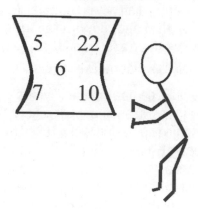

On the third or fourth day they were over the fatigue and started to concentrate on the numbers. I stood behind them and yelled out numbers. They have to hit the numbers with their hand as I yell them out. It makes them use both hands and focus on certain parts of the dummies.

The next drill is a partner drill. The players face one another, and they alternate back and forth. This is a pass-rush drill. I want them to be aware of where their hands are. The sled is stationary, but the partner drill is against a moving target. We start out with the progression of wrist, elbow, and shoulder. The first guy slaps the wrist down with his right hand on his partner's right wrist. He punches the right elbow of his partner in with his left hand. He finishes by punching the left shoulder with the right hand. As soon as one player does all three moves the other guy repeats the same three moves. He starts as soon as the other player's hand punches his shoulder. He starts by slapping the wrist of the hand that is on his left shoulder with his opposite hand. He punches the right elbow in with his left hand, and punches his partner's left shoulder with his right hand. They work back and forth on each other going as fast as they can.

Once they become proficient in the wrist, elbow, and shoulder, we add a swim or club move.

In another hand-movement drill, we practice pass-rush escapes. I teach them the club-swim, club-rip, chop-club-swim, chop-club-rip, and double-arm up. I teach these moves to everyone, but they only use maybe one or two of these moves when they pass rush. Along with the hand movement I teach short quick steps. When a pass rusher overstrides, it is easy for him to get pushed off balance. Once they

get past the blocker, they have to sink their hips and get their balance back. The pass rush is not over when the rusher beats the blocker; he has to finish the deal.

Another drill we do is the push-pull drill. This is a pass-rush move that does just what its name says. The move is to push back on the blocker and then pull forward and incorporate a swim or rip as you pull forward.

From individual drills, we go to group drills doing the same thing. We chop with the inside arm, club with the outside arm, and rip with the inside arm. In all these drills it is generally a three-step movement. We are trying to get to the back of the shoulder and pull it down.

At Oregon we don't play a lot of nickel defense. I have been blessed with linebackers that can cover in man coverage. That lets us keep them in the game in passing situations. Every day I do one of these drills out of this category. We do a trail technique, backpedal drive, and crossover techniques. I teach a couple reps of each move. The rest of the teaching is done in the 7-on-7 drill later in practice.

TRAIL DRILL

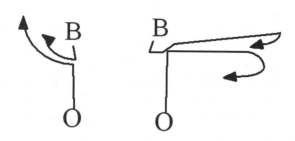

The next drill we do is called the *red ball drill*. I have these large red balls. I use this drill to teach linebackers to sink their hip so they can deliver a blow. The coach stands behind the red ball and pushes it toward the defender. He pushes it toward one side or the other of the defensive player. The defensive player has to shuffle to get in front of the ball and punch down on it with his hands. Every time they touch the ball, I want the weight on the inside foot, and the outside foot back. This also teaches the linebacker how to scrape. If the linebacker is scraping as a lineman tries to block him, it is important for the linebacker to get outside before he engages the block. If the lineman hits the linebacker before he gets outside, the lineman will grab him, and the linebacker will never make it outside.

RED BALL DRILL

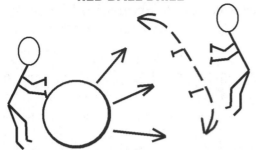

When I do the red ball drill, I have half of the linebackers doing balls and half of them doing *hoops*. One group starts on the hoops and the other on the balls and they switch.

HOOPS

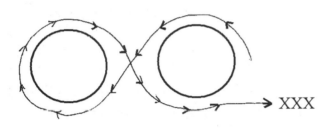

I don't do a lot on the hoops, but I do make them run one-and-a-half laps just to make them work on their lean. Some of our guys are stiff and can't do this very well. I stand in the middle of the hoop and pull them around the hoop. They don't particularly like that.

Last year we lost games to Wisconsin and Oregon State. In those games we screwed up our fits with our linebackers. In the Wisconsin game, their running back had 32 carries for over 200 yards rushing. He had three carries for 182 yards. On all three of those carries, our fits were wrong. We had the safety and inside linebacker outside, and the running back hit it inside and took it to the house. We did the same thing in the Oregon State game. We screwed up our fits, and the run went to the house.

This year we had one play where we messed up our fits. That was against Arizona State. Other than that play, we were damn near 100 percent on our run fits.

Linebackers have to get across the tops of blocks to keep from being blocked. They have to get to the outside shoulder of the blocker, or he will pin the linebacker in a heartbeat. But I don't want the linebackers to be robots. We play really deep. The offensive linemen learn where we are and run up the field to cut us off. We can't have our linebackers fighting over blocks six and seven yards down the field. If the linemen get too high or too far up the field on their block, our linebackers run underneath the block.

We work drills to teach that skill. As part of the drill, we put him close to the line and have someone try to cut him. That makes him play the cut block off and get downhill to make the tackle.

OVER THE TOP

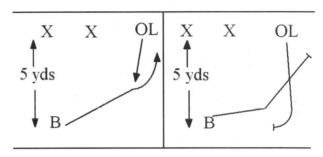

We can add a second part to the drill by including a ballcarrier. The linebacker gets over the top of the offensive lineman and secures the tackle on the ballcarrier.

OVER THE TOP TACKLE

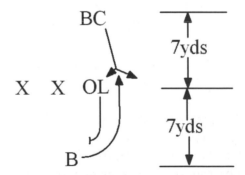

The next drill is the best drill I do. It is called the *fit drill*. It is a simple 1-on-1 drill. We have an offensive and defensive player. The defensive player is working to get his proper fit in the run game. The offensive blocker goes one way or the other. The defender has to get his proper fit and shuffle that way. We do this drill two or three times a week with two reps apiece. If the linebacker is an outside linebacker, he has to get to the outside of the blocker and shuffle that way. If he is an inside linebacker, he has to get to the inside and shuffle inside.

FIT DRILL

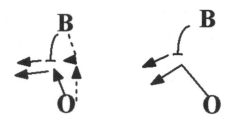

This next drill some of you might classify as a worthless drill. We line up our big pop-up dummies in a zigzag gauntlet-type alignment. Our guys run through the gauntlet clubbing the dummies with their outside arm. What this does is change the direction of their hips. Players are going to run in the direction their hips are pointing. Have you ever seen a pass rusher run right by the quarterback when he steps up? It happens because his hips are going in that direction and he can't turn back. This helps the linebackers to turn their hips and run downfield.

GAUNTLET DRILL

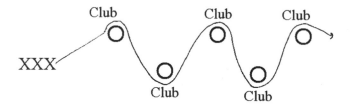

The last thing on this tape is some sled work. I give the linebackers a shoulder that I want them to hit the sled with. We are hitting with the shoulder and getting over the top. The sled is an imaginary man. The linebacker hits the sled with his right shoulder; he has to move to his right to get to the next pad. In this drill we work on footwork and blow delivery. We are working on hitting the outside pad of a man. We want to defeat half a man, not the whole man. The problem with a sled that has five or six stations is you don't know who is hitting the sled and who isn't.

When we work on the one-man sled, we make them push it. You can tell who is hitting and pushing the sled. That is what I like about it. If you have seven people on a seven-man sled, you could have three out of the seven just hanging on to the sled and the other four pushing. On the one-man sled, there is never any question.

Our goal as a defense is to play fast. I want my guys to be unbelievably fast. I tell my guys if they go fast, they can't be wrong. Just don't slow down and get blocked. There are lots of plays in a game where the ball keeps bouncing outside. We want to dominate the game. We only get two opportunities to do that. We do not play offense. The only ways we can dominate the game is on defense and special teams. If you are a linebacker at Oregon and don't play on the special, you will never play in a game. You earn your way on the field as a linebacker by doing something big on the special teams.

There are a couple of things we need to do off the field to dominate on the field. You have to know your defense from all positions. Knowing your opponent is the second thing we need to do. That means we have to study. They get out of school at one o'clock. Our meetings start at 1:30. When I walk into my meeting room, the linebackers have been in there for 30 minutes watching film. If I understand my opponent and understand my defense, I can control the opponent. You cannot control something that you don't understand. We teach the big picture. If you are a linebacker at Oregon, you are going to take reps at all three positions. When we get on the field, we do our thing and play fast. When we are in the drills, we do all the base fundamentals together. When you understand what everybody else is doing, it makes it easier for you to do your job. The defense can go faster when they know what everyone else is doing.

When we play, we have to be the "baddest" dudes on the field. I tell them that and they have to believe it. For them to be successful, I need to give them a bunch of weapons. We are playing in that five-yard battlefield against guys that are bigger then we are. They are guys who know where they are going, know the snap count, and in our league, have a license to hold. We don't get mad about someone holding us because the referees don't call holding where we play. That is the way it is and we live with it.

If we are getting a lot of a certain play, we change up how we play the blocks. The Sam linebacker may tell the Mike linebacker that he is going to cut all the blockers on the counter gap instead of simply spilling the play. That tells the Mike linebacker the play is going to break really wide. We are going to change up and take the fight to the offense. We have to slow down the offense and gain an advantage.

If you want to go fast, knowing who is going to block you will help your play. Never get stuck on blocks. We want to read and run and beat the blocker to the force spot. It is ridiculous to think a guard can pull from the other side and block the linebacker in the hole. The linebacker should be in the hole waiting for the pulling guard.

We have to believe our eyes. When I played, I didn't have the confidence to move. I didn't want to screw up, so I played really slow until I understood that I needed to believe what I saw. When the guys come to the sideline, I want to know what they saw. If they can tell me, I don't get on them. For those guys who don't know what happened, they catch holy hell.

I've got three minutes left, and I'll try to show you four plays of our mix blitzes on film. We see a lot of option. Because of that, we have a read-out function.

On certain blitzes, the linebacker determines who goes first. When people see our blitzes, there are a couple of ways to get outside of them. They screen and option to get outside on our blitzes. On these blitzes, we have one linebacker screaming through the line of scrimmage. The other linebacker moves laterally before he comes. If he sees anything that looks like a screen, he reads outside and gets into the play. That way we don't lose both linebackers on the blitz.

I did a better job of coaching that this year, and we were much better at the read-out function. We have a coverage control function also. That is so we don't lose both blitzes if a back swings in coverage. If the rover and Will linebacker are blitzing, in certain coverage they have to pick up a man if he releases. If the back releases and the rover back covers him, the Will linebacker keeps on coming on the blitz.

Quickly, I'll wrap it up. I appreciate the opportunity to share with you some of the things we are trying to do. The best thing we have going is a great environment and a bunch of good kids. We are really excited about our kids. I appreciate you getting up early and I really appreciate you guys not making me wear a shirt and tie. Once again thanks.

HOW WE APPROACH PRACTICE AND GAMES

University of Missouri

I am excited to be here. First I want to tell you this was a tough year for me. It was only my second losing season in 25 years. It's going to take a lot of energy to turn things around. There is a process to winning. It is not magic. The process to winning is that you must have a plan and a system in place. The thing that we do at Missouri is that we are not changing a thing in our system. We will tweak a few things offensively or defensively, but philosophically we will not change.

The thing we will do is change the people. We will change attitudes; we will become a lot tougher football team. We are in the process of getting that done right now. There are a lot of things that have to change, and I will change the people in it. That is the process. We believe 100 percent in the things we do. We have a great staff; they are soldiers and good people. And we have a system that we believe in.

What happens is when you go through adversity, and we all face it, the one thing the players do is try to see if you are going to start changing everything. Are you going to have a new offense or a new defense, or are you going to start lifting differently? Or now we are going to start getting tough on you guys. If you do that, you are going to start losing their confidence. I think one thing that our players see is the vision — that is my responsibility to make sure that gets done.

I also suggest to you that you need to know the influence you may have on people. I would suggest you probably do know this, and you do take that on as a responsibility. The players you coach watch everything you say, do, and the way you act. They watch everything! Some of those kids have no role models. They do not look anywhere else. So the things you do have a tremendous influence on those individuals. I take this real personally. This is a great profession. Even after being in some of the darkest days of the past season, which was one of the toughest in my life, I still love what I do. The thing, other than the winning and losing part, which is the most important thing, is the influence you have on them as a person. As a role model, you can influence young kids. You can change them. You don't think you do, but you do. You can help them well and beyond.

I would like to talk about practice organization and how we approach the game overall. We practice a certain way at Missouri. I do not know how other people practice, but we practice a certain way. I believe you can get an edge in the way you practice. You must practice better than anyone else. You learn how to practice, so you will be fundamentally better, and play better, so you will have more intensity. We try to have that edge in our program. We try to have an edge in everything we do. We try to have an edge in our weight lifting, in getting stronger, faster, and quicker. We try to do these things better than everybody. In our 40-hour preparation — everything we do will make us better. Practice is no different. What we try to do is practice with great intensity. We do not have clinics on the field. We try to get our players to play hard in practice. We want to get this to carry over to the games. We are now in the process of getting that done. We believe in, and have a certain way in which we do, everything we do.

During our drills, our coaches coach very hard. They are well-organized, and we get after it. I am going to go through some of the things we believe in related to practice and what we do during practices.

First of all, I clearly define what I expect of my coaches. I want them to get it to their players and define what their responsibilities are, and get the players to play above their potential. We measure by results, not efforts. That is what our business is. Nobody cares that we were 4-7. Nobody cares about our problems or personnel problems. This is a result business, not an effort business, and my guys know that.

You are responsible to have your position play at a championship level regardless of youth or experience. Every position should be motivated at practice to play at a championship level. We want to make sure every one of your players abides by the team covenant. We have a team covenant. If you are in the program, and you are part of our team, this is what you do. This is how you act. Right now, in this stage of our program, our coaches are policing it all the time; our players are not policing it. Next year our players will be saying, "We don't do that around here." So we have a team covenant that we sign. It is in their lockers. We read it to them, we talk to them about it, and we counsel our players in regards to it. It's the coaches' responsibilities to lead them in *who* we are and *what* we are all about. We stress our team covenant. Also, we constantly emphasize academics. Our players must graduate. We take that very seriously.

Here are some things we believe about our coaching and teaching. First, let your players know you care about them. Trust is earned, not guaranteed. You cannot expect your players to care about winning, and your program being part of their life, unless you care about them as people. There is no way it is going to happen. I am used to a different attitude than our team had this year, but we will get there. I'm used to guys where the program is part of who they are; I'm used to guys who live and die football, with passion – every single minute of their lives. We are still changing those kinds of attitudes. Before they change, they need to know we care about them.

The next thing is very important. We lead by example. Coaches, be good role models to your players. Honesty, respect, and loyalty are important. If you are not 100 percent honest, you will have no credibility. If you tell a kid something that is wrong or is a lie, or you are beating around the bush, they can see it. Your credibility goes down right now. You have none. It is really critical in our program for our players to trust everyone.

At times our players don't like what we have to say. You have to be careful how you say things. Be critique-oriented where by saying it you will not destroy the kid. At least they will respect you for being honest.

Get your kids to believe that you are the best coach-teacher in the league. If the players don't believe it we will not win. If you go into a position meeting and you are fumbling and not organized, or you go onto the field and you are not doing the drill properly, or not on top of things, guess what? They are not going to believe in you. This will carry over into winning and losing. We want our coaches to be great teachers. What you see on the video is what you coached. You see the bottom line. You have to be accountable. I ask my players to be accountable, and I ask my coaches to be accountable. I am accountable. And obviously what I saw, and what I coached last year was not good enough. I am going to work through that.

What I am doing with my coaches for the spring, and what I have done for the last eight years, is to have them write down every fundamental at the position they teach, and write down the drills that teach those fundamentals. Then we go back through those fundamentals and make sure we are fundamentally teaching and covering everything possible that we will be using in drills. We have to be a better fundamental team.

You are a teacher, and your teaching is evaluated by your players' performances. Professors can get A, B, C, D, and F students. Our players need to get all A's. Keep things simple, don't overcoach, and find the best way to teach. Kids learn differently. Kids are very visual, but they learn things differently. You need to find out about kids, and how they learn best. Teach fundamentals. Our goal is that each kid masters the fundamentals at his position. We have to become a much better fundamental football team.

Another thing our staff must know is what has to be taught. Our staff must have growth, improve schemes, and our philosophy must be declared.

After a tough year, you don't scrap your offense and scrap your defense. We talked about that before. You lose your credibility if you do that. We will absolutely evaluate everything we do. We will evaluate every phase of our program. We will find ways we can make ourselves better. But we will not scrap everything. That is not the way to develop a program.

We utilize teaching aids and change up the procedures at every meeting. If you teach the same way at every meeting, guess what? You lose the attention of the players. We have some great teachers, and some average teachers. Great teachers are organized and interesting; average teachers can go on and on. You need to change things up. You need to use teaching aids, and video breakdowns, marking boards. Also, accurate diagrams are critical. About 75 percent of learning is visual. When I was at the University of Washington with Coach Don James, I got up in front of the staff to draw a route, and it was not exactly like the route the tight end should run. He ripped me. If you draw something up improperly and it is sloppy, guess what? That player doesn't have a good perception of how the play is supposed to look. If it is done neat and it is proper, and in proportion to the other routes, it increases its chances for the carryover to the field. It may seem like a little thing, but all the little things make a difference. We feel it is important to use practice and scrimmage video, and we use training video.

When we first start our players' meetings, we assume our players don't know anything. We start from scratch. I was always impressed with the Dallas Cowboys and Tom Landry. The TV reporters were talking with Tony Dorsett when he was playing for the Cowboys. It was during the early season camp. I was coaching with Washington at the time, and I recall this conversation. They asked Dorsett what the coaches were working on with him. He said he was taught how to hold a football and that they worked on his stance that day. That was Tom Landry; he did not assume anything. Here Dorsett was, an all-pro, one of the great running backs who ever played, and he talked about Tom Landry, and what he was working on with him. He coached fundamentals.

Our players must be on time for every meeting. There is nothing worse than having a player show up late for a meeting. I treat our assistant coaches the same way. If you as a coach have a meeting at 7:30 p.m. and you walk in at 7:35, you lose your credibility.

We must be prepared for each meeting. If not, you crash and burn. That should not happen, and will never happen in our program. To be thoroughly prepared for a meeting, you have to have a plan for each meeting. You need to be the expert at that meeting. Our players do not just sit and listen. Our players have paper and pencils and write down what they hear and see. We make them write it down and take notes. Players must sit in their chairs, and make full eye contact. We don't have players lying on the floor or ground. That is not conducive to good learning.

We feel interaction at meetings is important. We do not just lecture. We ask players "Why did you do that?" After practice make some notes and run your notes off and give them to them as handouts. We will pick out five things or rules they need to know. They get it at the meeting the next day. We run it off and hand it to them. Even if you do not go through a video, it makes their learning visual. The players need something visual in front of them.

Coaches must watch their language on the field. Our coaches will occasionally slip up. But if you are role models, you don't need to use profanity. Some of you don't think it is a big deal, but I do. I want our players to know that you can be a tough son-of-a-buck as anyone in the country without using bad words.

Here are some general rules related to our program. We tell our players no tobacco product — staff or players. It is an NCAA rule. We will not lay a hand on the players. Our off-season program is at 6:00 a.m. in the morning, and it is much like a war zone right now. On March 1, we will be getting up like Special Forces in training. When I played at Kent State, we had a mat program that was high intensity. Then, coaches would just grab you or throw you around. If they did that now they would have 14 lawyers on their doorstep. It is also not the right thing to coach or teach. No matter how many times you feel like grabbing a player, we will not touch a player. Coaches will at times get mad and once in a while get up in their face. But you may have to back off a little and be smart about it.

You should have great enthusiasm, but not be a cheerleader. I believe in the 3-to-1 theory — three positives to every one negative. We are in a critique-oriented business. We will criticize performance and tell the players not to take it personally. We try to find things to be positive about. We are constantly critiquing, and coaching, to make our players better. When my coaches come out of a two-hour practice, they are absolutely drained. But they have to find positive things to talk about. We stress that 80 percent of the things they say must be positive. Sometimes, last year when things weren't going well, we had to work hard to be positive. It was tough, but we needed to do it to get the job done.

Something that is real important is consistency. Our players look for consistency in that they know where things are coming from. For example, if you lose a football game, then next week you go out in pads and beat each other up. You run them through walls. Then the next time you lose another game and everything is okay. They want consistency; they understand that.

All players must be team players and abide by our covenant. Consistency is the key to everything. We must praise and criticize all players. If you want to lose credibility, you criticize one guy all the time because he makes a mistake, but you let another player get away with it without criticism. Your credibility is shot. The players see all that stuff. For some players, you may have to pull their strings differently than other players. We all know that. But you still need a degree of consistency in how you handle things. You want your players to trust you.

Coach *toughness, toughness, toughness.* I am going to go over that, and underline it, with my coaches before we start the year. We are not a very tough football team. I understand that, but we can coach it. We want a 100 percent effort on every play. Play every play, every day. Play hard. We want players that play hard for six seconds.

Players must be on time for every meeting or practice. They must pay attention to detail. The guy who wrote the book *Don't Sweat the Small Stuff* — he and I wouldn't get along. I don't know what that little difference between winning and losing is going to be. To me, all the little things make the difference. We take care of all the details to make sure we get everything done.

We demand players compete in everything that we do. We want them to be six-second players. We weren't very good at that last year; we were off and on in that regard.

The last thing is: We want hard workers on the field. In practice we want to coach on every play. I had some new coaches on my staff last year. Some coaches have to learn not to put their hands in their pockets.

They were very good coaches but we want them to coach every play. We may say "good job," then wait two plays and say "do a little better." We want to coach every single play and give a coaching point to a player each play. That is what you are out there for. You coach every single play on the field. No hands in the pocket, no arms folded. How can someone get excited if he is coached by someone with their hands in their pockets?

We do not want our coaches to stand in one spot. If a coach stands around, so will the players. Get to where the action is. If you come to our practice you'll see us running 7-on-7, or 11-on-11. Our coaches will go get the players after the play, and coach them back to the huddle. Then we coach the next play. We believe in coaching on the run, and we are constantly teaching on the run. For the long term, that will pay big dividends. I know it will.

We do not conduct clinics on the field. That is why we have our walk-throughs, and that is why we have meetings. We do not run a play and then talk about it for three minutes. We make a coaching point, and then move on. We will not hold a clinic on the field. That is from my Don James background.

Our coaches run from drill to drill just like the players. Our players must run on the field. We run from drill to drill. We take pride in everything we do in practice or in games. You will never see our players walk on the field. When you run on the field it sets the tempo. When you do that, you tend to practice with a more upbeat tempo. You will practice better.

We do not allow our players to lie on the ground. There is nothing I hate more than a player laying on the ground. I just can't stand it. There is nothing wrong with getting knocked down. If you get knocked down, you get off the ground fast. If they can't get that done, we will have a little awareness training. We demand intensity, enthusiasm, and we insist that the players know their assignments. We are getting better on this phase.

As a coach, it is important not to try to emulate another coach. You must be yourself and develop your own personality. I read about coaches all the time. Brian Billick from the Ravens has a new book out on leadership. But I can't be a coach like Brian Billick. I can't be Don James. Don was a whole lot better at being Don James than what I can ever be. I made that mistake when I was at Toledo. I think it is important for coaches to know that you have to be yourself.

We never laugh or make fun of a player. We do not degrade players. We do not allow name-calling, or threats to players. "You will never play here if you don't start catching the football." My coaches aren't allowed to do that. We will not threaten a player with a statement that he won't play for us. If someone is going to make threats, I am going to do it at a time that I feel is necessary. As a coach you do not name-call, degrade, or threaten players. That is using fear for motivation, and I don't think that is very good.

Our walk-ons are treated like scholarship players: with respect. When a walk-on comes into our program, he is treated like everybody else.

In practice we believe you must control the hitting. We have three tempos. We tag off where we have all the players tag the runners. We play the ball live and then tag off. We have our thud tempo where we butt the ballcarrier but we do not take him to the ground.

As coaches we know that players must respect coaches and teammates. We must respect each other. The offensive coaches must respect defensive players and vice versa. Injured players need attention. They need someone to watch over them constantly. All coaches need to know about every player in our program. We want all coaches in the locker room after every practice, and that is mandatory.

Basically you must assess damage control. If you tear a guy's throat out in practice, or you are hard on him in practice, you must get to him after practice. You have to live with that guy. We have to pick him back up, and get him ready for the next practice. Players appreciate that and they need to know you care about them. We build players up after tough practice.

We must develop self-starters and leaders. A self-starter is the guy who turns his motor on and goes. It is fun to have a locker room full of, and a football team made up of, self-starters who just go. You don't have to bite off the head of a chicken and throw it against the wall; they just want to go.

You need to develop the team concept and promote the team concept. Promote the value of the game. Give players more responsibility and encourage positive peer pressure. We want to promote Tiger pride.

How do you get players to compete? I got this concept from the Dallas Cowboys. We talk about our players all the time being six-second players. It is hard to win if you don't have enthusiasm, and you don't play hard. It is hard to play hard if you don't know what you are doing. It takes no ability to play as hard as you can every single play. It takes no ability at all to know what you are supposed to do. If you're not going to do those things, you are not going to win. If you do those things, and if you get some good players, and if you coach them well, you are going to win. We talk about those things all the time.

How do you teach a player to compete? When Jimmy Johnson was with the Cowboys, and they had three losing seasons, he had to teach his players how to compete. These are his words:

"In every occupation it is possible to visibly see effort; but it is productive effort that counts. Competition in an athlete comes from an inner feeling, a willingness to allow oneself to extend his or her body beyond mental desire. So many athletes start out good, but don't finish strong. Many of these athletes think they are working hard. However, those that do not finish strong are not competitive. Once again the athlete who is the most consistent in effort is the most valuable type of player. The athlete who makes his body perform against all odds is a winner. We are going against all levels of resistance. That is what a competitor must do.

"Through a total competitive effort, you can see a burning desire without hesitation to get the job done. Look to see if a player is taking the easier way out of work. Is he avoiding physical contact by taking the long way around the play or deliberately arriving late at the point of attack? Remember, initial effort counts, but finishing the play strong is a sign of a good competitor. While evaluating your players on the field, you must constantly critique him as a competitor. Is he a three-second, four-second, or five-second player? We are looking for a six-second man. You can teach a player to be a great competitor."

What you want is a locker room full of competitors. Are they the most talented guy, the most athletic guys? Maybe not, but when you play them, you better hold on, because they are going to fight you to the end.

If you looked at our football team last year, you may have said we were not very good. I can only tell you this: We will get better. Thank you.

THE NO-HUDDLE SPREAD OFFENSE

West Virginia University

Thank you. I appreciate the opportunity to come down here and speak. When you go 3-8, you have to beg to get an opportunity like this one. My topic today should be "how to go 3-8 and get a contract extension." It is good to be here. Despite our record last year we feel very good about the direction in which our program is going.

We played last year with 53 guys on scholarship. We lost some players before we got there and some after we got there. Before we knew it, we were in a 1-AA status in our scholarship limits. We will recruit our maximum load this year and next year and we'll have it back to where it should be.

My topic today is the shotgun and no-huddle offense. I started doing this about 11 years ago. I figured I could find a quarterback that could do some things, linemen that were athletic not big, and a couple of receivers that could spread the field. I figured I could spread the field and make the defense defend us honestly.

What has developed in the last six or seven years is the running game. People get the perception that all we are doing is throwing the ball every down. The reality of the offense is we run the ball 53 percent of the time. Last year Clemson ran the ball from the shotgun 63 percent of the time. The quarterback made a lot of those runs in this offense.

Coaching the spread offense is a different system. I'm not here to sell you on doing the spread offense. You are going to do what you want to do anyway. If you think you can run the spread 15 percent of the time and do the other things you do in your offense, that is fine. For us we are committed to that type of offense. There is a lot more to the spread than being in a shotgun with four wide receivers. You have to do what you know. I'm sold on it because it has worked at different levels.

It didn't work so well for us at West Virginia last year, but execution is the key. We have changed our philosophy about the method we use to attack. I feel good about that and once our players learn what they are doing it will get much better.

You might wonder why Nebraska is good all the time. They train their offensive line the entire year and in the off-season. Everyone comes into the fall knowing the offense and who to block. Plus they have pretty good players and have been doing that for 30-some years.

I would expect West Virginia to be better in our second year and even better in our third year. Execution is always the key and everyone knowing his job.

That reminds me of a story about the old coach that got fired. He was looking through the want ads in the paper for a job. He found an ad for a lion tamer in the circus. He thought that might be an interesting job. He went to the circus to apply for the job. The ringmaster was doing the interview for the job. He brought out the current lion tamer to show the coach what he had to do. The lion tamer entered the cage with a 400-pound lion in the cage. He cracked his whip, and the lion got up on a stool. From the side entered a tall, good-looking blonde dressed in a long cape. The ringmaster told the coach to watch closely. The lion tamer cracked his whip and the blonde dropped her cape. She was wearing one of those Sports Illustrated bikinis. She was absolutely gorgeous. The lion tamer cracked his whip again and the lion began to lick the blonde up and down from head to toe. The ringmaster asked the old coach if he thought he could do that. He told the ringmaster, "Hell, yeah! Just get that damn lion out of there!"

The offense has two distinct advantages on the defense. The offense knows where they are going and when they are going. Everyone knows about the first advantage. But I'm not just talking about the snap count on the second advantage. I am talking about tempo. We can go in a fast tempo or slow tempo.

We run the no-huddle offense because it fits our philosophy, but it also controls the defense's ability to substitute situational players and to restrict their movement. Defensive coaches like to use different personnel in different situations. They want to bring the nickel and dime backs in on third down and passing situations. They want the heavy line in on first and 10 in a running situation.

The defense wants to substitute when the offense substitutes. They want to stem the front, show you one defense, and give you another front. If you snap the ball within five seconds of breaking the huddle, you will not see the defense making a lot of adjustments. We want to make sure what we see is what we get. We still have people move on us, but we want to play fast and control the tempo. We think we can go faster every year.

I heard Dennis Franchione from Alabama speak and he got into the nuts and bolts of their offense. A lot of coaches when they get to be head coaches think they have to become philosophers. I know you don't want to hear the philosophies, and I don't blame you. I'm going to give you some nuts and bolts to our offense. But we do have some philosophies that I have to cover.

These are things we can hang our hats on. Stretching the field both horizontally and vertically is the first thing we want to do. We are going to spread people out and make the defense defend all 53 yards of the width and 120 of the length.

Our entire running game is based on *numbers, angles,* and *grass*. The *numbers* in the box will tell us when to run and when to throw. If the defense has five to six in the box, we will run the football. If there are seven in the box, we have to pass. If there are three men on one side and four on the other, we are going to run to the three-man side. That is pretty simple. We try to keep it simple for our team.

Coach Rick Trickett, our offensive line coach, told me what he teaches our players is based on an 11 ACT score. Some of the coaches tell me that is what he got the sixth time he took it. Seriously, he doesn't talk over our kids' heads.

The *angles* are in relationship to the angles in blocking. It is easier to block down and kick out than it is to drive-block somebody back off the ball. And it is a more consistent style of blocking.

The *grass* means we want to run to the wide field if we can. If the numbers and angles are good, we want to go to the wide side of the field. If they aren't, we will run into the boundary.

Control of the tempo is the last of our philosophy. We are no-huddle all the time. We call our fastest tempo *Indy*. We want our offense to control the pace of the game. We want to get to the line and snap the ball. We go from fast to fastest as far as tempo is concerned.

When you run a spread offense, the spacing of the receivers is as important as anything you can do. We are mostly a three-wide and four-wide offense. Sometimes we get in three wide receivers with two backs. We will get into some I-formation or two tight ends with two wideouts. But for the most part we are a one-back offense set.

As I go through our formation, there is one consistent point. We want our outside wide receivers to be within 5 yards of the sideline. In general terms, the spacing for our wide receivers is to have 5 yards between the wideout and the nearest offensive player. If I am a slot receiver, I want to be 5 yards from the tackle. If I am an outside receiver, I want to be 5 yards from the slot receiver.

If you have 5 yards between the receivers, you will have enough room to create some space for blocking, running, and the route running. It is hard to find four good receivers. Last year we had a couple of good receivers. In high school you are probably lucky to have one good one. If you only have one good receiver, put him at the *X receiver*. The X receiver is our split end to the boundary.

That is where we put our best receiver. The second-best receiver is our slot receiver to the field, which we call the *Y receiver*. Our third-best receiver is generally our backup tailback. We put him in the boundary-side slot. He is called the *H receiver*. The fourth receiver is a good stalk blocker, and we call him the *Z receiver*.

I had a big booster's son playing for me. That guy gave more money to our program than God has. I promise you this boy was bad. I told the daddy if he would help us out and give us a little money for the program I would make sure his son got on the field. Well the guy gave us a bunch of money. I was in big trouble because if I played his kid he was going to hurt himself or somebody else. The rule in college football is you cannot break the huddle with more than 11 people or it is a penalty. I decided to use the no-huddle because there is no rule about the number of people on the field before the ball is snapped. You could have 20 guys on the field before the ball is snapped as long as you didn't huddle.

That is what I did. Before each play I ran the booster-boy out to the numbers and right back off the field. He got on the field about 25 plays and never played a snap. That is a good avenue to get a big booster involved in your program. All you have to do is tell him his son would be on the field at least 20 plays against our biggest rival. Make sure you don't promise him his son will letter.

Our favorite formation to run the ball from is what we call *reo*. That is a three-by-one formation. You could go into a two-by-two formation, but the three-by-one set makes the linebacker displace. If you go two-by-two, the defense can stay balanced. If you go to the three-by-one it forces the defense to show you which way they are going to shade. In this set we have the X receiver 5 yards from the sideline, and the Y receiver is 5 yards from the offensive tackle into the field. The H receiver is 5 yards outside the Y receiver, and the Z receiver is 5 yards from him. The quarterback is in the shotgun and the F back is in the halfback position to the wide side of the field.

REO

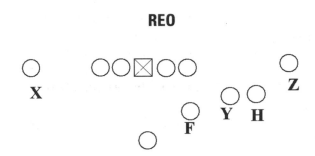

I'll show you our other formations and go through them quickly. The two-by-two formation is called *rip*. That is our double-slot formation. The H receiver is in the boundary-side slot, and the Y receiver is in the field-side slot.

RIP

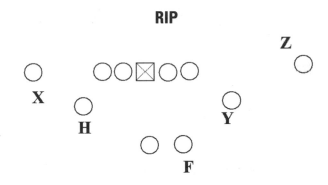

The *rip far* is a three-by-two empty set. It is like the rip set except the F back is outside the Z receiver.

RIP FAR

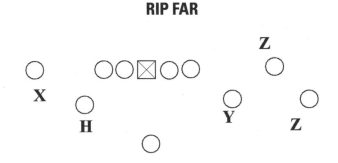

The *rip wing* is a double-wing formation with the F and H sitting in the wing sets off the tackle. The Y and Z receivers are bunched outside to the field side.

RIP WING

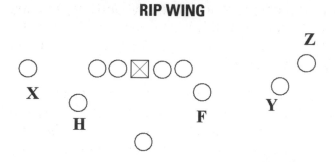

The *ram* is a three-by-one set with a tight end to the field. The Y and Z receivers are off the ball in a flanked formation.

RAM

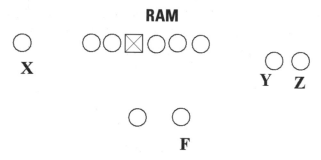

People say they don't have a quarterback who can throw the ball to the widest receiver into the field. It doesn't matter. If you put a receiver out there, I promise you the defense will cover him. It may be the worst defensive back, but someone will cover him.

Our offensive guards are in three-point stances and the tackles are in two-point stances. All the wideouts are in two-point stances. The line splits are about two-foot splits. If we have a tight end, he is split about two-and-a-half feet. They can adjust their splits if we are trying to move defensive alignments around. If we tell the offensive guard to split the bubble, he takes a wider split if he has a 3-technique aligned on him. If the alignment is a shade and a 5-technique, the offensive tackle widens to split the bubble.

The quarterback is 5 yards deep, and the tailback or F back is even with him. The snap in the shotgun is a learned skill. This year we had a center that had never snapped in a shotgun situation. It is like shooting a free throw or riding a bike: you have to do it over and over. We tell the center to sit on top of the ball. That means the ball is almost underneath him. We want to leave the ball flat with a V formed by the thumb and first finger of the hand, with the thumb on the laces of the ball. He snaps the ball back firmly. We don't snap it like a long snap with a spiral on it. The key is for the center to keep his butt down and step back slightly as he snaps the ball. He doesn't look between his legs. His head is up on the snap so he can see the defense.

If the center picks the ball up, he is going to have problems. He has to leave it flat on the ground. As he snaps the ball, he wants to release it before his hand crosses the back of his knee. If he lifts his butt, he will snap the ball high.

We always have about six offensive linemen practice the gun snap. They may have no chance to be the center, but we pick our six guys to practice this skill. Usually it is the six most flexible guys on the team. We want the snap to be somewhere between the waist and face. We don't want the quarterback to have to focus his eyes on the snap. We want him watching the defense.

We want the quarterback to make his checks and automatics, but we don't want him to give a verbal command for the snap. We used to give the leg kick for the snap. We don't do that any more. When you do those types of things, the defense will stem and change the defense. We change our indicator from week to week. We may use one finger for the ready signal one week while it could be two fingers the next week. After the indicator, the center snaps the ball when he is ready.

Our wideouts move on the movement of the ball. The linemen move on the center's snap. The center says, "Go," when he snaps the ball.

If the snap becomes erratic, the quarterback has to start watching the snap instead of the defense. We don't want that. We want him looking at the defense and seeing the snap in his peripheral vision. That is one of the negatives about the shotgun set. Our rule at West Virginia is any bad snap in practice or a game, means 50 snaps after practice. I've seen guys snap 300 snaps after practice.

We don't use a lot of motion in our offense. We feel it slows us down. Also if we bring someone in motion, it will probably change the defense we are seeing. The purpose of the fast no-huddle is what you see is what you get.

There is a common misperception that the quarterback in the no-huddle calls all the plays. I'm not going to put my livelihood in the hands of an 18-year-old kid that watches cartoons on Saturday morning. He is not making any calls for me. He is looking to the sidelines to see what to call. He gets the plays from the coach. If he wants to change the play, he looks to the sideline to see if it's all right. Our quarterback has to be a quick decision maker and an executor. He has to make the decision to hand the ball off or keep it and he has to execute the offense.

The decisions of which plays to run has to be removed from him until he thinks like a coach. You want your quarterback to think like you think. The more the quarterback thinks like you as a play caller, the faster you can run your offense. In my opinion, there is no one in a team game who has more impact on the outcome of the game than the quarterback. A pitcher in baseball probably has more to do with the outcome, but the quarterback is really ranked high. I tell that to my quarterbacks all the time.

You are not going to win the big games without outstanding play by your quarterback. We don't want to put a mental burden on our quarterback. The quarterback is the key to the spread offense. If you have a quarterback who can run and throw a little bit, the one-back offense becomes a two-back offense.

We have more runs out of the shotgun than we do under center. The philosophy in the spread offense is simple: It doesn't matter if it is man coverage or zone coverage, the defense generally covers all the receivers. If the defense leaves a receiver uncovered, you have to have the ability to get the ball to him. If the defense puts seven in the box, they are generally in man coverage with no help. The offense has to run the speed option or throw the ball.

My philosophy is the fewer people we have to block to get to the second level, the better chance we have. If we have to count on four real good blocks to get the play past the linebacker, we are hurting. If we can get two good blocks then we have a chance. We are demanding on our wideouts with their blocking. They do a good job of stalk blocking in the secondary. We have a basic rule for our receivers in run blocking: If it is man-to-man, run the defensive back off until he turns to come back. When it happens, you have to block him. If it is zone coverage, chase the defensive back out of his zone and get between him and the ballcarrier.

Our first three steps by the wide receiver are always the same. We drive three hard steps full speed at the defensive back's outside shoulder. We look right at the defensive back's eyes. If his eyes are on the receiver, we keep driving him off. If the defensive back's eyes go inside, the receiver stops and locks up on the defensive back.

With six defenders in the box, we want to run to the 1-technique defender. You could run this play toward the 3-technique, but we want to run it to the 1-technique because the angles are better. The center and onside guard are zone blocking on the 1-technique up to the linebacker depth. The offensive tackle reach blocks the 5-technique. We want to try to keep the defenders on the line of scrimmage. We don't run an inside and outside zone play. We run one zone play, and the back has to read the play.

The tailback is toe to toe with the offensive tackle. He is even with the quarterback, who is 5 yards deep. The tailback opens to the quarterback. He crosses over and takes his third step directly in front of the quarterback. On every run you have from the shotgun, someone has to be responsible for the mesh area. In the zone play, the back is responsible for the mesh area because the quarterback is reading the end to the backside. We never block the backside end. The quarterback is going to read him. If the end takes off inside after the back, he pulls the ball and runs the bootleg.

After the back takes his three steps, his eyes are on the playside linebacker. We tell him to press the outside hip of the playside tackle. The back screws up when he starts downhill too soon. He wants to stay flat and press the hip of the tackle. If the back stays flat, the linebacker will stay flat. That is what we want the linebacker to do. We want time for the guard to stay on the 1-technique until the center can get control. When it happens, the guard can come off on the linebacker. All we want the guard to do is get a hat on the linebacker and get run over slowly.

There are three things the back can do with the ball. He can bang it into the bubble, bounce it to the outside, or bend it to the backside. If we are playing an odd front defense with a head-up noseguard on the center, the back is going to bang it into the bubble or bend it backside. Against the even defense he is going to bang the ball into the bubble or bounce it outside. The 5-technique can sneak into the bubble if he is not careful. The track of the back is always going to be the same. The harder track for the back is to bend the ball back from the shotgun.

ZONE PLAY

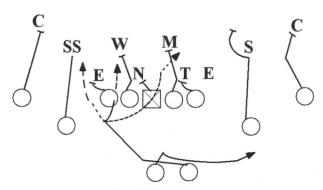

People like to play game on the backside with their end and Mike linebacker. They also get the Sam linebacker involved in defending the quarterback. We have answers for anything they try to do. If the defensive end crashes inside, that gives the quarterback a keep read. Some teams send the end down and scrape the Mike linebacker outside for the quarterback. Our answer is to turn out on the linebacker with the tackle and run up inside.

QUARTERBACK RUN

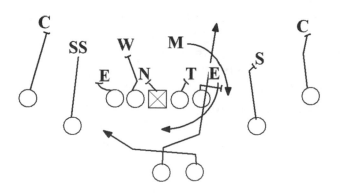

They also like to hang the Sam linebacker in the gray area on the backside. He is aligned off the slot back, but is hanging toward the inside. He is going to take the quarterback if he pulls the ball. He is covering the slot receiver, but at the same time he is leaning to the inside to take the quarterback. We have two answers for that technique. We call a quick bubble-screen play to the slot receiver that the Sam linebacker is covering. We do that from the sideline. The slot receiver gains a little width at half speed so we can get the pass completed. We want an easier throw than the full-speed bubble screen, so the receiver slows down and shows his numbers to the quarterback. It becomes a pitch-and-catch play. The line is blocking the zone play. They don't have any idea we are running the bubble screen to the backside.

QUICK SCREEN

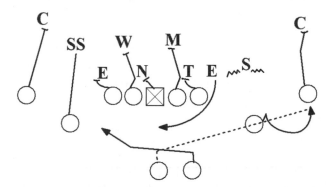

The other thing we can do is run an option with the slot receiver being the pitch back on the option. The quarterback pulls the ball and runs at the Sam linebacker. The slot receiver steps back to get a pitch relationship with the quarterback. They run a down-the-line option on the Sam linebacker.

OPTION

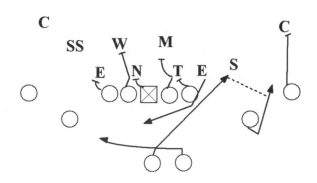

The first thing we tell our quarterback after he calls the formation and play is to look for any receiver uncovered. When we film our game, we have one camera that is not shut off during the game. We want to film what goes on between plays. We don't want anyone walking back to the line of scrimmage. That is part of their effort grade.

When the play is over, we are already signaling the next formation. The wideouts, tailback, and quarterback are looking at the signal. The quarterback yells the formation to the linemen. All that tells the linemen is their stance. After they get the formation, all their eyes go to the sideline to get the play. The key item when you have a no-huddle is to have simple signals. Some coaches get too complicated with their signals. They look like a third-base coach in baseball. I was like that for seven years. We don't worry about anyone stealing our signals. If they are looking at us, they are not getting lined up. If they steal the signal, they don't have time to communicate it. I don't worry about it.

When we are running the no-huddle, we have a rule that no one is allowed to bend over. We want to give the impression that we can run the no-huddle all day. We may be dog tired, but we don't want anyone to know it.

Probably my favorite play is the trap. I'll run this one from the rip set. We see the even front most of the time. We trap both the 3-technique and the 1-technique. When we go to four wide receivers, if I see a free safety in the middle of the field, I know there are six in the box. If there are two safeties on the hash marks, I know there are five in the box. That means we outnumber the defense seven to five in the box. If there are no safeties in the middle, we have to run the speed option or throw the ball because there are seven in the box. I like to run the trap to the 3-technique. The playside guard influences the 3-technique by pulling outside and blocking the end. Both tackles go for the inside V in the neck of the linebackers. If they can't get the cut off on the linebacker, they are to drive him past the hole. The center blocks back on the noseguard. The backside guard pulls and traps the A gap. If the 3-technique runs out of the play, or the Mike linebacker blitzes, the guard blocks the first man that shows. If there is no one to trap, he turns up the field and looks for another color jersey.

The quarterback is responsible for the mesh on the trap play. He takes the snap and steps up to mesh with the tailback. The tailback takes a 45-degree angle step. His second step is a 45, and his third step he is square to the hole. The quarterback makes the handoff and fakes the bootleg outside to hold the defensive end. If the end is squeezing hard inside, the quarterback can pull the ball and run the bootleg.

TRAP

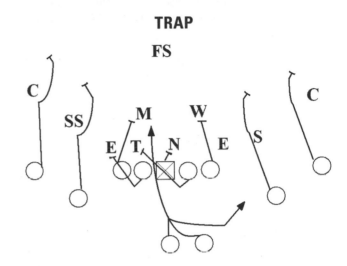

If the Will linebacker is cheating back to the gray area when the quarterback pulls, we run the option at the Will linebacker with the H receiver as the pitchman.

We could trap the 5-technique. If the noseguard gets tight on the center into a head-up position, we could trap the 5-technique. However we would pull and trap with the center instead of the guard. We can't pull the guard because the 3-technique would penetrate too much. The guard blocks the noseguard and the offensive tackle blocks inside on the linebacker. The center pulls and traps the 5-technique.

CENTER TRAP

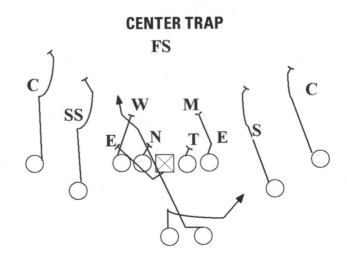

The running back has to align opposite the side the trap is being run toward. The defense started to adjust their front according to where the back aligned. If we moved the back over with an automatic, the defense changed their front to match the back. What we did to counter that was to let the quarterback run the trap. We leave the back where he is and fake the zone play to him. The line is running the trap; they don't care who is carrying the ball. The quarterback runs the trap. The quarterback does the same thing he did in the trap to the tailback, but after the back passes him, he pulls the ball and heads into the trap hole.

QUARTERBACK TRAP

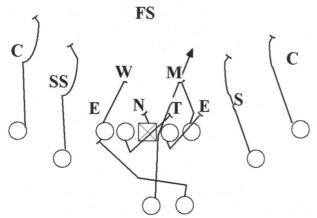

If you run the spread offense, you have to have a draw play. When we run the draw, the line blocks their five-man protection. We have a number of protections because we see a bunch of different defensive schemes. We have a gap protection, slide protection, man-to-man protection, five-man protection, and six-man protection. I match my protection to the personnel that I have. If I had a small athletic bunch, I would use man-to-man protection and get run over slowly. If I had a bunch of big hogs, I would gap protect.

In our quarterback draw, our tackle takes two hard vertical steps back. The guards set and protect the integrity of the pocket. They are thinking linebackers. The center has the noseguard. The linebackers playing on the slot backs fake in and out like they are going to blitz. We don't watch the linebackers. We watch the safeties. As long as the safeties are back 12 to 14 yards, the outside people are not going to come. If the safeties start cheating toward the line and get down to 7 or 8 yards deep, we are probably

going to get a blitz. The safeties are getting into position to cover someone man-to-man. That was a good key for us until we played Army. They kept the safeties deep and blitzed us off the corners. For that reason we run our slots on quick hitches in case the blitz does come. That gives the quarterback somewhere to get rid of the ball. That also keeps us from changing the play if we read the blitz coming. If the quarterback is going to carry the ball on the draw, he gives the illusion that he is dropping deeper on his pass drop. That way he doesn't have so far to get back to the line of scrimmage. If the back is going to carry the ball, he tightens up to the quarterback. When the ball is snapped, he shuffles over and meshes the ball.

DRAW PLAY

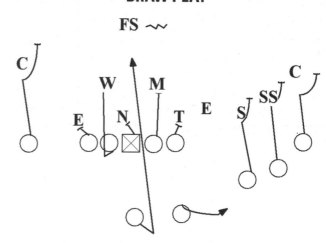

When you run the spread offense, if you can throw the quick game, you've got a chance. If you can't throw that pass at all, you are going to be hurting in the spread game. The quick game is the most important thing we do in the passing game. The quarterback wants to flip his hips as the ball is coming back to him. When the ball arrives, all he is going to do is get his fingers on the laces and throw the ball. The hardest thing a quarterback has to do in the shotgun is catch and throw. They have to catch and throw the ball in less than 1.5 seconds. From the shotgun we average about 1.3 seconds getting the ball off.

A bad snap changes the quick game because the quarterback's eyes have to focus on catching the ball. When he does that he loses his pre-snap read. What you see is what you want to get. That is especially true in the quick game. If you misread the quick game, your band will have to play the fight song for the other team, because that sucker is going the other way.

We don't read in the quick game. We don't have time to do that. The quarterback, in his pre-snap read, picks a side and throws that way.

I'm almost out of time, but I've got a couple more plays I'll try to show you. This is the *dart* play. On this one, the quarterback takes the ball and the tailback is responsible for the mesh. We are running a trap the other way. We seal down on the 1-technique with our guard. He is working on the 1-technique with the center, with one of them coming off for the backside linebacker. The tackle reaches the defensive end to his side like the zone play. The backside guard turns out on the 3-technique. The backside tackle pulls through the bubble hole on the other side and blocks the Will linebacker. The quarterback reads the defensive end as he did on the zone play. This play looks like the zone play to the bubble-side players. If the 5-technique aligns tight like he is slanting inside, the offensive tackle calls *tight*, so the pulling tackle knows he may have to go around the down block. If the 5-technique slants, the offensive tackle walls him to the inside.

DART

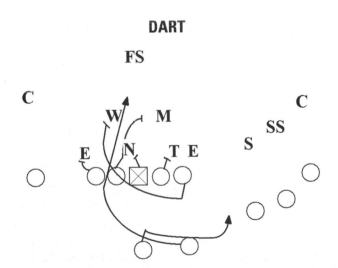

What could happen in this play is the linebacker moving up into the gap. If that happened, the tackle would block him down and the pulling tackle would trap the 5-technique. We have a couple of ways to run it.

From that play, we run the bootleg pass and the naked bootleg. On the bootleg pass, we pull a guard in the protection scheme. The naked scheme has no one pulling to protect the quarterback. We run the naked off a zone fake. The linemen run the zone play, but they don't go downfield.

If you have a young quarterback or you don't think he can read the defensive end, you can put a tight end in the game to block the defensive end and keep him from chasing the play down from the backside.

You can come to visit anytime you would like. We have an open door policy. You are always welcome at our place. The reason we will have success is because we will get players. The reason we get players is because you guys coach them well and allow us to come talk to them. I am a hillbilly from West Virginia. I call that place home. I am probably the tallest Rodriguez you've ever seen. I am Spanish, and every time I make a home visit and introduce myself, people look at me kind of strange. They think I should be a little dark-haired Spanish-looking guy. I've got a real good staff. Call on us if you need something.

Even though we didn't have success this year, I think we are almost there. Last year there was probably too much hype. Our motto last year was *spot the ball*. That was more of an attitude than anything else. The slogan was in reference to the referee marking the ball ready for play. Once he marked the ball and got out of the way, we were ready to play. That meant either side of the ball or our special teams were ready to go.

EFFECTIVE USE OF THE TIGHT END

University of Oregon

It is a real pleasure being here. I think coaches have a tremendous impact on kids. I have never coached at the high school level but I've always admired coaches and what you do. I really believe that what you do is so important. Don't ever underestimate that. Maybe the greatest impact a high school will have is on a player who doesn't have a lot of potential. He may not have a lot of ability, but he will gain confidence from being a part of your football team.

I take my hat off to high school coaches. We recruit the player you guys turn out and find they are well prepared for college football. The fact that you are here to learn more football, I think is a great tribute to you.

In coaching, I think the players are the most important things. The tight end and linebacker are not that much different, they are just on opposite sides of the ball. They are very unique individuals and have to be versatile in what they do. At Oregon we have been fortunate to have a great tradition of tight ends. We had another great one this year in Justin Peelle. You will see a lot of tape on him today. In addition to being a good tight end, he is one of those players you love to coach. The things that make him so good are the inner things.

He was highly recruited. He was a tight end/defensive end in high school. The only other scholarship offer he had was to Air Force as a defensive end. He had a lot of the intangibles. When it comes to players, we talk about three things. The first thing is their attitude about *hustling*. You have to be the most tenacious son of a gun on the field. You have to make sure you outplay the man you are playing against. These are things that your players can control. Players will buy into that. The way things are today, there are so many things that are out of the players' control. Outhustling someone is in the control of the player.

When you ask your players to play harder than the player across from them, the players don't think that is an unreasonable request. That is, until you put it on film and they understand the commitment they have made. When they see what they are accountable for, it raises their performance level. Great coaches get players to play above their ability levels.

The second thing we evaluate our players on is *hitting*. You have to outhit your opponent. Football is a game of hitting. I've been coaching this game for 26 years, and this game all starts with hitting somebody. When you look at football on any level, high school, college, or pros, the team that outhits the other usually wins the game. That generally is the team that establishes the line of scrimmage. That is a mentality that you have to get across to your players. Offensive players have to have that exact same mentality that the defense does. The offense has players that are a little more assignment-oriented, but they must have that mentality in order for them to be successful.

The third one might be the most critical and important one of them all. A player has to be *mentally tough*. That is how you react to adverse situations. People know as they go through life there are going to be good times and bad times. Life is a lot like a football game. In football games, sometimes things go bad. The character of your team is determined by how your team reacts to those situations. I really dwell on this point with all our players.

At Oregon this year, we went 11-1, which is a great season. When the expectations are high, losing that one game probably cost us the chance to play for the national championship. We lost that one game and had to go up to Washington State the next week and win a tough game. I talk to our players and tell them they are not going to win every battle on the field.

Someone is going to knock him on his ass. That happens; it is football. It happens to the best players. What they have to do is get by that and get to the next play. We talk a lot about playing the next play.

Hustling, hitting, and mental toughness is what we stress with all our players. Let's go to the objectives of our tight ends.

They have to *be smart*. That is a subject on which we can all improve. We want them to be smart in everything we do. Whether it is meetings, practice, scrimmaging, or playing in a game, we want to avoid penalties and assignment errors. One reason our tight ends have been so successful at the next level is because we train them for that. We play them at a lot of positions on the field. The tight end position is the second-toughest position to learn next to the quarterback.

He has to know blocking assignments on the run. We have 38 different routes for him in our passing game. He has to know pass protection. We throw hot patterns to him and keep him in to protect. We align him on and off the line of scrimmage. We will send him in motion and when he is in the backfield, he has to know the assignments of the running back. They have to know the protections and the routes of the running back. In addition to that, we split him out and he has to know what to do as a wide receiver. He has to be smart and take a lot of pride in knowing he has to know it all. They have to see the whole picture. They have to understand defenses and coverages. He has to know on a two-linebacker blitz, he is the hot receiver. He has to know that the fourth man to the strongside is his man in pass protection.

The tight end has to play with *high velocity*. When he does something, he does it full speed and to the best of his ability. That means we want him to play fast.

The last of our objectives is to finish. We want to complete the job. We want to block until the whistle blows. They finish the catch by tucking the ball away. When they are running with the ball, finish the run until they are on the ground. While he is running a pass route, we want him to finish the route whether the ball is thrown to him or not. If the ball is thrown to another receiver, we want to block for him.

The difference between winning and losing is about an inch. When I was with the Oakland Raiders,

Willie Brown, the all-pro defensive back, would always talk to the defense about that inch. If you can teach your players the importance of giving just a little more effort, it could be the winning edge.

The next thing in the tight end's learning phase is *efficiency*. He cannot have procedural penalties, line up offsides, or jump the snap count. When running the ball, he must carry it properly. He has to lock it away using four points of pressure to secure it. We cannot have turnovers. He has to know his assignments. The level of his playing ability has no bearing on efficiency. We can all become efficient.

The tight end is a hybrid. They are an offensive lineman at times and a wide receiver at times. Recruiting-wise, it is the toughest position to sign. We have to look for the all-around player who can grow in size and strength. The strength can be improved with hard work. There is "no gain without pain." We want them to be consistent and make lifting a part of their weekly routine, and it will become a habit.

Tight ends have to be fluid. They have to have good feet, control of their bodies, and know what they are doing. That is in some cases more important than a guy who can just run fast. Speed is important, but it can be improved by concentrating on form in running drills. Speed can be improved by running as fast as you can while we are competing. Football is a sport that is a lot different than basketball. In basketball one guy can dominate a game. In football it takes 11 guys.

It is amazing how many athletes playing in the NFL are good athletes, but not great athletes. The reason they can stay at that level is because they are smart. You get yourself into the league by your ability, and stay in the league by how much you know. It is the same thing in college. We recruit them because of their ability, but they perform because of how they develop and what they know.

One thing that I've found that has been very successful in motivating players is a player performance chart. I've been doing this for 10 to 15 years. I don't do this with every position I have coached. I make up a chart of things we want them to do to become good performers. I grade them every game.

When you grade players with a plus, minus, or zero, that is a subjective grade. We are all human; the grade a player gets may depend on the coach's attitude after a win or a loss. The things I put on this chart are objective things. I assign point totals to those things. The chart looks like this.

TOTAL CATCHING	NAME
Catch (+2)	_____
Break tackle (+2)	_____
Catch first down (+3)	_____
TD catch (+6)	_____
TOTAL BLOCKING	
Cut block (+2)	_____
Knock down block (+3)	_____
Block to score (+4)	_____
TOTAL BIG PLAYS	
Tackles (+2)	_____
Breakups (+3)	_____
Big hit (+4)	_____
Big play (+4)	_____
Recovered fumble (+5)	_____
TOTAL MINUS PLAYS	
Dropped pass (-2)	_____
Mental error (-2)	_____
Missed block (-2)	_____
Loaf (-3)	_____
Penalty (-3)	_____
Fumble (-5)	_____
TOTAL POINTS	_____

That chart is very objective and the players think it is fair. It is the first thing they want to see each week. They want to know how they did in the game. This is a pride factor.

The tight end has to block and do it well to be successful. It all starts with a stance. The tight end aligns on both sides of the ball. We let them align with their dominant hand on both sides of the center. The feet in the stance are about shoulder width. We allow a very slight stagger with the toe-to-instep relationship. The feet are slightly toed inside. When you are teaching someone to get in their stance for the first time, have them rock down with their elbow on their knees. After that have them roll their hand down and lightly put it on the ground. Don't let them put their knuckles down on the ground. Make them use their fingers. If they put the knuckles down, it takes them longer to get out of the stance, plus they get less push-off.

The most important thing about a stance is being able to get out of it. The tight end has to do everything out of his stance. He cannot have a heavy stance when he is going to block or a light stance when he is going to release. He has to go right, left, straight ahead, and drop back out of the same stance.

We want the back fairly flat, but the head has to be up so they can see. Years ago at Iowa, Hayden Fry had his tight ends stand up so they could see a lot more. It was amazing how well they could drive block from the standing stance. The only thing they got hurt on was the inside cutoff block. When our tight end gets down he has to be able to see. He has to see the safeties, linebackers, and corners. When you put them in their stance, walk around them especially in the front. Our blocking calls depend on how deep the safety aligns and how wide is the linebacker. It has to be a balanced stance that he can see from.

The next thing we want to do is explode off with the snap count. We vary our snap count. We have to use that to our advantage. We work hard on getting off on different snap counts. We go on set, one, two, and three. It is very important that your players are comfortable with your snap count. We want to own the snap count. That is one of the biggest advantages we have on offense.

Let's get into the basic fundamentals of blocking. I need a volunteer so I can demonstrate a bit. If the tight end is going to execute a drive block on the 9-technique, the foot he starts with depends on the tightness of the 9-technique. As long as the defender is in a wide technique, the tight end steps with his outside foot. However, if the alignment of the technique could threaten the inside, the tight end steps with his inside foot.

The first step is the most critical part of blocking and getting off the ball. So many times the first thing that moves is the blocker's hands. If they do that, they defeat the whole purpose of stepping. The biggest movement in the body is in the lower body. The first thing that has to move is the feet. The first step is a short six-inch step. When people overstride, they lose power. If the most important step is the first step, the key step is the second step. You have to get the second step back on the ground to create some power. The hands come with the second step.

As we come off, the tight end wants to get his hand right under the chest plate of the shoulder pads. Football now is all hands and feet. I put them down on a sled in a six-point stance. That is two hands, two feet, and two knees in contact with the ground. From there I give them a cadence. They pop their hands by and punch the dummy on the sled to get hand placement and hand explosion.

When I was coaching at the pro level there were rookies that came out of college and didn't know how to use their hands. In professional, you practice without pads for most of the season. It is amazing to me how good those players get with their hand position. We are talking about perfect hand fit every time.

From the six-point stance I put them in a three-point stance, which is a regular stance. I have them step with right foot first and shoot the hands. Then I have them step with the left foot and shoot the hands.

When I am drilling this movement, I have key words to indicate what I want them to do. When we get into the block with our hands positioned, the next thing is pad level. That means to roll over the toe and tuck the hips under to get lift in the block. I want control with my hands and my eyes are looking into what we call the triangle of the chest. That is where I have placed my hands on his chest. From there I drive my

feet and work for movement. The progression goes step, punch, pad level, and eyes. We drill this in a partner drill with the defender facing the offensive blocker.

BODY PART IN LINE OF FORCE

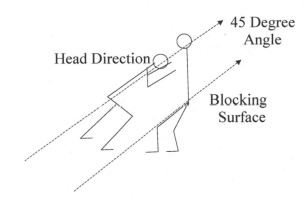

From there we go one step further. The defender leans into the blocker and the blocker tamps his feet and moves the defender back with short choppy steps.

Here are some valuable hints in the execution of a block. One thing that can really help the blocker is to know the offense and the philosophy of the play. Every play we run has a philosophy to it. Make sure your players know that. One basic thing in blocking is the offensive blocker getting his body between the defender and the ballcarrier. Make sure your players know exactly where the ball is going. Let the offensive blocker know when the ball is going to bounce and what the ballcarrier is reading off the block of the lineman.

The next thing is know the defense used by your opponent. They must recognize what defensive look the defense is in. We need to know if they stem the defense. If they do, we may have to change the line calls to match up with the defense. In addition to knowing the defense, the offensive blocker needs to know the personnel he is going to be blocking against. He needs to see film of the players he is going to block, so he can assess their strengths and weakness.

In leverage blocking, correct footwork is essential to gain the proper position. In our blocking scheme the tight end has to do a number of individual blocks. He has to drive, reach, rail, down, man-cut-off, search pull, and stalk block. He also has to work in combination with the tackle on a trey, six, and moon block. I'll show all these blocks to you on tape later.

I think everyone is familiar with all the blocks in the individual group except what we call a rail block. That is the type of block where the tight end is going inside to block a linebacker. In the combination blocks, the trey is a combination block with someone coming off for the first linebacker to the inside. The six block is a combination block with someone coming off for the second linebacker inside. The moon block is a combination block, which requires a switch by the tackle and end on a line stunt.

I'll show you how we coach our combination block. When we are going to combo block, we cut our split down a bit. The tackle steps with his outside foot. The tight end steps with his inside foot. They come hip to hip on this block. They come foot to foot and drive the 5-technique off the ball. The end has to block the linebacker, so he must feel the 5-technique but see the linebacker. The tackle is working for hand position on the 5-technique in the breastplate. The tight end has his inside hand on the 5-technique, but he keeps his outside hand free. He doesn't put it on the hip of the defender. The first thing we want is movement on the down man.

While the tackle and end are engaged on the 5-technique, the linebacker could shoot the gap inside the tackle. If that happens the tackle is coming off on the linebacker, and the tight end has to flush the 5-technique inside. That is when he puts his outside hand on the hip of the 5-technique and washes the defender to the inside.

TREY BLOCK

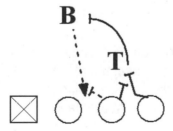

I want to show you some game tape, and I'll show you these blocks and talk about them at the same time.

When we work the reach block, we want to work for the outside armpit. We take a short lead step and a crossover step. If he takes a crossover step first and the defender slants inside, we are finished. The feet are backward to do anything to prevent the slant. If we take the short lead step, the end can step back in good balance to wash the defender down the line. With the outside arm, we punch on the outside shoulder pad of the 9-technique. That is to get the defender's shoulders turned. With the inside hand, we pull the inside shoulder around to turn the defender. The initial move turns the defender, which lets the end work his hands and feet around to where we have him reached.

A rail block is a block executed on the inside linebacker. We have to understand the linebacker is not going to stand still. When the ball is snapped he is going to mirror the path of the fullback. That means the attack angle of the tight end has to go where he is going, not where he is. On the videotape, Justin comes down on the linebacker, and the linebacker gets across his block. What he did well here is stay with the block, and he came back and blocked him off the play. We would prefer to have the linebacker blocked down, but you have to remember he is on scholarship too. The linebacker's coach is telling him he has to get across the tight end's block. If the linebacker gets across the block, stay with him and finish the block. If Justin had stopped when the linebacker crossed his face, the back would have been tackled for no gain. But he stayed with the block and came back on the linebacker, and the running back, with some extra effort, got into the end zone.

We want to have a change-up technique to keep people guessing. This is a change-up off the rail. We are coming down on the same path. We want to make eye contact on them. If they are looking in the backfield, cut him down. We want to aim for the hip and throw. We aim higher because when the block is thrown, they always end up lower than where they aimed. When we cut the legs out, we want to scramble and finish the block.

The next block is a cutoff block. If you watch Justin on this block he does a really good job. Too many times when you tell lineman to cut someone off, they make a big step, lunge, and fall down. He takes his first step and drives off his second step to get his penetration and then he lunges and drives through the knee.

The moon block is a backside block. The tight end and tackle are working together. They get hip to hip with the tight end taking anything that comes outside and the tackle taking anything coming inside. We get an ET stunt here. That is an end-tackle stunt with the end going first. We end up with the guard being pulled into the scheme, but that is normal because the defensive tackle was aligned in the tackle-guard gap.

MOON BLOCK

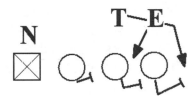

This next block is the search pull. This is a pulling guard type of block. We bring him out of the tight slot position. The guard pulls in front of him and kicks out on the force, and the end turns up inside like a pulling guard and finds the linebacker. The coaching points on this play are not to get too close to the pulling guard so that one defender can take out both the guard and the end, and secondly, get a slight bit deeper in his alignment.

SEARCH PULL

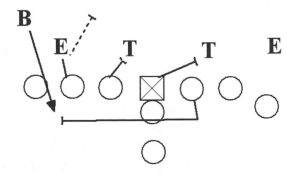

That is what we do in the off-season. We work on our hands and feet. We work on our hand strength and our footwork so we can run these types of plays. Watch Justin's hand placement. He doesn't lose his block, and he always finishes the block.

The last individual block comes off the arc block. The stalk block is what most of the wide receivers use to block defensive backs. We want to influence the defensive back to make him think it is a pass. Once the defender recognizes the play as a run, we want to break down and get in front of the defender. All we want to do is stay up high and in front of the defensive back. We want the ballcarrier to break off the block. The change-up on the stalk block is to throw at the defensive back's knees. You may not knock him down, but the next time you come out to stalk block on him, the stand-up stalk block will be more effective. Never try to block the defender the same way every time.

ARC BLOCK

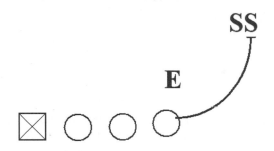

The passing game starts with catching the football. Before practice we have our receiver come out and do finger strengthening drills. We have the grip drills using the ball. They keep the ball in one hand with the hand on top of the ball. They quickly grip the ball over and over again releasing it and regripping it. We make them drop the ball and catch it one-handed before it hits the ground. We have them do that with each hand. We do all the basketball drills with the football. We do around the body and figure eight through the legs.

Our strength coach has buckets of sand out on the field with marbles in them. The players have to dig down in the sand and pick the marbles out. All these things build strength for catching.

When the tight end is catching the ball, he wants to catch it in his hands. We want to catch the front half of the ball. If the ball is above the chest line, we catch it with the thumbs together. If it is below our chest area, our thumbs are out. When we catch the ball, we want to take it to a tucked position. I want them to look the ball all the way in. We overexaggerate the tuck.

When we tuck the ball away, we want the point of the ball covered with the middle and first fingers of the hand split on either side of the point. We want to make sure the ball is touching our hands, forearms, elbow, and pulled next to our body. After we get the ball tucked away, we have a partner drill, where the partner hits on the ball from the top and underneath to try to knock the ball loose. I want them to catch the ball in a contested area and tuck it away. In every catching drill we have, I constantly try to knock the ball out of their hands. I do it to the running back also. Anyone who has a ball in their hands, they have to protect it.

We led the nation this year in fewest turnovers. We only had 11 turnovers in 12 games. That is the one thing I have found that has a high correlation between winning and losing. When I was with the Raiders, we were plus-18 in our turnover margin. Baltimore won the Super Bowl that year and they had a plus-24 in their turnover margin.

Defensive backs who chase receivers will try to pop the ball out from behind if they can see any part of the ball showing. If they can't see any of the ball they try to come over the top of the receiver's arm and try to pull his arm up to dislodge the ball.

I'm running out of time, but I want to show you our route sheet before I go. Like I told you before we have 38 routes for the tight end. We do a lot of things to utilize the tight end and get him the football. I didn't put all 38 on this tape, but I've got about 20 on it. I'll talk you through how we use them in the time I have left.

The first route that you see is what we call a spot route. It is a 3-yard by 3-yard route. Of course if you need 4 yards for the first down, the spot route becomes a 3-yard by 4-yard pattern. It is a control pass and safe pass. We like the quarterback to get the ball to the outside, so he can turn upfield quickly and get more positive yards.

The next pattern is a slant. We don't throw the ball to him this time. But when we run a slant from a flex formation, it is a look slant. We line up with our inside foot up and our outside foot back. We take one step with our outside foot and drive on an inside slant at a 45 degree angle.

A lot of the things we do with our tight ends are matchup situations. We want them to get matched up on people that cannot cover them. The next pattern is an arrow route. That is a shallow 3-yard pattern run to the flat. We want him to look back quickly to see if the quarterback wants to get us the ball.

The next one is a stick route. That is a quick 5-yard out pattern. They run that route in the NFL all the time. The toughest thing to teach tight ends is to run their route square. They want to round them off too much. We want to get the eyes around quick.

This pattern is a Y-read pattern. We throw this pass when the tight end is bracketed by two defensive backs. He is reading the coverage to see what to do. The coverage looks like a quarter- or half-coverage. The tight end reads what the secondary is doing and ends up running a post.

The sail route is a soft sponge route used to occupy a secondary defender. It is a decoy route. The sail route looks like a flat.

This next pattern is called a middle read. The tight end is reading whether the middle is open or closed. If the safeties are on the hash marks or outside of them, we call that middle open. The tight end runs a streak right down the middle of the field to the goalpost. If there is someone in the middle of the field, we turn it into an over route. The over is run at 15 yards and looks like a dig route, which can settle between the linebackers. When we call this pattern, we are looking to hit the defense with a big play.

On the flag route, we want to get to 10 to 12 yards and break it. When he feels he has the coverage beat, he breaks on a 45 and runs away from the coverage. The aiming point for the flat route is 25 yards deep. We tell the tight end to keep his pattern high in the zone and let the quarterback lead you low if he thinks the coverage is too tight. If the safety is beat, we keep the pattern high, and if the safety has recovered, we bring the pattern down low into the soft part of the outside zone.

At Oregon we have tree pass routes for our tight ends. The first tree has 15 routes in it. I'll list them for you and give you a short explanation of each one.

TIGHT END TREE #1

The first tree is:

1. Cross — TE box, feel coverage 6 yards.

2. Drag — Find hole in zone, run in man 10-12 yards.

3. Shoot — Angle 25 yards to sideline.

4. Delay — Replace LB on side 6 yards.

5. In — Throttle in hole off hash 10 yards.

6. Out — Break to sideline 10 yards.

7. Middle Read — Goal post on middle open, streak middle closed.

8. Flag — 10-12-yard break to 25 yards — feel coverage.

9. Quick Flag — 6 yards, 45 degree angle.

10. Spot — 3 yards by 3 yards turnout.

11. Arrow — Flat to sideline 3 yards, show number 5 yards from sideline.

12. Shake — Show arrow, turn up bottom of numbers, stay 5 yards from sideline.

13. Over 1 yard in route, throttle in hole off hash.

14. Streak — Straight upfield, keep stretch.

15. Hash — Bend to 2 yards outside hash.

TIGHT END TREE #2

In the second tree, there are 12 routes.

1. Choice — Option off inside backer, settle in zone collision back down stem.

2. Pump — 5-step drop — sell choice — inside plant, outside plant, bend over backers, keep thin.

3. Pump — 3-step drop — sell stick inside plant, outside plant bend over backer.

4. Pivot — 6 steps plant in flat 5-7 yards.

5. Flat and Up — 3 yards out, depth of 5 yards.

6. Slam Flat — Sell block used on boots 3-yard depth.

7. Stick Flat — Protect 4 counts, check down sideline.

8. Drag-in — 6-yard route to center, work back to Mike, stay in QB vision.

9. Slant — One step outside foot — back break inside — keep thin.

10. Crash — 2 yards outside far hash — middle closed — middle open — goalpost.

11. Stem — 12 yard out cut, work back inside.

12. Take — Thin post; close cushion on defender.

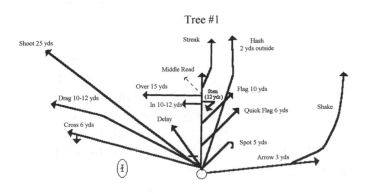

Tree #1

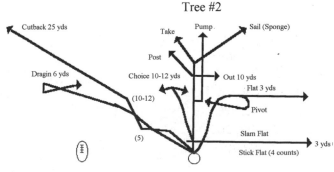

Tree #2

TIGHT END TREE #3

In the third tight end tree, there are 11 routes.

1. Loop — Opposite pivot 6 steps and plant outside.

2. Fin — 5 steps out — cut plant inside foot — snap head — look for ball.

3. Follow — Cross OLB — race four running steps — plant — take upfield.

4. Center — Inside release 10 yards over ball.

5. Stick — 5 yard out — cut plant inside foot — snap head — look for ball.

6. Read — Post or flag 10-12 yards off coverage man over top.

7. Leak — Inside release 5 yards hook over ball.

8. Post — 45 degree angle break to goalpost 10-12 yards.

9. Cutback — Push inside stem 5 yards vertical — stem 10-12 yards cross field to 25 yards to sideline.

10. Sail — Sponge safety — close cushion — pull safety outside.

11. Throwback — Post break 10-12 — corner break 12-14 yards to 25 or feel coverage.

I'm out of time. Men, I want to thank you for your attention and allowing us to visit with you. There are so many things we do with the tight end. I hope you got something out of this. If you have any questions, I'll leave my card here. You can call me or drop me a line. Thank you.

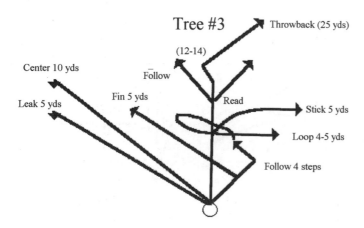

Tree #3

EIGHT-MAN FRONT AND MAN COVERAGE

Louisiana State University

I appreciate the opportunity to be here with you this evening. Everything that I know is something I learned from someone else. I have very few original thoughts.

From a coaching standpoint, I think we have a great responsibility. There are problems all over the place on my level, and I know you have problems on your level too. We have the 20-hour rule to deal with, but that doesn't seem like much compared to the problem you are going through. I know you high school coaches are having trouble finding assistant coaches. When you do have a full staff, you have trouble getting them all in the same building. The junior high are cutting athlete programs back as a money-saving effort, but the expectations on the high school coach to produce a winner year in and year out is still there.

At the college level, the NCAA is limiting the amount of time you can spend with your athletes, and yet we see examples every year of coaches being fired because they cannot produce a championship team every year. John Cooper at Ohio State and Jim Donnan at Georgia are two examples. Those coaches produced winners every year, but they didn't win big enough for the people who make the decisions. Both of those guys lost their jobs in years where they both won eight games.

The expectations are getting higher and the time to do it is getting less and less.

Coaching football is a lot like being a parent. I have a boy who is 15 and a girl who is 11. I would like to think that we will give them everything they need to be successful, but I'm not sure what is going to happen. I think my wife and I are good parents. There is so much going on today in our society that the future is hard to see.

My kids don't even know cause and effect. They don't get into many situations where they have to think about right and wrong. When we were growing up, we played checkers. If you made a wrong move, you got your man jumped. You got positive or negative gratification that you had done the right thing or the wrong thing.

My kid plays Nintendo. If he gets blown up, all he does is push the restart button and nothing happens to him. That is how the generations are growing up today. Kids in this day and age have a tough time making commitments.

There are four things you need to be a good coach. The first thing is commitment. If you talk about that word being so important to a program's being successful, there is a whole generation of people growing up that have a total inability to make commitments today. There are so many choices about what they do and what they don't do. As soon as something gets difficult or they don't get immediate self-gratification from it, they quit and go on to something else. My kids do it. I love them to death and try to break them from doing it, but I'm not having much luck.

There are too many choices. If they are shooting baskets and not making them, they'll quit and go hit golf balls. If they hit a couple of bad ones, they take off to the pool to see if there are any girls over there. They never sit down and say, "I've got to make this work."

All those things to me make it more difficult to coach. One thing to me about being a good competitor is you can never get frustrated. You can never feel satisfied about what you are accomplishing and be a good competitor. But at the same time, I have never played a game where everything went perfectly that allowed us to keep that kind of a disposition with all the people that are trying to compete.

It is a more difficult task for us to be good coaches. I look at all coaches as teachers. A good teacher always inspires harmony. A good coach understands that his biggest responsibility as a coach is to be there for his player. If the players weren't there, we wouldn't have a job. I think it is important to set a good example for every one of those players. I think you need to spend more time communicating with your players than ever before. They expect that, and they need it. You have to teach your players the fundamentals of the game with some kind of good progression, so they can understand it and stay interested in the game.

Somehow you need to make the game fun for them. Kids are wired differently now. We have a kid who is 6'5", weighs 310, and runs a 4.65 40-yard dash. He plays defensive end. When he wants to play, no one can block him. Before we got there, he had never played one play in two years. He did not practice and did not play. He sat on the field and did nothing.

I brought him in to my office for a talk. I told him I couldn't believe that he wouldn't go out on the field and compete. I told him he had first-round draft choice written all over him. He had the size, speed, strength, quickness, and the instincts that it takes to be a great player. He didn't say a word. The only thing he could say was that he was hurt and couldn't go today.

I had a sport psychologist who is a friend of mine come to talk to a couple of other guys and he ended up talking to this guy. We wanted to use all the resources that we had available to try to figure out what made this guy tick. The psychologist told me the guy was a leader. But he also told me not to depend on him playing at all. This kid had been the biggest kid around all of his life. Everyone had always told him how great he was going to be and how many records he was going to break. He told me this kid had been told ever since he could remember about how great he was going to be. He said the boy was afraid to compete because he was afraid to fail or hurt someone's feelings. He said if we could get him to focus on something else he might play. He said you can't expect anything from him or put any type of expectation results on him. He told me not to mention potential or greatness or anything like that and he may come out of it. That kid has been starting for us for two years.

I would never have thought that. I never understood that. I have never played with anyone that had

that type of condition. There is a real challenge to inspire guys and be a good teacher and teach in a progression. It is not enough to worry about the physical things that go on in the game, but now we must worry about the motivation and mental aspect of our players.

To be a good coach, you must be able to coach on the field. The biggest part of that is getting your team to play hard. You have to be a competitor. The number one thing about being a good competitor is never looking at the scoreboard. We all do it though. I'm 50 years old. If I get up 15-5 in a game of racquetball, for the next five points I loaf. I do that because I know I've got two more games to play. To be a good competitor, the score of the game shouldn't matter. If you are a good competitor you are going to compete whether you are ahead or behind. The score doesn't matter. There has to be something more important that you are trying to achieve or accomplish.

There is nothing more that I respect in someone than being a good competitor. There are some guys that can always make the best plays when the game is getting close and exciting. There is nothing I respect more than that. But the number one thing that kills that is great anxiety shown by a frustrated player. We as coaches condition that in our players. We do it all the time. When a player makes a mistake, we show our frustration in him for messing up.

One of the greatest true stories I can tell you about someone not showing his frustration in a game, is a middleweight championship fight involving Bernard Hopkins and a guy from East Lansing. No one ever heard of this guy. I knew him personally because he trained in a friend of mine's gym in East Lansing. He was undefeated when he got his shot to fight Hopkins. I think Bernard Hopkins is a competitor. This fight took place at the height of Bernard's boxing career. The fight came off at Caesars Palace. After the first three rounds, my man had won all of them. He came out in the fourth round and almost got killed. Bernard knocked him down three times and finally knocked him out. It was brutal. He went to the hospital and was really hurt. I saw the guy two months later and asked him what happened in the fourth round. I figured he would tell me that Bernard had hit him with a good shot and he couldn't defend himself.

He told me at the end of the third round he hit Hopkins with his best shot. It never fazed Hopkins. He told me he knew he couldn't beat him after that punch. I don't know whether Hopkins was hurt or not, but he showed nothing in the way of frustration or how he felt. He broke the guy's confidence and killed him psychologically to the point he didn't think he could win the fight.

I promise you the difference in our team at LSU is not the number of mistakes we make, because they make just as many mistakes as they did when they were winning three and four games two years ago. The big difference was how they respond to every mistake they make. No one shows any frustration about the last play or the mistake that was made. The only thing they are thinking about is the next play.

All the coaches I've worked with and all the coaches that I have hired think that they should be able to snap their fingers, say jump, and the players should say how high. It doesn't work that way.

We had some coaches come to watch practice. The whole time they were there none of the coaches raised their voices. The practice was fluid, everyone was hustling their asses off, and we had no problems at all. After the practice, one of the coaches told me he thought we really got after our kids. I said we do. They do it on their own. They take ownership in this program. They want to do well and compete. They understand that.

There are three things you've got to do to win at any level. You have to have effort. You can watch my films and you can find guys on every play that are not giving 100 percent. You have to be tough to play football. Players have to be both mentally and physically tough. If you are not tough you can't play the game of football. It doesn't take any God-given talent to give effort or be tough. Toughness comes from the heart, and it is choice. You can choose to be tough or not to be. Toughness is like fear. No one makes you afraid. It is like it comes from the dark side of the moon. No one knows what's on the other side of the door. No one wants to open the door because they are afraid of it.

The third thing is you have to take the responsibility for your own self-determination about what your job is. You have to know what your job is, how to do it, and why it is important to do it. That is the only way you can play together as a team. Some people think that has something to do with God-given talent because you have to be smart. I don't think you have to be smart. I think you have to be persistent and go the extra mile to get it done. You may have to stay in the meetings 10 minutes longer.

There is one more thing that goes with those three intangibles, and that is conditioning. That is the answer to all the questions. When is a player going to loaf? When is he going to make mental and physical mistakes? Remember what the great Vince Lombardi said: "Fatigue makes cowards of us all." That is why the fourth quarter is so important to the conditioned teams. They know they can win the game in the fourth quarter when everyone else is trying to hold on. When a player gets tired, he is not the same player. That's why you have to have a well-conditioned team.

There are three things that lead to teamwork. You have to have a good product, know your opponent, and you've got to get people to play the game. Division from within will kill any organization faster than anything. We are in a day and age now when everybody is more selfish than they have been. They are more self-absorbed than they ever have been. All they think about is how does this affect me?

If something goes wrong, the leader of the team stands up and says we are not playing well on defense because the defense is too complicated. He is saying it is not my fault, we can't learn it. He is blaming someone else without saying it. It is the coaches' fault. That fractures your team because if the leader says it's too complicated, then it must be. Then you have a big problem.

To have a good product, you have to have a road map of how to get there. You cannot go anywhere and not know where you are going. I don't know many people that take off driving and don't know where they are going. You always have a map, plot your course, and know your destination.

In football everyone should have a goal for what they want to accomplish. I don't go into a recruit's home and say we want to win the national championship. That is not the goal of our program at LSU and it wasn't at Michigan State either. Our chief goal is a mission statement. We want to create an atmosphere and environment where players can become more successful as people for having been involved in our program. They are going to develop the character and attitude it takes to be successful, so they can have the consistency and performance that it takes to be successful in whatever they choose to do.

The second thing is we are committed to making sure they get an education. That change will affect the quality of their lives more than anything else they do.

The third thing is to compete for a national championship. We were very proud to win the SEC championship this year and qualify for the BCS series in our home state.

I am from West Virginia. I grew up in a small town. When I was a senior in high school, we won the state championship. They erected a sign in the town that still stands today that reads, "West Virginia Class AA State Champions 1967." Every time I go home, I ride up there and see the sign. We have won a bunch of games at the college and pro levels, but that game is what I am proudest of.

I want every guy in our program to have the opportunity to experience winning a championship. Those are the goals of our program.

The last thing we try to do is use every resource that we have available to us to help these guys launch their careers, whatever they may be.

When players develop the character to give consistency and performance, it will help you win football games. The players start thinking about what is important to them. From there they start to make commitments. They learn from their mistakes, believe in themselves, overcome adversity, and they are better people for it. The choices that a player makes either make him successful or unsuccessful.

I'm going to tell you the greatest coaching story that I know. When I was at Ohio State in 1980, we lost the Rose Bowl to Southern California 17-16. Southern Cal had five players on that team that eventually became NFL Hall of Fame players. John Robinson was the USC coach at that time. They went to their two-minute offense at the end of the game and ran the isolation play eight times in a row to score.

In 1980 we were rebuilding and hadn't had a very successful season going into the Michigan game. We were 8-2, which was a disappointment for the Ohio State fans. We were a 17-point underdog. Michigan was leading the Big Ten in scoring at 35 points a game. The fact was, if we could win the game, we could tie Michigan for the Big Ten Championship.

The last week of practice was cold and snowy and we practiced like we didn't want to play the game. Usually the week of the Michigan game we always had to be careful in practice because we didn't want to get anybody hurt. During that week, guys went crazy, they were so hyped up. That was not the case this year. We were getting some heavy criticism from everyone, and the kids just didn't think we had a chance to win. I even felt that way. I don't think anyone thought we could win the game. We had a tradition at the last practice, where all the seniors would make their last tackle. They each hit the bag for their last tackle, and we had a speaker come in to address the team.

Earle Bruce was the coach then, and Woody Hayes had not had anything to do with the team or the school since the incident in the bowl game against Clemson. We got him to go on a trip with us and to address the team. His speech centered on this statement: *"There can be no great victories in life unless there is tremendous adversity."* He talked about all the adversity of having to go play Michigan. He talked about the point spread, the weather, and all the other bad things that were surrounding the game.

He turned all the adversity into opportunity. He equated it all to the war in the Pacific during World War II. He said the war in the Pacific was the greatest victory ever for the United States because to win that war we had to go through tremendous adversity. He went on to talk about Pearl Harbor and the role it played. By the time he was finished, the whole team had come from doom and gloom to looking at this game as an opportunity to do something great. I felt the same way.

We had an opportunity to go to Michigan and do something special. We went to Michigan and played our butts off. They didn't score a touchdown. We won the game 14-9. After the game, Coach Bruce said he was glad we didn't have a game the following week.

He felt there was not a team in the country we could beat. He was probably right. We were so emotionally high for Michigan, if we had tried to get up the next week it would have been a disaster.

The way that opportunity was presented to the team changed their whole outlook of that game. There was no fear of losing; there was only the opportunity to win.

Bill Belichick is probably the best planning coach that I've ever been around. He works his plan and plans his work better than anybody I've ever been around. He had great success this year as an NFL coach. His success was due to his organization and planning. Bill had a plan and he went out and built the team he wanted. They won the Super Bowl because they outhit St. Louis. St. Louis was the most skilled team, but New England took the fight to them and won by being physical. It was because they were made that way, he picked them that way. He drafted and traded to get that type of team. Bill Parcells is the same way.

You have to know how to define your product because as coaches, our product goes back to the people that are going to play. You have to know your competition. But the other side of that is you have to know yourself. There are a lot of coaches that play a system. It doesn't matter whether the player fit the system, that is what they are going to play.

When I was 15, I was a sophomore in high school. I was the starting quarterback, and we played a team at the end of the season for the right to go to the playoffs. We played at their field, and they had bad lights and a graveyard at the end of one end zone. We had to walk about half a mile from the dressing room to the field in the dark. They were leading us 18-0 at halftime. I was the quarterback and called all the plays. We had a great coach. He is still alive today. He had won a number of state coaching awards and many Coach of the Year awards. He would never call a play in the games.

We came back in the second half and we got the ball with two minutes to go, behind 18-12. We got down to their 25-yard line with 25 seconds to go in the game. It is fourth and 12 and Coach called time-out. I was relieved because I thought he was going to call the last play and take it out of my hands. If we won that game we were going to the playoffs. If we

lost we were through for the year. They were third in the state and we were fifth. I went to the sideline to find out what we were going to run. Coach told me he wasn't going to call the play. He told me I had to call the play. I asked him what he wanted to do. This is what he told me. "We have the fastest guy in the state playing left halfback." By the way, the halfback ended up an All-American at West Virginia. He went on to say, "We have an All-State wide receiver. I do not care what play you run, but make sure the ball is in one of those guys' hands at the end of the play." I went back in the game and called a play-action pass. I faked the ball to the left halfback and threw the ball to the split end. We scored a touchdown and won the game.

I never wanted to be a coach even when I graduated from college, but I've been coaching all these years. I have never felt like I was going to work. I learned a valuable lesson that day. When you come to a critical time in the game, always think of the players you have playing the game and not the play. I learned a lesson and I carried that with me to this present time.

When I was at Michigan State, we lost a game to Penn State and Joe Paterno. We were ahead 20-17 with eight seconds to go in the game. It was third and eight on our eight-yard line. They had two great wide receivers playing for them. They had no time-outs, so we felt they were going to throw two times into the end zone or try for the touchdown on third down and kick the field goal on fourth down and tie up the game.

They called a jailbreak screen to their stud wideout. We had five guys on him in a blink of an eye. The guy ended up breaking three or four tackles and got into the end zone and we lost the game. At first I thought that was the dumbest call I've ever seen. After I thought about it I realized it was a good call. You put the ball in your best player's hands and let him make a big play. All these stories relate to knowing your competition, but sometimes you need to know yourself.

I heard it put another way by a baseball coach. He told his pitcher, who had retired 26 guys in a row using a fast ball, "Please don't lose the game throwing the 27th guy the change-up."

I think getting players to play together is the hardest thing there is to do in football. Everybody has an ego and is self-centered. We all think of ourselves first. It is human nature to do that. You are asking egotistical self-centered people to give up themselves and do things for the good of the team. That means you are willing to put the team first in importance. You might be criticized for making the commitment to the team. You might be singled out and ridiculed for doing it, but you can have great success if you can get everyone to do it.

I have been in lots of locker rooms where we have won big games, and you have some guy sitting in the corner mad because he didn't catch enough passes. That is unbelievable to me, but it happens all the time. But it doesn't happen on real good teams. Winning becomes more important than the individual himself.

The one thing we all have to do to get the players to play together is show respect for each other. You have to show them respect and in turn they will respect you and trust you. That respect and trust will lead the players to come together as a team.

In football there are two things that you have to do. You have to be able to *run the football,* and you have to be able to *stop the run.* This year our team passed for more yardage than we ran for. We passed the football for 300 yards a game while only running it for 150 a game. You have to run the ball to win. When you get into the red zone, if you are a throwing team, it gets harder to throw the ball down there. If you can't run the ball, you are going to take a lot of field goals instead of touchdowns.

If you go back to the big comeback the Buffalo Bills had against the Houston Oilers in the championship series several years ago, you will understand what I'm talking about. Houston was ahead at halftime 35-0 and lost the game. What happened to them? Did their defense break completely down? Their offense was throwing the ball every down and not completing anything. They were throwing the ball three straight times and taking 19 seconds off the clock each time they had the ball. If they had run the ball and never made a first down they probably would have won the game.

On the other side of the ball, if you can't stop the run, the offense will never try to pass it. There were two statistics in the NFL this year that were the most significant things in winning and losing games. The turnover ratio and the big play ratio were the two statistics that had a great bearing on winning and losing. A turnover ratio is the number of turnovers you gave up as to the number of turnovers you got. The big play ratio is the same thing. The number of big plays you gave up as to the number of big plays you made.

Your offensive and defensive systems have to fall into those categories if you plan on being successful. The other thing I think is important is third-down efficiency. We led the SEC this year in third-down conversions. We converted on third down this year at a rate of 50 percent. On the other side of the football, when you get the opposing team in a third-down situation, you want to stop them and get off the field.

Those three things in combination are the most important things in winning and losing as far as I am concerned. You have to have a way to measure those types of situations. We think we have a unique system to evaluate our team.

We grade the film, but we don't give each player a percentage grade of how they played. We don't believe a guy could have a winning performance when you lost the game 42-3. We grade the team individually, but what we give them are areas in which they did well, areas in which they did poorly, and areas that they can improve upon.

The team is graded purely on down and distance. We win or lose every situation in the game based on down and distance. Let's say it is first and 10 yards to go for a first down. On that play the tackle and end got hooked, the safety got cut, and a linebacker missed a tackle. The offense gained five yards, and we lost that down situation. That is a losing situation for our defense. To win the down, the defense can't give up more than three yards. If the offense had second and seven for a first down and they gained five yards, we lost that down. If an offensive team had third and 19 and gained 17 yards, the defense won the down because the defense didn't allow a first down.

When we show the film to the players, that is all we say. We tell them why we were successful and why we failed. The players start seeing the chance to be successful depends on them doing the job.

You have to find ways to reinforce position performance. We use production charts. Players are scored and awarded points for positive and negative things they do in the course of the game. These points are very objective points. The more hard evidence you have, the better off you are. If a guy recovers a fumble or intercepts a pass, that is very objective. If he makes a tackle, that is also clear. If you jump offsides or commit any penalty, that is not a debatable point. We score the good things with a plus value and the bad things with a minus value. We score and post those charts in the locker room for all to see.

I know that works to motivate players. I know that because it works in the National Football League. Players that are making upwards of four million dollars are concerned about the performance chart. That is the first thing they look at when they arrive on Monday morning. I've seen that firsthand, and I know it works. They are looking for self-gratification from their peers as to what they have accomplished. They want to be recognized as people who are doing the right things.

What I am going to talk about today is the eight-man front with man-to-man coverage. This scheme can cover an offensive personnel package and not have to substitute any personnel.

We are going to play a defense that is based on a 3-on-2 principle. We are never going to have a player who has a run/pass conflict with his run gap and coverage. In our defense, we are a four-man under front as far as alignment. We have a Sam linebacker on the tight end. Our defensive ends are in 5-techniques. The defensive tackle to the tight-end side is in a 1-technique or center shade to the strongside. The tackle to the open side is in a 3-technique. Our inside linebackers are in a 10-technique strong and a 40-technique weak. The strong safety rolls up into the box five to seven yards deep over the strong offensive tackle. The linebackers and the strong safety have the two backs in the backfield. The Sam linebacker has the tight end in man coverage.

The offensive team is going to have a hard time blocking us because we have more defenders than they have blockers. The corners are in man coverage on the wide receiver, and the free safety is in the middle. The key thing that I want you to understand is the 3-on-2 concept in the middle with the strong safety and two inside linebackers.

BASE UNDER DEFENSE

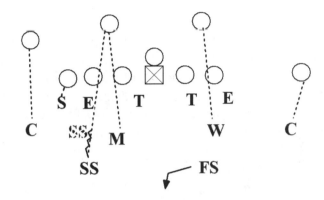

If the backs in the backfield split in their flow with each back going in opposite directions, the Will linebacker and strong safety have those backs in man coverage. The Mike linebacker is the free player and he drops to the short-middle hole called the *rat hole*.

SPLIT BACK FLOW

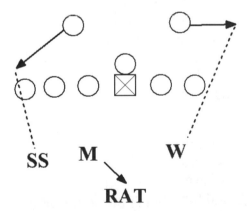

If both the backs full-flowed to one side or the other, the defender to that side plus the Mike linebacker would be in man coverage on the backs, and the remaining linebacker would become the middle-hole player or *rat*.

FULL FLOW RAT

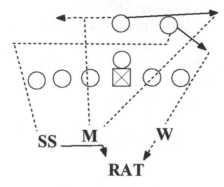

If the off-tackle power is run to the tight end, the flow of the linebacker is normal. The Sam linebacker is coming outside to play the kick-out block. The strong safety is coming up outside because he is man to man on the first back his way. The Mike linebacker has second back to that side and is now reading run. The Will linebacker has to get over the top of the down block or go underneath it. But it is full flow away from him, which means he is the rat player if it is a play-action pass. He has to hustle out of run support and get into the deep middle.

PLAY-ACTION PASS

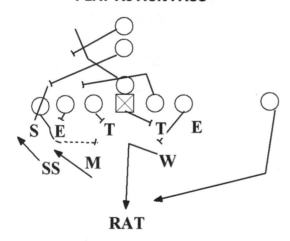

If the offense comes out in a twin set to the defense's right, we flip both corners on the wideouts. If you don't want to flip-flop your safeties, you roll the free safety up, and put the strong safety into the middle. The principle of 3-on-2 is still in effect. The free safety is up in the box with the two inside linebackers and is covering the first back his way. On full flow away from him, he is the rat.

TWIN SET

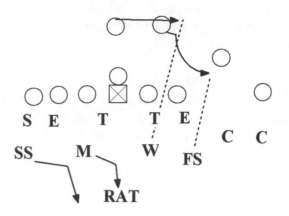

With two tight ends and two backs our adjustment is the same. We can play the second tight end two different ways. We can bring the corner into a head-up technique at linebacker depth, or we can put the end in a 7-technique with the corner outside. Everything else is the same.

TWO TIGHT ENDS

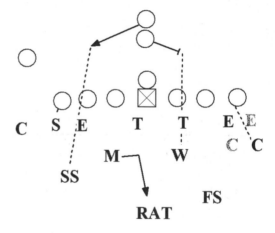

In the spread offense, we disguise the coverage but do the same thing. The only adjustment is we probably would bring a nickel back into the game for the Sam linebacker. The corner would take the outside receivers. The nickel back would take the slot back to the strongside. We bring the strong safety down and play the same way.

SPREAD OFFENSE - TWO BACKS

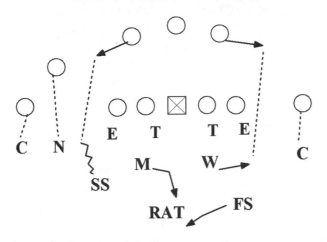

SPREAD SHOTGUN - ONE BACK

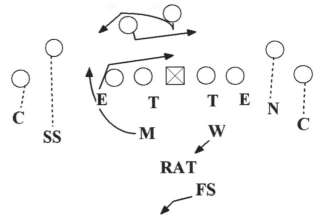

The spread offense can use a tight end in their scheme. If there is a one-back set with a tight end, we still work the same principle. The only difference is we consider the tight end as the fullback. If the tight end ran a drag route to the defensive right and flared the one back strong, the Mike linebacker would always take the second coverage on full flow. That means he would have the back on the flare. The tight end is going backside or away from the strong safety. That means the strong safety is the rat player, and the Will linebacker takes the crossing route.

SPREAD TE - ONE BACK

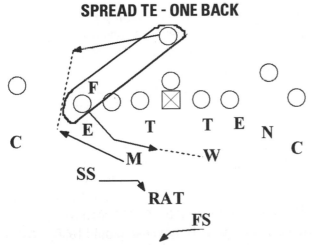

People like to run the ball out of the spread offense using a read option away from the back fake. If you crash your defensive end inside, the quarterback will pull the ball and run a naked bootleg or an option play with the wide receiver as the pitch back. We exchange gaps with our end and linebacker. That lets the end chase down the line and the linebacker scrape on the quarterback. If we don't want to pull our safety down in the box this offense, we can play two on one with our linebackers and the one back and still get a hole player.

If we want to play split safeties and an eagle front, we go to quarter-half coverage. We call this defense "*41 short.*" We are going to run an X stunt with our short-side tackle and end. The linebacker is fitting outside the stunt in the C gap, and everything is bounced to the corner. Behind the front we are playing a quarter-quarter-half secondary scheme. The free safety is in half coverage behind the corner to his side. The defense looks like a 4-4 with our alignment, and we outnumber the offense on either side. When we freeze the corner in the support game, we call that a *cora*. The corner in his alignment is bump and run. The corner cheats off the receiver and to the inside. If he gets a run key, he takes off inside. That way the wide receiver doesn't have a chance to block him. That leaves the corner up in quick support on the run. The corner has no deep coverage on this coverage. He is leveraging the run and playing short-side flat zone.

41 SHORT

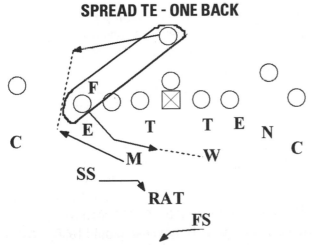

The short defense is meant to bounce the ball in a hurry. We want a quick bounce to the corner. That is why we are stunting. That shortens the bounce time of the play.

In the *41 short* if the linebacker calls short, the defensive end and tackle slant to the inside. If we want to run the three-man game with the shade tackle coming all the way around the defensive end, we call pirate. The nose tackle reads the block of the center before he does anything. If the center is reaching weak or pass sitting, he does the stunt. If the center is reaching toward the defender, he stays at home and plays the run.

41 SHORT - PIRATE

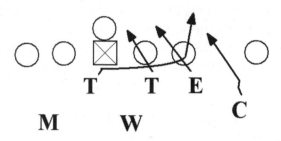

The linebackers are in fast flow in this defense if they get full flow inside strong. The Mike linebacker fills his gap right away, and the Will linebacker plays over the top in a fast flow because he has no backside gap.

41 SHORT - RUN STRONG

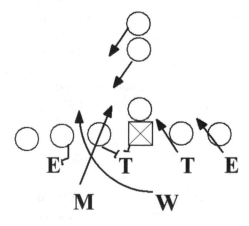

Against a trip set we can play the same coverage. To the short side, we run a cora for our corner. That freezes the corner in the short-side flat. If we are not comfortable with the corner on the run support, on the snap of the ball, we run the corner to the half coverage and bring the free safety for run support. You are reversing the assignment of the corner and free safety.

We are playing quarter-half as our coverage to the strongside. We call the strongside of the formation *stout*. The star in the diagram is a nickel back. The strong safety is keying the number three receiver first. If the third receiver runs a short or out pattern, he moves his focus to the number two receiver and runs a robber coverage on the second receiver.

If the third receiver runs deep, the strong safety takes him on the deep route. If the third receiver goes short, the strong safety goes to the second receiver, and the Sam linebacker has the post cut. The offense's answer for this coverage is to go four verticals. If they bring the trips set and the single receiver vertical, we have the single receiver doubled, and the three receivers deep to the stout side are covered by the corner, nickel back, and the strong safety. In addition we have the Sam linebacker to help also.

The reads to the trips are simple. The Sam linebacker has the third receiver on all short patterns. If the third receiver runs a vertical, the nickel back has to carry the second receiver on all patterns, except the smack route by the first receiver. The smack for us is a quick hitch by the receiver. If the wide receiver runs the smack, the nickel breaks back on that route and the corner takes the second receiver deep. The Sam linebacker expands under the second receiver in the curl area.

If the second and third receivers go vertical, the corner has the first receiver exclusively except on the smack. What we are doing is playing robber coverage on three receivers instead of two. We are reading outside breaks to always run someone under the inside break, no matter who is running the inside cut. Basically, this alignment gives us seven people in the box, plus maximum cover on everything else.

QUARTER - HALF COVERAGE VS. TRIPS

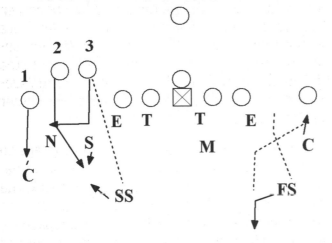

THREE DEEP - MAN FREE

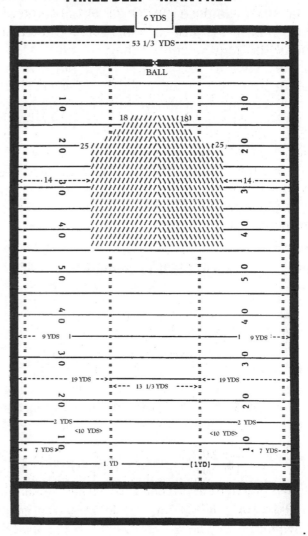

Let me explain the theory about the split safety coverage. If you are playing any kind of a three-deep coverage, the middle safety has to cover from hash mark to hash mark. If you are playing a three-deep zone or man under and a free safety, the area from hash mark to hash mark is the area the safety is responsible for. The problem is the alignment of the corners. The numbers on a football field are within 10 yards of the sideline. We say any receiver inside the numbers is in the relative distance to the middle safety and in his responsibility. The corner is told that if the receiver aligns within the area of responsibility of the middle safety, he aligns in an outside position and forces him inside. If the receiver aligns in a position outside the middle safety's area of responsibility, the corner aligns in an inside position and plays his inside technique.

The problem for a three-deep or free middle safety is created by four vertical routes. If the offense runs four verticals, you have to have someone carrying the seam receiver or reading off the seam receiver. What we mean by carrying a receiver is having someone cover the receiver until he enters the area of responsibility of the middle safety. If we are reading the seam, we have someone running with the receivers all the way.

When I talk about split safeties, this is a two-deep scheme. Our corner alignment on receivers is such that we wall the receiver out of the middle until they get deep down the field. The thing that people don't understand about pass defense is control of the receiver. You have to keep the receivers cut off. Once the receiver gets on top of the defender, the defender has no control of where the receiver runs.

As long as the defender is on the high shoulder of the receiver, he can impede his progress on the field. He can lean on him, bump him, or punch him. However, when the receiver gets on top of the defender, and the receiver is on the receiver's low shoulder, the receiver can go anywhere in the field he wants to go. The defender has no control and has to follow him.

All defenders have to carry their receiver at least 10 yards down the field in the receiver's pattern. After that time, if the defense has any rush at all, it is too late to throw the ball in a place that can hurt the split safeties. The defense has to decide whether to play hard or soft and how to carry receivers to the area of responsibility. We want to keep receivers out of that area. When we have split safeties, we are going to play hard corners. The defense has to make a decision on how to play the defense. That all boils down to whether the corners can play or not.

If the corners can't cover, it puts limitations on what kind of defense you can run. When you start to game plan how to play your defense, you have to use one of the two concepts I showed you to stop the run. You have to use the cora adjustment, where the corner can roll up for support and not have to play the receiver alone. Or, I showed you how we play the eight-man front concept, which kept them from running the ball.

It all comes back to the point of whether our corners can cover the receivers, or are we in mismatches on them. If you have a mismatch at the corner, the offense is going to go after him until they hit one. To stop that, you have to play split-safety type coverage, but that puts you in a position of not being able to stop the run. That is the key. You have to get in the two-deep look and play eight-man fronts out of it.

I would rather play against a team with a great runner, than a team who has skilled athletes at the quarterback and receivers. A great runner is the easiest thing to stop. Teams like that I call "wad ball." That means if you wad up your defense in short area, you minimize the athletic ability of the runner. The trouble is when athletes get the ball in space. That is when it is hard to get the guy on the ground. That is when the five-yard out cut ends up in the end zone.

The last thing you have at your disposal is pressuring the quarterback. There are a lot of people blitzing the quarterback and trying to affect his throwing. I like to blitz and hit the quarterback, but when I coached in the pros and we called a blitz, all the secondary coaches folded their hands and prayed. We prayed that we didn't hit the quarterback. We could sack him, but we didn't want to hit him. If we did the coordinator would blitz 50 times that game.

If you can play with your corners in man coverage, you have to do something else. You play zone and blitz the quarterback by bringing four defenders to one side of the protection.

I'll show you the blitz everyone is running from the 4-3 front. The open-side defensive end fakes rush and drops to the weak flat area. The 3-technique loops outside the offensive tackle. The shade tackle comes across the center's face to the backside A gap. The 5-technique defensive end slants inside and upfield. The Sam linebacker comes from the outside. The

Mike linebacker scrapes behind the slanting tackle and blitzes.

The strong safety creeps up and plays the tight end wall to flat. The Will linebacker plays the hole in the middle. The drop end plays wall to flat on the weakside. The corners are locked up on the wide receivers, and the free safety is in the middle.

STRONGSIDE BLITZ

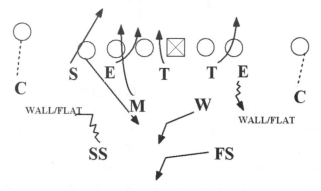

The offense could devise a scheme to block that stunt, but they can't from the other side. We slant the tackle inside, blow the Will linebacker and bring the corner off the end. The defensive end draws the block of the tackle and then drops into the wall to flat drop. The free safety rolls to take the wide receiver in man coverage, and the strong safety goes to the middle zone.

CORNER BLITZ

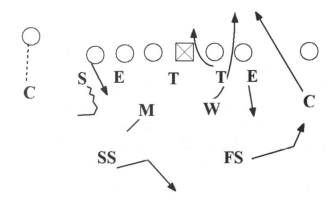

I did not have time to get into a lot of techniques. Hopefully you can use some of the schemes in your system. I enjoy talking football. You're always welcome at LSU. Thank you very much. I appreciate your time.

THE GEORGIA SOUTHERN OPTION GAME

Georgia Southern University

This is my very first clinic of the year. I'm not in shape for the clinic season. I will probably have to catch my breath a couple of times during this lecture.

We are an inside veer team. We run the football effectively and take what the defense gives us. We are a run-and-shoot team. We run first and shoot second.

The only thing I know is this offense. I'm going to tell you the things I know and explain it to you like I do my players. I will give you all the secrets, the snap counts, and the formula.

The first thing you have to do is to get a base play. Our base play is the triple option, and that comes off the inside veer play. The offense gives you the ability to control the clock by running the football. This type of offense creates a north-south running attack. I watched Air Force, Army, and Nebraska, who run the option, and we are different from them. We don't stretch ours out the way they do. We go north and south with our plays as much as we possibly can.

When you play this offense, both sides of the ball become more physical. We do the sleds and bags, but we have a 25-minute option period in spring and fall drills. We run the offense just like we do in a game situation. We let our slot receiver go inside and get physical. We cut linebackers, we let the fullback get tackled, and we let the quarterback get tackled. We are smart about it. We don't clip people and if someone has a good shot at the quarterback they don't kill him. But we are aggressive with our drills. Our defense learns how to defend blocks and come off blocks. We have to have 18 inches of movement at the point of attack. The only way to get that type of work is live blocking. We have to come off the ball and get physical.

The offense is good anywhere on the field. I have put the football down on the goal line where the offensive line is in the end zone. The quarterback is taking the snap from a yard-and-a-half in the end zone. It puts stress on the quarterback to make sure he gets the center-quarterback exchange. It puts pressure on everyone up front to make sure they are driving their feet to get out of the end zone.

Then I turn the ball around and put it on the nine-, three-, or one-yard line going in. We still run the same plays we did on the other end. We run the veer, trap, and midline in both places.

This offense eliminates the weather factor. We have to play whether it is cold, rainy, or sleeting. I have had good days in the rain and bad days in the rain. For the most part, our winning percentage at Georgia Southern is awfully good. We are 59-10 in the last five seasons there. Our seniors are 39-1 at home. We went 10-3, 14-1, 13-2, and 12-2 the past four years. We didn't play all those games in sunshine. This is a fast-break offense that gives the quarterback a bunch of 2-on-1 opportunities.

I've said it before, and I'll say it again: let your rabbits run. We have some good athletes and some good players. The quarterback is a threat to run the ball, and that means the defense has to account for another back.

The offense puts stress on the defense and spreads them out. It makes them cover the field from sideline to sideline. It forces the defense to be in a balanced alignment. If they don't balance the alignment, I will take advantage of numbers, angles, or the field.

We have a chance to hit four vertical routes every time we line up. If the defense doesn't play cover two on us, we are going after them with four verticals.

We take the emotion and enthusiasm out of the opponent's defense. They must start playing responsibilities. The offense can control a good player on the line of scrimmage and slow down the linebackers. If someone doesn't play their responsibility, we are in the secondary. Our athletes are good enough; when they get going they are hard to bring down.

In this offense you don't have to block the 7- or 5-techniques to run the ball at them. We let them take themselves out of the play. We let them come to us and neutralize them.

When you run this offense, you will see five base defenses. You will see a 50, 6-1, 8-man front, and some kind of stack defense. The other front is going to be some kind of defense that has a 3-and-3 alignment. It will either be some kind of bear front or a double eagle. Other than that, you won't see any other defenses.

We can create personnel mismatches with the formation we use. We line up in the spread, trips, or double wing. What we are looking for is a linebacker trying to cover one of our slot players. We have slot backs that can run.

Since we only face five basic defenses, our blocking rules are simple. They see these defenses the whole time, so they have a good understanding of what is coming at them and how fast it goes.

An important thing is the repetition we get in practice. The things we are doing on August 5 is the same thing we are doing on December 5. We get to practice the offense over and over. There is a saying down in Georgia: "If you don't beat Georgia Southern by the time the frost is on the pumpkin, there is a chance you won't beat them." That is a fair assessment. By the time the frost gets on the pumpkin, we have run our offense over a thousand times. It is like Mary Lou Retton. The first time she went over the vault, she didn't get a 10. But she kept working at it until she did. That is the way we run our offense. The first time we run the option, it is not going to be as good as it is later on.

Speed and execution is the secret to this offense. This offense allows the quarterback to get you out of bad plays and into good ones.

The last point is probably the most important to the offense. We can recruit to the offense. We don't have to get big fullbacks, huge tight ends, or mammoth offensive linemen. When I see us coming across the field, we don't look like much. I know one thing about our players: they have big hearts and play with a lot of emotion.

If you ask a defensive player what is the most important play, he will tell you it is the next play. If you ask a Georgia Southern offensive player what is the most important play, he will tell you the most important play is 12 and 13. That is their bread and butter. When all else fails, we can run 12 and 13. In spring practice, when I set the ball down on the 35-yard line and tell the offense to run 12 and 13, the quarterback looks at me like I have just given him the keys to the Cadillac. Everyone knows how to run the play from any formation. That play is the inside-veer play, with which we had great success.

Since 1983 Georgia Southern has won six national championships. Every head coach over that period of time has won a national championship. We played in eight national championship games. We have had seven Southern Conference championships since joining the league in 1993, with five in a row. For 15 consecutive years we have been in the top six in rushing yards in the nation. We have had two losing seasons in 15 years.

We have been very successful with what we are doing. A lot of it has to do with our scheme and our kids.

Our base formation at Georgia Southern is called *spread*. We line up in a double-slot formation with the quarterback under center and one back in the backfield. We put the X-receiver to the left all the time. The Z-receiver is always to the right. They both are on the line of scrimmage in our base set. The slots are called A-backs and the single back behind the quarterback is the B-back.

SPREAD

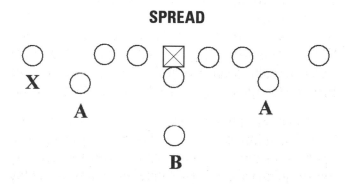

In the offensive line, your best lineman has to be the center. He has to be quick and have some power. He is going to have a noseguard on him so tight that he could tell you what he had for dinner. The last thing we look for in the center is speed.

The guards need to be powerful guys. The second physical feature they need is speed. The third thing in their makeup is quickness. Our offense has counters, quick traps, long traps, counter option, dive counter option, and speed option.

Our tackles have to be quick off the ball. They need some speed because they are going to have to chase linebackers and secondary personnel. The last requirement for the tackle would be their power. Of the tackles, the left tackle needs to be your best tackle because he has the backside protection in the passing game.

Our offensive line has to be able to come off the ball. We don't want heavy guys that can't get out of their own way. We want guys that can come off the ball, smack the defender in the mouth, and get 18 inches of movement.

The offensive line we have coming back is going to be good. My center is 265, and the guards are 303 and 306. Both the tackles are converted tight ends from high school. One of them is 255 and the other is 285. The oldest player in the group is a junior. They will all be back for two more years.

If I were going to put together a high school team, my quarterback would be a great runner. He has to make good decisions, have quick feet, and be able to throw a little.

The best thrower on the team would be my second-string quarterback. When I do my option drills, my first quarterback would get 75 percent of the rep and the second quarterback would get 25 percent. When we had passing drills the first and second quarterbacks would each get 50 percent of the work. When we come to the game I have a good mix of what I want. If I didn't want to run the clock out and wanted to extend the game, I could use the second quarterback.

The next player I want to talk about is the fullback. The fullback has to be able to give you big yardage runs; he has to give you that 60-yard run. The guy who is going to give you 6- and 8-yard runs can't play in this offense at that position. He also has to have good hands because we have to pitch it to him all the time. If I have three guys with the same ability, I put the biggest guy back there. We want players in this position who will fight to get the extra yard.

The A-backs are interchangeable. You can play them right or left. Backs like this are a dime a dozen in Georgia. Every high school has one playing for them. One of our slots is only 4.8, but when he catches the ball he is running downhill and he looks fast.

When we played Youngstown State in the national championship game, he rushed for 639 yards in that game. Everyone we had was going the distance on them. We have two kids that can really burn. They are both in the 4.4 categories, but the rest of our kids are average at best in their speed.

The wide receivers must be able to make the defense pay if they make a mistake. They have to be great stalk blockers.

The center is in a four-point stance. His feet are a little wider than shoulder width. I try to get my linemen in this position. I want a flat back with his hips and shoulders on the same plane. I want the knees ahead of the hips and the ankles behind the hips. He has a 60/40 weight distribution from his hands to his feet.

I want his off hand grounded with the hand on the football between the second and third laces of the ball. We want the ball snapped with a quarter turn and firm against the quarterback's hands. He is going to snap and step at the same time. The quarterback has to ride him out as he takes the snap. When the center steps right, there is no problem, but when he steps left both center and quarterback have to really concentrate on what they are doing. The reason for that is the hand the center uses to snap. The quarterback wants to pressure the butt of the center so he can feel his hands.

The guards are going to have three-foot line splits. The grounded hands of the offensive guard are on the knuckles of the toes of the center. It doesn't matter whether these guys are in a left- or right-handed stance. I want them to be in a comfortable stance. The guards come to the line and get down immediately and the tackles align on their stance. They have a three-foot split from outside shoe leather to inside shoe leather.

The A-backs are 3 feet from the tackle and 1 foot back. The A-back is in a stance with his inside foot back. His shoulder and chest are ahead of his knees, and his stance is straight down the field. He is not cocked in like they do at Air Force. We want him to be able to see everything happen in front of him.

If the ball is in the middle of the field, the wide receivers split the numbers. If the ball is on the left hash mark, the X-receiver aligns 4 yards from the sideline. The wide receiver to the field, which is the Z, will align on the top part of the numbers. If we are on the right hash mark, the receivers reverse their alignments. The X-receiver will be on top of the numbers, and the Z-receiver will be 4 yards from the sideline.

The heels of the fullback are 5 yards from the football. Our fullback's stance is about the length of the football. It is a narrow stance, but balanced. He is in a three-point stance with a weight distribution of 60/40 from his hands to his feet.

SPLITS

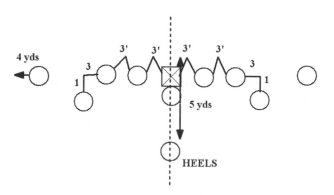

The quarterback puts the pressure on the center's ass and lifts him up a bit. Our center's feet are shoulder width, and so is the quarterback. He has his knees bent. He is not under the center in a straight-legged position. When the center takes the cheat step as he snaps the ball the quarterback is going to take one also. His weight distribution is 50/50 on his feet.

When our quarterback comes to the line of scrimmage, the first thing we want him to do is put us in the right play. We have a system to count the defense. We count the defense starting outside the veer read. If the defense is a 50-cover-three look, the 5-technique is number 1. The 9-technique end is number 2. The strong safety is number 3. Going the other way the 3-technique is number 1. The 5-technique is number 2. For this clinic talk I will put the support safety inside and call him number 3.

NUMBERING SYSTEM

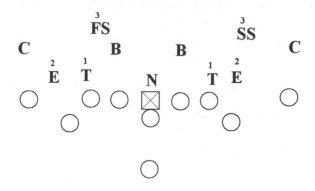

There are two different ways we run the option. When the run support is outside, we run an *up scheme*. When the run support is inside, we run a *load scheme*. The first thing the quarterback does is find the free safety. If the free safety is in the middle of the field, he counts the number of linebackers in the box. If there are two linebackers in the box, he knows he has the load scheme one way or the other. The free safety is off the hash mark, so he doesn't know whether the coverage is cover two or four.

After he counts the linebackers and finds the free safety, he listens to the linemen for their technique calls. The linemen are going to call the technique of the people aligned on them.

We number techniques like everyone else. The head-up positions are 0, 2, 4, or 6. The shoulders of the linemen also have numbers. The guard has three shoulder techniques on him. His inside shoulder is a 1-technique, inside leg is a 2i, and the outside shoulder is a 3-technique. The tackle has the same numbering system. His inside shoulder is a 4i, and his outside shoulder is a 5-technique. The slot back's inside shoulder is a 7-technique and his outside shoulder is a 9-technique. The techniques are the same to the right and left of the football.

We count gap players simply. If there is a defender in the A-gap we consider him a 2i player. If there is a player in the B-gap he is considered a 3-technique.

The quarterback has 9 feet to his read key. That should give the quarterback enough time to read. When players start getting in gap, they will start screaming off the ball. You may wonder when a 4i becomes a 3-technique. As long as the defender is splitting the crotch of the offensive tackle, that is a 4i.

The offensive line in this scheme is responsible for anyone from the B-gap inside. The quarterback is responsible for the first two players outside the B-gap. The 5-technique tackle is the read key for the quarterback and the defensive end is the pitch key. The quarterback handles both men by reading one and pitching off the other. The wide receivers and slots are handling everyone outside.

The A-back is blocking the run support on this play. He arc releases outside the end and stalks the strong safety. The wide receiver pushes the corner off in a pass route. He is going to try to get him to run. If the corner stops and starts back to support, the receiver breaks down and attacks his playside shoulder.

The tackle will call his techniques. He calls *5-technique-backer in or out.* He is telling the quarterback that he is not sure if the linebacker is in the box or out of the box. If the linebacker is in the box, we are going to run the load scheme. If he is out of the box, we are going to run the up scheme.

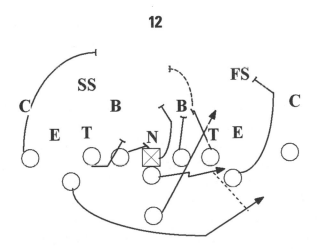

12

Let's go to our 13 play. When we call our plays, all even-numbered plays go to the right, and all odd-numbered plays go to the left. The playside A-back has to block the run support. The run support in this case is outside. The A-back takes a drop step, crosses over, and gains width. He wants to attack the strong safety to his side. When the strong safety sees the drop step and crossover, he flies to the line of scrimmage. That is the reason we have to be aggressive going after him.

We use the drop set to time up the play. When the A-back was in the wishbone his block on the run support timed out good with the option. Since he is in

the slot he has to delay his time so he doesn't block too early. If he gets there too early he cannot sustain a block that long. If he knocks down the strong safety, the strong safety can get up and recover. You want the block to occur at the time when the pitch gets there.

The tackle has the playside linebacker. The tackle can go inside or outside the handoff key. If the guard is covered, we want to run the ball in the B-gap. It is the tackle's job to make sure we can run the ball in that gap. We come off the ball with a 6- to 8-inch power step. Every step the linemen take should be the same. The tackle's first step should be at the inside foot of the 5-technique. He wants to get the second step in the ground quickly to get the third step upfield. The shoulders should precede the knees, and the knees should precede the toes. The eyes are the sights, and his hands are his guns. The tackle is trying to get north and south as fast as possible. He wants to take three steps straight upfield.

When he hits the linebacker, he wants to shoot his hands inside on the breastplate and turn. He wants to get his hip between the linebacker and the ballcarrier. The tackle is trying to lift the linebacker and strangle him with his own shoulder pads. The tackle has a simple rule: If the tackle is uncovered, he goes outside number 1, and blocks the quarterback to pitch; if the tackle is covered, he goes inside number 1, and blocks the linebacker.

The playside guard blocks base. That means if he has a 1-, 2-, or 3-technique aligned on him, he base blocks on that man. If he is uncovered, he checks the playside linebacker. The first guy on the defense to get the triple option is the playside linebacker. In this situation we have the tackle and guard on the playside linebacker. If the guard gets the linebacker, the tackle works laterally to the next level and picks up the safety. We work linebacker to safety with the guard and tackle.

To the backside, we are using a scoop block in tandem with the guard and tackle. The noseguard in a 50-defense is generally slanting one way or the other. The center is scooping on the noseguard. The center, backside guard, and tackle are in a scoop scheme. The center has a scoop from half the front A-gap to his crotch. The backside guard scoop path is from his crotch to the center's crotch. The tackle's scoop path is from his crotch to the guard's crotch. They have a scoop area.

The center is using a short scoop. He takes his first step at a 45-degree angle, his second step is on the spot where the ball was, and he turns north and south as fast as he can. He is looking for the backside linebacker. He doesn't care about the noseguard; he is trying to get up to the backside linebacker as fast as he can. If the noseguard slants backside, the backside guard is full scooping on him and the center is on the backside linebacker. If the noseguard stays to the playside and continues to try and cross-face the center, the backside guard climbs to the backside linebacker.

We have three types of scoop schemes in our offense. There is a short scoop, full scoop, and a tight scoop. The short scoop is a 45-degree step and a 90-degree step.

The backside A-back is coming in short motion. The ball is snapped about the time he gets to the backside B-gap. He is taking three steps and hitting it hard north and south. The backside receiver is selling a backside post. The first time they don't respect that move, it is a touchdown.

The track of the fullback is the inside hip of the playside guard. His second step is going toward the crotch of the guard, and his third step is outside the guard. As the fullback comes into the mesh area, he is going to put a soft squeeze on the football. He is going to take the football when he clears the frontside leg of the quarterback. He will know he has the ball because the quarterback is going to press it into his stomach. We tell the fullback to keep two hands on the ball to the linebacker. He doesn't try to cut until he is clear of the line of scrimmage. When he gets the ball, he wants to cut north and south.

The quarterback takes the snap and his eyes are focused on the handoff key. He extends the ball for the mesh area. The fullback is responsible for the mesh area. It is his job to get over the ball. The quarterback rides the ball in the fullback pocket from his back leg to his front leg. If he leaves the ball with the fullback, he steps around the heels of the fullback and carries his fake-out downfield.

If he keeps the ball, he steps around the fullback and gets back downhill. He has the ball up in the chest area and tries to get his shoulders square to the next key. We don't want to take a big step. We want the defense to come to the quarterback. If the 5-technique can make a play on the fullback and tackle the quarterback, the fullback is too soft.

We want to make the pitch read commit to the quarterback. Both the A-back and quarterback are turning north and south at the same time. The A-back is flying because he has had a running start. If the quarterback reads his pitch-key crashing, he stops and pitches the ball.

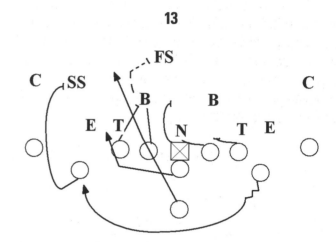

13

In the midline scheme, we have two plays. The plays are 10 and 11. 10 goes to the right, and 11 goes to the left. We have two ways to block the 10 and 11 play. The first way is called *10-right*. The second way is called *10-twirl*. On this technique, the playside A-back comes in motion. On the snap of the ball, he twirls back and applies his blocking rules. The playside A-back has two rules to apply on this play. He has a one-back rule and a two-back rule. If there is one linebacker in the box, he blocks the outside linebacker. If there are two linebackers in the box, he blocks the playside linebacker. The backside A-back on the 10 play starts in motion and runs the pitch path.

The playside tackle's rule is base to outside. He blocks out on the first down lineman on him or outside of him. The playside guard veer-releases and blocks the playside linebacker. The center and backside guard are responsible for the area from the head up on the center to the backside A-gap. The center will base to a reverse ace. If the center is covered, he base blocks. If there is a backside gap player, he combination blocks with the backside guard, with the center trying to get off for a second level block. The center and guard are trying to knock the gap player out of the hole.

The quarterback steps back to give the fullback his path off the hip of the center. The fullback is responsible for the mesh area and sees the handoff key. If the 3-technique penetrates, he has a lead block on the middle linebacker by the playside guard. If the handoff key takes the fullback, the quarterback pulls the ball and makes a square cut north and south in the B-gap.

We want to make sure the playside guard never blocks a 2i tackle. His block is the linebacker. The playside guard can widen his split a bit to make the 2i tackle become aware of his inside responsibility. The 2i player will fall inside and take the fullback. The playside guard is the lead blocker on the middle linebacker for the quarterback.

MIDLINE 10

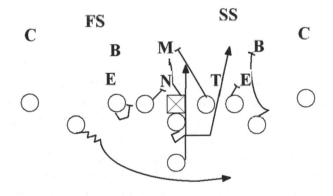

Against a 50-defense, I like to triple-team the noseguard with the two guards and the center. Since there are two linebackers in the box, the playside A-back comes through the crotch of the offensive tackle and blocks the playside linebacker. The tackle will base block out on the 5-technique defender. Everything else is the same.

MIDLINE VS. 50

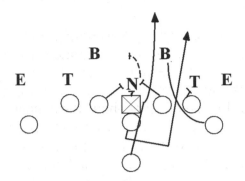

I like to block that play like that and so do our kids. If you go to a scoop scheme against the 50-defense, you may as well run the triple option.

I want to show you one formation that drives people crazy before I stop. We call this set *heavy*. We go unbalanced with both tackles to the same side and bring in one of our split ends to the tight position away from the two tackles. The A-backs are in a wing-and-slot formation, but that is all that changes.

HEAVY

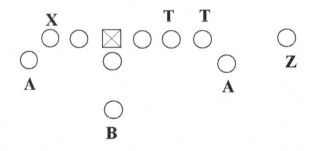

We don't run the outside veer because we feel the footwork is too radically different than the inside veers. We want to get repetition on our footwork and ride techniques. The midline and inside veer are not that different as far as footwork and mechanics. Remember, the more work you get on the veer, the better you become. Thank you, gentlemen, I appreciate your attention.

DEFENSIVE SCHEMES AND TECHNIQUES

University of Louisville

It is a pleasure to be here representing the University of Louisville and Coach John L. Smith. This has been a great year at Louisville for my family and me. We have settled in and love the city. We are really excited about being here. Before coming to Louisville, I was linebacker coach at Minnesota. I came from Minnesota to Louisville for one reason: the snow. I grew up in New Mexico. I never saw any snow there. I found myself living in a place where every house had a three-car garage. The third stall in that garage was for the snowblower. They even had headlights on them.

I want today's presentation to be very informal. Anytime you have a question, step up and ask it. Hopefully when I finish today, you will have learned something, or at least reaffirmed your beliefs. If I cover something that you want to get deeper into, just hold your hand up and I'll do it for you. I hope I can spark your interest.

What I hope to do today is give you an overview of our defense at the University of Louisville. The first thing I want to start with is the defensive philosophy we have at Louisville. If you know me, you know I am not a philosophical kind of guy. I'm a hands-on type of person. But I do believe there are major points within your defense that you have to stress and hang your hat on.

The second thing I would like to cover is our basic techniques and our fronts. We are a very multiple-front team. Our base front will be an eagle look with two backs in the backfield and a base 4-3 with a one-back set. In both fronts we utilize a man-free coverage.

I am going to touch on our base techniques in our defensive line. I will go into detail on what we call a *9-jam 7-technique*. It is a new technique for me. It is a unique technique.

The third part of my talk will be on pass rush. When other coaches come to visit us, the thing they want to talk about is our pass rush. I'll cover our philosophy on the pass rush and get into our teaching sequence.

The last thing I'm going to do today is go over some defensive-line and pass-rush drills. I've brought one of our drill tapes, which I'll cover later.

The first thing I'll talk about is Louisville's defensive philosophy. The most important thing that we have to do is to *stop the run*. In Conference USA, everyone throws the ball all over the place. But if you can't stop the run, you are not going to win. To stop the run, you have to *keep the box full*. That means you need more defenders in the box than the offense has blockers. The best way to get that done is to play man free in the secondary.

If you have two backs in the backfield, we are going to be in an eagle look. We use a gap-control defense. To the split-end side, we are in a 3- and 5-technique with our tackle and end. To the tight-end side we are in a 1- and 5-technique with the tackle and end, with a 9-technique by the outside linebacker. We play 4-3 personnel with two ends and tackles and three linebackers. The strong safety aligns on the tight end and is responsible for the tight end. If the tight end blocks, the safety is heavy on run support.

EAGLE VS. TWO BACKS

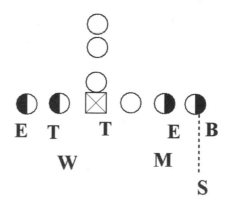

Against a one-back set, we go to a base 4-3 defense. To the split-end side we are in a 5- and 1-technique with our end and tackle. To the tight-end side we are in a 3- and 9-jam 7-technique with our tackle and end. The bandit linebacker adjusts toward the passing strength and the strong safety aligns on the tight end.

BASE 4-3 VS. ONE BACK

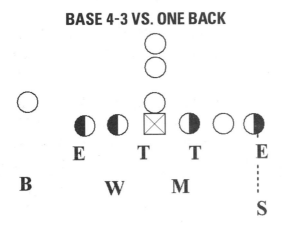

We are going to teach aggressive techniques. At least once a week we are going first offense against first defense in a live full-contact team drill. To play an aggressive defense, you have to keep the rules for the line very simple. We don't want to burden these guys with too many rules. We want them to play loose and aggressive. The same thing is true with our linebackers. There may be a slight shuffle step, but most of their technique is played downhill.

Our four down linemen and the three linebackers have a foxhole mentality. In gap-control defense, the defenders have a foxhole to defend. If we can be aggressive and stay sound we have a chance to be good. We constantly talk about *squeeze* and *spill.* When we squeeze, we take blocks on with our inside shoulder and force the ball inside. When we spill, we take blocks on with our outside shoulder and force the ball to the outside. We want everyone on the defense to be on the same page. That requires communication that they understand. We don't huddle as a defense. We get the calls from the sideline. You have to be great communicators to get aligned properly.

We work each week on defensive concepts. The concepts we work on weekly are counters and options. The team we are playing that week may not have this in their scheme, but you have to prepare for that type of scheme. You can't do it in one week. That keeps you from being surprised by some team with something they haven't shown before.

The next part of our philosophy is *pressuring the quarterback.* The first thing we want to do is utilize the rush position. We name our defensive ends the *rush* and the *stud.* The rush is our best pass rusher. We want to get him into the best position from which to rush the quarterback. We want to give him some freedom and try to keep him out of a situation where he can be double-teamed easily.

RUSH ALIGNMENT

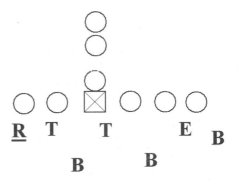

In the eagle defense, the rush end will be toward the open side. We hope he gets more one-on-one blocking schemes. In our dime package, we want him to the open side to avoid the tight end.

DIME PACKAGE

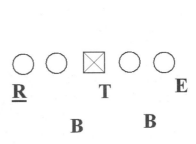

We also put the rush at a linebacker's spot. We do this with game planning. When we back him up as a linebacker, we have a number of places we can put him to blitz. By playing him at multiple spots, it gives him a chance to get to the quarterback. We can align him on the offense's worst pass blocker.

LINEBACKER BLITZ

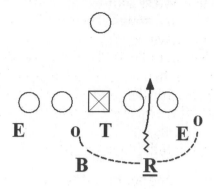

We use a zone blitz scheme to put pressure on the quarterback. We are going to play the run first in the defensive line. On the pass, we can drop defensive linemen out of the line of scrimmage to cover receivers or zones. This helps us to cover the hot routes a quarterback is looking for when he sees the blitz coming. Or they could be sight-adjustment routes when he sees a defender vacate a zone. We can use the zone blitz from our base defense. It allows you to bring linebackers and still cover their responsibilities. On the one I'm going to show you, we drop our rush end and nose tackle. We blitz the backer off the edge and the Mike linebacker through the B-gap.

ZONE BLITZ VS. PRO I

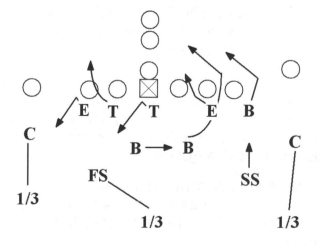

The next diagram shows the same zone blitz against a twin-wideout situation.

ZONE BLITZ VS. TWINS

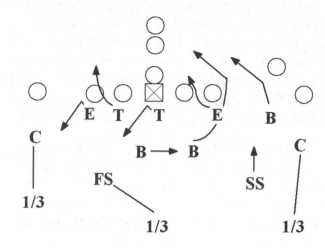

This is a safe concept. It allows you to blitz on first and 10. It is also great on field position. If the ball is on the 15-yard line, you can zone blitz and not worry about giving up an 85-yard touchdown.

The last thing in our defensive philosophy is trying to create turnovers. Louisville has created more turnovers in the last two years than anyone else in the nation. We do a good job in this area for three reasons.

The first reason is *pursuit*. Pursuit is an attitude. We practice each day on getting our entire defense running to the ball. If you get a lot of people around the ball, someone is going to get a good hit or make a strip of the ball.

The second reason is *tackling*. Everywhere I've been, I've worked on a tackling circuit at least once a week. I think it is important to break down the techniques of tackling and emphasize those techniques. Everyone knows the fundamentals of tackling, but you have to emphasize those fundamentals. There is a new concept in tackling. It recommends that you don't talk to your kids in terms of "breaking down."

Tackling is not a natural concept. It is not natural to tell a 200-pound athlete to bend his knees, keep his eyes open, and run into another guy going full speed. Don't use the words "break down" when you are teaching tackling. When we hear the words "break down," that means bend your knees, spread your feet, and slow down.

We feel like the running back is going to be a better athlete than the defensive lineman. If we tell the defensive lineman to break down, the running back is going to beat him every time. We take our shot and tell them to run through the tackle. If they miss the tackle, we want them to miss it in a certain way. If we miss the tackle, we want to do it in such a way that the ballcarrier is forced back into the remaining pursuit.

To create turnovers, you have to talk it up with your players. You have to mention it as often as possible. They have to understand the importance of turnovers. Make it part of their mindset when you practice tackling or any other drill relating to tackling.

At the University of Louisville, our defensive goals are set up into season and game goals. Our season goals are as follows:

- Number one in total defense in Conference USA.

- Number one in defense vs. the score in Conference USA.

- Number one in defense in forced turnovers in Conference USA.

- Number one in defense in sack production in Conference USA.

Our game defensive goals are more detailed in what we are trying to do and what we hope to accomplish. Our game goals are as follows:

- Win.

- Allow no 10-play series or scoring drive 80+ yards.

- Score defensively or make a goal-line stand.

- Win the fourth-quarter battle.

- Create four turnovers.

- Win third-down battles (67%).

- Have no penalties that keep a drive alive.

- Make one sack out of every 12 pass attempts.

- Win the sudden-change battle.

- Make a 100% effort to swarm to the ball.

We continually show our players what we expect of them. We expect to win every game. All our game goals come down to playing hard at all times. We strive to have no loaf plays during a game. The unique thing about Louisville is that we define what a loaf play is. When we go to the field on Sunday, our defense lines up on the goal line and we do an up-down for every loaf we have in the game on Saturday. It is not a conditioning drill. It is a pride drill. If we had six loaf plays, the team does six up-downs.

We have some posters in our meeting room that define loafing. First is *"No change of speed."* If a player is running in pursuit and the ball pops loose, we want a change of speed after that ball. If there is no change of speed, that player is loafing.

Next is *"Not turning and going to the ball."* If a defensive lineman is rushing the quarterback, as the quarterback throws the ball, the defender better turn and chase the ball. If he just turns and looks, that is a loaf.

Third is *"Laying on the ground."* If a player is on the ground and doesn't get up, that is a loaf.

The fourth definition of loafing is *"Getting passed by another player."* As he is running to the ball, we don't expect him to be passed by another player pursuing the ball.

"Turning down a hit" on someone is a loaf. That means the defender turns his head on the tackle or doesn't tackle with toughness.

The mental toughness we are trying to develop ties into our philosophy of stopping the run, pressuring the quarterback, and creating turnovers. Those are the things we are going to sell our kids on. That is how we win football games.

We use a production chart to grade the production of our players. These are the areas we want our players to be aware of. We grade them as to the following criteria:

- Tackle (primary) — 2 points

- Assist — 1 point

- Tackle for loss — 3 points

- Sack — 4 points

- Assist sack — 2 points

- Pressure (force bad pass) — 1 point

- Batted pass or breakup — 2 points

- Interception — 4 points

- Score — 2 to 6 points

- Cause fumble — 4 points

- Fumble recovery — 4 points

- Great effort — 1 point

- De-cleater — 2 points

- Loaf — -3 points

- Ignorant penalty — -4 points

- Critical error — -4 points

- Missed tackle — -1 point

This is a good way for us to evaluate the way our players are playing, and everyone can see what we expect from them.

In our eagle defense, we put five guys on the line of scrimmage instead of four. That helps us in run defense. We are in man-free coverage, which also helps us on the run. In this coverage the corners and strong safety are always going to have help on the high post. That is an advantage for the corners, and they can funnel everything inside.

The strong safety is aligned over the tight end. He is going to take anything vertical by the tight end or anything over the top of a linebacker. The Will and bandit linebackers are what we call width droppers. The Mike linebacker is a middle dropper. The Will, bandit, Mike, and the strong safety are responsible for the tight end and two backs in the backfield.

The Will linebacker is aligned on the weakside. He is responsible for the flat to curl on his side of the ball. The bandit linebacker is aligned in a 9-technique and has the flat to curl on the strongside. If the tight drags to the weakside, the Will linebacker is responsible for that also.

Before I go any further, I need to show how we get the strong safety involved in run support. If we

get an isolation play at our Mike linebacker, he is going to spill the ball outside. He takes the fullback's block on with his outside shoulder. The strong safety is reacting up outside. The Will linebacker doesn't need to get over the top and fills the cutback lane in the A-gap. That is an example of man-free coverage allowing us to outnumber the offense at the point of attack.

EAGLE VS. ISOLATION

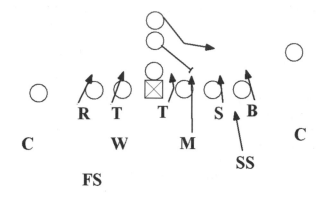

At this point, I'm going to quickly go through our down-the-line defensive techniques. Our defensive line aligns with the inside foot back and the inside hand down. We key the ball and react off the ball. We are going to throw our pads and place our hands. In the placement of the hands, I want the down hand in the breastplate and the outside hand tucked under the outside shoulder pads of the offensive lineman. You have to play with your hands. If you don't, you are going to get held by the offensive lineman. To combat that, you have to utilize your hands to get separation. We play with our thumbs up. I want my hand on the offensive lineman's shoulder into the gap I'm responsible for.

VS. BASE-PRESS OUT AND DEFEND GAP

I don't get too concerned about foot movement. If I get off and place my hands, that will lead my feet to the proper place. If we get a down block, the defender automatically goes down with him because of my hands. Coach your players in terms of eyes and hands. After that it goes back to the foxhole mentality. I have my foxhole, and I am going to protect it.

On a reach block, the defender does the same thing. He reacts, gets his hands placed, and takes short steps in his movements. On a reach block the second step of the offensive lineman is the important step. If the defender takes a short step and gets his foot back on the ground, the offensive lineman has no power in his second step. If the defender takes a long second step and allows the offensive lineman to complete his second step and get his foot back on the ground, the blocker can break the defender down.

The defender wants to bench-press toward the pressure of the block. He is working for a spot 2 yards outside and 2 yards deep. When he gets there, he sits down and plays football. If the ball gets to that point, it will have to cut back. If the defender stays on the line of scrimmage, the ballcarrier can go anywhere he wants to.

VS. REACH-ANCHOR AT 2 X 2

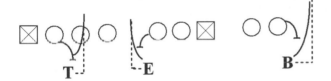

A lot of people think if you get penetration you are susceptible to the trap. If you are playing with hands when the blocker goes down, we go down with the block. We get penetration, but we are squeezing the air out of the charge, and there is nowhere for the trapper to go. We are pushing the down blocker into the next foxhole. That works well on the zone play too. If the trapper tries to trap the defender, the defender takes him on with the outside shoulder and spills the ball outside.

VS. VEER/CUTOFF-SQUEEZE AND SPILL

Coaches have some different ideas about reactions to the double-team block. We coach to stay up on the double-team. We don't want to go to the ground. With the zone schemes today, the double-team block becomes a base reach or a cutoff block. We want to dip the shoulder, get into the crease of the two blockers, fight pressure, and be a football player. If the tackle comes off for the linebacker, the block ends up being a base block by the guard. If the guard comes off on the linebacker, the block becomes a cutoff block by the tackle. We want to get our butts down and react to the block. I don't believe in sitting down and trying to take two blockers on. If you do that, you are no help to the linebacker, and then you can't make a play either.

VS. DOUBLE PRESSURE

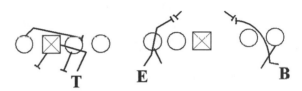

If the tackle gets a down block from the outside, he steps into the down block and presses the block back out. He makes sure the ball clears his gap, pulls the blocker inside, and cross-faces him into his pursuit angle. Some coaches teach to get in the guard's hip pocket and follow him on a down block-pull situation. The problem is the split by the guard and tackle. If the split is tight, it makes it hard for the defender to follow the guard. The offensive line is coached to not let the defender do those things. They are good athletes too. I've found it extremely hard to play that technique, unless the split between the guard and tackle is large. That is why we teach a cross-face move.

VS. DOWN-SECURE GAP, PRESSURE

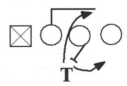

In a nutshell, that is all our defensive line does on their run reactions. We keep the teaching simple. That is all our kids know. I drill that in individual drills. We do a lot of half-line and inside drill work to try and perfect those techniques.

Our *base-1* defense is our 4-3 look. When we get the one-back formation, we like to go to the 4-3 look. We make all of our adjustments with our linebackers. The stud and rush ends are in a 9- and a 5-technique. The tackles are in a 3-technique to the tight end and a shade on the center to the open side. The bandit linebacker covers down on the slot player. The strong safety is still on the tight end, but from a disguised position.

It looks like a two-deep zone, but it is a man-free concept. The Mike and Will linebackers have the remaining back in the backfield man to man. If he goes to the left the Mike linebacker takes him and the Will linebacker becomes the low-hole player. If he goes right, the Will linebacker takes him, and the Mike linebacker becomes the low-hole player. That still gives us seven guys in the box.

The difference between our eagle and the 4-3 defense is the *9-jam 7- technique* played by the stud end in the 4-3 scheme.

BASE-1

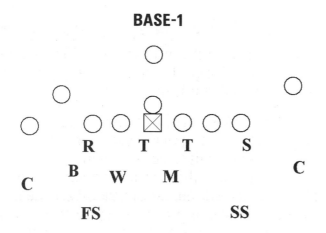

I believe the 7-technique, or inside eye of the tight end, is the hardest technique to play. The defender is aligned inside the tight end protecting a gap that the tight end has a natural inside blocking angle on. We play a *9-jam-7*, which is a new technique for me.

The alignment for the end is a 9-technique on the outside shoulder of the tight end if the split of the tight end is small. The wider the split gets, the tighter the alignment of the defensive end becomes. If there is a wide split by the tight end, the defensive end lines up in a 6-technique. However, his gap responsibility is the C-gap. He wants to get his hands on the tight end's breastplate and drive him down the line and close the C-gap. He is an on-the-line defender. We don't want too much penetration by him. We want the lateral gap closed.

He has a number of keys that can help him. He keys the ball, the chest of the tight end, the tight end's split, and offensive tackle's stance. He reads the blocking triangle of the frontside guard, fullback, and backside guard. We want him spilling the blocks of all those guys. If the tight end is trying to release on a pass, we read that as no pressure and get back inside. However, if the end is trying to execute a block, he will be exerting great pressure, which we fight.

As the tight end comes off the line of scrimmage, the defensive end wants to jam him down into the C-gap and make the football come to him. He squeezes the C-gap with the tight end's body. He works off the tight end's hip with his eyes inside. We want him to spill all blocks at him and react to the bootleg and cutback. He is basically taking two blocks out if they try to run the ball at him with a kick-out scheme. He has taken the tight end off his block and spilled the kick-out block.

Another advantage is on the pass rush. He has outside alignment, and containing the quarterback is his responsibility. He is already outside, so containment is automatic.

VS. BASE

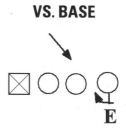

If the tight end tries to reach block the defensive end, he drives the tight end back. He wants to stay square and press out on the tight end. He keeps his eyes inside and defends the C-gap. If the tight end is arc blocking, the defender keeps his eyes inside and plays all blocks coming from inside. We want him to spill all blocks outside. We don't expect the defender to beat the reach block. It is all right for him to be underneath the block.

If they try to cut him off, he benches to the pressure. He accelerates his feet and uses the tight end's body to control the C-gap if the ball cuts back. If the tight end is taking a huge split so he can get inside, the defensive end moves head up and stays inside.

If the double-team comes from the tight end and tackle, he wants to stay square and create a pile. The safety is filling outside of him so he can't get turned out. If he has to slant into the C-gap, it is all right. His help is outside. He can't allow anything to come inside of him.

On an option play the defensive end has the quarterback. We slow-play the quarterback. We don't attack him. If he pitches the ball, the defender turns and sprints down the line to junction the pitch man.

I want to talk about our pass-rush teaching sequence. The first things we teach are *stance* and *takeoff*. We have a pre-snap agenda we consider. We want to know the down and distance. We want to know the formation the offense is in. Eye contact is a big thing in the pre-snap agenda. I want to know who is looking at me. If the fullback or guard is trying to find me, I know I'm going to get some action. Watch the stance of the offensive lineman for tips as to what they are going to do. Are they heavy or light in their stances? Is the weight on the hand or feet?

The defensive end's alignment and foot position will be different according to down and distance and what the scouting report tells us. If we read a high release by the offensive lineman, we get up the field immediately.

We want to react to ball movement not cadence. Use the ball on a stick to get your people to react to the right thing. If we see any movement in the line, we are coming off.

The second idea in the pass-rush sequence is the *break down*. Before we can get to the quarterback, we have to break down the offensive lineman. The first thing we use is speed. If the defensive end can sprint up the field 4 yards, he can break down the offensive blocker. The offensive blocker gets too high and off balance. His feet also have a tendency to get too close together.

We emphasize pressure points to break an offensive lineman down. The offensive lineman wants to create and stay in a perfect position. If the defensive end can grab the wrist, elbow, or shoulder, it disrupts the offensive lineman's perfect position. I can punch him in the chin, which breaks down his position. The last pressure point is the offensive lineman's chest. If the defensive end can punch him in the chest, we can get him to raise his shoulders and take the bend out of his knees.

The next thing is the *step-through*. The most important thing to do in this move is to release the hips. The hips turn sideways at a 45 degree angle. Turning the hips will put the pass rusher in a position to be looking at the offensive player's helmet ear hole. If he keeps his hips square, all the offensive lineman has to take is one drop-step, and he is in position to get back on his block. The second part of the move is to step through with the same foot and same shoulder. When we step through, we try to step on the heel of the offensive blocker's outside foot with our inside foot. We rip or slip with the inside arm as we step through.

After we step through, we want to get the knee and toe pointed at the quarterback. Most of the pass rush is a desire to get to the quarterback. We want to aim at the ball and low.

We also must learn a counter move. We teach two counters. That gives us something to fall back on. When we can't get around the corner of the shoulder, we stop, plant the outside foot, club or pull with the inside arm, and come around the other corner. We can plant and spin, but we must be conscious of our rush lanes. We spin off the inside foot. We throw the outside arm, spin around, and attack the other corner.

We have to work hard on these techniques in practice to perfect them. We have to confuse the offensive linemen and get them out of their comfort zone.

Let's watch some drill film, which illustrates these points. We do the hoop drills to help us with our inward lean. It helps you lower your center of gravity and run. You have to bend in at the end of the pass rush to get to the quarterback. If you don't learn how to do that, the offensive tackle will continually push you past the quarterback.

Thank you very much. I really appreciate it.

INSIDE AND OUTSIDE ZONE AND MIDLINE SCHEMES

University of Nebraska

First I want to tell you I am glad to be here. I attempted to get here last year but got stuck in a snowstorm and was stranded at the St. Louis airport. Things just did not work out last year, but I want you to know I did make an effort to get here last year.

I really do not know where to start today. I will talk about the inside and outside zone plays. I have been at Nebraska a long time. There are advantages and disadvantages connected with that deal. One point is that you do have continuity there. The disadvantage is that every year you think you need to add something different. Sometimes we do become concerned with the amount of offense we have. We have eight sets of running plays. We have eight to 10 pass protections. You would not know it if you watched us play but we do work on pass protection.

We have two coaches at Nebraska that work with the line. Dan Young is responsible for the pass protection, and I am responsible for the running game. We work on throwing the ball in practice more than any team in the country. That is for the fans that like to watch practice. We do not throw the ball a whole lot. We may have to throw it more now because teams are starting to load up on us by putting more defenders in the box.

I want to talk about the zone plays. We put the scheme in our offense in 1989. We were scoop blocking, but it really was not what we call the inside or outside plays. We went to visit Howard Mudd. He was with the Chiefs at the time. He talked one day each on the inside and outside zone plays. The inside and outside zone scheme is the easiest scheme in football. The thing about the plays is that you do not need to have rules for the blocking. You are going to be a covered lineman or an uncovered lineman when the ball is snapped. That is very simple, and our players like it. When you have a lot of rules, you get bogged down and you lose track of technique. You spend all of your time teaching rules. So this style of play made it simple for us to teach and coach.

COVERED OR UNCOVERED

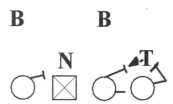

There are a lot of plays you can run from tackle to tackle. The only play we have from tackle to tackle is the isolation, where we block it as an inside zone play. I am convinced you can run any play from tackle to tackle with an inside scheme of blocking if you are not pulling the guards.

The nature of the scheme is very simple. We tell our linemen they are considered covered if a down lineman is over them. If the down lineman is not over any part of his body then he is uncovered. We simply say they are covered or they are uncovered.

We have pinned the terms for our linemen, so we can communicate with them. If the lineman is covered, we call it a stretch base. The terminology comes into play on a lot of our plays. Stretch base to me is not firing off the ball to get the defender. If we tell him he has a lock-on-block and you tell him he must block the man wherever he goes, you will not have as aggressive a football player. This is because the kid will be worried about what the defensive man is going to do on the play. The nature of the inside zone is that it gives you a chance to lock onto someone without just sliding off the defender.

We have three concepts on the zone-blocking scheme. To describe the blocks, we have come up with these terms over the year. We have a rip reach, a stretch double, and a straight base block.

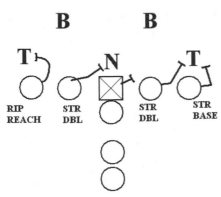

The principle of the scheme for the inside-zone stretch base is this. If we are covered with a defender and we are going to stretch the play laterally, we must turn the outside foot toward the call and invite movement that way. The second thing we must do is to redirect the second foot. The entire body must stretch laterally. You teach this technique from the side. If the player is leaning, there is no way he is going to be able to redirect his step. The nature of the thing is to step so it is more a timing step. It is not a big step and it is not a slow step. We do not want the body projecting forward initially. The reason for this movement is to buy a little time so we can see what the defender is going to do.

The second step is always to the cylinder of the body. By taking the first step laterally, it allows you to redirect the second step, which is just as important as the first step.

The first step is lateral. I do not care what the defense does, the second step is going to be in the cylinder of the body. It is a quick step, and then we redirect that second step.

The thinking behind this is because of the slanting defensive lineman. If he is slanting, we can stop his slant on that second step. We do not want him crossing our face. That is where the foot should go on the second step. We want him to go for that back leg of the defender. Before the ball is snapped, we tell the lineman to pick a spot behind his leg. That is where the second step goes on the inside zone play.

If the center is going to help the guard with a stretch double block, he wants to step at the spot behind the defender's leg. He does not want to put his head underneath the defender we are going to double-team. He wants to stick his head on top of him. If the defender is there to double, we are going to double him. If he has worked outside of the stretch set of the covered lineman, then I am not chasing a shadow. So if the guard stretches and the defender goes outside with him, then the center is at the linebacker on his second step. He does not need to double on the play. We already have the defender moving and we have more room in that area. The nature of the inside zone is to create some inside crease along the line for the back to run in.

Let me show you what to do with a 2i technique on the right guard. That guard is covered, and it does not make any difference whether the defender is head up, inside, or outside the guard. If the defender is heads up or to the outside, we tell our linemen to stretch block to the callside. If the defender is lined up in an inside shade technique, we tell the linemen to eliminate the stretch step. We are going to assume the defender is going to cover that gap if he is lined up inside. We eliminate that first step and go right to our second step. We tell the right guard to step with the inside foot or his second step immediately and smoke the defender in the gap.

We are playing the odds the defender is playing the inside gap. He could loop on us, but we are going to play the odds that he is playing that gap. If we see an inside shade on the playside, we do not stretch the block. We will still double the crap out of the man and go to the next plateau.

The thing about the inside zone is this. Technically, the uncovered man is responsible for the linebacker. But he does not have to worry about the linebacker until he comes to him, or the two blockers double the down lineman back into the linebacker. When they get to the linebacker level, the uncovered man comes off and gets what he can against the linebacker. We tell the uncovered man that if he has to slip off the double-team block to get to the linebacker, he did not keep the double-team block long enough. They really can hang on to that block.

This is a blocking scheme where you can get two blockers on one defender regardless of the size of the players. It is a neat scheme. One thing we tell the center: Regardless of where the defender shades him, we want him to stretch it as far as he can stretch. Even if the defender is offset to the backside, we still want the center to stretch on the play. We do not want the center to allow any penetration. All he has to do is to maintain the line of scrimmage. You cannot have penetration because if you do, you do not have a frontside play or you do not have a cutback play. So we want the center to stretch his butt as hard as he can and to prevent any penetration across the line of scrimmage. If he can do that, we have a chance on the front side and on the cutback.

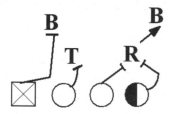

Everyone has that same rule. From the backside guard to the tight end we have the same rule. If they are covered, they stretch base and if uncovered they stretch double. The only player that varies from this rule is the backside tackle. The first thing the backside tackle looks at is the status of the guards. Here the guards are not covered. Now all the tackle has to do is a rip reach block. He does not want the defensive man to cross his face.

We tell all of the linemen all they have to do to line up is to break the belt of the center. We tell all of the linemen their hands should be down on the heels of the center. When the center gets down, our linemen align their down hand on the heels of the center. This allows for space for the linemen when they take that second step after the stretch step. If they are stepping properly, they will at least have a chance to make contact.

We found out we could not block the down linemen if we crowd the ball. If the defense loops or slants, it is tough to block them from that distance. We used to do that, and we found out we were putting our kids at a disadvantage. If both the offense and the defense are crowding the ball, it is difficult to block anyone. It was the slants and loops by the defensive line that convinced us to back our linemen off and give them a chance to play. At least we have a chance to make contact now that we have backed off the ball some. That concept is tied into the zone principle. It allows us to do what we need to do with those people.

The hardest thing in coaching offensive linemen is this: We do not want to allow the defensive lineman to become an alley player. We do not want to just let the man go by. You have to give the blockers a place to step, and tell him which foot to step with, and give him a place to aim. We want to give the blocker a place to set and a place to aim. If the defender is not there it is not his fault. You as the coach must determine where you want that step by the nature of his play.

If we face a 4-4 defense this is how we block it. We say the 7-technique is on the inside shoulder of the end. He is going to block him with the tackle blocking on a stretch double. The tackle is in a 3-technique. The only way the outside linebacker is going to get involved in the play is for him to slip back underneath the play. We should get a blowout on the 7-technique man. They have a stretch double on the man with the tackle and end. The center and guard have the same block on the 3-technique and inside linebacker.

On the inside zone, we have a little curl dive to the fullback that is off the pitch action. We run it by blocking the inside zone. We run the midline fullback dive. If we were running an inside zone play, we would always go toward the strength of the defense. To me the tight end side is the strength of the defense. The defense is reduced on the backside, and the strength is over on the tight-end side. If we were running a one-back play, we would want to run the play to the strength of the front.

If you want to run the inside zone to our split-end side or the reduced side, then we want to make sure we have an extra player over to that side. That means we need to have the other back available to block on that side. We would send our fullback on the backside to get that end man that you would not be able to block if we split the backs. To keep from changing our alignment, we just call it a draw so the fullback knows where to block on the play. It is not really a draw. It is really the weakside isolation. We use terminology to determine the way the fullback is going to block.

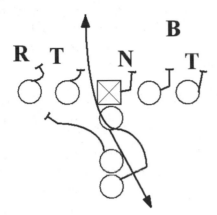

Now I will talk about the outside zone play. It is the basis for all of our option game. It includes the speed option, dive option, and the arc option. If you run a lot of inside zone plays and you face a team that is running a lot of stunts and twists and loops, it is not a very good play. It is not a good scheme against that type of defense. You are lucky if you can pick up the stunts by the defense. If we face a team that stunts a lot, we do not think inside zone.

The outside zone is a play that will take care of all defensive stunts and blitzes. We get a lot of different crap when we run our option offense.

On the outside zone, we give the players a rule: covered or uncovered. If the lineman is covered we want him to use a rip reach block. We are trying to get the ball outside. We must be able to outflank the man. If we can get outside on the down lineman, we can option on the secondary support. We try to outflank the defender the first two steps. On the outside zone, we let our linemen cross over on the second step. We tell the blocker to cross over on the second step as long as it is upfield. He wants to get started upfield because he is going to come off on the next level. We call it a rip reach because we used to take the inside arm and rip it across the outside arm of the defense. We changed that block a little. We still call it a rip reach but we are trying to put both

hands on the far side shoulder pad. It has helped us keep our shoulders pointed upfield. It has also helped our team by letting our buddy know we are gong to help our buddy.

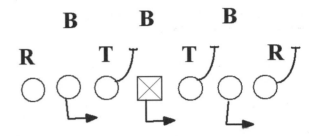

When you run the outside zone scheme, you cannot have big splits by the linemen. We tell our linemen one foot is the split we want on the alignment. This is for the uncovered lineman. We tell the man that is uncovered that he is going to pull and overtake. When you pull, if you will put the lead foot where it is supposed to be, the rest of the body will come with you. We want the pulling guard to get depth and distance on the pull. We want him to get depth and distance. He picks the foot up and puts it in the direction we want him to go. We tell the pulling guard before he can overtake the linebacker he must get beyond the man before he can come back on him. If he tries to pull and come around the backside number of the tackle, he will never get it done. So we tell the guard he cannot get the linebacker until he gets there. They know what we mean by that statement.

If the defense is playing a 3-technique or a 5-technique, realistically they are there for one reason. The defense does not want the offensive man outside of them. If you put a 3-technique on the guard, there is no way he should be able to reach the defender. We recognize this fact, and the kids recognize this fact. Against the 5-technique the guard is going to get a 5 call. That means the tackle is telling the guard he has a defender on his outside. The guard will pull, but he must check to see if the tackle is slanting inside like some teams will do to screw you up. He will pick the man up if he slants. But what is automatically going to happen is that he is going to pull around the tackle for the linebacker.

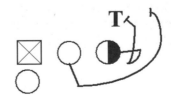

We try to stop the 5- and 3-techniques by stretching and scrambling if the defense stays in those positions. I would stretch and scramble rather than just go down and scramble because if the defender does scramble you have lost that man. If the blocker takes that stretch step and he slants, he will have enough balance to get up to the next level. If the tackle dives on the ground rather than taking the stretch step, he won't be able to pick up the linebacker.

Here against the 3-technique we tell the center the only time he has that man is if he slants. We do not run into a lot of those situations but that is how we block it.

If we get to the two-tight-end set, we will "either-or" the option. We would rather run the play to the reduced side of the defense. We do have change-ups on the play, but we could run it either way.

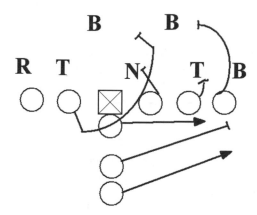

For us to run the stretch play, we are aiming for the outside of the tight end. We can full zone that play. It does not make any difference where we run the play. The back reads what happens to the defensive end. The back can cut the play back underneath the end.

We change up a little on the outside zone on the stretch play. Most of you have seen that play. The pros run three plays on this. They run the inside zone, outside zone, and counter play. That is just getting us warmed up at Nebraska.

If the defense is playing an offset nose and a 5-technique to keep us from going outside, we make

this change. We will go into a game and tell the linemen we are going to change the blocking on the stretch play this week. We tell them we are going to pin shade. On anything that is shaded to the call we are going to pin them. That means we are going to down block on them.

We tell the end he has to come down on the 5-technique. We tell the tackle he has a high pin block on the linebacker. He wants to get him behind the defender and anticipate his flow. We want to pull him flat. If the linebacker comes outside too quick our back will cut back inside on him.

There is nothing tougher for the center than to block the offset nose man. If the nose man is any good at all, he will go with the flow, and if the back breaks the play back inside, the nose will make the play. So we pull the center on the play. This frees the fullback up for the secondary support.

If we are running our arc option to the strongside and the end is skating or slow playing it outside, there is no way they can take the play away from you if you run it right. If we are running our 41 speed option, we would add the word "seal" to the play. That tells everyone we are going to seal inside and pitch on the end man. We seal inside and arc block on the secondary man with our fullback. If the defense has a 9-technique to that side, we will never try to zone that look. It becomes an automatic pitch on the end man for us. We are not going to force something the defense does not want us to do. If the defense is in a 6-technique we will try to run the zone play. But if he is in a 9-technique we will not try to block him. We will pitch off the end.

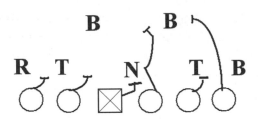

We can run the play to the short side as well. We tell the onside guard to check the onside linebacker but to come off on the backside linebacker.

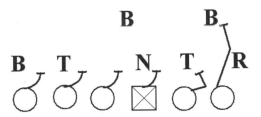

We can run a dive option and run it into any technique. We do not use the seal principle on the dive option. Let me show you what I mean against this look. We have a 3-technique on the guard and a man on the outside of our tackle with a linebacker in between the guard and tackle. The guard and tackle cannot block the 3-technique and linebacker and the rush end. We still run the play, but we make a "solid" call to the fullback. This alerts the fullback that we cannot get the linebacker on the outside zone scheme. On the solid call, we run it this way. The fullback is responsible for the onside linebacker.

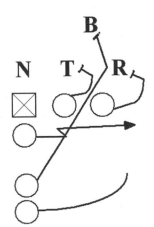

When you run the option you are not going to have every play go for a big gain. But if you can gain 4 or 5 yards per play on a "duck" play, it is not bad. In the 1990s we won three national championships, and we only averaged a little over 5 yards per play. We won the national rushing titles as well. You do not need to gain 10 yards per play to win a championship. You need

first downs to win national championships. So we would love for the defense to force our quarterback to keep the ball 20 times per game if we can get 6 yards a shot on the play. Just because we do not get to make the pitch does not mean it is not a good play.

If you are good at option football the defense must take something away and they must give you something. That is what it amounts to. If the defense gives you the I-back, pitch the ball to him. If they force the quarterback to keep the ball, that is all right as well. The ideal thing is to be able to get the ball outside. But defensive teams are not going to let you do that. Miami did some cute things to us, but we still had three or four plays that were good for us where we had the quarterback keep the ball on the option.

There are not a lot of different blocks involved in line play. We say the inside and outside zone plays are a separate bag of tricks. But on the other plays, you have four types of blocks. You have a down block that we call a pin block. You have a man-on-man block, which we call a lock-on block. On the lock-on blocks we run one play, and that is the isolation play. The fourth block is the combo block, which is a double-team block. The other type of block is the trap block. But you do not have a lot of different types of blocks.

If we are going to run the isolation play, and we are going to lock on the one gap, we are going to protect the inside gap. We tell the linemen if they have a lock-on block, the first step is straight ahead with the near foot. They aim at the middle of the defender. We want them to aim at the cylinder or the numbers. We do not want to get beat inside on the callside. We tell them to go straight ahead with the inside foot or they will get their butt in trouble.

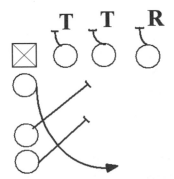

The only time we tell the line to cut the splits down is when we are running the outside zone play. If we definitely know in the huddle that we are going to run the outside zone play, we tell them to tighten their splits. On the inside zone and the other plays, I do not think the splits make that much difference. We do not want them to bunch up. Normally we tell the guard to split 2 feet, the tackle 3 feet, and 3 feet for the tight end. When you get down to the goal line you see teams go foot to foot. The defense gets tight and they are foot to foot as well. We want to spread them out a little so we have a chance. I see a lot of teams that bang, bang, and bang inside on the goal line. Nothing happens because everyone is in there so damn tight. We tell them to keep the splits. We tell them when we need 1 yard, we want to split the line out a little more. This gives us a chance to get that yard. If you run the option down on the goal line and you are lined up tight, it is not that bad, but we like to split them out. If you are going to hammer at them, you need to get the splits.

The first thing we are going to start out with in the spring is the stance. This is critical. If they get lazy in their stance they are not going to be a good football player. We do not want to have an alley player. We want to get them into a stance where they can step anywhere we want them to step. They cannot have weight out on the hand. If they do that they can't run the inside zone because they cannot pull unless they adjust their stance. If they do that they give the play away. We want to get them into a stance where they are relaxed. You are never going to hit a man in your stance. When you get to the man is when you kick butt. We want to align them in a position where they can move. They should not have to adjust their stance on the pin move, pull, or the stretch move. We do not put the weight on the down hand. It is used just for a balance tool. We are flat-footed in our stance because over 99 percent of our offense is not there first. If you have too much weight on your hand or you are up on your toes, you can only go in one direction. You must be able to step properly on all blocks. A general rule for the guard and tackle is this: If they have a lock-on block, they step with the inside foot directly at the man. They do not want to get beat inside.

On the pin block, the angle the tackle steps is determined by the play. On a toss sweep, the guard is pulling, so the defender is going to try to go over the top of him. That is where we use the high pin. We want to take away the thing that will hurt the defense the worst.

We tell the tackle any time he gets a down call, he must adjust his path. We tell him to aim at the cylinder. Try to play the odds. What can the defender do to hurt you on the play? We do not want penetration on the play, so he must aim a little flatter on his block.

Any time a player is told to trap, it should trigger a word to the buckler. It should trigger the word "climb." The second step is a climb move. The guard pulls here and on the first step he gets depth. The second step is back toward the line of scrimmage. The only thing that can hurt the play is for the 3-technique man to come inside on the play. You can take the tackle and fan him or turn him outside.

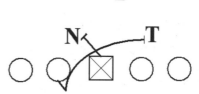

The pulling guard takes the second step into the line and comes off the center's rear and steps up inside and climbs the tackle. He is going to fan until he gets that man. We want to take the inside angle first and then we can make sure we get him.

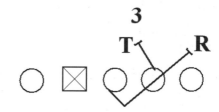

You can have a rule for every play that you run. On the inside and outside zone plays it is a matter of being covered or uncovered. But we do have rules for those plays. If we are running our isolations or toss sweeps we have rules for those plays. If the defense does something to break down our rules, we have calls to adjust on the plays. We have struggled with different words and we have used a lot of different calls. We are very simple.

We number our holes from the right to the left starting with 1. We do not use odd and even like a lot of teams use. The tight end is the #2 hole. He is also the #2 tight end. The right tackle is the #4 hole and the #4 tackle. You see how we number the hole and the man. If the right guard makes a #3 call to the right tackle, that means he wants the #3 tackle to come down inside on the block. It is that simple. That is the reason we say when a tackle is called on a "down" block, he has to step a little different. All systems do not have to be complicated. The defense does not know what we are calling. We have other calls that do not mean anything. It is not complicated for us at all. On all #2 hole plays, the tackle has the same responsibility.

Every team becomes known for something. People tend to think of Nebraska as an option team. But we run a lot more offense than the option. Last year we did everything we could out of the shotgun formation to free up Eric Crouch. He was our game breaker and he could take it all the way. We ran everything we could with him involved in carrying the ball. We ran the option, trap, counter trap, and quarterback-keep plays with him. If you have a quarterback that can run the ball, we have a lot of offense that helps the quarterback. I do not have time to talk about all of the things we did to keep the ball in the hands of the quarterback.

I do want to talk about our midline series. We started this in 1997. We do not block the midline like we used to block it. We used to run the zone block on the backside like the Air Force people do. We used to zone block the backside. Other teams would read the defender on the give, and zone block the backside. That scheme is good if the defense plays the way you expect them to play.

We run the option, the trap, and the quarterback-keep play on the midline. The three interior players give you some picture. We do not like the zone or pull scheme here. We had the read possibility in the play, but we never really ran the read play. We ran it in practice, but when we got in the game, we said we were going to run the option, the keep, or the trap.

If we are running a fullback midline trap we give the ball to the fullback over the center's crack tight.

The one thing we cannot have happen is to allow a defender to roll over the top. That center knows he has a high pin. He is the only man that is specifically placed on his pins. On the fullback trap he knows he has a high pin. He is going to take away the possibility of the defender rolling over the top.

If we are running the counter trap where the two guards are pulling, we are worried about penetration and rollover. We cannot block both the linebacker and the down defender. We use a cylinder fill on the lineman and aim at his middle. If we are running the counter sweep we do not worry about the man coming over the top because he may get caught up in traffic because that play breaks a lot wider. But the counter-trap play could break over the guard area. We cannot take care of both the penetration and the rollover. So he takes the best path he can take. That is a cylinder-fill block on the down lineman. He is aiming right at the middle of the man.

If we are running the counter sweep, we tell the center we are not worried about the man rolling over the top. So we tell him to take away penetration. That is what we call a shallow pin. Most of the time the center is pinning back on the power midline or lead play.

Let me go back to the midline plays. First is the midline option. Again, we are not zone blocking the backside. We are not reading on the play. One reason we do not zone the backside is because we are concerned about blocking the backside linebacker. Another reason we do not zone on the backside is because the defense can take away the option by bringing the 3-technique down inside hard, taking away the dive, and scraping the linebacker over the top. If they do that, we do not have an option play. The only difference in the three plays, the option, trap, and quarterback keep, is this. On the trap, on the second step, the pulling guard climbs. On the option or keep, we do not climb block. We did not say "trap" so he does not climb. He pulls flat and secures the line of scrimmage. That means he has to block the 3-technique if he stays the 3-technique. We do not want him to chase a ghost. By that we mean we do not want the pulling guard to go for the 3-technique if he comes down inside. We will let the fullback collision him if he comes inside. If the guard stays at the 3-technique, we think we have a chance to get around him to the inside linebacker.

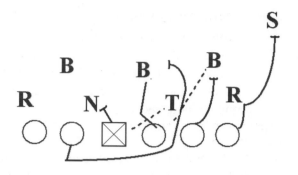

If we are running the play to the side of an inside shade technique, which we would prefer to do, we have the onside guard make a "6" call for the pulling guard. That call lets the pulling guard know he does not have to worry about the shade on the inside. The call tells the pulling guard he has no on-line responsibility. The 6 is the number for our pulling left guard. Now the pulling guard knows he can start looking for the linebacker as he pulls around the center. He is not concerned about the shade man.

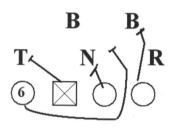

On the midline option we are always going to pitch on the end man. If we are running to the split-end side, the tackle blocks the linebacker. I promise you he will get the linebacker because of the midline fake to the fullback. It is not like a dive option or an arc option where the linebacker is going to run outside. The reason the linebacker will not come inside is because we run the quarterback-keep play and the fullback trap on the action. The linebacker is not going to run outside and the tackle can block him.

If you are running the play to the tight-end side against the 4-3 defense, they have a safety setting back deep, playing halves. The tackle takes the frontside linebacker. The tight end arcs on the safety. Because of the threat of the quarterback ducking it up inside, it prevents teams from sending secondary people to fill the alley. Between the end and tackle they will block the linebacker and safety.

We line the fullback up with his feet 5 yards from the football. He blows straight up the pike. The quarterback must clear the midline action. He does more than a 180-degree pivot on the midline action. He cannot just turn around because he will run into the fullback. If we are running the midline to the right side he has to bail out with his left foot so he can make the pivot on the offside of the center. The guard can clear the quarterback and fullback on his pull.

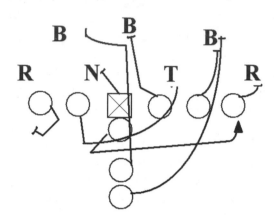

If we are running the quarterback keep on the play, we still run the midline action. We call it 34 quarterback keep. It is the same action in the backfield except the I-back is going to be blocking outside. Now we are going to block the flank with the tight end or tackle. The backside tackle executes what we refer to as a swinging gate. Now we are going to block the flank with the tight end or tackle. The backside tackle executes what we refer to as a swinging gate. If we release the tackle for the tackle, the backside end can run the play down because it is a slow developing play. We assign the fullback on the backside linebacker. So theoretically we have someone blocking on everyone on defense.

The question is what we do if the 3-technique is blowing up the field. We are pulling the guard flat and he tries to kick the man outside. The quarterback has to duck and get upfield and get what he can on the play. If we have to run that play very many times we will come back and run the trap all day long.

Another thing that would force us out of the quarterback keep on the short side would be for the defense to put two men on the tackle. They can put a linebacker up on the line. If they do that, the I-back would have to block the extra down man. We would probably check out of the play and go to the speed option or the arc option. We would run something that would help us against the assumed slant defender.

That is a hit-and-miss lecture on the midline series. We have made some good adjustments on it over the years. Against teams that are stronger than we are in the line, we can double on the lineman. We used this play in the Big 12 championship game a few years ago on fourth down and one to go. We call it 42 power midline. It is the same action for the backs. But now we can double-team the 3-technique. At least we have a chance to create a stalemate with them and he is not going to disrupt the play. We based the tight end on the outside man. We pulled the offside guard on the Mike linebacker and sent the I-back on the outside linebacker. The quarterback kept the ball and ducked up into the hole. It was fourth and one from the 32-yard line going in. Our quarterback broke the play for a touchdown. It was a midline play but we secured everything on the inside, and the defense was not ready for it. It has become a good play for us in certain situations.

This leads me to our counter offense. We have a counter trap, counter sweep, and our lead play. We have those schemes all together because our linemen all have the same rules. We try to combine as many of our plays together where we have the same rules. The rules are the same on four or five plays and that makes it a lot easier for the linemen.

(Editor's note: Dan Young, the other offensive line coach at Nebraska, covers the counter trap, counter sweep, and lead plays in his lecture, also included in this book.)

I hope I have not put too many of you to sleep with this because a lot of the blocking is the same. I like to tell people our linemen get more sleep than our other players. Not the night before the game, but in our meetings where we put them to sleep with our similar blocking rules.

I will show the film of these plays if someone will show me how to run the video. I do appreciate your attention. Thank you.

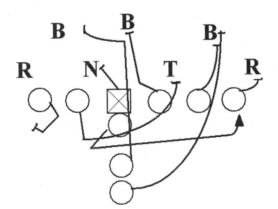

THE INSIDE POWER RUNNING GAME

Ohio State University

The last 12½ months have been quite a whirlwind for me. I had 15 wonderful years at Youngstown State. In fact all the places I've coached, I would have no problem sending my children to those schools. They were wonderful places. I could have stayed at Youngstown State for the rest of my life if they would have wanted me. It is a wonderful place. But you never know what God has in store for you. The last 12½ months have further etched that in my mind. I had the great fortune to get the opportunity to become the head football coach at Ohio State. It is a tremendous place within a great community. There are great people there. The tradition at Ohio State is second to none. We have great players at Ohio State and a wonderful student body.

The changes that have occurred in my life were only minor as compared to the changes that we went through as a result of September 11. The world as we knew it changed overnight. As I looked into the eyes of my players, I knew it was a fearful time for all of them. They had never experienced anything like they had on September 11. As our team came into the Woody Hayes athletic facility that day, they had a concerned look on their faces and a lot of questions to be answered in their minds and hearts. I'm sure the exact thing was true in your particular team situations. We all have to deal with that situation.

This calendar year has been a wild one, both personally and professionally for me. What September 11 reinforced to me was how important we are. Today coaches and teachers are so important. This is such a fast-paced world. We have to make sure we stop and evaluate things as we go through our lives. I think it is important to stop and reflect spiritually.

The morals, beliefs, and values are the center core of who we are. As we reflect on what we are doing in here this morning, it is much like spiritual growth. Sometimes we don't spend enough time growing spiritually. When we sit in here and exchange ideas about football, it leads to professional growth. We get so busy doing so many different things, that we do not do the central core things.

It is nice to get away from the rat race of recruiting. It is nice to sit down and talk football. We have been flying around the country trying to attract good young people to the Ohio State football family. It is refreshing to me to sit down and talk about coaching.

The next two or three minutes I want to share a thumbnail sketch about coaching. After that I will talk about our inside power running game.

We constantly remind ourselves at Ohio State that the most important thing we do doesn't have anything to do with X's and O's. I heard this quote from an engineering professor at Ohio State. I was sitting in an engineering lecture with my son. He was on a recruiting visit at Ohio State when he was trying to choose a college to attend.

The professor told his students this story before he got into the subject of how this form of engineering was going to change society. Throughout the talk, there was one thought that came up. We keep this thought in mind in our department at Ohio State.

"Concern for man and his faith must always form the chief interest of all technical endeavors. Never forget this in the midst of your diagrams and equations."

That was an engineering professor who could have been a football coach. He was quoting Albert Einstein. The same thing has to be true in football. Before we draw up one X or O, we better understand that concern for our players is the most important thought. That is the chief interest. Once we understand that concern, we can talk about our schemes and packages.

Coach John Majors was up here when we started. He has invested his whole life in our game. He has invested his whole life in his players. His father did the same thing. The things that his players carried with them as they left Tennessee, Pittsburgh, and Iowa State, were the things that had to do with the core values. We have to make sure we do the same thing as we make our way in this world.

My topic today is the inside running game. When you become a head football coach, it is important for you to find a philosophy that you totally believe in. There are a couple of plays that every coach believes in and can count on in any situation. I don't want to sit here and try to tell you this is the only play we run. But this play *is* the basis of our offensive philosophy.

I have to trace my college career to find out how I decided on this type of offensive game. When I played for my father, he was a run-and-shoot coach. Later, I went to work at Miami of Ohio with Tom Reed. We ran the veer offense. Then I went to the University of Syracuse as an assistant coach. Coach Dick MacPherson was just coming out of the pro game at that time. He liked to run the power-off tackle, but it was from a weak backfield set instead of the I-formation. It wasn't a pound-it-at-you type of offensive play.

When I went to Ohio State the first time as an assistant, I worked for Coach Earle Bruce. That is when I met "Dave." Dave was the name for our off-tackle play at Ohio State. I was an assistant coach at Ohio State for three years before I got the opportunity to be a head coach at Youngstown State. When I got to Youngstown State, I had to decide what type of offense we were going to run. Earle Bruce was running the I-formation when I was at Ohio State. At the time, that was the freshest offense in my mind, and so that is what I chose to run.

When you go to a clinic, you should always think through what you are going to do before you do it. If you are going to make a change, think through that decision before you do it. Don't just change to be trendy. Find something that you believe in and stick with it.

The reason we chose the power-off tackle as our base play at Youngstown State was because we felt that was the way we needed to start our program. We wanted our offense to be physical, tough, and simple. Another factor was the fact that we were starting from scratch. We needed a play to hang our hat on. We felt we knew how to teach that type of play. It is so important that you know how to teach in coaching, and especially the plays you are going to make your bread-and-butter plays.

We found out if we could run the ball for 200 yards a game, we had a good chance to win the game. If we could score 24 or more points a game, we could win most of our games. If we could win the turnover margin, we could win most of our games. As these facts became clear to us, they became our philosophy.

We did a study when we got to Ohio State. We wanted to see if the same things were true at Ohio State as they were at Youngstown State. I gave one of our graduate assistants the task of finding out the answers by researching the past 10 years of Ohio State football. At Youngstown State, we had a coaching tool we called a production index. We added the number of first downs we made to the number of points we scored in each game. From that total, we subtracted three times the number of turnovers we made. If the answer came up to be greater than or equal to 40, we won most of those games. If the answer was less than 40, we did not win those games.

The findings in all of those games were very conclusive. In the past 10 years, Ohio State's record was 56-2 when they rushed for more than 200 yards in a game. When their production index was greater than or equal to 40, the record was 67-2. When the production index was less than 40, they were 24-27-2. That meant they won 24 games playing good defense, but lost 27 games because of offensive failures. When Ohio State scored 24 or more points, the record was 76-4.

This is a measuring stick for our program. We can tell our players if they do these things, they will win the game. Our players want to know what we expect of them and what we want them to do. Once you find out what you need to accomplish, the next thing is to find out how to do it.

At Youngstown State, when we ran the same off-tackle play 250 times or more in a year, we were National Champions. That meant if we were good enough to run the same play off-tackle 250 times, we probably had a good football team. We probably played good defense as well.

The most important statistic about any given play is the percentage of consistency of the play. The yards-per-carry statistic is often skewed by long runs. The consistency of the play is what is important. That means the play got the yardage it was supposed to get, and at a very high percentage of the time.

We had a consistency formula. On first down, we needed four yards. On second and long yardage, we needed to gain half the yardage. On third down, we needed the play to get a first down. That was how we measured a play for its consistency. The off-tackle power play got what we needed 56 percent of the time in 1999.

I don't want to mislead you. We do more than line up in the I-formation and run off-tackle. College football today is throwing the football. We are no different than other teams today. But we are never going to lose sight of running the football inside.

The most important concept of college football is utilizing the talents that you have on your football team. If I could point to one thing over the course of the last 16 years as a head coach, that is one area in which our offensive staff has done well with that concept. We have done a good job of utilizing the strengths of our players.

The worst thing you can do with a young man is to ask him to do something he doesn't have the ability to do. We want to make sure we do not ask our players to do more than they can handle mentally. The greatest threat to successful offense or defense in my mind is outsmarting our players. We can get very competitive in trying to outsmart the opposing coaches. In this age of video wonderment, with so many things available to us, it is a challenge to keep things simple for our players. We have to make sure we do no more than our players can handle.

At Youngstown we went four straight years where we played 15 games. We went to four straight National Championship games from 1990-1994. We played 60 games in a four-year span. We had some guys who played in 58 and 59 straight games. We lost 26 seniors after that fourth year. In 1-AA, that is a lot of guys to lose when you only have 63 scholarships.

In 1995 I made the biggest mistake I've ever made as a head coach. After the graduation of so many seniors, I didn't go back to basics with the young group we played with the next year. We simply kept on doing the things we had done, without the experience we had enjoyed for four years. We didn't do a good job and the coaches got ahead of our players in the mental approach to the game. It cost us because in 1995, we didn't have a good year. Fortunately, we knew what we had done wrong, and we took the blame. It was our fault, not the players'.

We want to be able to run base running plays that can be run from different formations. Teams that scout your team know what you are doing. We need to know as much about our team as they do. We need to scout ourselves during the season to see what the opponent is seeing.

We felt at the beginning of the season we had to change plays at the line of scrimmage. We didn't want to play a guessing game from the sideline. We think the only way to keep that from happening is to have a simple enough scheme to automatic at the line of scrimmage. We had to have the ability to check out of bad plays.

We have to work to get efficient play-action passes off our base runs. If we get good at our base runs, people will commit more defenders to the run. You have to take advantage of that by being effective in play-action passing. We want to strike the area where the extra run-support players come from. We must do a great job with play-action passing because it will complement everything you are doing in the running game.

We want the threat of the run-pass balance from all of our different formations. The players coming into college football these days are really smart football players. You are not going to outsmart too many college players today.

We have to utilize different personnel groupings. If you watch our defensive coaches during the course of the game, they always want to know what personnel group is in the game. We want to utilize our personnel groups to get the most out of their ability. We may bring in our jumbo group and throw the ball. We want to force the defense to play an honest defense regardless of whom we have in the game.

One time I heard a coach say foo tball was a game of pressure. Does the defense have the pressure on the offense? Or does the offense have the pressure on the defense? I believe the offense can put pressure on the defense if we give them less time to think. If you line up and the defense knows what is coming, they have a better chance to stop it. If we vary what we do and force the defense to think about their adjustments, we stand a better chance of a successful play. We have to keep the pressure on the defense.

We must have the threat of attacking the entire field. You can't get so caught up with being such an inside-run team that you forget to attack the rest of the field. If you do that, you allow the defense to play only the field you are using.

If the inside-run game is going to work, you better have some other plays to get outside with. Our inside power run worked this year because we could get outside with a stretch play or a toss-sweep play.

The offense must have the ability to change the launch point of the thrown ball. Defenses today have outstanding pass rushers. If they know exactly where you are going to throw the ball from each time, they will sack you. We can't give them that advantage. We have to throw the ball from a variety of different places.

We have to utilize the three-step-drop passing game. Today, defensive teams love to blitz. We are in the age of defenses that like to blitz and pressure the quarterback from a variety of different areas. It is the age of the attacking defense. They try to pressure the offense into making mistakes by attacking them.

We must make sure we have a passing game that can take advantage of the defense when they bring more defenders than we can block. We want to be efficient in the passing game. You can't run the football effectively until you are efficient in the passing game.

All of these things I have been talking about played a big part in being able to have a power inside running game. Without being able to do the things I have been talking about, we can't run the ball. Keep all those points in mind as I show you the power off-tackle running play. We want to use it as our base play. This is our big play. It may not be the one you would choose. Jim Dennison, who coached at Akron University, has made a living running the isolation play. That is his play. He knows how to teach it. He believes in it. His players believe in it. That is the play he hangs his hat on.

We picked the power inside run, because we think we can run it against all fronts. It is better against some fronts than others, but our guys know how to block it against anything the defense can put up. It is the one play where we can call it and run it. We don't have to worry about calling an automatic to get out of the play.

In the heat of the game, when you ask your players what they want to run, you better have one of these plays. It is a play they have confidence in. Everyone needs a play they can run against any defense. You have to run this play from multiple looks. You have to be willing to run the play anytime or anyplace on the field. We can run this play in our sleep and in any situation.

I'm not saying this is the best play to run. I'm saying this is the best play for us to run for what we want to accomplish. It has simple execution, and our players believe in it.

Our basic power inside run can be run to the tight-end side or the split-end side. The tight end has to block the C-gap. The onside tackle blocks the B-gap. The onside guard blocks the A-gap. The center blocks the backside A-gap. The backside tackle has to block both the B- and C-gaps on the backside because the backside guard is pulling. He has to get his big bootie in the B-gap and turn back on the C-gap. It sounds simple, but it isn't.

You get too many different looks from the defense. They give you varying techniques that make it tough to run this play and be effective. We tag the play now to remind the linemen to block their gap. We call it "21-gap," to remind the linemen that this was an area blocking play.

The fullback blocks the onside D-gap. The backside guard pulls and finds the onside linebacker. He has to stay square and get his eyes on the linebacker. The fullback traps the D-gap. The aiming point for the fullback is the hip of the tight end.

The tight end, tackle, and guard are blocking their gaps. Most likely there will be a double-team block with two of these three blockers. On most defenses, one or two of the offensive linemen will be uncovered. When the blocker is uncovered, the gap they are responsible for is not threatened immediately. The uncovered lineman must watch the linebacker for a blitz. The uncovered lineman can come off slow and help the covered lineman with his block. Any of the three blockers can call the outside lineman down anytime they need to. The center and backside tackle have to secure the backside A-, B-, and C-gaps.

The term "Dave" was Earle Bruce's name for this play. For all I know, it could have come from Woody Hayes. But to Earle Bruce, "Dave" meant down blocking for the line. The guard, tackle, or tight end in this scheme has to block the backside linebacker. The backside linebacker in the 4-3 defense is the Mike linebacker.

On defenses today, no one lines up in pure vanilla. They line up in one defense and angle out of it into something else. They try to guess what you are running and stunt to where they think the offense is going. The thing the offense has going for it is that they know where they are going from the outset of the play. The rules for this play are good. The key to the success of any play is what the offensive line does after they block their rules.

Later as we watch the film, you will see what I am talking about. When there is no one to threaten his gap, a lineman can give help to one of his teammates.

If we run the play to the split-end side, it is the same play, and it has the same rules. Everyone blocks down. The backside guard pulls, and the fullback kicks out. It is that simple.

DAVE

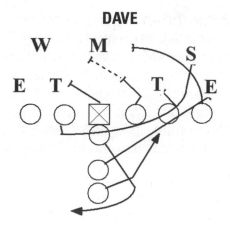

The only difference for the fullback is this. He is trapping the C-gap instead of the D-gap. His aiming point is tighter at the tackle's hips. The play is tough to run this way, but it can be done. It is harder to get to the backside linebacker.

DAVE OPEN SIDE

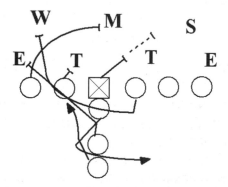

If the tight end doesn't have anyone in his gap he blocks the backside linebacker. In this case, he bypasses the Sam linebacker and blocks the middle linebacker. The Sam linebacker is blocked by the pulling guard.

Jim Bollman is our offensive line coach at Ohio State. He has a coaching point that applies to a player blocking the backside linebacker. When our players have to block a backside linebacker, we want them to attack the linebacker's backside number. They attack the linebacker's backside number and make him bubble over the top of the block to disengage from the block. We can attack his frontside number and push him back on the chalkboard. But in reality, we can't get him going backward by attacking him on the frontside number. That is an important coaching point. Attacking the backside number allows the lineman to get square on the linebacker.

The fullback tracks the hip of the tight end. He kicks out the defensive player in the D-gap. The tackle comes down on the 3-technique. The guard has no one inside of him in the A-gap. He comes off the line slow and helps the tackle on the 3-technique, keeping his eye on his gap for a possible run-through by the Mike linebacker. He doesn't block his gap until it is threatened by someone.

All we are trying to do is get the tailback to the line of scrimmage. If we can do that, the tailback will make yardage. As the season went by this year, our tailbacks got better and better. We want the tailback to hit the line of scrimmage with his shoulders square. If he hits the line of scrimmage with his shoulders square, he has a chance to be creative.

We don't want to coach the tailback too much. We want to slow him down. We want him to get his shoulders square, and let him do what we recruited him to do. We don't want to get too scientific. He is the one on the field, and he has to make the decision where to run. Let him be a tailback and run the ball.

If the 3-technique slants inside, the guard takes him and the tackle goes all the way to the Will linebacker. He works for the backside number on the Will linebacker. What this technique allows the blocker to do is to get square on the linebacker as he tries to pursue. When the linebacker tries to bubble over the block, our blocker can get square on him. We don't want the linebacker to get square and run downhill at the line of scrimmage.

DAVE VS. STUNTING 3-TECHNIQUE

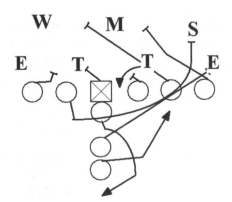

We can run this play with our fullback aligned in the wing position to the open side. We can bring the fullback in motion and get into the same position as he was in the I-formation. If the frontside linebacker blitzes the C-gap, the tight end walls him off to the inside. The pulling guard turns up in the hole and blocks the next player to show. We don't want him to slow down and look around for someone to block. He fires up into the hole and finds someone to block.

DAVE VS. STUNTING SAM

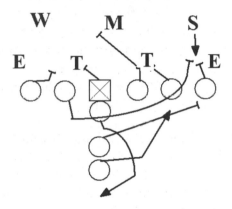

If there is more than one player coming to the D-gap, we block the first one that comes. We feel the second defender cannot get flat enough to get in on the play.

On the goal line we generally get into a two-tight-end set. In this set we have our fullback in a halfback set. We like the Dave play because the angles are good for us. The defense is bringing everyone who is eligible to play. We area-block the gaps. The fullback has to take a step up to get on the proper track to kick out. Everything else is the same.

We want the safeties to have to make the tackle on our tailback. The tailback has to remember we want at least four yards out of the play. He can't get fancy with his footwork. He must get square and then hit up in the hole. He has to be a football player. He has to make defenders miss him, and he has to split people, run over defenders, and still be an aggressive football player.

We can put an extra lineman in the game and get into an unbalanced line. We have a four-man side and a three-man side. Nothing changes for the play. We block it the same way and we can run it either way. The advantage of this play is you can run it with any formation you line up in, and you can run it against any defense they can put up.

We have to give our tailbacks freedom to run where they want to. We do not want to overcoach the tailback.

DAVE FROM THE UNBALANCED

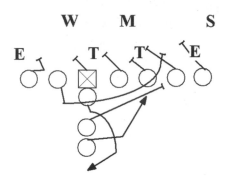

Any lineman can call the outside lineman down for help if he feels he needs it. When we talk about the backside linebacker, it is the Mike linebacker in a 4-3 defense. The Will linebacker is the third linebacker.

On this play, we cannot block the safeties. They are always going to be unaccounted for if they come into the box. That is why the tailback must be a football player. If they make the play, we feel it is going to be down the field. If they are making plays at the line of scrimmage, they should be set up for the play-action pass.

Defensive coaches teach their defensive ends to wrong arm on kick-out blocks. When that happens, the pulling guard has to be alert. If he sees the wrong technique by the defensive end, the fullback will log in the defensive end. The guard goes around the log block and turns upfield for the linebacker. The tailback has to take his time and not rush the play. He must read the log block and the guard pulling around the block, and then he takes the ball outside.

DAVE VS. LOG KICK OUT

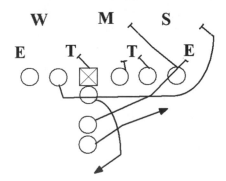

Our tailback is lined up six-and-a-half to seven yards deep depending on the tailback. We have an adjustment we make if we are getting a lot of heavy wrong technique for the defensive end. We call it "Dave stick." This is to help the fullback from having to root out the defensive end. The tight end sticks the defensive end over him. Everyone else blocks the same. The fullback comes through the hole and takes the end's blocking assignment. He is working for the backside linebacker.

DAVE STICK

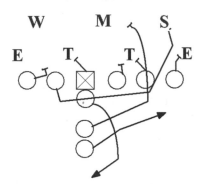

When we run this play to the open side, the kick-out block gets on the fullback real quick. The C-gap is one gap closer and the defender gets on him in a hurry. The fullback has to get low and get really tough. As I said before, the tailback has to break a tackle if he wants to score. What he doesn't have to do is break that tackle behind the line of scrimmage. We are always going to make sure the tailback gets to the line of scrimmage before he is hit. If you can read the back's number in the film, that means he is square to the line of scrimmage. That is the way he has to run the ball.

Well, that is the end of the film. Thank you so much. Our doors are always open. We have a great staff of coaches. Many of them have coached in the high school ranks and they care about young people. You are always welcome at Ohio State. Thank you.

OFFENSIVE MODES AND PASSING GAME CONCEPTS

University of Illinois

It is great to be here. I want to thank Nike for the great job they do to promote college football and high school football. I think it is great that Nike sponsors these clinics across the country. I was in Minneapolis last night for a Nike clinic, and they had some great speakers there. It is a privilege to be here to speak along with the great speakers you have for this clinic.

I know many of you were here for the lecture by Mike Cassity earlier. I am thrilled to have Mike on our staff. I knew the defensive style of play that I wanted, and Mike was the person everyone told me could do the job. I used to stand on the sideline and call the plays. I would look beside me, and all of the offensive players were standing next to me. We could not get on the field. We were playing a conservative style of defense, and we could not slow the teams down. We did not have the size up front to line up and stop teams against the run. They would take the ball down the field methodically, eating up the clock and putting points on the scoreboard. So I knew what I wanted in a defensive coordinator. I talked to people around the country and Mike's name kept popping up. He came in and did a good job. We wanted to make something happen on defense. I did not want to sit on the sideline waiting to get the ball back.

Shortly after I hired Mike Cassity as the defensive coordinator, I got a little nervous. I went down to the convention, and a lot of people told me they knew Mike well, and many of them told me they had worked with him. All of the coaches that had coached with Mike told me he had a great card trick. Not one person told me about his coaching ability. But he did a great job with our defense. He brought in a new attitude and confidence that we could play the style of defense we wanted to play with.

I watch my two young boys play sandlot football. I never see them playing zone coverage in those sandlot games. All they want to do is blitz in those games.

That is what Mike brought to us. That is the style our players could react to. It gave them confidence in what we were doing.

First I am going to talk about some philosophical things, and then I will talk about what we do offensively at the University of Illinois. I hit on these points every time I speak. I want coaches to understand and not lose sight of the fact that we must respect the game of football. It has been around for a long time. The game is bigger than any of us or our programs. It is a great game. We must have respect for the game and the way it is played. We must have respect for the people that play this game today and for the people that played and coached this game before. The game has been around a long time, but there are so many other things for young people to do now, and so many distractions — we are losing a lot of kids that once played football who are now going in different directions. We must do everything we can to keep the young people involved in this game and help them to enjoy this game. That is what it is all about. I have a great deal of respect for this game.

The key to football is that you are enjoying what you are doing. I tell our players not to forget that it is only a game. It is true at all levels. There are more pressures to win for coaches today, but the bottom line is that it is a game. We want to keep sight of this and make sure we always enjoy it. We must enjoy coaching, enjoy the kids, and enjoy the competition. If we are not enjoying the game, we are not going to have the respect for the game. It will be hard for the kids to enjoy the game as well. You must be intent, but you need to enjoy the game.

You must make sure you enjoy all of your wins. Wins are hard to get. You have heard the expression, "Boy, that was an ugly win." There is no such thing. Wins are hard to come by. It is not like basketball where you play 40 to 50 games or baseball where you play 80 to 90 games. If you get a win in football you should take the time to enjoy it. They are hard to come by.

Have fun with what you are doing. Have fun with the kids. Do not be afraid to smile. Let them enjoy the game. The game must be fun for the young kids or they will not come back.

Develop a passion for the game. You cannot win without developing a tremendous passion for the game. We have a saying at our place. "Work hard but work smart." I have been around coaches that stayed at the office until 3:00 a.m. every night. They were working hard but not very smart. They think this is the way to outwork people. You should work hard, but then get away from the office. I have to throw Mike Cassity out of the office. Our defensive staff accuses Mike of having the defensive staff meetings in a submarine. That submarine goes down at 7:00 a.m. and it does not come back up for air until 11:00 p.m. I have to go to Mike and tell him to let them out. I used to work late at night. What I found was that I was not coaching very well. I was too tired and grumpy. I was irritable and I was not doing a good job of coaching. Now I try to quit work at the office by 10:00 p.m. I can come back the next day recharged and ready to go. If I do not do that, I find that I am not doing a good job. Work hard, but work smart.

Believe in yourself. Have an attitude, have a plan, and believe in it and stick with it. When you have adversity, you better believe in yourself because not a lot of other people are going to believe in you. There are millions of people out there that think they know the game better than you do when you are not winning. You had better believe in what you are doing, and you better stick with it. That does not mean you cannot make adjustments. It means you develop a philosophy and you stick with it.

I think it is important to be a good role model to the student athletes. Many times the coaches are the most influential male figures in a young man's life. I know because I was raised in a single-parent home. I was raised by my mother. The most influential people in my life were my coaches. This was true from little-league baseball, to Pop Warner football, to high school football and basketball, and college football. Chester Caddas of Murray, Kentucky, was my head

coach in college at the University of the Pacific. I still talk with Coach Caddas once a month. We talk all of the time. He was one of the father figures in my life. The same is true for a lot of you that are coaching today. No matter how old you are, you are still the father figure for many of these kids. They are watching everything you do. You need to be a positive role model for them.

I am going to get to some X's and O's now, but those are some things I try to hit on every time I talk at a clinic. I think it is important to stress those points.

We won the Big Ten Championship this past year. One thing I know is this: You better play good defense. You are not going to win the championship if you cannot play defense. You must be able to stop teams from running the ball. That is number one in defense. We are going to apply pressure, but we are going to stop the run. You have to play good defense to win championships.

You must also be able to run the football to win. That does not mean you have to run the ball for 250 yards per game. But you have to have the commitment to the running game to win. If we run the ball and gain 1 or 2 yards, we are going to stick with that play. We are going to run the power play to both sides anywhere from 15 to 22 times per game. Against the University of Louisville, we ran the power play 26 times. We keep running the play. It sets everything else up for us. We must be able to run the ball and play great defense to win the championship.

I also believe you must score points. You must be able to put some points on the board to win a championship. You can win some games by playing great defense and running the ball. You will stumble in the big games if you cannot score points.

To score points, you must be able to throw the ball down the field. We have made a commitment to the power running game, and we stick with it. We have made a commitment to a high-percentage ball-control passing game, which is my background. I was with Dennis Green at Northwestern in 1981 and 1982 running the so-called "West Coast" offense before it was called that. It is just a high-percentage control passing game. That offense is my background, and we have stayed with it over the years. We have used that offense along with the power running game.

I believe you must have a strong commitment to throwing the ball down the field as well. You must be willing to take your shot at the long ball. You have to work on this, and you have to spend time on it. You have to execute it just like anything else. You do not need the best athletes in the world to do this. It helps to have great athletes, no question about it. We have some of those great players, but we have a lot of other players that are not great athletes that make some big plays down the field for us. Our players know we are going to throw the ball down the field early and often. We are going to take our shots. Hopefully we are going to hit some of them. We are going to make some big plays. If we do not hit the big plays, at least we will keep the defense honest and keep them a little softer to keep them from coming up and squeezing us.

It is so difficult to methodically move the ball down the field unless you are so much better than the team you are playing. It is tough to move the ball first down after first down. It is hard to move the ball down the field without getting a big chunk of yardage along the way.

I want to talk to you about the things we do to get the ball down the field. Our commitment has started to pay dividends for us. In 1999 we were the highest scoring team in the history of Illinois football. We only had one defensive touchdown, and we did not have a very good defense. This past year, we broke the 1999 record. We have been a high scoring team two out of the last three years. This year our defense helped us a lot more. We had two touchdowns, and we got the ball in good field position a lot more this year. It all works together. But throwing the ball down the field has helped our offense.

The number one job as coaches is to give our players the opportunity to make plays. In the last few years we have done that. We have speed on defense. We have turned our players loose and allowed them to make plays. We do the same thing on offense and defense in this regard. We try to get certain matchups. If the defense is going to play man coverage, we are going to go one-on-one and give that receiver a chance to make a play. If the defense is playing zone coverage, we are going to flood the zone and get the ball down the field. We want to take advantage of the holes in the zone defense. The bottom line is that we are going to give our guys a chance to make plays. Our players know this. If the defense is playing one-on-one, the ball is going up in the air. It is the job of the receivers to go up and catch the ball or make sure it does not get intercepted. If the ball gets intercepted we are not going to throw to that receiver a lot. Our players know we are going to give them a chance to get the job done.

I am going to go over a couple of concepts. Throwing the ball down the field is no different than anything else. You must commit to it, but you have to focus on the details. It is not just a matter of running a player down deep and throwing the ball to him. Our concept is sound against the man defenses and the zone defenses. This concept puts your players in position to make plays, and it allows them to go one-on-one in the matchup that you have. It is about out-executing people. It is about doing what you do. It is not what you do, it is how you do it. You can run a variety of defensive packages and a variety of offensive packages. If you run them well and you do them better than what your opponent runs their offenses and defenses, you are going to be successful. *"It is not what you do, it is how well you do it."* We are going to try to out-execute people. We want to do what we do better than what other people do with their program. To do that, you must get a lot of reps.

We teach a concept and make sure everyone on the team learns that concept. Then we will apply the concept to every formation you can imagine. The concept does not change when we change formations.

The first concept I want to cover is our alley route, which is with four vertical receivers. We focus on this play and teach the details of it from day one. Everyone runs a four vertical route. We really emphasize and teach everything related to the play. We want everyone to be exactly where they are supposed to be, which includes the depth, width, splits, and everything they are supposed to do against the different coverages. After we have covered the concept, we practice the play over and over. No matter what defense we see, we feel we have a chance to be successful.

I am going to go through each position against the man and zone defenses. The outside receivers take a normal split. We are very concerned about our splits. When we look at the film, if the players are one-half of a yard off of where they are supposed to be they will get downgraded. If the ball is on one hash mark and they are to be 3 yards outside the other hash mark, they had better be 3 yards outside that other hash mark. We do not want them to be 3½ or 4 yards off the hash. We want them exactly 3 yards or whatever we tell them to be for that game.

If the ball is in the middle of the field for us, the outside receivers are going to be 1 yard outside the numbers on the field. Here we have a tight end on one side and a receiver in the slot. The slot is going to split the difference between the wide receiver and the next man on the line. We are very precise where we want our receivers to align.

FOUR VERTICAL

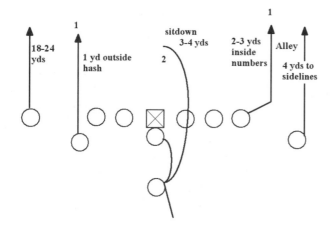

I am going to talk about the zone coverage first. If the defense is in a zone defense, it becomes a *landmark pattern* for us. Everyone has a spot on the field they have to get to. We are not too concerned about beating defenders necessarily. We are concerned about getting to our landmark. The wide receiver on the tight-end side is going to push off the ball vertical and get downfield. When he gets 15 to 20 yards downfield, he has to get to his landmark. His landmark is 4 yards from the sideline. He wants to get to that area against the zone. Everything we do is vertical down the field. He is going straight down the field to put pressure on the defensive backs.

The tight end wants to get width and to get vertical on his release. He wants to get down the field and get into the alley. Some coaches call this the seam. If the ball is over on the hash mark and he is into the short side of the field, he is going to get 2 to 3 yards inside the numbers on the field. We want to get separation with the two inside players. If the ball is in the middle of the field, the tight end is going to get 5 yards outside the hash mark and take it up the alley.

If the ball is in the middle of the field, the outside receiver opposite the tight end is going to get 5 yards outside the hash mark. The man in the slot is going to get 1 yard outside the hash mark and take it up the seam. He takes it up the field and gets 1 yard outside the hash mark. The fullback comes through the line and sits down over the ball in the open area 3 to 4 yards deep. If we are in a no-back set, one of the receivers will come inside and get to that spot. It is still the alley concept with four vertical routes and someone coming underneath. Those are the landmarks we use against a zone defense.

The quarterback has two things he has to read against the zone defense. He has two things he must be aware of against the zones. First is the middle of the field. It is either closed or open. We talk a lot about this in our meetings because it gives the quarterback a good idea of what is going to happen when the ball is snapped. It is a very simple concept. That is the first thing we want the quarterback to be aware of.

The second thing the quarterback must be aware of is whether the defense is playing zone defense or man-to-man defense. Is the defense playing man or zone? They can find this out very quickly. If a defender locks on to one of our receivers and runs with him, it indicates some type of man defense. If the defense is dropping to their zones on the field, it indicates a zone defense. It is very simple.

If a free safety or strong safety man rotates back to the middle of the field, it is closed. If someone goes back to the middle of the field, it is closed. If the ball is on the hash mark and someone on defense is rotating back to the middle of the field, it means the middle of the field is closed. If the middle of the field is open, the two safeties drop back and out.

OPEN MIDDLE

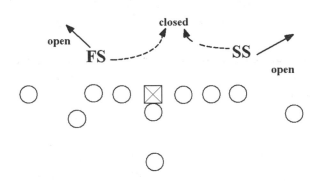

If the middle of the field is closed and the defense is playing zone, we have a tremendous play in the alley. You put this play in to attack cover three or a closed zone defense. It could be cover three, or the defense could roll a corner into the middle of the field. They may kick the safety over the top, but it still is a closed middle zone to us.

If the middle of the field is closed in a zone, we are reading the inside receivers first. The quarterback reads the two inside receivers as number 1. The fullback inside is the number 2 receiver. As the quarterback drops, he can see the middle is zoned. He knows he has receivers that are getting separation on their routes. They are getting width and getting up the alley. The quarterback retreats and eyes the defender that is closing the middle area. On the first three steps, the quarterback holds the safety man. On the next two steps he comes back to the alley on the opposite side. If he can throw the ball in the area at 18 and 24 yards deep, we will take it. If the linebackers have dropped underneath the seam route, we do not want to force the pass to the seam. If he throws the ball 28 to 35 yards deep, the safety and corner will collapse on the ball. We want to drop the ball in the hole at the seam. We want to keep the receivers wide to keep them away from the safeties. If the linebackers cover the seam, we drop the ball off to the fullback. It is a high percentage pass. Our players know we will call this play several times per game. We are going to take our shots on the play.

Next is the middle of the field with an open zone. The defense is playing a cover two or a type of corner coverage. This means the safety is keying our number 2 receiver. If our tight end runs a crossing route or runs an out route, the safety comes up to help. He doubles the area in the post on the tight-end side. Now the quarterback reads the play to the weakside first. He reads the slot receiver as number 1, and the outside man on that side is number 2. The fullback is the number 3 receiver on the check down.

Our weakside inside receiver has what we call a bend rule. If the middle of the field is open, he will push it upfield 12 yards and then bend it inside. The angle he breaks the route depends on two things: first is the safety man, and second is the linebacker. If it is a cover two safety playing deep, the receiver can keep it outside and keep it skinny. The quarterback can hit him on the route 18 to 24 yards just inside the hash mark.

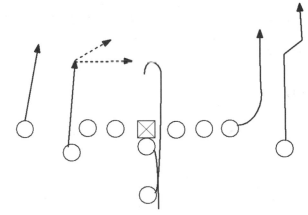

If the safety is squeezing the play like a lot of teams like to do, the receiver breaks the route inside across the face of the defender a little flatter. If the linebacker is running with the receiver, he tries to get him on his outside hip and then brings him inside. If the inside man is covered, the quarterback looks to the fade area. If we get the fade route open, we want him to take it. If the fade is not open, he drops the ball down to the fullback.

On middle open, the quarterback goes to the weakside. Against the middle closed zone, he is going inside. It does not matter what formation we are in; it is the same.

If the middle of the field is closed and the defense is playing man coverage, we know we are going to get man-to-man cover on the outside. It may be a man-press technique or the off technique. We know we are one-on-one on the outside. We are going to take a shot on the man. If the middle is closed and it is man coverage, the outside receivers know the ball is coming to one of the wide receivers. It does not make any difference if the man is open or not; we are going to throw the ball deep.

The most important point about running the deep route is this: If the defense is playing off man and we tell our receiver to run a go route against the zone coverage, we run a landmark route. Against man coverage it becomes a *win* route. The receiver does not have to get 4 yards from the sideline. He is told to win the route. He must beat the corner on the go route.

Everything we do is vertical. Our players get tired of hearing this. We want them to get down the field. On the go route, the receiver goes vertical and then goes inside or outside. We prefer for the receiver to go outside on the route. Once the receiver gets by the defender, he must get vertical again. We run the pat-and-go play. We do it every day. We line the receivers up on the outside edge of the number, and this includes running backs, ends, and anyone that may catch a pass. The receiver starts his route. He makes his cut, and the quarterback pats the ball. The receiver stays on the edge of the number. The receiver runs the fade route and the quarterback throws the ball to the outside to the receiver. We want the receiver to stay vertical and catch the ball on the outside shoulder away from the defensive back.

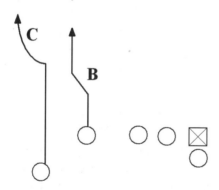

Here is another thing we do. I got this idea from my brother. I went to San Diego to see him and to see practice. They had lines on the field 4 yards from the sideline. I asked him what those extra lines were for. He told me they were to remind the receivers not to get closer to the sideline than 4 yards. That gives the quarterback a chance to throw the ball into that area. That has really helped us.

With man coverage, we are one-on-one on the outside. Our quarterback is going to take a shot on throwing the ball deep. If the receiver is even with the defender, we are going to throw it deep and give our man a chance to make the play.

The inside receiver against man coverage still runs his landmark. He makes an outside head fake as he comes off the ball, but he wants to get back on the seam route. The ball should be going outside.

Against man coverage, the back checks his protection first. He runs through the line. If the defense picks him up, he runs away from the man. He can go one way or the other. He keys the linebacker. He wants to get 3 yards deep on the play. If the linebacker is playing him man, he pivots and goes either left or right. He sticks the near foot in the ground and pivots away from the defender.

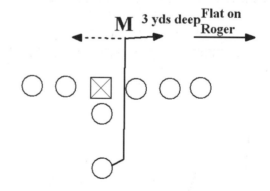

If we call alley-F roger, the fullback checks through on the play and then goes to the right flat. The quarterback knows the fullback will be in the right flat. If we call alley-F lucky, the fullback goes to the left flat.

If the middle of the field is open against man or zone coverage, the receivers on the outside have to win, and the inside receiver is the bend player. If you get a lot of reps on the play, it will pay dividends. If you focus on the details, the players will have confidence in the play.

We use different formations with the alley pass. We use the double set with two tight ends and two wide receivers. The weakside number 2 receiver is the number 2 man, and he is the bend receiver. We can line up with a wingback with the tight end. We can motion the wingback and have him run the same route. It can be a back or an extra receiver in that position. The wingback ends up as the outside receiver, so he has to get to his landmark, which is 4 yards from the sideline. The tight end runs the same route as before.

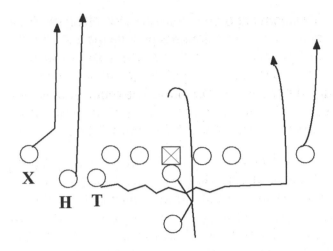

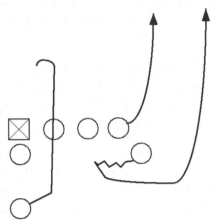

Here is an I-slot look. We run the ball out of the I-formation, especially in the red zone. It is a good red zone and two-minute drill concept as well. We can motion out to a double receivers look. Now the halfback has to get to his landmark because he is the number one man. He must get 4 yards from the sideline. If it is man coverage, he has to win the battle for the ball.

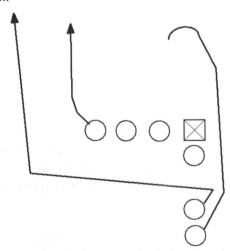

We can run it from the trips look as well. We can motion the tailback across the formation and have him run the inside seam.

If we run it out of the trips look, we have to make a few adjustments. As you can see, there is not a 2 man to the weakside. If there is not a bend player on that side, the next man on the other side becomes the number 2 receiver. He runs the bend from the other side. The two outside receivers run their regular patterns.

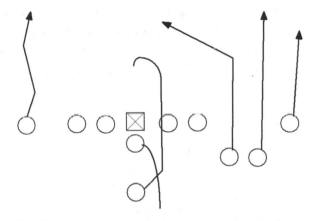

Nothing for the quarterback changes on the play. If it is against a zone, he is reading the free safety. It is a real good play against teams that check to cover three when you go to the trips set. If the defense is in a cover two look and the middle is open, the quarterback reads the receiver to the bend side.

The quarterback must distinguish the situation in the middle of the field. It is either the middle of the field closed and a zone, or middle of the field closed, and man coverage. Or it is middle of the field open, a zone, or middle of the field open against man. That is what he is looking for.

A drill we use most every day is a simple passing drill for the quarterback. We line up two receivers on those seams 12 yards deep. The receivers can be managers or kickers if they are not working on a kicking drill, or other players if you do not have the receivers available. We put a safety between those two receivers. The quarterback is going to look one way and throw the other on the alley route to one of the two stationary receivers. After the quarterback has completed a few passes to the stationary receivers we add the defensive linebacker. We put the linebackers at a depth of 12 yards. We put two dummies or managers between the receivers and the quarterback to simulate linebackers. Now, the quarterback has to drop the ball over the head of the linebacker. The pass is 18 to 20 yards deep. The defender at 12 yards is jumping up trying to get to the football. The quarterback has to put the ball in the hole to the receiver. It is the kind of throw the quarterback is going to make in a game situation.

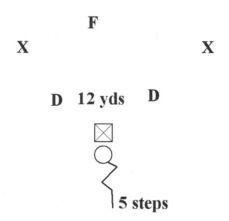

To change the play up, we will have the linebackers drop back to cover the deep pass so the quarterback has to drop the ball off to the fullback. We run the drills over and over. We do the same thing with the middle open. We will put a defender outside to force the receivers to run the proper route. The drill with the quarterbacks can be done anytime. If the quarterback is not involved in special teams, he may be doing this drill instead. We like to run this drill early in practice. Then we bring the receivers and backs together and run the drill. Then we come together and run it as a team.

We start every practice with a walk-through. A lot of players can learn from the chalkboard. Others can learn from watching film. There are a lot of players that cannot learn this way. We do the drill on the chalkboard, on film, and then we go out and do a walk-through. It takes 10 to 15 minutes to get through the drills. Then we do a quick warm-up and then stretch before we get into the practice. In the spring we practice for two hours to two-and-one-half hours. During the season we never go more than two hours. Early in the year our Tuesday practice will be two hours. On Wednesday we practice one hour and 45 minutes. On Thursday we cut down to one hour and a half. Later in the season we cut the practice time by about 15 minutes for each of those days. We are not on the field long, but we go at a very upbeat tempo.

We do run the same patterns with our play-action passing game. We do run the one-back draw play a lot. We run the play-action off the one-back draw play. On the regular alley patterns, the quarterback gives a token fake to the fullback. On the draw, he looks to the receivers.

In spring practice, we go 20 to 25 minutes of 7-on-7 every day. If we go for 25 minutes, we get about 40 plays in. In 20 minutes we can get in 36 plays. During the season, we go 20 minutes of 7-on-7 on Tuesday, close to 20 minutes on Wednesday, and cut it way down on Thursday. During the practice sessions, we do not script anything. The only thing I may script is our blitz period. We do not script 7-on-7 or the team period. I do set the down and distance. We never run a play without the chains on the field. I always want our guys to be aware of down and distance. This is true on offense and defense. We have managers, trainers, injured players, or someone to hold the chains. We do not script the plays. We will put down the hash, down and distance, and yard line. I want to know who is going to be in the huddle before I call the plays. I want to be aggressive in play calling. After the practice, I will go back and chart the plays and take a look at practice to see if we are hitting on the long passes down the field. We chart everything we do in practice.

We go into a game with 25 to 30 passing-game concepts. We have another 10 or 15 plays for third-down plays. We have another 10 to 12 plays for the red zone. Then we have all of our running game plays. When we add them all together with our protections, it is over 100 plays, but in actual concepts it is not that much. We do give the players a playbook. We diagram every play we are going to use in the game in a game book for that week.

During the regular season we script everything including down and distance, yard line, hash, the play, the defense, and the defensive front. We want to simulate game day as much as possible.

I have one more concept that I want to cover, but I will not have as much time to go into as much detail. I have film of the plays and I will show those to you later. It is a very simple base play, and we have had some big plays with this concept. We call the concept *blade.*

Offensively, we use terms that fit into packages. We have plays that we call our cutlery package. They include the blade, knife, scissors, swords, and others. We have a geographic package with cities in the package. We use cities and states in this package. All of these terms tie in with our packages. The players know the plays are related with other plays. We even have a cigarette package. We put that package in a long time ago. We have the Winston, Marlboro, Camel, and other names come off the package. The blade is part of our cutlery package.

We put the blade package in to attack corner coverages. It is a good route against cover two. If the tight end blocks down, the safety man comes up for run support right now. If the tight end runs a cross route or an out route, or anything except a vertical route, the safety drops back to double the Z receiver.

The wide receiver is going to make a sharp break to the post. His aiming point, regardless of where the ball is on the field, is the near upright of the goal post. I do not want him to make the break at 15 yards. The quarterback is going to lay the ball up high for the Z back to run under. The tight end makes his cut at 12 yards and goes outside. He runs the pattern at 12 yards to hold that safety. If the safety turns his head to the post man, the quarterback comes down to the tight end or back in the flat. If the tight end can keep the safety man concentrating on him, then we can hit the Z back behind the safety on the post.

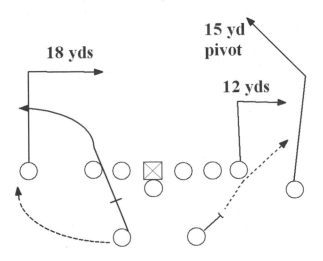

A change-up on the play is very simple. The tight end runs to the corner or flag instead of breaking outside. That is a simple change-up. On the strongside, we have a post route, an out route, and a flat route. On the backside, we have a dig route with the split receiver, and the back runs the flat. The back can swing outside to hold the linebacker.

It is middle of the field open or middle of the field closed. If the middle of the field is open, the quarterback is going to stay to the strongside to the Z back, the Y end, or the back. We can put both backs to the right side if we call roger. Then the backside guard covers for the H back.

If the middle of the field is closed, the quarterback is going to look to the weakside. On that side, we have a dig and flat route combination. We have a flat or a wide route to pull the linebacker off the dig route.

The concept is simple. If the middle of the field is closed, he goes to the weakside. If the middle of the field is open, he goes strong. If you quarter coverage, it is a good play. We run the play from a variety of formations.

You can run the same play from the trips look. It is the same concept. We have averaged about three touchdowns per year on this play. We hit the man deep for the score about three times per year. You can run the concept from several formations and get the same look.

You can run the same concept from a bunch look. It is the same concept. You want to make sure the patterns are run properly from each formation.

I hope you got something out of this lecture. There are one or two plays that could help you. I think the key is this: Regardless of what you do, it is how well you do it. It matters how well you run the routes and execute the concepts. We have made a commitment to get the ball down the field. Our players believe in it. They have a lot of confidence in the system. This has really helped our program.

It has been a pleasure to be here. I hope you got something out of this lecture. Good luck to you. You are welcome to come to our 7-on-7 tournament June 15. We have linemen that come to the camp at the same time. The quarterback camp starts that same night. Again, thanks for your attention. It has been my pleasure to be here. Good luck to you.

DEVELOPING THE GAME PLAN

University of Miami

I want to talk about the success we had back in the 80s. We had a bad image and lots of people didn't like our kids. We deserved a lot of it, and we know that now. Coaching friends of mine thought it was terrible having to work with our players. They thought they were thugs and convicts. My answer to those inquiries was, "Come down and visit us for one week. You will fall in love with those kids." Michael Irvin probably is not a good example to cite after all the problems he has had the last few years. But when he was at Miami, he was a tremendous competitor. When he stepped on the practice field, he competed more than anyone I have ever seen.

That led to everyone else competing also. It didn't matter whether it was in the weight room, or—whatever he did, he wanted to be the best. That is how our guys were on the field. We had a lot of off-the-field incidents, and the behavior on the field was not the best, but all they wanted to do was to win.

Butch Davis did a heck of a job getting that attitude back into the team after it went down. We continued what he started, and now we are doing things within our program with class. For me, it was not just the winning. I wanted to win, but do it with class. When I went to the national coaching convention in San Antonio this year, I heard nothing but praise—not only about the way we played, but about how well our team displayed sportsmanship. The NCAA has set the rules to where you can't do things like we used to do them. I think it has been good for the game of football.

There are a number of things that have made our program successful. I can give you an example. When we got back from the national championship game this year, as coaches, we had to hit the road recruiting. The players didn't get back to school until January 14. I flew back into town that day. When I got back to the office, our All-American quarterback was in the film room watching tape. It wasn't the Nebraska tape; it was cutups of drill work on drops. This was the first day back after we had just won the national championship.

The NCAA allows players to go out and throw or do whatever they want, as long as the coaches are not there. We had recruits in Friday night and our players showed them around and made sure they had a good time. At ten o'clock Saturday morning, they all showed up to play 7-on-7. There must have been 50 guys out there. We didn't tell them to do it. They didn't have to do it. They just showed up and played because they wanted to get ready for next year.

That is the kind of attitude our guys have. It filters down to the freshmen when they come to school at Miami. A new kid that comes in may not be a player that has a lot of character, but when he sees how the other guys work, he either turns into a player with character and a hardworking kid, or he goes someplace else. Most of the players we sign stick with the program.

We work hard to make these guys take responsibility for what goes on within this program. We are seeing the fruits of our labor and it makes it easier on us. I think Coach Davis had a lot to do with that, but the current coaching has certainly picked up where he left off.

Obviously, we have great players. I don't mean to sound like we won all these games by the grace of our coaching. We have great players, but you have to get them in the right positions. There are a lot of schools out there at the college level that have great players. I really feel like what we did this year with our game planning and preparation was as good as anyone in the country.

We didn't play well against Boston College and Virginia Tech. When we came to a point where we didn't play well as a team, we had answers to what the opponent was doing. Our kids believed in what we were doing, so we found a way to win. We looked at other teams that were just as talented, and maybe better than we were, but when they got into a tough situation, they ended up losing.

What I am going to talk about today is our game planning and what we go through in a week to prepare. I coached high school football for seven years, and I know there are differences, but if there is one point in what I have to say that will help you in your preparation, I think it would be a good situation for you.

You have to sell your game plan to your players. If our players don't think our plan is very good, it doesn't stand a chance of being successful in the game. Even if it is not a good plan, if they think it is, we have a shot at being successful.

The first thing we tell our players is we are going to run our offense. We are not going to let the defense dictate what we are going to do. That is what we tell the kids. Obviously, we are going to game plan as to what the defense is going to give us. I want our players to believe this is our scheme and the defense has to stop us. We are going to find certain plays that can attack a certain area that the defense is giving us. You don't have to have a lot of plays to do that. I will get to how we break it up later.

If they are supporting with a safety that gives us an opportunity to hit a big play over the top, we are going to come up with one play that will do that. You don't need nine plays to do that. We are not going to call that play nine times.

The big thing that I am a proponent of is trimming down the offense. We start out the week with 500 plays on the board. As we start watching film, we start dotting the ones we like. After we get it down to 100 plays, we start tearing it down. When we get into the game, if the defense does something, we know where we are going with the ball. The players know before we call the play, and they know it is going to be the correct play for the situation.

We want to use motions, formations, and different situations to keep the defense off balance. I would like to go into a game-running plan with the exact same plays as we did the week before, except from different formations. The defense is looking at that play as something different, but our players are practicing the same play over and over again. If we can keep the defense off balance, we will have more success.

We call plays to set up big plays. I may call a certain play, motion, or formation a few times to set up a tendency, so that later in the game or in next week's game, I can run a play off that tendency that could lead to a big play. When we get into a game with a team like Florida State, it is usually one or two big plays that make the difference. Generally, those types of games will be close and low scoring. One big touchdown could be the key to winning or losing. When you play against those guys, you have to work for everything you get.

You need to know what the defense is going to do to stop what you are doing. I want to know how a team is playing our power off-tackle play. If they are spilling the play, I have a play that can be run off that type of defense. During the game, you have to be able to make adjustments by the way they are trying to stop you. That to me is the big key between a good coordinator and a great coordinator. The guy who can make the changes in the middle of the game is going to win.

If you know the situation before you go into the game, you are a step ahead. Have the counters in your mind before you get to the game.

We will have six to eight base formations for each game. On the board, we will have a big list of all the plays from that formation. From that base formation, we need four to six runs. You don't need nine or 10, because you can't run them all. Don't waste your time practicing them. Practice the plays you are going to run in the game, so the players have confidence in them. Off those runs, we want two to four play-action passes. We want four to six dropback five-step passes. In every formation we have, I want at least two to four three-step passes.

As long as I have been watching pass cutups of our game, we keep wondering why we didn't throw more three-step passes. It is always a 70 to 80 percent throw. You catch it for five yards and run for five more yards. In some cases, you break it for the score. If we had that kind of percentage on a run, we would run it every play. I want a couple of gimmick plays off the plays we are running all the time. That is how you get the big play.

I want to make sure we are calling in the game what we are practicing throughout the week. If we have a play on our list of plays, that play is going to get called. I script my plays for the game right off the game-plan sheet. If I see an opportunity to run a big play, but it is not on the game plan, I don't call that play. If we haven't practiced the play in practice, we will not run it in the game. I am only going to call plays that we have practiced and that are in our game plan.

Plays that are scripted for practice are plays that come off the game-plan sheet. In the game plan, I want to break tendencies. As we look at the previous week's play calling, we can find tendencies. For instance, we may have run only one play from a certain set, and we ran it five times. That is a tendency. It will appear on the game plan to run the play-action off that play.

I will show you our game-planning sheet. It is an 11-inch by 14-inch, two-sided sheet. Our board has little boxes across the top. In those little boxes are our formations. Under the formations, in categories, will be our plays. They will be grouped as runs, passes, screens, play-actions, protections, gimmicks, and whatever we think is important. Every play that we could possibly run will be in these boxes. We have about 20 formations listed on this board. Some of the formations will have limited amounts of plays under them. But a formation like the I formation may have 50 plays listed.

When we start viewing the I formation cutups, we start as a staff to dot the plays we like. We keep paring that down until we have only four to six runs. Once we get all the plays selected throughout the week and decide those are the plays we like, we put them on the game plan. That will be the sheet I have in the press box. I know these are the only plays we worked on all week and those are the plays I am going to call on Saturday.

We list all the different passes and play-action passes we want to throw. That includes any deep passes we want to throw against them. It lists our screens and any type of special play. It also has our four-minute game plan when we are ahead. If we are ahead with four minutes to go in the game, we want to run the clock out. We have a plan for that listed on the sheet. That is the make of one side of this sheet.

The other side of the sheet has our playlist. We do the same thing Bill Walsh did when he wrote about scripting 15 plays. When we heard about him doing that, we went to visit the Forty-Niners, when he was the coach there. I thought the third play of the game came off the sheet, whether it was third and one or third and 18. That is not the way it works. We have situational columns and field position columns on the back side of our playsheet. One column is headed as minus-11 to plus-31. We consider anything between our own 11-yard line and the opponent's 31-yard line as the freewheeling zone. We have a list of plays that we can use in that zone on first or second down. If the actual game situation does not fit the situational sheet, I skip down and pick up a call from the call list that does fit that situation.

I want to stick as close to the script of plays as I can, because we are going to be practicing those exact plays all week in practice. The first play of the game is going to be the first play we have been practicing all week. When we decide what we want to run, it is going to be run. If we work these plays all week in practice, they will be called in the game, and the kids know that.

If the first play of the game is going to be the off-tackle power play, the second play of the game is a counter to how we thought they were going to try to stop the first play. If they spilled to stop the off-tackle power, we run the sweep on the second play. If we thought they were going to run the play down from behind, we run the naked on the third play. That would be a little three-play package.

If the first play of the game is a real stinker, I put a mark through it. If it is because of the defensive scheme and we don't have a counter for it, I won't call that play again. If we made an assignment mistake, I will put a star next to the play. That means we will come back to that play. As an offensive staff, we have to know why that play did not work. Our staff on any one play are all looking for different things. The coordinator is watching the point of attack. The receiver coach is watching the secondary to see what they were doing. If it is the safety that is flying up to make tackles, he will know that. The second offensive line coach will be watching the backside. The line coach will be watching the frontside. We have guys watching for a way to counter anything the defense does.

On the first play, if we gained five yards, we go to the second play on the script. If that play ends up being a first down, we go to the third play on the sheet. If the offense is getting a bunch of first downs, we could go right down the sheet.

After we get through the sheet, we go back and look at the plays that are starred or circled. Circled means we should have run another play in that situation and that play is listed. From the original sheet, we make a new sheet. After I have done that, I have a pad of paper where I keep a list of six or seven plays that we are going to run the next time we get the ball. While we are playing defense, we are talking as an offensive staff about what we need to run the next series of downs.

We do the exact same thing when we get in the red zone and when we get in the tight red zone. When we get in closer to the goal line, we will call different plays.

We do the same thing coming out of our end zone. We consider that to be the minus-eight and in. The passes that are thrown down here are more cautious in nature.

The next set of situational plays is the third-down plays. About 70 percent of the game's plays are called from this area. We are not in the red zone or coming out that much during the course of a game.

We break down our third-down situations into three groups. The first one is third and three to five yards for a first down. The second situation is third and six to nine yards for the first down, and the third situation is third and 10-plus yards.

In practice, we will have five minutes to work on third and three to five yards for a first down. I want the player to know that the first play to be run on a third and three to five yards is going to be a particular play. If we call a pass in this situation, the quarterback and the receiver know that particular pass is going to be run. If your players practice all week and never know if their play is going to be called, they won't work as hard. If that receiver knows he is going to get the ball on an option route on the first passing play on third and five yards, he will work his butt off to make sure that pass is a success.

On my situational sheet, there aren't going to be too many run plays listed in the run block for third and six to nine. The pass block column on third and six to nine will be full of plays.

At the start of each season, we have a list of about 15 gimmick plays that we like. We research these plays and get a list of plays that we can run within our scheme of offense. I don't think we have any gimmick plays that we just call. They are all set up off of actual plays we run.

When I was at Murray State, the week prior to a game, we used a motion scheme to block our outside zone plays. I must have run it 10 to 12 times in that game. The following week, we sent the man in motion, the safety flew up, and we threw a halfback pass on the first play of the game for an 80-yard touchdown. We set the gimmick up the week before.

If the gimmick gets on the game plan, it is going to get called. We do the same thing with the two-point play as we do with our gimmick play. We have five or six two-point plays. We may go for weeks without running a two-point play. That particular play may be the first play listed for four straight weeks. If we run it one time, it goes to the bottom of the list.

We have our short-yardage and goal-line plays listed. The short-yardage and goal-line plays are the same set.

We have a two-minute package we call *Indy*. That name is in reference to the Indianapolis 500 auto race. We are trying to hurry up and get plays called. We have 10 plays that are in the Indy package. They are the same plays every week. All the players know the plays, and we practice them weekly. The quarterback doesn't have to wait until the last two minutes to call any of the plays. He can come to the line of scrimmage at any time and call Indy-five. That means the fifth play in this list will be run. It is the same play all year long. I got this from Tulane two years ago.

On the sheet, there are plays of consideration. These are notes that I write to myself during the week or during the game. They are plays that I want to run in upcoming games. We are running a certain play that I like. I know the defenses in the coming weeks are going to do something to stop it. I write a note to run a certain gimmick off this play in two weeks.

In the press box, I have a graduate assistant keeping a chart for me. His job is to keep track of the deep passes we throw. If we call a screen, gimmick, or play-action pass, it was his job to keep track of them. After three or four series, if we hadn't thrown any deep balls, he was supposed to tell me.

That made me think about doing it. It really helped me because in my mind, I want to throw the ball deep four or five times a game. It doesn't matter what action we use; I want the ball thrown deep. At Miami, we have guys that can really motor. You could get a big play out of it. But even if you don't, it puts the defensive backs on their heels. We want the defense to think we could do that at any time. People that are scouting your films will see the same thing. I can't say this enough; the plays we run on Tuesday, Wednesday, Thursday, and Friday are actually called in the game.

We start our week on Sunday. I don't like to spend a lot of time grading the film from the previous week. I want to go through as a staff and figure out what we did wrong within our scheme. I want to see it and get it over with. We let the kids see it and get on the practice field and get the mistakes corrected. That game is over, and we need to get it behind us. We need to focus for the next week's opponent.

We are going to break down the opponent's film as a staff. I don't like to separate the staff and have them doing their own thing. I want to sit down as a staff and talk about what we are seeing. I don't let the GAs break down the films. I want to make sure we are all on the same page. We have to talk about what we are seeing because we have to get it in the computer. The GAs may break the film down, but the staff is going over that film before it goes into the computer. I want to know that we are all calling everything the same thing.

We have another big board in the back of the room for nothing but coverages and blitzes. Every coverage and blitz that our staff sees goes on that board. Everything I do with the game plan is to try to save time. It takes a long time to put all this together.

The next thing we do is to grade our opponent by position. I started doing this a few years ago. I think it has been really good for us. This is the last thing we do before we go home. We grade one-half of our opponent's personnel on ability, knowledge of the game, and how aggressive they are. Each coach grades the people they will be facing. The offensive line coach grades the defensive line. The receivers coach grades the secondary. The quarterback coach grades the linebackers. After we finish that and have a short meeting about what we have seen, we go home for the night. We want to have some idea about who to go after and who to stay away from.

On Sunday, we have a short practice, no-pad workout with the players. The first 15 minutes is the special teams period. That is when I take the quarterbacks and get some individual time. As a quarterback coach, I get almost no individual time. When we are in individual period as a team, the quarterbacks generally are working in someone else's drill, handing off or throwing passes.

The next 10 minutes are spent in correction of the previous game. We are not concerned with individual breakdowns. If there is some problem with the scheme, that is covered during this time.

From there, we go to an inside run drill with our base runs against their base defenses. It is a walk-through. We are not going to show them anything strange that would cause them to ask a question. We want it to be our simplest plays versus their simplest front. We script up 18 plays and let our guys see what their fronts are going to be. We don't want to start answering questions about the opponent because we haven't seen their films. We will watch the film after practice. The base fronts come from the graduate assistants, who have watched the film.

After that, we spend 15 minutes in pass skeleton working base passes against base coverages. Then we spend 20 minutes in team running base against base.

Monday starts the big workday for the coaching staff. The players have Mondays off. That is according to the NCAA. The first thing on our agenda is to go to the board and talk about our protection and how they hold up against the blitzes we have seen. We make sure we have an answer for every blitz scheme they have. We want to point out the problems we are going to have. If we have something in our protection scheme that is going to be a problem, we won't run it that week. We don't spend time trying to figure out a way to make it work; we just eliminate it from the game plan for that week.

We split up and do our scouting reports. This is something that you have to do, but I think it is wasted time. Even the kids that are your hardest workers don't pay much attention to them. That is probably the most overrated thing in football. We practice against those schemes during the week and give them a test at the end of the week, which I think is much better than a scouting report.

The big thing we do, and probably the most important, is our formation cutups. We take the first formation, which might be the pro set, and match it with our playlist. There may be 60 plays to choose from. We boil the list down to 20 plays. We will whittle that down more as the week goes on. That is the first basis of what our game plan is going to be. That takes a while because we have to do that with all our formations.

Once we get that done, we are going to set up our script plays. I wanted the staff to feel like they had some input as to what was going to be called in the game. I had those guys write down their 16 favorite plays, run or pass. They each are doing a script. When we got it done, I would write down each coach's list. Every time a play appeared on a list, it got a check mark. The plays with the most check marks went into the game plan.

The whole staff has taken ownership of the game plan. I had the final say on all plays. If there were a play that I liked but no one else did, it was probably going to make it on the list. If the other coaches liked a play and I didn't, I put it at the end of the sheet and tried to eliminate it.

Each day, there were some plays that we took out of the game plan. If a play didn't look good in practice, why try to run it in the game? If it doesn't look good against the scout team, why run it against Florida State?

When we leave at about 10 o'clock on Monday, the scripts are done. Those were the plays we were going to work on in practice and the ones that were going to be called on game day.

The first thing we do on Tuesday when we meet is to review the script. There may be some alterations we want to make after we have slept on it for a night. We do that every day. We want to make sure we feel good about the plays we are going to run. Once we feel good about it and decide that is what we are going to run, we have to get into our situational plays.

In our short-yardage play box on our game plan, I would love to keep the same play in every week. If we play teams that use a 6-2 short-yardage defense week after week, we will keep the same plays in our short-yardage box. I may change up the formations or motion scheme, but I want to run as close as possible to the same plays. We have about five or six plays in that package.

The same thing is true about our third-down plays. We have a few plays we call in the third and three to five yards that are good against anything the defense does. We have a lot of plays that have zone beaters on one side and man beaters on the other side. That doesn't mean we don't watch the third-down cutups, because we do. If we find something that is obvious, we will put that in the play selections.

Last year at Miami, our third-down percentage was 29 percent. We were 11-1 and had a percentage like that. It was ridiculous. They never had a third-down block of time in practice where they went over what they were going to run in that situation. This year, we really practiced it and made the kids understand how important third down was.

We don't spend enough time talking to our quarterbacks about third down. If a quarterback throws an incomplete pass on a fade in this situation, instead of taking a short, sure pass completion, that is like a turnover. It is like gambling. If you throw the fade on first down, you have nothing to lose. If you do it on third down, you are going to lose the ball. Get the ball to the kid that can get you the first down.

Once we have decided the situational plays, we put them on the game plan and those plays are in for Saturday. After that, we work on our practice script. Each coach takes a different situation and draws up the defenses for that situation. They do that from the film cutups.

When we get back from lunch, I have a script meeting. In the meeting, we look at all the defensive cards to make sure they are drawn correctly. Then we talk about how we are going to do the things and perform the techniques that are involved. We go over the hot routes, blocking schemes, and blitz schemes. The worst situation that can happen in coaching is two coaches talking about something on the field that should have been covered in a meeting. It will happen, but if you have the script meetings, it won't happen very often. If there is a problem, I speed it up to the next play. I don't want the players to think for one second that the coaches are not on the same page.

In our practice, the first thing we do is a team takeoff period. We take five minutes and run any new formations, motions, or plays. During this period, we work our cadence really hard. We do the little things that you don't think about when you get into the normal team practice. I chart the cadences to make sure they are varying the snap count and work on the hard counts. If you try to draw someone offsides and never practice it, it will backfire on you every time.

The next period is a 10-minute special period. After that we do a 9-on-9 drill. This is the first year we have done this, and it worked well. It is a half-lines drill in the red zone against our first defense. We go for five minutes and we can get six reps; three reps with the first unit and three reps with the second unit. They get one at the 15, one at the 10, and one at the five. It is a non-contact period. This gives us reps against faster players.

From there, we go to an individual period for 10 minutes. The team gets 15 minutes of inside run drill. All the plays that are called in this drill come off the script. This is all first- and second-down play situations. The next drill is a skeleton drill, with the first 10 minutes being first- and second-down passes from the game plan. The last five minutes is the third-and-three to -five situations. We have the chains out on the field and we emphasize getting the first down.

We have 10 minutes of short yardage and goal line against the scout team. From there, we go to the blitz pickup period for 10 minutes. After that comes the script play period for 15 minutes. I script our hardest plays during this time. That gets our players into the proper mind-set. As we go through the week, I want this period to get easier and easier. By the time they get down to Wednesday and Thursday, I want them to think they have the game plan down cold. Tuesday is when we get in their kitchen. We are after their butts on Tuesday. If we play a weak team, we are twice as tough on them. We don't want them to think all they have to do is show up.

By Thursday, there is no screaming or yelling. We are calm and getting ready to play. The last thing we work on Tuesday is the third-and-short situation with the chains. Then we go to our condition period. During the course, I chart all the plays we are going to run and passes we are going to throw, and make sure we run them against all the defensive fronts possible. I put that on my play chart so that as we run the script, the person calling the defenses gives us the changing defenses we need to see. The plays are called each day against the defenses we need to run or pass against.

On Wednesday, the coaches review the script and see if we are still happy with it. This is the time when plays are dropped from the script. We work on our third-and-six to -nine passes, third and 10-plus plays, and screens that we are going to throw from the script. From there, we go to the red zone and get those plays on the game plan. We prepare the script for practice. After lunch, we have our script meeting before we go out to practice.

Practice on Wednesday is just like practice on Tuesday, except we change the situational plays and we add a pressure passing period. During that period, we are working our passing game against our first defense. They are blitzing on almost every play. It gives us a chance to work against the speed and better personnel. We end up throwing a lot of hot patterns against them. In every situation we are in, the players know the first play we call in that situation is the play that will be called in the game.

On Thursday, the whole staff reviews the game plan. Everything is done on the game plan. We go over it one more time to make sure we are doing what we want to do. If there is a change, it will be plays dropped, not plays added. I would rather trim the game plan than add to it. We work on our backup offense, which from week to week is about the same. It is usually something conservative.

The script for this practice is going to hit all the situations. We are going to move the ball down the field. This is a practice game for the offensive coordinator. We do everything in game types of situations. The first drive will be a 12-play drive. We put the second unit on, and they drive the other way. After they score, the first team goes back in and drives the ball out from the five-yard line. Our goal there is to get two first downs before we have to punt. After that, we go to the two-minute drill. We try to run this where we get eight to 10 plays in.

The last five minutes of practice is spent running special situations. We go over the Hail Mary alignment. Hopefully, we don't have to throw one of those, but you have to cover it so they know what to do if it ever happens.

We go over our last play of the game plan. That is the one you call on the last play of the game with no time-outs. It is the same play all year. We do this versus air in practice. We take a safety and take a knee, and act like we had just won the game and go in.

On Friday, the day before the game, we have a basic walk-through. Then we have a test meeting with the players. Our offensive line, back, and tight end coaches do a better job with this than anywhere I have ever been. They do an excellent job. Everything that was covered in practice about tendencies and keys is on that test. They have a play that they put on the test and all the players have to draw the play up with what everyone on the play does. The running back has to know what the line does.

The last thing we do on Friday is to have our Friday-night film. We have about 30 plays on the tape. There are formations and defenses that come up on the screen. All the positions sit together. When the formation and the defense come up, all the receivers and offensive line have to make all their calls that they would make in a game situation.

The quarterback looks at the defense and makes an automatic if he has to. If he doesn't automatic, he calls good. We are playing the game in our heads. We get 30 snaps, which takes about 45 minutes. After that, we put them to bed.

On Saturday, we have individual meetings with our position groups. Then we get together for a clap drill. It is basically a walk-through. The quarterback calls the play, breaks the huddle, moves to the line of scrimmage, and calls the cadence. At the point in the cadence when the ball is supposed to be snapped, everyone claps and then they point to who they are supposed to block.

We go through the script, short-yardage situations, and take a knee. From there, we load the bus and go play the game.

By the time we get done on Saturday, we have sold the plan to the players. If they believe in it, you have a shot to win. Years ago, my dad told me a good coach was not someone who could come up with a hundred different plays. A good coach is somebody who can run one play and get his players to believe in it. If your kids believe in what you are doing and you have a plan about how to attack people and keep them off balance, you have a chance.

I want to thank you for showing up tonight. Good luck to all of you next year.

ORGANIZATION AND CHECKLIST FOR SUCCESS

University of Notre Dame

Thank you. I am here today to talk to you about the limited amount of football I know. I am one of the coaches that believes there is so much about this game that you can always learn. I hope what little I know may help some of you.

I'm going to talk on a couple of general things, and then I'll get to my specific topic. I don't have all the answers. I am not sure there is any one coach that has all the answers. I am lucky to be where I am. But I think there are some other factors that go into it also. As I present things to you, please don't assume this is the only way to do them. These are the things that work for me and my system.

I walked on at Michigan State in 1972. I was a high school player like most of the players you turn out. I was 5'6" and 139. I thought I could be somebody's college quarterback. As a coach today, I can truly say I wouldn't have recruited me. But I tried. I went to Michigan State and played for a legendary coach, Duffy Daugherty. In fact these clinics are named after him. Duffy said a long time ago that *it was bad luck not to have good players*. I don't know of any statement any truer than that one. Good players make good coaches. But also good coaches make good players.

I advanced Duffy's adage a bit and I believe this wholeheartedly; *it is bad luck not to have good coaches.* What I have tried to do in every program I have been in is to make sure Tyrone Willingham is the worst coach on our staff. That is part of my job. Because if I am the worst coach on our staff, I think we have a chance to be okay. The key to success in life is to surround yourself with good people. I am blessed and believe we have an excellent staff of coaches.

My topic today is developing a checklist. A checklist is critical to your program. A checklist gives you an inventory of things to look at every week. Every week you take the time to go through systematically every item on that checklist. We do it week, by week, by week, so we don't let anything slip through the cracks. The one time you let something slip is the one time it will bite you. That is when you end up with egg on your face.

When I go to the grocery store for my wife, I have to have a checklist. If I don't have one, I'll forget half of the things she sent me to the store for. That is not a pretty sight to see when you get home without the things you went for. Having a list is important to my coaches, my players, and me. This is one of the ways we make sure that everyone is on the same page.

Some of you have been on staffs where all the coaches have not been together. It is amazing how sometimes you can be in the same room having a discussion, but when you leave the room there is no evidence that we had ever been together. When we get outside the room, there are two different opinions on what was discussed. When we do our checklist, it allows us to put it on paper. It allows us to put the answers on paper and allows us to be on the same page.

What I am going to start with is our offensive checklist. These are things we must prepare for every week, and for which we need a plan.

The first thing on that checklist is *the creation of a theme*. That doesn't sound very important. I think creating a theme is part of the imagination that coaches have to have to get their players where you need them to go.

In 1999 we had a football season at Stanford that was spectacular. It was the first time in 28 years that we had won the conference championship. We tried to make sure our kids had something to tie them mentally to the things we were doing.

We had gone to Washington and gotten beat. Everyone around us thought the championship run was over. Everyone felt the best we could do was tie for the title. We went to Arizona State the next week and won, while Washington was losing to UCLA. That put us back in the race for the conference championship. We gave them a theme the following week. It was "to share or not to share." That was a play on Shakespeare's line, but our players really liked it. They saw the championship rings that were theirs if they didn't share the title and won the championship outright. They rallied around that theme.

Each week we gave them themes of that nature. We gave them things that they could really get excited about. We want something to capture the imagination of our players. We want them excited about the upcoming week. We want to make that week unique and special.

The second thing on our list is to *work to our strengths*. We want to work at what we are good at. That is critical for us. We want to make sure we *identify and attack personnel*. I picked this up from the years I spent with the Minnesota Vikings. In pro football, each coach looks for every weakness a team has. Everything is analyzed, and they find a way to exploit that weakness. From that environment, I brought those things back to my college philosophy.

Every week we make sure we *study ourselves*. We want to see our offense as our opponent sees it. We have to scout ourselves, so we can prevent establishing tendencies. We have to see what the opponent is going to do to us.

On offense we want to make sure we *develop a plan to defeat the blitz and the zone blitz*. We have to know how they are going to blitz us each week. We have to know when and where they are going to blitz. We have to know how to attack what they are doing to us. We want to be successful in those situations.

When we are creating a game plan, we have to *develop a plan for the eight- and nine-man fronts* we will see. Along with zone blitzes, the eight- and nine-man fronts have proliferated in football. Everyone in college football is running some form of that front. We have to develop a scheme to get a blocker on the extra defender in the box.

One of the most important things we have to do is *develop a plan for things that you can't practice*. Basically, our checklist will line up everything we are going to do in a week of practice. It gives us basics for setting up our practices to make sure we cover all the areas we need to cover. We have a 20-hour rule in college. In our system, we feel the mental approach is as important as the physical time you spend on the field. We meet for two hours daily. That means that somewhere in the next two hours of practice, you can't get to everything you need to. At some point, you have to have a plan for things you can't get to in practice.

One of those areas for us was the four-minute offense and the backed-up offense. We spent time weekly practicing how to run the offense in the last four minutes of a game. We covered both situations of being ahead and being behind. We also practice coming out from our goal line. We evaluated what we were doing in practice and felt like we were spending time on something that occurred rarely in a game. We felt we were practicing things that we didn't do a lot in a game.

Some weeks we practice the four-minute drill and the backed-up drill, and some weeks we don't. But every week we had to have a plan for our four-minute offense or the coming-out offense, whether we practiced it or not.

This next point comes from the Bill Walsh school of offense. We *script anywhere from 12 to 18 plays* of offense for each game. The number of plays depends on whom we are playing. We wanted to make sure we had those plays firmly in mind. This is not only for your coaches, but for your players as well. It is amazing when you script your plays how many times you take the first drive down and score. I think that happens because your players are so familiar with the plays that are being run. They know what to anticipate and how to perform.

We think it is important to script our plays and that the players rehearse them. We do it in a walk-through or on the practice field. If we do it on the practice field, we can anticipate the plays, the defense we might get, and the reaction of that defense.

People ask all the time if we stick to our script regardless of the situation. We do not stick with the script if the situation does not call for that play. The script for us is base plays and special plays that we want to run early in the ball game. If we get to a situation at play number four on the script, we may jump off the script and run a play designed for that situation. As soon as we handle that situation, we bounce right back on the script with play number five.

We may see something that is going on within the script and rotate a play up in sequence. Also, we could rotate a play down depending on where we are and what we are seeing.

An example of that occurred in one of our games last season. We had a special play we wanted to run early in the game. We were backed up inside our 20-yard line when the play came up on the script. It was not such a terrible situation, but we felt it was a little risky for us to run that play at that time. We simply dropped that play down and picked up another play from the script.

We don't repeat the script once we have gone through it. I don't assume the defensive coordinator on the other side is dumb. Most of them write down the plays in the order you run them. They would pick up that pattern right away.

At halftime we may write out another script. The first thing we do is go to our team, put the script on the board, and have them visualize what is going to happen at the beginning of the second half.

We want to *list plays that fit certain situations*. I want to outline the situations that are included in our offensive checklist. The first play grouping is what we classify as *second down and short yardage*. That is important to us because that is classified as a waste down. Of course, that would depend on whom you were playing. If the play situation is second and one or two, there is a good chance we are going to take a shot at the home run or big play. However, in other games we may feel we have to be more conservative and simply go for the first down. The rhythm of the game may be such that we don't want to be in a third and short or medium situation.

The next situation is the *third and long* category. We make sure this is a concise plan for this down and distance. I have one pet peeve about third and long with our offensive coordinator. I never want to be caught throwing hot on a third-and-long situation. Our protection has to be able to let us have a chance to get the first down. We don't want the quarterback to have to dump the ball to a hot route because we couldn't pick up the blitz. If you allow a team to force you to throw hot on third and long, you are in trouble. If we allow that to happen, I don't call that good coaching on our part.

The *third and medium* situation is our next grouping. On these plays it is all right to throw to hot receivers because they have the opportunity to run for the first down.

The *sudden change* is more of an attitude than it is a situation. But we want the offense to understand, in this situation, the defense is reeling. The defense is coming on the field thinking they can stop the offense, but in most cases they are not prepared to do that. We want to give a mental advantage to our offensive team. We tell our offense the defense is on their heels. We want to attack them and make something happen in the sudden change. No matter how you cut it, you are dealing with young people who have emotional ups and downs. We want that to work in our favor. There is a good chance when we come out in a sudden-change situation, we are looking to strike for a big play or score.

We want to run a reverse, a fake reverse, or a pass. We want something that keeps the defense on their heels and makes them doubt what they are doing.

We have to have a plan for when we are *backed up*. These are a set of plays to call when we are trying to get off our own goal line or inside the 10-yard line. In this situation, we must get at least one first down. If we don't get the first down, we have to get enough room so the punter can get his heels off the end line and punt the ball.

The next play situation is *short yardage*. I put second down back into this grouping in case we don't want to waste the down. I also include our third-down play calls in this section.

The next situation is critical to our system. We want to know what we are going to do in our *goal-line offense*. In this section we include what we call "one play with no time on the clock or no time-outs." It is not necessarily the play that is a factor. Instead, it is the situation and emotions that are involved in that situation. If you don't give your players a chance to practice that situation, when it happens in a ball game, it is totally different. You have to practice that play so your players can feel the emotions that go with the importance of the play. Asking your players to execute a play with no time on the clock, in a win-or-lose situation, is a pressure-packed situation. You have to practice that. You may have run that play in your goal-line offense, but if you didn't put them in that situation, which requires a different emotional level, they won't know how to react.

I hope what you are hearing about our system is that everything we do is dominated by down, distance, emotion, and game dynamics. The mental approach to our practice is game-focused every day. We want to play the upcoming game three or four times during that week of practice. We want to handle all the emotions and mental training before we get to the game.

When it comes down to a last-play situation, the offensive coordinator makes that call. I don't override his decision. We have spent the entire week going over that situation and reviewing it. That situation has already been covered before we get to the game. My opinions have already been noted. We decided during the week what was going to happen in that situation. The checklist allows everyone to be on the same page. We know as a staff what we are going to do.

What is nice about the modern-day football game is the information you have available to you. Because of the information available to us, I know how many third-and-one situations we are going to have in Saturday's game. On Saturday we will have a maximum of three third-and-short-yardage plays. In our game plan we will have four calls on our call sheet in the third-and-short situation. If you only have four calls, Stevie Wonder could figure out one of them. The coaches are on the same page. But more importantly the players are on that page too. They are in the game with the coaches, and they know what is going to be called.

If there is something different called, it will come from a discussion of the four offensive coaches and the head coach. One coach will not make that call.

On our script sheet, we have additional information on the sheet besides the play. Everything is scripted in categories on that sheet. We have formations listed with right and left options as to where the ball is on the field. We also include any motions and the backfield sets. On each situation, the total information required on the play being run is written down.

If you don't have that information written down, at some point of the game you will freeze. When the pressure builds, it becomes harder to recall things quickly. The coach only has five seconds to get the play to the quarterback. Everyone in the stadium can see the 25-second clock. They know when the play is late coming in the game. If the quarterback is looking to the sideline and waiting, it builds pressure on the whole team. If you don't have it written down, you'll freeze. When the play comes into the game on time, with all aspects of the play covered, that gives confidence to your team.

If you send a play into the game, and the set or motion is wrong, your players lose confidence in you as the coach. If the play comes in without any hesitation and is a proper call, your players feel good about the play.

Your players today are affected by every motion you make. I laugh because at the end of the year, we have our rookie skits. That is when you find out that everything you do as a coach, your players mimic. If you have a certain smile or eyelid movement, they pick up on it. They are watching every move you make and evaluating and making decisions on everything. It is a shame, but it is true.

Writing down your play calls doesn't stop you from being creative. There are going to be some moments on the sideline when you can put some things together that weren't on the script. As long as you can get those thoughts to your football team, it is fine to freelance. But when crunch time comes, the clock runs faster. The five seconds you've got to call the play seems like one second. If you have it written down, it works better.

We practice the *four-minute drill*. If we are ahead and trying to protect the ball, there are certain things we want to try to do. We want to stay inbounds with the ball and keep the clock moving. We want ball security to become a major focus of the ballcarriers. We want control passes thrown and catches made to keep the clock running. If you practice those situations, you stand a better chance of executing them when the time comes.

The *two-minute offense* can come before the half or at the end of the game. We work the two-minute drill two to three times during the course of the week. The two-minute offense gives you a chance at the end of the game to win the game. The mechanics that go with the two-minute drill are crucial. We have to practice how to use the clock play to kill the clock. You have to get out of bounds to conserve the time. Hustle to the ball while the chains are being moved after a first down. We drill all kinds of situations. We put them in all kinds of positions with limited time and time-outs. We want our players in a realistic situation.

I have had practices where the pace was boringly slow. You could look at your players and see they were in a funk. They seemed like they didn't want to practice. Some days I look at my players and feel like I have to be a dentist. Because I know practice is going to be like pulling teeth. I control the practice schedule. I don't like to jump around and alter the plan, but I control that schedule. On days like that I go to a two-minute drill right away. If you think about the two-minute drill, it's an instant tempo lift for everyone.

When you get into the two-minute offense, the defensive linemen get in their racehorse stances and fly off the ball. The offensive linemen know the defense is flying, so they pick up their speed. It automatically picks up the tempo of practice. In our two-minute drill all of our plays come from two formations. That keeps us from having to change personnel.

When we call plays off the sideline, we use hand signals. The quarterback can change the play if he needs to. I believe the game of football is too fast for us coaches. Think about that statement for a second. Let's suppose we have a particular situation in the game on Saturday. We have practiced all week to use this particular play because we believe it will be good against the defense the opponent runs in this situation.

The opponent, for whatever reason, decides he is not going to play that defense in this particular situation this week. We are in a bad play for that situation. From the time we sent the play in, things have changed. The only way to get out of that situation is to let the quarterback change the play and get you into one that fits the defense.

In my opinion your players are always evaluating their coaches. If we have four or five bad plays a ball game, the players start to doubt your ability as a coach. We want to always give ourselves a chance to be in a good play. Of course, there is always the possibility that the quarterback can screw up the play. But I prefer to take that risk than to have us as coaches calling bad plays. I think that is a no-win situation.

If we had an injury during the game and had to replace a running back, we will make adjustments to our script. We would pick offensive plays that will play to the strengths of the back we had in the game. Remember what I said in the beginning. We are going to do what we are good at. We play to our strengths and not our weaknesses. At Stanford we had two backs. One of them was a quick slasher type of runner, and the other was a big power runner who caught the ball well. If one of those guys went down, we would work to the strengths of the other back. We would not have two scripts. If one of them were injured, we would pick plays from the script that fit the remaining back and eliminate others.

The next situation we deal with is *fourth-down calls*. The last couple of years, we found ourselves in the gray area on fourth down. You are almost too close to punt, but not close enough to try a field goal. We were in the area where turning the ball over on fourth down would not hurt you that much. We have regular base calls that we practice every week for this situation.

Our *red zone* starts roughly at the 25-yard line. In this situation, we look for the tendencies of our opponent and try to score touchdowns. There were some interesting statistics done by some pro coaches a couple of years ago. They looked at the top five teams in the league and compared them to the bottom five teams in the league. The percentages of times in the red zone for all teams were almost the same. The difference between the top and bottom teams was the percentage of touchdowns in the red zone.

The key is not getting in the red zone. The key is scoring touchdowns when you get into the red zone. That is what we try to do. That is something we have scripted, practiced, and given great thought to during the course of the week. We just don't want to kick field goals. We want touchdowns.

Our next category is what we call *must-win plays*. At the national coach's convention two years ago, I listened to a pro coach talk about this. He had it on his checklist. We have a list of plays that we call if we have only one play left to try to win the game. We have one play each from the 40-yard line, 30-yard line, 20-yard line, and 10-yard line. We practice those plays every week. We prepare for that situation if and when it arises.

One of the big plays in college football is the *two-point play*. We give this play great thought. We always know where to position the ball. As soon as we know we are going for two points, our quarterback goes to the official and tells him where to place the ball. Our guys know exactly what we want to do.

We always want to make sure we have our special and trick plays. A trick play will work if it is done at the right time. I learned this next point from Dennis Green. He made sure the football team understood that a trick play was no different than any other play. All he wanted from that particular play was four yards. If you get four yards every time you snap the ball, in three downs you make a first down. If we had a loss on a trick play, the mentality told them it was just another play. That way you don't have the emotional drop that you might have if you featured this play. That is the mentality we want to create with our special and trick plays.

We have to plan to get our *base runs* into the offensive scheme. We always have 10 to 12 base runs. We have to make provisions for our *draw plays*. The last and most important thing with the running game is our *best running plays*. We want to always remember where our strength lies.

When we game plan our passing game we start with our *base passes*. Not counting formations, we will have 18 to 20 base plays in our game plan each week. We have our quick-passing game. That is our *three-step drop-passing game*. Within the passing game, we have to plan our *play-action passes* to correspond with our running game. On this game we are dropping seven to nine steps and looking to get the ball downfield to our receivers. We want to have provision to move the quarterback out of the dropback scheme. We call those types of passes *movement passes. Special passes* that are put in for particular defenses are part of the game plan. These are not trick plays as such, but serve a special purpose. Two years ago against Washington, on the third play of the game, we faked an isolation play, continued with a reverse fake, and hit the wide receiver over the middle for about 50 yards. That is a special pass we put in because of something we had seen in their secondary.

The *screen pass* is an important part of our game plan. It is a play that we put into another category called *blitz breakers*. The screen we like against the blitz is the jailhouse screen. That is the middle screen to the wide receiver coming back over the ball, while releasing all your linemen downfield. We ran this play against California three years in a row for touchdowns. California was a man-to-man blitzing team. Three years in a row we caught them in a blitz and hit that screen.

The last part of our passing game play is the section called *best passes*. This year in the Seattle Bowl, we weren't successful. We were struggling. We weren't having the offensive production we were accustomed to. One of the things we did was to go to the chart to our best passes column. What we found there was our best passes to our best receivers, and we got some things done.

I have been talking about the offensive checklist, but we do exactly the same thing on defense. I'm going to show you some of our defensive checklist, but I'll go a little faster. If you have questions about them, make sure you ask.

I want to cover a point about our theme planning. We can have team themes each week. That means the offense or defense can't come up with individual themes for each team. The offense may have a theme they want to gear up on. The defense may have a theme that they want to emphasize. For that matter, the special teams may want to do the same thing. But they all come from the same umbrella of the team theme. You must remember you are a team. The thing that you don't want is a separation of your team.

We saw a perfect example of team play in the last Super Bowl. No one gave the New England Patriots a chance to win that game. They played as a team and overcame the odds. Anytime you can keep everything within your team structure, you are better off.

My number one job as head coach is to keep our team fresh and healthy. I believe a healthy team and a fresh team wins games. Monday is our off day. Tuesday and Wednesday are our full-pad days. Thursday is a shell day. That means we are in shoulder pads and helmets. Friday we practice for exactly 37 minutes with no pads.

As we go through the year, I trim our full-pad days down. That means we go to full pads on Tuesday. On Wednesday and Thursday, we were in shells. On Friday we were still practicing exactly 37 minutes with no pads.

As we got further into the season, our practice on Tuesday and Wednesday was a shell day. Thursday and Friday were no-pad days. The last couple of weeks in the season, we may be in no pads the entire week. My job is to keep our team fresh.

You learn football from so many people. I learned this from Dennis Green, who comes from the Bill Walsh school of thought. My record at Stanford for the month of November was 28-8. I'll take that as a record. One of those years, we lost three games in November. We have a good record during the month of November because the team is healthy. You have to work your team, but you can't beat them up in practice. The other side of the coin is they are mentally fresh.

I want our players to hear everything I say. I have found that when the voice level goes up and the browbeating starts, the ears close up. That is why we don't browbeat our players. I want them to hear everything we are saying. I believe we recruit players that have the same goals I have. We tell them that from day one. We want to win on the field. You know what happens to coaches that don't win? They put a new coach in that slot.

I want to win in the classroom. Smart players win games. They make fewer mistakes. They have to be good athletes too, but the game is about mistakes. He who makes the most mistakes probably will lose the football game.

I want our players to be quality people. If I recruit players like that who have the same goals, drive, and desire that I have, I shouldn't have to browbeat them. Do you have to get on their ass a little bit every now and then? Yes you do. We all need a kick in the butt sometimes. I need one. But I shouldn't have to constantly browbeat them to get them to do what we want them to do. If I have to do that, I've got the wrong guys.

To get a defensive checklist all you have to do is flip over your offensive checklist. They are very similar in content. I'm not going to have time to go over all the things we do. I'll try to hit things I think are important.

The first thing I want to talk about is prevent-defense. There is a saying about prevent-defense. The only thing a prevent defense does is prevent you from winning. I don't believe that. Prevent-defense doesn't mean we put three guys back deep and not rush. You practice prevent-defense the same way you practice regular defense. What you want to create is a mindset that the defense is preventing the offense from scoring. Part of the prevent-defense mentality is keeping people inbounds. Don't let them catch the ball and run out of bounds. Blitzing can be part of a prevent package. It doesn't have to be so generic in its approach. There is no law that says you can only rush three in a prevent defense.

Instead of blitz-breakers on offense, we want protection-breakers on defense. If we know the protection of the offense and they are consistent with it, we can get to them on the blitz.

You can do the same thing with your kicking game. Make a checklist of things and situations that occur in a football game. Make sure you cover it in practice before it happens to you in a game. Try to think of every possibility and problem that might occur, and design some practice time to cover that facet of the game.

Gentlemen, it has been my pleasure to be here. Thank you.

THE TACKLE TRAP AND COUNTER TRAP SCHEMES

University of Nebraska

I want to thank Nike and Earl Browning and Tom Cheaney for having me on the Hawaii clinic again. I have been here three times in the last seven years. I do enjoy the opportunity to get out of the cold weather of Nebraska. I can assure you I am looking forward to going back on Monday and sweeping eight inches of snow off my driveway.

I do have a story to tell about Earl and Tom. They were friends for a long time and they both died and went to heaven. When they got to the pearly gates, St. Peter met them and asked them if they would like to have a female escort while they waited to be processed into heaven. They thought about it for about 10 seconds and said, "Yes, we need some company. Bring them out."

About five minutes later St. Peter came back with an ugly looking woman. She walked up to Earl. He looked at her and turned to St. Peter and said, "What is the deal? Why did I get such an ugly female?" St. Peter said, "That is your penalty for all of the sins you committed on earth." Earl agreed he did have a few sins and that he probably deserved what he got.

About 10 minutes later, St. Peter came back with another female. Here came a beautiful lady. St. Peter walked her over and gave her to Tom. Earl just gets irate. "What is the deal here, St. Peter? Tom's woman looks like she is just out of *Baywatch*. I just do not understand this at all." St. Peter said, "Earl, that is *her* penalty for all of the sins she committed on earth."

Players from all over the country come to our football camp. We have a great camp, and it is one of the least expensive camps of its kind. We have four sessions and they cost $210 per session. The camps start June 5 and run through June 25. They last for four days each. We have over 400 players in our camp each session. Most of the players on scholarship at Nebraska attended our camp at one time or another. The people that have been to our camp have good

things to say about our camp. We do not just cater to the very best players. We work with everyone.

I think it is amazing what Nebraska has accomplished with the football program over the past years. It has great tradition. The population of Nebraska is only 1.5 million people. We cannot just depend on getting players from the state of Nebraska. We recruit all over the country. We have had four players from Hawaii in the last few years. We must recruit all over the country to be successful. The players are a big part of our tradition.

We have had over 40 consecutive winning seasons. We have been to 34 consecutive bowl games. In the last nine years we have played for the National Championship five times. It is a high profile job as far as getting the job done. Also, we have done a good job as far as the graduation rate for our athletes. We have some great academic players as well.

Traditionally, Nebraska has been a running team. When you play in the Midwest area where we are, it is difficult to have a consistent passing game. Toward the end of the season you get all kinds of adverse weather. It could be 10 degrees and snowing with the wind blowing. We get all kinds of inclement weather. You must have the type of offense that can move the ball in all kinds of weather. We have had some outstanding linemen, outstanding running backs, and some very mobile quarterbacks. That combination of players has helped to make us a great football program. When you have those ingredients, you can control the clock, and you can physically defeat teams. I have not done a study on this, but I would like to see the record of the teams we play for the week after we play them. I would think the chances for them to win the next week would be a lot less than it would be otherwise. That is just because of the physical type of game that we play. We stress the physical aspect with our players. We do not have mountains or water to detract the players. All we have is football players. There are no pro teams in Nebraska. We are the only Division I school in the state. We have great fan support. All of these factors help draw good players to our program.

In our offense we feature three phases of the running game. First is power football, which includes isolation and the inside and outside zone plays. The second phase is option football. We have mobile quarterbacks that can make decisions at the crucial time. The third phase of our offense is our counter game. That is the subject that I want to address today. When you have those three phases of offense, it is hard for the defenses to zero in on one thing. When the defense only has a week to work against our offense, it makes it hard to get prepared. I think we have a good play-action passing game with these three phases of offense. We have play-action off most of our plays.

Today I am going to cover our counter series. We have one counter that comes off our inside zone play. That is what we call our tackle trap. We show flow one way and bend back the I-formation running back. That is off our inside zone action. It is called tackle trap.

The other phase is our counter. We run counter trap, counter sweep, and our lead play where we lead off tackle. It is like a power play, but we run a counter action, where the quarterback opens and the I-back steps one way, and he counters that move. The three plays, counter trap, counter sweep, and lead play, are all about the same play. As far as blocking rules, there are only a few changes the linemen need to know.

Basically, in the counter game we are talking about two different schemes. When you are setting up your offense, it is important to set up plays that are similar, so you can teach things that way. There are some differences, but those are the two schemes we use. As I said, our play-action passes come off the same schemes that we use on our running plays.

On the tackle trap, we run it to the I-back and to the quarterback. We have our quarterback tackle tray. It is the same play as the counter trap and counter sweep. We fake the ball one way or the other, and the quarterback keeps the ball on the sweep. We like to involve the quarterback in the same scheme. When we get into the one-back set it

spreads the defense out. This enables us to make a lot of big plays using our quarterback on these plays.

As far as the blocks we use, the most important is the combo block. This is where we are blocking with two offensive players against one defensive player. After contact, one of the blockers comes off the block to the linebacker. This is how we teach the block. We tell the lineman that is covered to take the defender on his own. We tell him, "He is yours." He steps with the inside foot. If the defender slants inside, he has to take him 1-on-1. The reason we do not slant with the outside foot is because we do not think we can pick up the slant as easy. So we tell him to step with the inside foot first.

The blocker that is going to help on the combo block is going to pin high. We expect him to be able to get off that block. We do not want him to come down flat. If he does, he will get tangled up in the block and can't get off the block to the linebacker. We work on the combo block all of the time with the different combinations the defense can give us. This includes the linebacker on the blitz and the slant inside by the down defensive man. The blocker that is going to pin-block high must come down with his inside foot. The most common mistake on the pin-high block is where the blocker takes a drop step. This happens when they have their stance too wide, and they have to step back to get balanced. We check our linemen all of the time to make sure their stance is tight. The blocker pins high on the defender and helps the blocker. Then he has to know who they are going to block late when they come off the pin-high block. Sometimes it is the Mike linebacker and sometimes it is the backside linebacker. They must know whom they are going to block when they come off the block late. The further away the linebacker is, the longer he can stay on the double-team block.

The other blocks are important to our offense. The center has an important block and that is a 1-on-1 pin-back block. That is the most difficult block for the center. We work on the same techniques with the center. He cannot take a back step. He must step toward the defender. We do not want any wasted movement when we are pinning back.

We work on our techniques of pulling quite a lot. The big mistake pulling linemen make when they go to pull is they drop the shoulders to get the near foot around. We tell our linemen we want them to take the drop step but we want them to gain some distance where we are going to, so we do not lose ground. If they have a wide stance, they cannot take that lead step because they are all spread out. We work on a tighter stance so they can get some distance where they can get in a position to pull to the position where they want to go. We tell them to "lose ground but gain distance." The thing we stay after them on is the first two steps when they pull. Once they get those first two steps down, everything else falls into place. To get them out on the plays, we tell them to lose ground and gain distance. We want them to point the toe in the direction they want to go.

When we run a counter trap we tell the players we are going to kick it. This means he is going to climb the hole. When they hear trap, they think climb. On the inside trap and the counter trap, we do the same thing. We take the same lead step on the trap, and the second step is back up into the hole. We are climbing the hole. The tackle is going to get under the kick-out block.

When we run counter sweep, we are taking the same step. We tell the pulling guard to get a least 1 yard deep. He does not climb on the counter sweep. He is pulling flat and getting some depth.

It is the same thing for the tackle. He is pulling flat. We tell him to get 2 or 3 yards deep. We do this so he can get around the stack on the end. We can log the end, or we can load on the defensive end with the fullback. We are getting the guard around for the linebacker. The tackle is up on four or secondary support.

The technique we teach on the inside zone play is this. The playside guard is going to stretch, and on his second step, he wants to get to the defender's crotch. We do not want him to cross over. That is the biggest mistake linemen make when they run the inside zone. The move is basically a change of direction. I must be very quick. He does not want to be caught going sideways. We do not want to allow penetration. We tell him to step, and then the second step is into the crotch.

When we teach the inside zone, we ask the players this question: Are you covered or uncovered? The uncovered lineman steps at a 45-degree angle. He aims for a spot on the backside hip. If that spot disappears, as long as the hip is there he is going to work on it until he can come off on the linebacker. Those are the basic fundamentals on the plays I am going to cover.

First is the tackle trap. The fullback comes outside where the tackle is pulling from. He skins his butt and protects to that area just like he would on a lead play.

When we call our plays, the 3-hole is to the right and the 2-hole is to the left. We block the play like a dive play. We call dive right and tackle trap left. This is our 43 tackle trap.

43 TACKLE TRAP VS. 4-3 DEFENSE

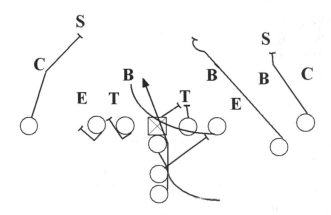

We call the play to the dive side even though the play is coming back the other way. This is the blocking scheme we would use on 43 tackle trap. Again, we are calling the play to the right but it is coming back to the left side. The zone block is by the guard and center. The guard makes the contact and the center comes over late to help before he comes off on the linebacker. On the other side, the guard and tackle pivot on the inside foot and go after the down linemen. They want to create space inside. The pulling tackle comes around and reads the block of the left guard to determine if he goes around him or inside his block. That is the 43 tackle trap against the 4-3 look.

Against the 50-defense, it is not an ideal play. If we do run it against the 50-look, we are going to trap on the line of scrimmage. Most of the time, we are going to be trapping the down lineman on the 50-defense. We let the pulling tackle know we are going to trap on the line. The guard and tackle on the trap side let the pulling tackle know to block the down lineman.

43 TACKLE TRAP VS. 50-DEFENSE

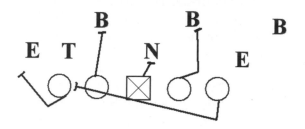

When we run this play we trap the linebacker most of the time. If we do trap the down lineman, we let the pulling tackle know the defender will be on the line of scrimmage.

The defense we like to run the play against is the 4-3 over look. The defense has the noseguard shifted over to the formation or tight end. Now we can have the two guards and center run the inside zone block. The tackle pulls and traps the linebacker.

43 TACKLE TRAP VS. 4-3 OVER DEFENSE

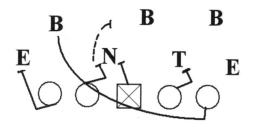

The two looks we get the most are the regular 4-3 defense and the 50-look. The stunt we see the most is when the 5-technique is pinching down inside, and the Mike linebacker is scraping through.

47 TACKLE TRAP VS. 5-TECHNIQUE

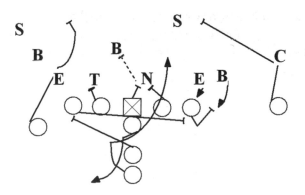

We can run the play from one back as well. Here we have the tight end protecting on the backside inside of the fullback coming back on the outside man.

4-3 TACKLE TRAP - ONE-BACK SET

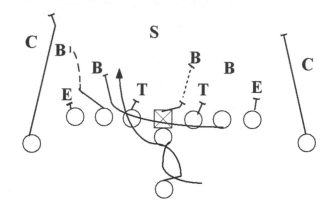

All of our linemen are numbered. We go from right to left. The tight end is 2, the right tackle is 3, the right guard is 4, the center is 5, the left guard is 6, and the right tackle is 7. We can make a 7 call, which tells the left tackle he is blocking on the line of scrimmage. On some calls the number means something different. We can run the play to the tight-end side. You can run the ball to the tight end.

NUMBERS FOR LINEMEN

Here is the same play out of our gun left formation. We have loaded the left side with trips. We generally have a tight end in the slot next to the left tackle. You need some type of protection to cut off the backside rush. If we were in a two-back set, this is the man the fullback would be assigned to block. This is from the shotgun set. We do have plays where we give the ball to the I-back and run the inside zone play inside. This is the counter to that play. Now we run 47 quarterback tackle trap. We fake the ball to the I-back coming across the set. The quarterback follows the tackle as he comes across on the trap. He does the same thing the I-back does on the tackle trap. If you have a quarterback that can run a little, it can be an effective play. We got this play from

Northwestern a couple of years ago when we played them in the Alamo Bowl. It is a good play because a lot of the time teams do not account for the quarterback as much as they do for the running backs.

47 QUARTERBACK TACKLE TRAP

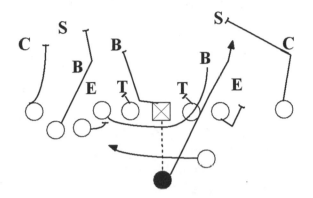

There is nothing new for the linemen on that play. We usually get fewer defenders in the box when we are in this formation. The defense has to cover the receiver and they are spread out.

Next I want to talk about our counter trap. First I want to cover the blocking. We start out looking at the under front. The first thing we must know is this: Is the tackle *covered or uncovered?* That is the first thing our linemen look for. If nothing is called, the tight end knows he is going to combo block at that point. If the tackle is uncovered, he calls out the number 3. That means there is a 3-technique in the gap. Now the tight end does not have to double-down because the tackle is uncovered. This tells the tight end we do not need help on the 3-technique because the tackle can block him alone. On the 3 call, the end is on his own, and more than likely the tackle and guard are running the combination block. But this is an example of no 3-technique call. When we run this play, we are looking to let two defenders go free. We are going to pick those defenders up by the pulling guard and tackle. Here we have an example of the linebacker plugging and the end or tackle coming off the block.

42 COUNTER VS. UNDER SPACING

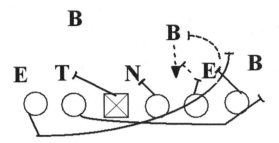

Our I-back is running to daylight. A lot of time the play will be broken inside the double-team block because the defense fights outside so hard. The crease comes inside the double team. When we run to the tight-end side, the tackle must know if he has a 9-technique or a 7-technique. If he has a 9-technique, the tight end can release to the linebacker.

42 COUNTER TRAP VS. 9-TECHNIQUE

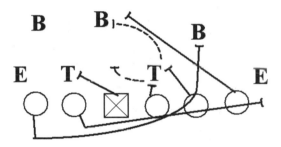

Now we know the double team can go all the way back to the Will linebacker. He can hang on to the double-team longer. We try to create a crease in there and drive the down man of the line as far as we can. We kick the 9-technique and get under on the Sam linebacker.

The key coaching point is to make sure the two pulling linemen are stepping toward the defense. We do not want them to take false steps and we do not want them to lose any time getting there.

42 COUNTER TRAP VS. 7-TECHNIQUE

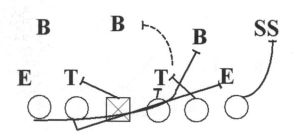

42 COUNTER TRAP VS. 50-SPACING

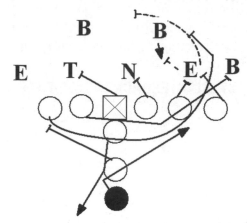

If the defense plays a 6-technique or 7-technique, the tight end is going to release and block the first man on the outside. Our linemen know if the defense has a 6-technique or 7-technique, he is going outside. We are still going to combo block, but the combo is going to be inside.

We run the play out of a lot of different formations. We run *ace trips* with two tight ends and two wide receivers. We have been effective by shifting the tight end back to the wing position and have him go in motion across the formation. One of the receivers on the formation sidesteps up on the line to make it an unbalanced set. We get the secondary over reacting to motion side, and we run the counter trap back to the short side.

42 COUNTER TRAP - ACE TRIPS - SHIFT

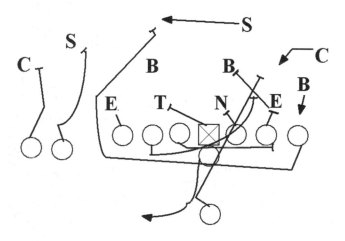

When we run the counter trap against the 50-defense we have to get the double-team on the tackle. If we do not get the 3 call, the tight end knows he is working with the tackle on the combo block. If the linebacker plugs, the tackle has to come off the block and pick him up.

This is the look we see a lot against the ace set. Teams will widen the Sam linebacker and put him into the coverage. We do not have a 3-technique, so the tackle would make a 3 call. The tackle is uncovered, so the end knows he must block outside. He takes the first man outside. We are going to trap the 7-technique rush. The key block is the center coming back on the fill block for the pulling guard.

43 COUNTER TRAP VS. EVEN FRONT VS. SAM

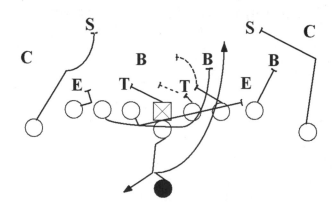

Here is another one-back set. This is trips left for us. We are going to run 42 quarterback counter trap - lead. We use a lot of different schemes against the rush ends. We attack them several ways and from several angles. We bring the fullback out at the rush end. A lot of times this will widen the rush end. This sets him up for the guard trapping him. Just as the defensive end is set to take on the fullback, the pulling guard traps him. The quarterback runs up the crease. We have the tight end to the backside to protect the play.

42 QUARTERBACK COUNTER TRAP - LEAD

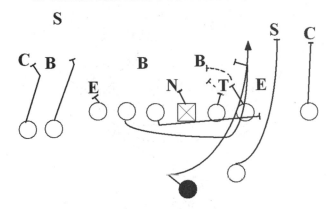

This is a very effective running play. Our line does not care if the fullback or the quarterback is running the ball.

We can run the same play to the tight-end side. The tight end is coming outside because he has a 6- or 7-technique on him. Nothing really changes on the play for the linemen. Now it is a different ballcarrier. The defense is spread out and it opens it up more on the backside. You do not have to throw the ball in third-and-long situations.

42 QUARTERBACK COUNTER TRAP

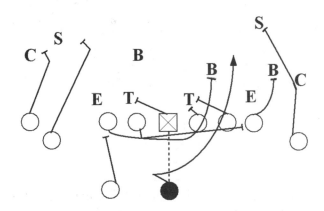

Another play that has been good for us is what we call 42 counter trap read. We run the 42 counter trap and the quarterback eyeballs the rush end. If the end slow-plays it or shuffles and does not commit to the rush, we are going to give the ball to the I-back on the 42 counter trap. If the end comes down and plays the trap, the quarterback keeps the ball and gets in the crease behind the two wide blockers.

42 COUNTER TRAP - READ DEFENSIVE END

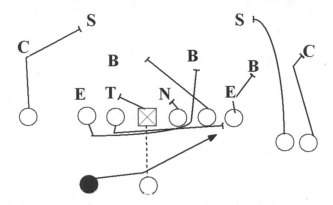

This year we scored twice on the play as Eric Crouch kept the ball. It was a big play against Kansas State as the defensive end came flying down inside to stop the trap. If the defense plays the quarterback, we run the regular counter trap.

We do not run as many counter sweeps as we used to run. We have not been able to log the end as well as we used to. Now we are running the counter sweep, and we are loading on the end man with the fullback. When we run the 42 counter sweep-lead, the pulling guard does not have the end man line he did when we ran counter sweep. In the old counter sweep the guard pulled and got 1 yard deep and logged the end man. The tackle pulled deep at 3 yards and came around and blocked the linebacker. Now we pull the linebacker on the linebacker and the tackle has the secondary man coming up.

42 COUNTER SWEEP - LEAD

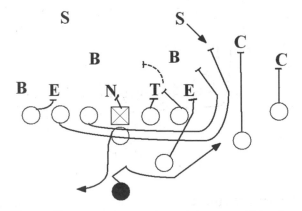

The pulling guard gets 1 yard deep and blocks the first linebacker. The pulling tackle gets 2 to 3 yards deep and blocks the deep secondary player that shows. Our I-back flattens out more to stay behind the two pulling men. On the counter trap he takes it upfield a lot harder. Here he runs more like a sweep play.

A similar play from the trips set is our 48 quarterback counter sweep - lead. Everything is the same for the linemen. We have the load block by the fullback. Again we have the defense spread out, and we are using the quarterback as a runner. We do not have to throw the ball on long yardage situations.

48 QUARTERBACK COUNTER SWEEP - LEAD

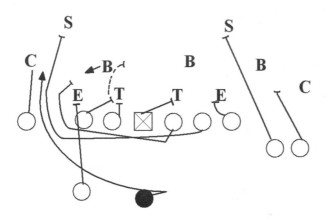

Our next counter is our 42 lead. It is the same blocking for the line except the fullback is going to block the end man instead of the pulling guard. The guard now pulls for the first linebacker. That is all the line has to know that is different. The other point is that the backside tackle is no longer pulling. He is a swinging gate man on the backside. He steps down inside and pivots to the outside and protects on the backside. The pulling guard is thinking first line-backer instead of kicking out like he would on counter trap. The I-back takes a short step left and then comes back to get the ball and gets upfield in the open hole. As I said before, at times the back hits the play inside the double-team block. It does not always hit where you think it is going to hit.

42 LEAD VS. UNDER DEFENSE

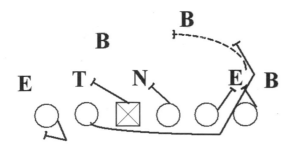

Against the 4-3 defense the tight end does not block down. He base blocks the 9-technique or the end man. The backside guard pulls and picks up the linebacker.

42 LEAD VS. 4-3 DEFENSE

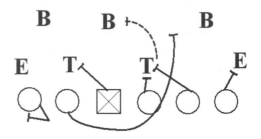

If there is no 3 call, the fullback has the end man. The guard still has the linebacker. The important block is the center's block on the fill for the pulling guard.

Against the 4-4 look, the tight end does not get a 3 call, so he takes the man on his outside. Now we pull the guard a little tighter around the combo block so he can get upfield on the linebacker. The fullback finds the other linebacker that is walked off the line. As you can see, there are a lot of similarities between the counter trap, counter sweep, and the 42 lead.

42 LEAD VS. 4-4 DEFENSE

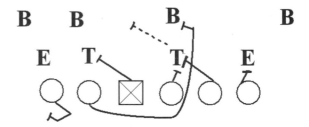

We do not always have to run the lead with the fullback. We can run it with our tight end because our tight ends are good blockers. We have been able to run the play from our ace shift set. Here the pulling end makes the block the fullback would make.

ACE SHIFT 42 LEAD VS. 4-4 DEFENSE

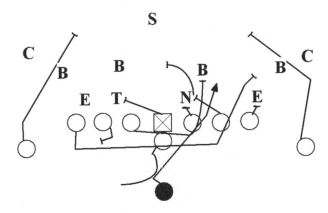

On the goal line, we can get a double-team block on the defensive end with our motion man. We call the play 42 lead-motion. We bring the back in motion and have him double on the 6-technique end. We block the double-team inside and have the tackle seal inside on the off linebacker as before. We still pull the guard around on the front side linebacker. The fullback leads the play between the double-team blocks. The I-back follows the fullback and cuts off the double-team blocks. This has been a good play on the goal line for us.

TIGHT - 42 LEAD - MOTION

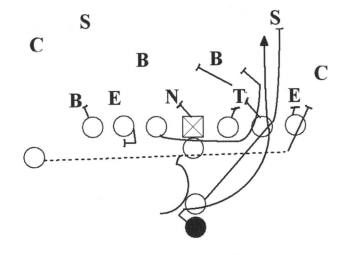

Here is our 42 lead against two linebackers. The tight end base-blocks. The guard pulls and comes around on the linebacker. The fullback always blocks the end man.

42 LEAD VS. TWO LINEBACKERS

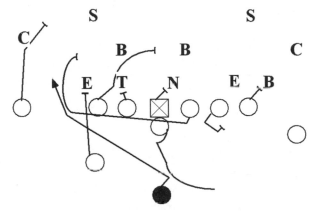

I want to thank you for your time. We appreciate the invitation to come to Hawaii. We always enjoy our visit here. If you get back to Nebraska, feel free to drop in to see us. If you have any questions, I will be around. Mahalo!

QUARTERBACKS AND THE ONE-BACK PASSING GAME

University of Florida

From that introduction, you can see I have coached at several schools. I enjoyed the years at Marshall University. I am looking forward to working at the University of Florida. I know it has been interesting the last six weeks.

In today's world, coaching football requires motivational techniques. To motivate, you must be able to communicate. When I was a young boy, my dad used to make me speak with marbles in my mouth. As I got better at speaking, I was allowed to take out the marbles one at a time. When I lost all of my marbles, I went into the coaching profession. I am sure we all can appreciate this point of view.

As coaches we can have a lot of good ideas of what we want to do and how we are going to do things. But you must be careful you do not try to do too much. What you know is great, but the key is how much your players know and what can they do. That is more important than anything you know. I can draw up the best pass pattern in the game of football, but if my quarterback cannot make that throw, it is not a good play. It may be a perfect play to use against the defense employed. But it is not a good play unless the quarterback can make the throw.

The same analogy applies in coaching quarterbacks. There are a lot of coaching points you can get into. I tried to keep things as simple as possible without cluttering the quarterback's mind with a lot of coaching points. It is different for me at the college level because we recruit players. If a player cannot throw the ball, he should not be in the program as a quarterback. We recruit good players, but we still have to put them on the right page to do certain things.

In working with young kids in camps, I do the same things. To me the important thing in working with quarterbacks is to *keep it simple*. There are two basic drills for working on the mechanics of throwing the football. They need to set the ball in the drill. They get tired of doing this but they need to learn how to set the ball. They do not want any wasted motion or any dipping of the ball. If you have a quarterback that is having problems, have them work on setting the ball in the throwing stance. Have them work on holding the ball where they want it.

After they learn to set the ball, they must learn to step and throw. Next, they practice a few motions, and then you put the actions together. That is how you want them to throw the football. Everything else is extra. Any other motions are wasted. If you can get them to do the basic things upstairs, you have a chance. Spend most of your time where it is important. That is down on the feet. That may sound crazy because you are throwing with the motion of the upper body. Watch the quarterback when he plays "catch." If he can be accurate in that drill, he has a chance to be successful. He knows he can make the throw. It is the job of the coach to put him into that position after he has dropped. It may be a play-action pass, a bootleg, or whatever type of pass it is, but you need to put him in that same position so he can make the same throw. You have to put him in that position over and over again. That is the whole purpose of the pass drop. We want to put the quarterback in a position where he can repeat the throw.

The basic things we tell the quarterback in throwing the ball is to start with the weight on the inside of the rear foot. The gun is loaded. If the ball is up in the set position, the gun is loaded. If he is sprinting out, he must have the weight on the rear foot, so he can step and throw the ball. Everything moves toward the target and he must follow through. It sounds simple. I know guys are different, but any coaching you do should be to smooth that procedure out and to make him consistent.

When I went to Marshall University and went to practice that first day, I met Chad Pennington. Actually I had met him the day before spring practice started. I got there the night before and we practiced at 6:30 a.m. I introduced myself to Chad. "I am your new coach." I told him I did not know the plays and that he could coach the plays. I told him I was going to work on the techniques. I watched him for about five seconds and decided that Chad could throw the football. Even my wife could tell this guy could throw the football. I could see he did not need a whole lot of coaching. Everything from the shoulders up was as good as you could get. The only thing we needed to work on was balance.

When a quarterback can set and throw without pressure, most of them are pretty good. When they have to move around they get off balance, and this is when they have a problem. They are not consistent. This is what I work on with them.

If the weight is on the inside of the rear foot and the quarterback moves, he must get the weight on the rear foot to throw the football. We work on this over and over again. We are concerned about being consistent in throwing the football. We are interested in the quarterback being a high-efficiency quarterback as far as completion percentage is concerned. This does not just mean dumping the ball off. I want them to be consistent down the field as well as on the short routes. The only way to do that is to have him do the right things over and over again.

At the same time, we work on some of the off-balance throws. We do that because the quarterbacks are going to throw off balance at some point in time. So we work on them doing drills where they have to set their feet and throw the ball. After a few throws as they are warming up, I want them to start moving their feet. We do not want them to stand in one spot and throw for very long. We are going to be moving. It does not have to be a long throw. We want them to move for four or five yards and set their feet. The weight is on the inside of the rear foot every time. We do not want them to get off balance. That will happen sometimes. We do not want them to throw off balance if they do not have to. We repeat this process over and over.

I can live with the quarterbacks releasing the ball from different spots. As long as the elbow is shoul-der-high so everything is moving in the same direction, he should be fine. I have had some quarterbacks that threw the ball with the ball a foot outside the shoulder. But they knew where the ball was going. When the elbow starts dropping down, you get a lot of rotary action, and the ball is going to take off in different places. As long as the ball is set, and the ball is above the shoulder, he should be able to throw the ball.

We do a lot of work on the abs with the quarterbacks. They are important for the quarterback. But the point I make to them all of the time is this: The strongest muscles they have are in the middle of the body. The abductors are very strong muscles. There are very few players that have a "strong arm." Not many of them can stand flat-footed and throw the ball 70 yards. I have only had one quarterback that could do that. I have been lucky. Most coaches never have a quarterback with an arm that strong.

Most people have a connection with the ground. A lot of you play golf. If you did not use your legs you would not hit the ball very far. It is the same with the quarterback. He must get in a good position with the weight on the inside of the rear foot and step and throw. I keep repeating this because that is how I coach it. We keep running the basic drills over and over again. I do not want the quarterbacks thinking about the mechanics of throwing the football.

When we practice, we go through sequence just like most teams do. The first part of practice is the individual phase. This is when I want the quarterbacks to think about mechanics. Then we go into other phases where we are working with other players. Now we are thinking timing, spots on the field, and other related aspects on the passing game. When we get into the pass skeleton drills, we start thinking keys in the secondary. The last phase is when we get into teamwork. This is where we tie all of the passing game together. This includes protection and the keys.

When you get into teamwork, you cannot spend a lot of time on technique. If you do this, you are losing focus on the most important things you are working on at that time. If you need to get him out after practice and work on techniques, don't dilute what you are trying to get done by spending all of your time working on correcting techniques. If there is something that is a real flaw, you may want to make a correction, but you really try to minimize what you are doing. You can make a note of it and work on it later. With young players, you may have to do more along those lines.

There have been a lot of coaches that do more on details related to the quarterbacks. I like to recruit good quarterbacks and teach them where to throw the ball. It may be more than this and we may have to be a little more specific, but when we have camp and have eight-year-old kids, I still get them doing the five-step drop with no wasted motion. I get them stepping and throwing with the weight on the inside of the back foot. They get the ball up and turn the palm down and the ball comes out in a spiral for them. The body falls in line. To get the bottom line done, the body will adjust.

If you are the quarterback coach, or any other position coach as far as that goes, and you cannot give the player enough detail about the position and put it in writing for him, then you do not know enough about the position. For example you must be able to give him the details on how to read different defensive coverages. He must be able to determine where to go with the ball. You must be able to give him the details on how to do those things.

Once you have given him the details on those things, you can ask him for feedback. That is very important. If he can't tell you what you want to know, then he does not know the system. If you cannot tell him, then you do not know. The first thing you must know when you put in a new pass play are the details related to that play. What does the quarterback do if something goes wrong? "If the receiver falls down, what do I do? If the defense is not in the coverage we expected, what do I do? Is the play still a good play?" You better know the details, and you better be able to communicate the details clearly.

I do not think coaches get enough feedback in the classroom setting. I am not talking about on the field. Coaches get in such a big hurry they do not give the players the opportunity to provide feedback in the classroom setting. I want our quarterbacks to be able to get up in a meeting and draw up a formation and what the receivers are doing on a play. I want them to be able to draw up the protection and I want them to be able to draw up the defensive fronts and coverages. I want them to be able to show me how the defense lines up to disguise their coverages. I want

them to be able to draw up everything about the play. We have to spend time with the quarterback teaching this information if we expect him to know all of it. The front end is really loaded for the young quarterback coming in for the first time. We spend a lot of time teaching defensive concepts and what we want the quarterback to do against those concepts. How do you attack defenses? What are the good plays to run against each of the defenses we face? If the defense lines up wide, we run inside. If the defense lines up tight, we run outside. If the defense lines up in two deep, we attack the corners. If the defense lines up in three deep, we attack the seams. We work on those things over and over again, so they can attack what they see on defense. The more the quarterback knows and the more they can use, the better coach you become.

If you saw Marshall University play this past year, you know our quarterback had a lot of freedom in the offense. We gave him a lot of choices in the concepts we gave him. I would call the formations and tell him to watch for certain things from the defense. "The first time we see three deep, we want to run four verticals." He knew what to do when the defense gave us that look.

If you sit down and study a game, you will find there are six to 10 times per game when you have the right offensive look against the defensive look that gives you a chance for a big play. Not very often do you have a chance for a big play in the game. If you really study the situation, you will see you only have a chance for a big play six to 10 times per game. You do not want to waste those opportunities. If you concentrate on this point just one more time per game it will result in an additional touchdown. If you can communicate this to the quarterback, now you have a chance to do it.

We put it down on paper for the quarterbacks. We teach them defensive theory. Things have gotten a lot more complicated in college football in coaching quarterbacks than they were when I first started coaching. When I first started coaching, the defense lined up in three deep or two deep. The defense played zone or man. Then the defense started playing quarter coverages. Now we see brackets, combos, keys, and cross-keying is the thing with the defense.

All of this makes it tougher to coach the quarterback. In some ways, this has changed how I coach the quarterback about defenses. We teach him basic alignments, but once the ball is snapped, we teach him concepts. Is there a safety in the middle of the field? Are they playing the deep secondary with two half safeties or not? We want them to know our plays, but we also want them to know what to expect on defense. By the time the quarterback takes that first step he has a good idea of what is happening by the flow of that middle safety. By the time the quarterback gets to his second step, he knows if a blitz is coming or not. If the blitz is not coming, he knows he has a zone or man coverage, and any other factor that he needs to know about the play.

We use drills that apply to game movements. I will line up as the free safety in front of the quarterback. I will take two steps and the quarterback must tell me what the concept is. We want him to tell me right now what the defensive concept is that the free safety is executing. We want to teach him what is good and what is not good.

Another example of what we are trying to get across to the quarterbacks would be this. Let's say you have a real good play to the backside. If the defense has four defenders sitting over on the backside, it is not a good play. The quarterback has to know that is not a good play and he has to be able to change the play. We do not want to waste a play.

We use visualization with our quarterbacks. We want them to see themselves making plays. We want them to go through the keys on the play. Today I was talking to some coaches about working on drills with the quarterback with his eyes closed. Some of you may say I am crazy. How can a quarterback work with his eyes closed? When we are working on fundamentals it has nothing to do with seeing the defense. We tell him to close his eyes and take a pass drop. The quarterback comes back and sits up. He may be off balance but he will be aware of it. There is no reason he cannot set and be balanced with his eyes closed.

Then we go to the next step. We have a man that runs for four steps and we throw him the ball. He takes a balanced step and throws the ball to the receiver at five yards. There is no reason he cannot do this. We do this drill until they can hit about every pass. I make a point to them. "Use your eyes to watch the defense. It has nothing to do with passing the ball." I make them go through the sequence.

It is important to make the players give you feedback. I have to know if they understand what we are trying to accomplish. Make sure they know the details. Make them draw it up on the board. Give them a study sheet to take home. If they can't put it down on paper, they do not know it yet. You may have to find another way to teach them. Do what you have to do to teach them the concepts. That is why you have "coach" in front of your name. Figure out a way to get it done.

I have gone to a lot of practices from grade school to high school to college to the NFL. Over the years I have seen a lot of great drills. The thing that struck me about some of these drills is that they did not have anything to do with football. They were creative but they did not have much to do with what takes place in a game. To make a point make sure your drills improve a specific skill.

We want our quarterbacks to practice all of the different kinds of passes. If you have a quarterback that wants to practice in the summer, but does not have his receivers available, here is what he can do. He can put up a net, and throw toward the net. He can get a bucket or trash can, and throw at the bucket. He can just throw to that spot. When we throw the corner routes, this is about where the ball should be. Tell him this in an outline that he can take home with him. The corner route for us is 26 yards deep and two yards from the sideline. If we are working the seam route, it is going to be 18 to 20 yards deep and two yards outside the hash mark. He can go through all the motions of throwing to the sideline on a flat route.

While the quarterback is working on this in the summer I want him to visualize the whole pass route. He can practice all of the throws in the passing game without his receivers.

Let me cover one point about teaching quarterbacks. How you say things is more important than what you are saying. Most of you teach the curl-flat combination in some form. Most teams teach the quarterback to read the strong safety or the flat defender, or whoever it is, to decide where to throw the football. You teach them to read the defender and throw the ball opposite that man.

Defensive coaches know this as well. They will screw the quarterback up by having the safety hang around on the curl until the linebacker can get depth and then the safety will cover the flat. The quarterback is sitting back in the pocket trying to figure out what to do with the ball. He is making snowballs. He wonders why the curl-flat pattern is no good.

Try telling the quarterback something like this on the play. "Here is what I want. Run the curl-flat route. You throw the ball to the flat unless you cannot throw it there." Now he comes back on the drop, looks at the receivers, and throws the ball to the flat. Next play he does it again. No one covers the play. Now the defensive coach gets on the safety to get outside and cover the flat route. The next time he drops back, he runs the ball. We want him to make the defense define what they are going to do quicker. Make them commit quicker than they want to. We do not want them to call the route unless you are satisfied with the flat route.

The next point I want to cover is how to teach the quarterback to throw the ball over the head of the linebackers and in front of the safeties in the hole. It is the same area on cover two on the fade route between the corner and safety. We want to work on improving the throw down the field. We take a receiver and place him behind the goal post at about seven to eight yards deep. We have the quarterback and a center set up inside the 10-yard line. We want the quarterback to take the snap and throw the ball to the receiver behind the goal post. If he is making the correct throw, the ball will skim the crossbar. If he floats the ball, there will be air under it. If he tries to muscle the ball to the receiver, it will go underneath the crossbar. He has to put the touch on the ball. We tell him to hit the receiver in the mouth with the ball. Players love this drill. We throw the ball at an angle. We can change the angles up and have him throw four or five times from each side. We do not let the quarterback look at the crossbar. Once they get the feel of it they will take it over the ball and in front of the safety. The player does not have to be a pro to make that throw. You have to let them get a feel for the throw and a sense of dumping the ball over the rushing linemen and dropping it to a back. The goal-post drill can be a good instructional tool. You can use different angles with this play.

We do a lot of timing with our receivers. We want the quarterback to be able to let the ball go when he hits on his fifth step. He wants to set up and get the weight on the inside of the rear foot.

I am not going to spend much time talking about teaching the drop. I teach it the same way as I did when I first started coaching. We teach the drop with no hitches in the drop so we can throw the ball on time. Hitches will come when you need them. We work on this. When they finish on the drop I want the weight on the inside of their rear foot. If the weight is on the front foot when they finish the drop, they cannot throw the ball on time.

We encourage our quarterbacks to stand up and throw the ball. Some quarterbacks want to get bent over and throw the ball bent forward. We want the spine up so everything is normal. If we are throwing the ball deep, we may tell them to tilt the spine back a little. This will help them get a little more air under the ball.

On the five-step drop timing, we teach it like this: 1-2-3, 4, 5. On the first two steps we are getting depth. On the last couple of numbers we are not getting depth anymore. This is how it goes; 1-2-3, 4, 5, and then you can get into the throw.

I am going to touch on the one-back passing game. There are a lot of different forms of the one-back offense. There are a lot of different ways to do things. The one-back passing game is a game where you can use the concepts that you have been taught since you were in junior high school. You can have different combinations of passing routes. You can have curl-flat routes, corner routes, vertical routes, hook routes, and three-step routes. It is all the same stuff. You do not have to come up with a lot of different combinations. You have the ability to put in a few plays here and a few things there. You do not have to be the most creative quarterback in the world to complete a pass. It helps to have an extra receiver out on the play. It is not against the rules to have the curl-flat route on one side and the curl-flat route on the other side. It is a lot simpler for the quarterback. We say *less is better; less is more.*

Have some things in the offense that you know they can run. Then you can go to the quarterback and tell him because the defense is playing in such a way we are going to put in three plays for them. It could be something we know the quarterback can do. I have our receiving coach make sure we did not put in too many running plays. We had our five base running plays and three additional plays we just put in. Now if we wanted to put in another play, that receiver coach would ask what play are we going to take out if we are going to add another play? It is the same thing in the passing game. The offensive line coach is in charge of that aspect of the game. If we want to add five new routes, the line coach wants to know which five routes are coming out. If you keep adding five plays each week at the end of the year you have a list of plays that is a mile long. You have plays so you can attack any defense in football. The problem is the players can't run the plays because they have not practiced them enough. If you have an experienced group, you can do more things. Make sure the lowest common denominator does not get wiped out. Make sure you put people in position for success.

One thing I like about the one-back passing game is that you can spread the field out. Obviously, that helps in the running game as well. The mentality of most defenses today is to stop the run first. This is true with teams that throw the football. Teams still line up to stop the run first against us at Marshall. We obliged them by throwing the ball. We threw more in some games than we did in others. When we sit down at the end of the year and take a look at the balance between the run and the pass, it comes out that we pass about 55 percent of the time. Some people think we throw the ball 80 percent of the time, but we don't.

In the one-back passing game, if you have some athletic players, it gives you a chance to take advantage of their skills. You can put players in a 1-on-1 situation where you can be successful. If you do not have better players than what you are playing against, it still gives you a chance to utilize the skills they have by taking advantage of matchups.

You can go away from the one-back set and run the empty set. You can get four receivers to one side, or three receivers to one side, or two receivers on each side. If the defense keeps too many players inside, you have them outflanked. When you have them outflanked, there are not many defenders to make the play. You always want to have something on offense that can take advantage of the defense when you use the different formations. You may use the sprint-out game, the three-step screen game, or anything that takes care of the defense when they do not have enough players in a certain area. The quarterback must be schooled on what he is looking for in each situation. If the defense is spread out all over the field, then we should be able to run the football.

Just because you are in the one back does not mean you cannot use play-action passes. Sometimes it is even better from the one-back set. It does not matter if you run it from the shotgun or from under the center. It is hard for the defense to see the ball when you are in the shotgun. The pop pass to the tight end is better out of the one-back set than it ever was out of the two-back set. In the one-back set, there are more defenders out of the picture. They are not in the way like they are in the two-back set.

The theory of the one-back offense is that you have taken the fullback out of the picture and you are putting him in different places. It may be that you have a receiver playing for the fullback or you have a more skilled player at the fullback position. Sometimes it is easier to find another receiver than it is to find another fullback.

It helps the quarterback to see the blitz from the one-back set. When everyone is bunched up on the two-back set, it is hard to tell who is going to blitz.

A lot of teams like to disguise their coverages. At Marshall that was the reason we went to the no-huddle offense. After 10 or 12 plays into the game, that disguise in the secondary is gone. We snap the ball fast before the defense can change up. Now the defense is out of position, and they are sitting there looking at their wristbands looking for the call and the ball is snapped. They are out of position when they get to the sideline. Now the defense has to play us honest and the quarterback can see this and take advantage of the situation.

Some offenses attack everywhere along the line of scrimmage with the run. They only attack the passing game in a few areas. In the one-back passing game, you can attack the entire field. You can make the defense cover the entire field. You can get more people into more protection even though it appears that you are in a wide-open formation. You can still get six- or seven-man protection from the one-back set.

At different times in my career, this has been a big factor. You do not have the big linemen up front, and you cannot knock them off the line as well as you would like to. A lot more linemen can learn to get in front of a man and try to keep him out of the way than can knock them off the ball. The defenses have such good athletes today it is hard to knock them off the line. You have a better chance of preventing the defensive line from overpowering you in the one-back set than you have trying to knock them off the ball in the two-back set. If you have linemen that can knock them off the ball, it is even better. Now you can spread them out and still run the passes as well.

I like to move the pocket around. You can run bootleg, spring-out, or stop-out behind the tackle. If the defense knows where you are going to set up all the time, they attack that spot. If it is six or seven yards behind the center, they are going to go for that area. They attack that spot. They can get good at it because they know that is where the quarterback is going to be. But if you are there 60 percent of the time and somewhere else 40 percent of the time, it is a lot tougher. Even if you just move around 20 percent of the time it makes it tougher for the defense.

We like to run our basic routes and a lot of different combinations. One of my favorite routes is a 10-yard hook route. You run down the field 10 yards and turn around and look for the ball. We can be in four wide receiver and all four receivers run the hook route. We can be in all combinations and still run the same route. It does not matter what formation we are in, we can run that route. The quarterback takes his five-step drop and throws the ball. It puts a receiver against a linebacker. We run it over and over. Then the defense thinks they have us figured out. Now we run four verticals on the same path. Zoom, we are gone. We run four verticals.

The one-back set lets you use your strength. You can find a way for one of your receivers to take advantage of someone on the defense. You must use your strengths to take advantage of the defense.

I do not have time to go over everything we do in the one-back set. I want to talk about some different concepts that you already have in your offense that you can use. You can get into your three-step drop game. Run the hitch routes. You can run the hitch or the quick-out routes. Not every quarterback can throw the quick-out routes. At Marshall we had a quarterback that could throw the quick-out route.

The slant route is very important. Make sure the receivers run the correct angle when they run the slant route. Depth is important to a certain point where you are not being jammed. The receivers must know when it is time to break. They must break on the right angle. The quarterback can adjust to the depth of the route. Basically we are going to take three steps and cut at a 45-degree angle inside and separate. The big problem is when the receivers do not take a good angle and the defender is too close to them. You must have a way to account for him to clear or you must have another receiver inside. The receiver has to beat the corner and then run at the angle.

We want to be able to throw the fade route on the deep outside. We want to be able to throw the ball in a hurry. We do not just throw this pass on the goal line. It may be when we have a tall receiver and the defense is covering him with a short player. Find out who the best receiver is to run the fade and use him for that route. Not all receivers can run the fade. Even the good players cannot always run the fade route. When you find a receiver that can run the fade, you must take advantage of him.

We have routes that go to certain spots on the field. We talked about the hook route. We send the receiver down 10 yards and have him come back toward the quarterback. That is a simple concept. It has been effective for a long time. You can use different combinations on these routes. The receivers get good at running them. All positions for us learn how to run a hook route. We can split the running backs outside and have them run the hook.

We talked about the curl-flat route. Teach them to run that pattern. I have run the curl 12 yards to 16 yards. What determines the depth? It depends on how fast the receivers are. If your receivers run 5.0 for the 40 then you are running them 16 yards deep. I would speed up something because you cannot protect the quarterback that long. The curl route is not a route that you throw on time. On the hook route it is a five-step drop, and set the foot, and then throw the ball. The curl is not thrown on time. There is an extra count in there. If you take the five steps and set and throw the curl, it will not set up. It takes a hitch step first before throwing the ball.

There are more routes than those, but these are examples of the ones we use the most.

Here are some routes we use on movement. First is the out-cut. Some coaches are afraid to throw the out-cut. If the defense picks it off, it is a touchdown. It is not a problem if your quarterback learns to throw the route properly. If the defense is covering him, the quarterback should not throw it over there. The quarterback must have confidence in the throw because you were confident enough to call the play. When you are working with the quarterback in the preseason and you are in pass skeleton drills, I want him to take chances with the football. I want him to see if he can "fit" the ball in on a route. Otherwise he will never know if he can make that throw or not. If he gets it intercepted in practice, you can work with him to improve his throw. Until he tries the throw, he will not know. I want him to be aggressive. We can always back him off a little. We can go over his mistakes and make corrections after he makes the mistakes in practice. We do not want to wait until the game to make the mistakes and the corrections.

The out and comeback routes fall in the same category. The question is how deep the receivers run on the route. On the comeback, we go 18 yards deep and come back to 15 yards. If we have a fast receiver, we may send him 20 yards deep and back to 17 yards on the comeback. Also, it depends on the quarterback action. If we do a bootleg, we will send the receivers a little deeper. That gives us more time to run the deep route.

If you are scared to throw the out route, you can move the pocket for the quarterback over toward the side of the pass. You do not have to run a full sprint out for the quarterback. You can run half-sprints on the out-cut to get the quarterback close to the receiver.

The one thing teams do not do enough of is to attack down the field. You do not just have to throw streak routes or post routes. There are a lot of different routes you can use.

We like to run deep crossing routes. The defense tends to lose the receivers on crossing routes. You will need some time, but you can run bootlegs and other actions.

We love corner routes. We run these routes against two deep and against man coverage. We do not run them against three-deep coverage. We are gong to throw the ball away from trouble against the man coverage.

On the streak route, we like to run four vertical receivers down the field. We try to find out who can run the best vertical routes and who can catch the long ball. The man that can play the ball in the air is the man you want to throw the ball to. Throw it to the man that can make the catch. How do you find these things out? You have to try it, and you have to practice it. You can find out if you can run that play or not. We run a couple of post routes. We have a skinny post that we throw on time. On the deep post, we are going to throw the ball deep down the field.

There are two basic concepts on the play-action pass. First is the quick series. This includes the plays where you are attacking linebackers. If the linebackers step up into the hole, the quarterback throws the ball to the tight end on the pop pass. We want the high percentage and high efficiency passes on this throw. These are not touchdown plays. They are efficiency plays. These plays slow the blitz people down.

When you go deep on play-action, you want to work on the safeties. Corners should not bite on play-action plays. The safeties are the defenders that come up to stop the run to quick.

We like to run the screen play. In the one-back, that is the way we run a sweep. I like to get the ball outside. If we get five yards on the play, we are happy. If we get the all-out blitz, we want the big play. One of the hard things about practicing screens is getting a good look on defense. Scouting teams do not run the right defense. So we practice them on air most of the time. We put the bags outside where the defenders are supposed to be, and we go block on the bags. If you do takeoff drills at the beginning of practice, it is a great time to work on your screen plays. If you put the ball on the 10-yard line and you are running plays into the end zone on goal line drives, you can run the screens on the calls. You can get a sense of rhythm on screen plays.

I hope this gives you a concept of what we are trying to do in the one-back offense. We repeat those concepts over and over. We run a few crossing routes, a few corner routes, a few hooks and curl routes, and we throw the ball down the field. We keep putting our quarterbacks and receivers in those situations over and over again.

I appreciate your attention. Thank you very much.

ESTABLISHING A DEFENSIVE PHILOSOPHY

University of Florida

The last eight weeks have been very exciting for me. For the last six years, I have been coaching in the NFL. I became the head coach at Florida in January and have been going at a very fast pace ever since. It is going to be a little different at Florida next season. We have a great staff. Several of our coaches have recruited in the state of Florida in the past, and some of the staff will be new to Florida high school coaches. We are all at Florida for the same reason and we all are looking for the opportunity to visit with the high school coaches.

As I said before, for the last six years I have been coaching in the National Football League. As coaches, we used to talk a great deal of the time about the University of Florida being the best coaching job in football. We talked about Coach Steve Spurrier having the best job in football and the fact he made a lot of money. Now, I do not make as much money as he did, but I am happy now that I am the head coach at Florida. When I was an assistant at Florida, I had the chance to recruit the state of Florida. So I know about the state of Florida. Now I feel I have the best job in football. If there is anything we can do to help you with your program, we will do it. We will spend as much time with you as we can.

I want to talk about a number of things. I am not a big tape guy at a clinic. It is hard for some people in the back to see what is on the film. For that reason, I do not show tapes at clinics. I want to talk about the things we did the last six years in the NFL. I will use a lot of the same terminology as we use in the NFL.

The first thing we wanted to do when we got to the University of Florida was to get the offensive staff set. The athletic director kept asking me who the defensive coordinator was going to be. I told him I was not too concerned about the defense. I could coach the defense if necessary. I wanted to get the offense set. We brought in Ed Zaunbrecher as the offensive coordinator. He was at Marshall University before and has the same philosophy of throwing the football as Coach Spurrier.

We selected Coach John Thompson as the defensive coordinator. He was at Arkansas before. I was not concerned about the defense as much as I was the offense. I knew the players wanted to know if we were going to run an offense similar to what they had run in the past. On defense we want our players to have fun. That is the type of defense Coach Thompson employs. We want the defense to play hard and have fun playing the game. John Thompson has a similar philosophy as I do. Our terminology may be a little different, but basically we are going to be an eight-man front football team. We are going to be a pressure defensive team.

The things I want to talk about now are the things we are going to do at the University of Florida. We are working on terminology with the staff, so we are on the same page.

I want to talk about the philosophy of our defense. This is how we started off on defense. Any time you start a new program or start a new year, you must have a philosophy. We start with the fact that our defense must be able to stop the run. You must be able to stop the run on defense at all levels. It is true in high school, and it is true in the NFL. You must be able to stop the run.

When you talk about stopping the run, you must have a goal. When I met the team for the second time, I told them the only thing I was concerned about at the present time was the indoor program. That was all we were concerned about at the time. We were not worried about spring practice, fall practice, or what was going to happen in a particular game. We were only concerned about getting bigger, faster, and stronger, and becoming a better football team. We worked out at 6:00 a.m. Our staff tried to get around to see everyone. I was so impressed by how our team responded to our early workouts. I was impressed with their attitude and how they attacked the workouts. Our strength coach has been at Florida for the past seven years, and he said the workouts were the best he had seen in those seven years. The players were continually pushing themselves and encouraging each other. But we were only concerned about the early workouts and nothing else. After the early workouts we gave them a few days off. Now our next goal was spring football.

We talked about the things we could do to get better in spring practice. Again, we were not worried about the summer, the fall, or what was going to happen in a particular game. We were concerned about spring football. We have 15 days of practice. We have to install a new offense, a new defense, and we have to install new special teams. We are only worried about our players getting better in that short period of time. That is all we are worried about.

People ask me how we coached the players in the NFL. I was there for six years, and I coached them the way I coached the college players. I never changed my style of coaching from the time I left the University of Florida and went to the NFL. I coached the players the same way I coached the college players. People tell me that I can't coach the players in the NFL the same as you do in college. Bull! They say you can't coach college players the same way as you coach them in high school. Bull! Football is a game. Now, I know there are a lot of things that are different in many respects, but you coach the same at all levels.

We wanted to decide what our team was going to work toward as we approached spring practice. We needed to decide what we wanted to accomplish in those spring practices. Obviously, you want to become a better football team. When you say you want to become a better team, what is becoming a better football team? Do you want to become a better offense, defense, or better special teams? You have a better chance of accomplishing that goal if your players know what that goal is. We are going to have a goal we want to accomplish at the end of spring football.

A lot of people are telling us we cannot win with the consistency that Coach Spurrier won with at Florida. To me that is a challenge. Now, make no mistake about it, Coach Spurrier did a great job. The night I got the job at Florida, Coach Spurrier and his wife, and me and my wife, went out to eat together. I told Steve he had really screwed the Florida coaching job up. "You took the best job in football and screwed it all up." I looked at Jerri Spurrier and told her she had just made it worse by adding Miami University to the schedule. "Both of you have screwed this job up." She replied, "Steve wanted to play Miami." I assured her that I knew why he wanted to play Miami because he was not going to be at Florida when the season starts. We had a lot of fun with the situation.

But all kidding aside, we have something to prove at Florida. Everyone says we cannot continue with the winning tradition. I have assured the players they are the ones that will determine if we win or not. Now, the players know there is a challenge out there for our team. I have seen how the team works and how they have approached the season, and I can tell you they have taken to the challenge. Our coaching staff has accepted the challenge as well.

It is the same for you in your situation. That is why you coach. That is why you teach school. It is for the challenge of coaching football. It is a challenge.

When our team takes the field on August 31 next year, we are not going to be thinking about winning. We play against the University of Alabama—Birmingham. They were fifth in the nation on defense last year. It is a challenge for our team. It is the same as the other situations. We are going to prepare for that one game, and then we are going to take the next step to the next level. Winning will take care of itself if we take care of the other things.

You must develop the same chemistry and work habits on a team. In our first season at New Orleans with the Saints, we had a big turnaround season. The reason we had a big year was because everyone had something to prove. If you can find one thing in the number of practices you have that the team has to prove during that time period, they will get better. For the Saints, each member of our defense had something to prove. The coaching staff had to prove they could coach in the NFL. I had to prove I could be a defensive coordinator in the NFL. Everyone had something to prove. If you can get your team to believe that everyone has something to prove, they will work harder. They are not going to worry about who will get the credit. They are going to be concerned about proving a point. This is the way we are approaching the spring practice. We all have something to prove.

Everyone is looking at Ron Zook at the University of Florida. Can Ron Zook and his staff win at the University of Florida? We tell the players that everyone is looking at them to see if they can win at the University of Florida. When you have a team that is working for something, obviously they are going to work a lot harder. Not all practices are going to be easy. As coaches, we must take the hardest game there is and make it fun. It is going to be hard to start the season. Not all days are going to be good practices. But you cannot let the players know it is hard work. The players must believe it is fun. You have to take the players and make them work as hard as they can to make them as good as they can be.

I said our defense was going to be an eight-man front football team. I do not care if we are rushing three men and dropping eight men. We may not be gap-sound in some long-yardage situations. But when the offense breaks a run, they will know who is responsible for each gap. We are going to chase the football on defense. Chasing the football is a habit.

You cannot expect a player to chase the football in a game if they do not chase the ball in practice. We insist on the players chasing the football when we are in shorts, in pads, in practice, and in a game. We are going to run back to the huddle. That is the tempo we are going to practice in. That is how we play the game.

When the people leave the stadium after a game, I want the fans to say our team is having fun. If we can get the fans to say the Florida players are having fun, we will be all right. We want them to have fun and to chase the ball. If they are uptight, they are not going to have as much fun.

How do you get your team to play the hardest game there is and still have fun doing it? It is not easy. If we knew the answer to that question, we would not be here.

There is no margin for error. We know what we have to do, and we must do it fast. I talk fast. I want everything moving fast. It is a habit. People tell me I talk too fast. Sometimes that may be true. But do you know what? It is a proven fact that a person can listen faster than anyone can talk. If you force yourself to concentrate, you can listen faster than anyone can talk. I am not going to slow down; you guys will have to speed up.

Not all players in the NFL are great players. You would be amazed at some of the players in the NFL. There may be some guys in the NFL that you do not understand how they got there. But here is what happens in the NFL. The great players bring the other players up to the next level. They force the lesser players up to the next level. It is the same thing in forcing yourself into talking faster.

Doubt will defeat aggression. Frank Beamer taught me this more than anyone in coaching. You are better off doing less and doing it fast than doing more and not doing it as fast. If your players are thinking, you are in trouble. A lot of the coaches here today know as much football as I do. But the thing is we are not playing. The players are the ones that are playing. I used to tell the defensive backs this: If you lose one step going full speed, it is a total of three yards. If the defensive back takes a false step, he loses three yards. It makes the defensive back look like he got beat bad. If he hesitates for one second, it costs him three yards. You are better off doing less and doing it fast.

As coaches, we sit around and talk about game planning. We want to game plan this and game plan that. I am as guilty as anyone. Now, in the NFL, you have to do some things differently, or the players will get stale. You must add some things to keep them stimulated because they are playing 16 games. But, if they are not playing fast, they are in trouble.

We talk about emotions. We ask this question: Is he a racer or a screwup? If you are playing with a lot of emotion and flying around on the field it will take care of a lot of screwups. We have all been guilty of this. A play starts out as a bad play and then something good happens and it turns out to be a good play. "Oh my goodness — oh, great play."

We always talk about rules. I am not big on rules. Coach Spurrier had a rule about wearing a hat in the building. I thought this was a good rule. I see guys in the NFL that wear hats inside. At times I wished we had that rule when I was in the NFL. Here is the situation about rules for me. If you make a rule, then you have to make sure you enforce the rule. Sometimes when you have a lot of rules, you are just asking for more problems. This is the same about making the rule on wearing hats inside the building. I am not going to lose any sleep over this rule.

When I was at Ohio State, Coach John Cooper said the players could not wear earrings in the football facility. Now, I do not know what the right answer is to these rules. You must do what you believe in as far as the rules. But, if you make a thousand rules, then you must enforce them to the hilt.

We insist that our players be on time for everything. Everyone in coaching has this policy. What are we going to do if the players are not on time? What are you going to do? Everything we do is important and we treat it that way. The NFL is no different than high school or college in this regard.

We start practice with a run-through. It is really a walk-through. It is before the stretch session. It is a way of getting in about 20 plays within a 15-minute session. It is a way of getting more reps for us.

We have three types of practice. We talk a lot about keeping players practicing and keeping them fresh. I am from the school that believes you must hit to be effective. I grew up that way. You have to hit to get tough. Today in football, we all have numbers problems. If we are thin on offense or defense, it does not make any sense for us to go out to practice and beat the crap out of them. If we do that, they do not practice hard, or they end up missing practice. You must make it tough for them, but they are there because they are tough. Hopefully we do not have to go out and beat the crap out of them to find out who is tough.

Again, we have three types of tempo in practices. We are going to take off and tag the ballcarrier. If I am a defensive back and the ball is over on the other side of the field, I am going to pursue the football and touch the ballcarrier. Everyone on defense has to touch the ballcarrier. The offensive and defensive linemen are both trying to win the scrimmage. You may ask why we do that. We feel you must try to work together in practice. The defensive lineman gets into the blocker and then he gets off the block and chases the ballcarrier.

The next tempo is what we call *thud*. On thud we front up. You come off the ball on the line of scrimmage and smack the assigned man across from you. We do not want anyone on the ground. We want them to move their feet but we do not want them on the ground. It is a pop! It is one or two steps full speed and then bam! The defense can hit the ballcarrier, but then they let him run after they make contact. We do not want anyone on the ground. We use the thud tempo more than the others. There will be some contact in this tempo. But you must teach them to stay off the ground in the drill. Don't let them get on the ground. You can practice that way. I did not believe that until six years ago. But now I know you can practice with a thud tempo.

The third tempo is live contact. Football is a hard, tough, physical game. You must have live contact somewhere in practice. I know this about contact practice. No coach in this room wants to lose a player due to contact. Not one coach wants to lose a player. You have to be smart about the practice and contact. Contact is the nature of the game of football. We insist that the defense stays away from our quarterbacks. At any level, if you have a quarterback you must take care of him. We know the quarterback has to be tough and all of that, but you must protect him as much as possible. You can practice just as fast and just as hard without beating up the quarterback. You can practice at the same tempo and not tackle the backs.

We want to get in and out of the huddle as fast as we can. If the players slow down, I am going to be chasing them in and out of the huddle. We want them to chase the ball, and *we chase them to the huddle.* Soon the players will start doing it themselves. If the head coach cannot take care of this, then one of the assistant coaches can chase them in and out of the huddle. If he can't do it, have one of the managers do it. Have someone chasing their butts in and out of the huddle. What happens is this: The players will run back to the huddle sometimes. You stay after them and make them do it all of the time. "Get to the ball, get to the huddle." Soon it will become a habit. Basically, the human being is lazy, and you have to make them do it your way.

What do we expect from our players? We expect the best effort from our players on the field and in the meetings. We want them to ask questions. We do not want them to be afraid to make mistakes, but we do not want them to repeat mistakes. It is hard to get the young players repetitions. If that second-string player is on the bench, he is only one play away from being the starter. He does not get the same amount of reps as the first-string player? No! But during the games you want that second-string player paying attention, and you do not want him to make the same mistake the starter makes. If someone makes a mistake, we do not want another player to go out and make the same mistake. We want them to pay attention at all times.

I let the players determine how long practice is going to be. We have a team period. We run 25 plays in 20 minutes. If we get to the number 16 or 17 play and we run out of time, we will go on to the next period. We do not want to run the same plays over and over if we make mistakes. You could run the same play over and over all day if you do not follow the script. You decide in your practice schedule how many plays you want to run in a period. We do not want to run plays for 30 minutes. If your players know they can determine the length of practice, it is easier to get them going. If you have two hours and 15 minutes scheduled for practice, but the team gets the work done in two hours and five minutes, what is wrong with that? If you get the same amount of work done, there is nothing wrong with this. You must determine what you must get done in practice. We simply tell our players we are going to run a certain number of plays, and we are going to get the job done. The same thing is true in watching tapes. That is a mental rep as well. If they are concentrating, they know how many plays they have watched.

Next I want to talk about common goals. In addition to common goals, we want our players to have individual goals. I am living proof of a person with an individual goal or a dream. I have dreamed of being the head coach at the University of Florida since the day I got into coaching. It has been a dream come true for me. You talk about being blessed — I have been blessed. I really mean this. I really wanted to be the head coach at the University of Florida. I first came to Florida when I was nine years old. I was from Ohio, and I did not like cold weather.

After I got into coaching, it was hard for me to go coach for the Pittsburgh Steelers. In Pittsburgh when the sun goes down in November, it does not come out again until May. I like it in Gainesville, Florida. I wake up and wonder if I am still at Florida. The point I am trying to make is this: You want your players to have a goal and a dream. We all know there are individual goals and individual dreams.

However, the football team must have one common goal. It must be the same goal for everyone on the team. That is the next problem for the coach. How do you get the team to strive to achieve the same goal? How do you get them all to want the same thing? I will tell you this. If and when you do get them striving for the one common goal, you have something. If no one is concerned about who is going to get the credit, you have something. The players must realize individual goals must come after the one common team goal. Those goals will happen for them if they can achieve the team goal.

Our defense will be adapted to the players that we have on our squad. Our offense will be adapted to the players we have available. In football at all levels, your offense and defense must be flexible enough so you can adapt it to your personnel. Your system must be flexible enough to adapt to the people you have to work with. Just because one player can do something very well does not mean all the other players can be as good as that one player. Coaching is putting your players in positions where they can be successful. I believe this with all of my heart. You must put the players in positions where they can be successful. If you have a corner hung out on an island, and you expect him to do something he cannot do, it is a bad situation. You want your players to play with a lot of confidence. You must put them into situations where they can do their best. We know this is impossible to do 100 percent of the time. But if the players really believe you are trying to put them into situations where they can be successful, they are going to play harder.

(Editor's note: The last 15 minutes of the lecture was not recorded due to technical difficulties.)